INTRODUCTION TO POLICE ADMINISTRATION:

A SYSTEMS/BEHAVIORAL APPROACH WITH CASE STUDIES

ROBERT SHEEHAN
College of Criminal Justice
Northeastern University

GARY W. CORDNER
School of Criminal Justice
Michigan State University

ADDISON–WESLEY PUBLISHING COMPANY

Reading, Massachusetts
Menlo Park, California
London
Amsterdam
Don Mills, Ontario
Sydney

This book is in the Addison-Wesley Series in Criminal Justice
Consulting Editor: Robert Sheehan

ISBN 0-201-06777-3
ABCDEFGHIJK-MA-79

For Evelyn W. Cordner, Carol Lee Sheehan,
and Tom, Mike, Tim, and Bobby Sheehan
and in loving memory of
Charles H. Cordner, Ellen Walls Sheehan, and Thomas W. Sheehan

PREFACE

This book is a basic introductory text written for both students and practitioners interested in the elements of police administration. The subject matter is presented in the simplest of terms from two major and, we think, extremely important perspectives—the systems perspective and the behavioral perspective. If organizations are to function productively and effectively, they must be understood conceptually not only on the basis of their component parts and structures, but also in terms of the people who work within them and make them function.

Police administration has traditionally been studied primarily on the basis of individual police tasks and specific police duties and responsibilities, with little or no consideration to the way in which human behavior and the interrelationships of people and the functions they perform impact on the process. Although we attempt to describe this process in the most elementary way, the administration of any organization is extraordinarily complex. It involves a great deal more than understanding a few basic management principles and being able to apply them in the most simplistic fashion. Rather, organizational administration involves the behavior of people, the way they perceive themselves and others, the way they communicate with one another and work together, and the way they relate to one another within the organizational setting and to their clientele outside of the organizational setting.

Most police administration texts give too little consideration to the significance of human behavior as either a constructive or a destructive element of major importance in managing police departments. In this book we have emphasized human behavior as a relevant ingredient in the administrative process and have attempted to describe those aspects of behavior which we believe most notably affect the management of police organizations.

We see police organizations as open behavioral systems made up of interdependent and interrelated subsystems (people, bureaus, divisions, units, squads, teams, beats, etc.). Each of these subsystems may be looked on as a system in and of itself or as a subsystem interacting with the total system or with other subsystems.

We consider the historical, social, political, and democratic aspects of administering police agencies and examine a number of concepts and concerns which have been traditionally central to police administration, such as police tasks, structures, principles, and functions. Indeed, a number of police administration texts do not go beyond this narrow traditional perspective. We see these considerations as being important, but only as building blocks for more advanced practices. The traditional perspective provides little more than the fundamentals. Unfortunately, many police departments are managed on the basis of these fundamentals and little else.

Because management is sometimes described as the business of getting things done through other people, we believe that people and their behavior are important inputs to the management process. We look at people's behavior from a number of different viewpoints. We discuss the behavior of people in organizations, focusing on attitudes, roles, self-concept, motivation, perception, and communication. In so doing, we attempt to gain insight into why people behave the way they do in organizational settings. We also look at organizational behavior sociologically, or on the basis of the way groups behave, and we consider the intangible qualities of leadership in terms of functions, styles, and theories.

Organizational interactions and managerial guidance mechanisms are emphasized in our treatment of the flow perspective of police administration. Here we discuss the importance of information as a resource as well as the flow of information within the organization.

We also borrow techniques for organizational improvement from the fields of business, industry, and public management, where they have been successfully applied, and attempt to demonstrate how they may be used in police organizations.

Although we have included a number of case studies we hope will give the reader some opportunities to apply theory to practice, our intent in writing this book was to provide the reader not with specific management techniques, but rather with conceptual theoretical tools which we believe will help tremendously in identifying and analyzing organizational problems.

We hold that there are no easy solutions; in fact, we postulate that many issues in police administration defy resolution. To the extent possible, we identify and define these issues with the hope that all our readers may develop a greater appreciation and understanding of them and, therefore, make a more meaningful and constructive contribution to society in whatever roles they may play in the police administrative process.

Boston, Massachusetts   R. S.
East Lansing, Michigan   G. W. C.
January 1979

ACKNOWLEDGMENTS

We are grateful to those who contributed to this book by reading the manuscript at its various stages of development and making valuable suggestions and comments, by providing us with ideas and research contributions, by giving us direct editorial input, by furnishing us pictures for the text, by shaping the attitudes and philosophies that we have taken with us into this book, and by encouraging us and being patient with us during the long four-year period it took to write what *finally* is within these covers. For their help and their kindnesses, we thank the following people: George E. Berkley, Boston State College; William Blake, Chief, Wayland, Massachusetts, Police Department; Arthur F. Brandstatter, Federal Law Enforcement Training Center, Brunswick, Georgia; the late James J. Brennan, Michigan State University; Pierce R. Brooks, former Director, Department of Public Safety, Lakewood, Colorado; David E. Burns, San Jose State University; Robert Croatti, Northeastern University; Maurice J. Cullinane, former Chief, Metropolitan Police Department, Washington, D.C.; Frederick Cunliffe, Northeastern University; Edward M. Davis, former Chief, Los Angeles, California, Police Department; Shirley Davis, Northeastern University; Frank D. Day, Michigan State University; Romine R. Deming, Northeastern University; Walter T. Driscoll, Jr., Chief, Scituate, Massachusetts, Police Department; David G. Epstein, Chief, Savannah, Georgia, Police Department; Francis X. Finn, Chief, Quincy, Massachusetts, Police Department; Robert R. J. Gallati, Northeastern University; A. C. Germann, California State University at Long Beach; Harrie C. Gill, former Superintendent, Rhode Island State Police; Robert Gillis, Brockton,

Massachusetts, Police Department; Richard P. Grassie, National Issues Center, Westinghouse Electric Corporation, Arlington, Virginia; Jack R. Greene, Michigan State University; Peter J. Grimes, Nassau Community College; Rev. Gerald J. Hickey, Associate Pastor, St. Thomas Aquinas Church, Jamaica Plain, Massachusetts; Larry T. Hoover, Sam Houston State University; Howard R. Leary, former Commissioner, New York City Police Department; Myron J. Leistler, Chief, Division of Police, Cincinnati, Ohio; John T. McCool, former Chief, Bureau of Police, Wilmington, Delaware; Henry F. Maiolini, Chief, Bourne, Massachusetts, Police Department; Robert J. McCormack, John Jay College of Criminal Justice; David McCutchen, Lieutenant, Chatham County Police Department, Savannah, Georgia; Lynne M. McLeod, Georgia State University; Timothy F. Moran, Northeastern University; Patrick V. Murphy, President, The Police Foundation, Washington, D.C.; Peter J. Pitchess, Sheriff, Los Angeles County, California; Norman Rosenblatt, Northeastern University; Daniel J. Roberts, Jr., Northeastern University; Kenneth G. Ryder, Northeastern University; Hrand Saxenian, Concord, Massachusetts; Frank O. Shaw, Chief, Weston, Massachusetts, Police Department; Wallace W. Sherwood, Northeastern University; Frank A. Schubert, Northeastern University; Paul M. Shields, Fairfax, Virginia; Eugene O. Tobin, former Lieutenant, Everett, Massachusetts, Police Department; Lavell Tullos, Chief, Jackson, Mississippi, Police Department; Ralph Turner, Michigan State University; and Hubert Williams, Director, Newark, New Jersey, Police Department. Very special thanks go to our friends, our colleagues, and the members of our families for their patience, understanding, and help; to Tom Sheehan for composing the index; and to our editors at Addison-Wesley—David Geggis, Patricia Mallion, and Evelyn Wilde—whose personal and professional inputs made the project both viable and worthwhile.

CONTENTS

PART I
BASIC CONSIDERATIONS

The two chapters in Part I serve as introductions to the study of police administration as it will be presented in this book. These two chapters discuss several important frames of reference that the police manager and organization analyst alike must appreciate.

Chapter 1 considers briefly the historical, social, political, and democratic contexts of American law enforcement and police administration. Simply stated, we strongly argue that policing can neither be understood nor fairly and effectively practiced except in terms of these contexts. The police manager's job is greatly influenced by historical, social, political, and democratic factors; an understanding and appreciation of these factors will help police managers adjust to their roles and be more effective.

Chapter 2 introduces the systems approach to police administration. Readers well versed in systems theory will recognize that the approach is used here in its most elementary form. We believe that the most important contribution of the systems approach is its holistic perspective. That is, the systems approach encourages us to look at things, such as police departments, as wholes rather than as mere collections of independent parts. It helps us to realize that police organizations are interrelated with other entities as parts of larger systems and that they are composed of interrelated subsystems and subsubsystems.

A few additional basic elements of the systems approach are presented, but the key concepts are interdependence and interaction. These concepts and the holistic perspective force us to broaden our treatment of the topic of police administration. In Part II (Chapters 3–6) the traditional approach to police administration is presented. Parts III, IV, and V present material once not considered truly germane to police administration, but which our new, wider perspective requires be given attention.

CHAPTER 1
POLICE ADMINISTRATION
IN HISTORICAL AND SOCIAL
CONTEXT

LEARNING OBJECTIVES

1. Cite the year that marks the origin of organized, paid, civilian policing.

2. Characterize policing prior to the year cited above.

3. Cite the first two fundamental principles of Peelian reform.

4. Identify the organizational models available to Peel as he began designing his police force.

5. Compare Peel's personnel practices with those of the military at that time.

6. Summarize Peel's approach to police administration.

7. Identify two obstacles to the adoption of Peel's approach to police administration.

8. Characterize the view of police work held by Vollmer, Smith, and Wilson.

9. Describe the current state of police administration in terms of both personnel standards and organizational structure.

10. Cite a reason for the apparently constant dissatisfaction with the police in American communities.

11. Characterize the police role in crime control.

12. Identify the relevance of the doctrines of checks and balances and separation of powers for policing.

13. Identify the impact of federalism on policing.

14. Characterize the conflict between policing and democratic values.

15. Identify the basic problem in our pursuit of ordered liberty.

16. Characterize the difficult position of a police administrator in a democratic society.

One of the fundamental and recurrent themes in this book is the systems approach to police administration. Basically, this approach emphasizes the interrelatedness that characterizes modern society and the necessity of viewing people, organizations, and processes as parts of larger systems. In order to understand the behavior of an oil company executive, for example, one must look at the oil company, the pertinent government regulatory agencies, our capitalistic economic system, and the worldwide multinational economic system. All of these systems, and others, impact on the executive and in turn are influenced by the executive. As another example, explaining the process of government in Topeka, Kansas, would certainly require consideration of the state and national governmental systems, as well as the economic and cultural environments of the city, state, and nation. In short, the systems approach, with its stress on interrelatedness, helps us to keep these external influencing factors in mind. And as the forces of change, complexity, and interdependence in our society continue to grow stronger, as they certainly will, the need for the systems approach to organizing and managing will increase.

The systems approach is both present- and future-oriented. It examines the ways that people, organizations, and processes fit together, the effects that changes at one point have on other points, and the relations between systems and their external environments. It focuses on *how* and *why* in order to *explain* and *improve.*

Explanation and understanding also require some backward looking, however. Current behavior, practices, and structures are to some extent based on past ways of doing and organizing and on past experiences with other alternatives. In other words, where you *are* at a given moment depends on where you *were* previously.

The purpose of this chapter is to briefly discuss where police administration is at present and where it is coming from. We hope that this discussion will give you a useful framework for reading and thinking about the rest of this book, which deals with the behavior, processes, and organization entailed in police administration.

THE DEVELOPMENT OF POLICE ADMINISTRATION

The development of police administration, of course, had to await the development of policing. The year 1829 marks the origin of organized, paid, civilian policing. In that year the Metropolitan Police Act became English law, culminating a long and emotional debate. Prior to that time, law enforcement in London and elsewhere had been the province of private citizens, volunteers, night watchmen, private merchant police, and personal employees of a few justices of the peace. This informal and unorganized law enforcement approach, which had proved satisfactory for centuries, was overwhelmed by the Industrial Revolution, which spawned rapid urbanization and spiraling crime rates.

The Metropolitan Police Act of 1829 authorized Sir Robert Peel to establish a police force for the metropolitan London area, and 1000 men were quickly hired.[1] Where no police force at all had previously existed, there suddenly stood a large organization. The basic organizational and managerial problems faced by Peel and his police commissioners were essentially the same as those faced by police chiefs today. How were they to let their officers know what was expected of them, how were they to coordinate the activities of all those officers, and how were they to make sure that directions and orders were followed?

Some of Peel's answers to these questions can be found in the fundamental principles of his Peelian Reform:

1. The police should be organized along military lines;

2. Securing and training proper persons is essential;

3. Police should be hired on a probationary basis;

4. The police should be under government control;

5. Police strength should be deployed by time and area;

6. Police headquarters should be centrally located; and

7. Police record keeping is essential.[2]

The foundation of Peel's approach to police administration is in his first principle. For although he felt strongly that the police and the military should be separate, distinct agencies, he turned to the military for his model of efficient organization. He also turned to many former military officers in recruiting his first police officers.

That Peel should borrow his organizational styles from the military was not at all unusual. The military and the Church were actually the only large-scale organizations in existence. Both were organized similarly, although their members bore different titles. Both were centralized; a few people held most of the power and made most of the decisions, whereas many people just did as they were told. Also, both operated under a system of graded authority; for example, generals had full authority, colonels and majors had a little less, captains and lieutenants had less still, sergeants had only enough to direct their privates, and privates had none at all. The same held true with the Church. The Pope had full authority, with lesser degrees of authority being delegated to cardinals, archbishops, bishops, monsignors, pastors, and priests.

It was natural, then, that Peel should borrow the centralized organizational form of the military model. His personnel practices, however, were not copied from the military, which at that time was peopled largely by debtors, criminals, and draftees, with officers drawn from the wealthy and aristocratic classes. The military was chronically in need of people and so would accept anyone into its ranks. Peel, in choosing his police, however, was highly selective. Only a small percentage of applicants was accepted, and a probationary period was used to weed out those whose performance was not satisfactory. The standards of conduct were very rigid, so that many officers were dismissed, especially in the early years of organizational development.

Peel's approach to police administration can thus be summed up as follows: centralized organization with graded authority and selective and stringent personnel standards. He fashioned his approach in 1829, and in some respects we still fall short of implementing it.

The primary obstacle to the adoption of Peel's approach, which we will call *traditional police administration,* has been the enduring sentiment that police work is essentially undemanding, physical labor. This widely held belief has prevented the establishment of the rigorous personnel standards advocated by Peel. As a result, the pay and status derived from police work have tended to be low, and the job, until very recently, has attracted mainly those whose job prospects elsewhere were bleak.

Stringent personnel standards in the early days of American policing were also subverted by the influence of local politics. Local politics served as the vehicle for bringing immigrant groups into the American social structure, and police jobs were part of local political patronage. Initially police work was the domain of certain politically powerful ethnic groups rather than the profession of highly qualified people who could meet rigid standards. Consequently, police officers were likely to be dismissed by their agencies not because of unsatisfactory performance, but because they belonged to the wrong political party.

Strong criticism of the view that police work was undemanding did not emerge until the beginning of the twentieth century.[3] Since then, however, police practitioners, academics, and investigating commissions have decried the poor quality of police personnel; pointed out the need for intelligence, honesty, and sensitivity in police officers; and thus reaffirmed Peel's philosophy.

Among the individuals most vocal and noteworthy in support of *traditional police administration* and higher police personnel standards were August Vollmer,[4] Bruce Smith,[5] and O.W. Wilson.[6] Each strongly believed that police work is a demanding and important function in a democratic society, requiring officers able to deal with a wide variety of situations in a wide variety of ways. They agreed that physical power is an important attribute, but felt that good judgment, an even temperament, and other human qualities and skills are more important. In their roles as police administrators and recognized police experts, they promoted the adoption of *traditional police administration.*

Supporting their views were the findings and recommendations of investigating commissions, most notably the Wickersham Commission[7] in the 1930s and the President's Crime Commission[8] in the 1960s. The first found that the American police were totally substandard; the second found that relatively little progress had been made during the period between the commissions. Both found that the quality of police personnel was low, in terms of carrying out the job to be done and in comparison to the rest of the population, and both called for substantial upgrading of police personnel.

Through the mid-1960s the problem of poor police personnel dominated the literature and practice of police administration and detracted from the consideration of other important matters. In particular, the organization of the police in centralized military fashion went largely unchallenged. As a result, only in recent years have alternative organizational schemes been seriously considered and, in some cases, adopted on an experimental basis.

Police administration today reflects this history. In most major jurisdictions the need for intelligent, sensitive, flexible people in policing has been or is being accepted. Better-educated people are being hired as police officers.[9] Police salaries are improving, as is occupational status. Because police agencies are getting more and more applicants, they can be more selective in choosing their officers.[10] In general, the quality of American police personnel seems to be on the rise.

For the most part, however, police organization and management have not changed, and this is the crux of the problem. The rigid, military approach does not seem to fit the demanding, variable, discretion-laden nature of the police job today. Nor does it seem appropriate for the management of the better-educated, more knowledgeable police officers of today. Other kinds of organizations, in both the business and government sectors, have abandoned the centralized, military form of organization in favor of more flexible arrangements. There is consensus today that the upgrading of police personnel must now be followed by some radical changes in police organization and management.

Later in this book we will discuss some of the approaches to police organizational improvement that have been suggested and implemented. First, however, you should have an understanding of the historical context of police administration. We have been nearly 150 years trying to attain Peel's model of a centralized organization with rigid personnel standards. Now that police service is approaching the level of high personnel standards that he envisioned, increased criticism of his centralized, military model of organization has developed. This latter problem now dominates most of the literature and discussion with respect to improving modern-day police administration.

In this section on the historical context of police administration, we have, of course, covered only the most rudimentary elements of what is involved in organizing and managing a modern police agency. Later chapters address those topics in considerably more detail.

THE SOCIAL CONTEXT OF POLICE ADMINISTRATION

Just as current police administration can be explained in part by its past, so too can its form and substance be explained in part by the general social structure. We have already mentioned, for example, that the low status of police work in America helps to explain the unsatisfactory quality of police applicants and thus the inability of police administrators to implement stringent personnel standards.

The police seem perpetually to be the brunt of scathing criticism. One reason for the apparently constant dissatisfaction with the police in American communities is the lack of agreement in the society about what the objectives of policing should be. General agreement does not exist in the society on the most important goals of policing, not to mention the means of attaining those goals. In addition to the disagreement among people about what the police are supposed to be doing, individuals often change their opinions and priorities over time or in response to certain perceived emergencies, so that the unfathomable "will of the community" is always changing. As a result, even the police administrator who tries to provide the community with the type of police service that it desires is unlikely to escape criticism.

To the extent that policing and police administration do have identifiable goals and objectives, they are not attainable by police action alone. For example, crime control is a generally accepted objective of the police. In actuality, however, the police play a secondary role with respect to crime control. Families, peer groups, churches, and schools have a more primary role, and in a sense the police become involved only with the failures of those social organizations. Even when they do become involved, the police are dependent on victims, witnesses, prosecutors, and the courts in their efforts to achieve crime control. Crime control is not solely a police function, although it is generally considered to be one.

The social implications and the environment of policing have been highlighted in recent years in discussions and debates about police-community relations. Mass altercations between certain ethnic groups and the police, and students and the police, in the 1960s dramatically demonstrated that police relations with at least these communities were less than ideal. In urban areas the estrangement of the police and the community extended beyond civil disorders to everyday policing, as many other groups seemed also to regard the police as an army of occupation.[11] The problem of police relations with these and other segments of the community made it clear that the police operate in a social system that they can neither take for granted nor totally control. Different community groups view the police differently and have varying notions of the priorities and objectives of law enforcement and criminal justice.

THE POLITICAL CONTEXT OF POLICE ADMINISTRATION

Part of the social environment of police administration is the governmental and political system. We have already noted that during its development, policing was closely tied to local politics and that this relationship had important consequences for police decision making and police personnel standards. Although this undesirable political relationship is greatly diminished today, the political environment of police administration is still an important factor to consider in understanding and explaining police behavior, practices, and organizations.

In our junior high school civics classes we all learned about the American government's system of *checks and balances* and *separation of powers.* The Founding Fathers dispersed authority among the legislative, executive, and judicial branches of government in order to prevent any one person or branch from becoming all-powerful. The legislative branch was assigned the roles of enacting laws and appropriating funds. The executive branch was given the tasks of implementing and enforcing the laws. The judicial branch was directed to review the constitutionality of legislative enactments and to adjudicate alleged violations of the laws.

The police are a part of the executive branch of government. Their role, then, is to enforce the laws enacted by the legislature and to refer alleged violations of those laws to the judiciary. In actual practice, of course, policing is considerably more complex and less mechanical than this description suggests. Police officers utilize discretion in such a way that they do not enforce all of the laws all of the time; their efforts are not universally reviewed by the courts; and many of their practices involve activities not related specifically to law enforcement. Nevertheless, it remains useful to keep in mind that the police do not make either the laws or the decision between the guilt or innocence of a suspect brought to court. These matters, though important to policing, are within the domain of other branches of the government.

Another important characteristic of our governmental system is *federalism*. Besides being distributed among different branches of government, power in our system is also dispersed through several levels of government. As a result, some functions are performed by the national government, some by the states, some by counties, some by local communities, and some are shared.

Policing in America is basically a local function, although the states and the national government are also involved with law enforcement and cannot be ignored. With respect to objectives, priorities, and budgets, police administrators deal primarily with city councils, city managers, mayors, and other local executive and legislative units. State and national law enforcement organizations, of course, deal with state and national executive and legislative bodies, respectively. Even local police, however, have relationships with the state and national governments. The law that most police enforce is state law enacted by state legislatures or local law enacted by city councils or town governments. Also, in many areas the correctional and judicial systems, both of which are important to policing, are operated by counties and by states. Finally, in recent years many local police administrators have had increased contracts with state and national government officials who control special anticrime funds and other federal funds that can be used to augment local law enforcement budgets. These funds have become available during a period of local budget belt-tightening; therefore, the competition for them has been intense.

Although the political environment of local police administration varies from agency to agency, some regional patterns can be discerned. In the Northeast states, local city and town government is very strong and partisan. Police chiefs and other administrators are frequently changed after elections, and local partisan politics have a strong influence on day-to-day policing. In the West, by contrast, local politics are much more likely to be nonpartisan, with college-trained city managers exercising much of the authority wielded by elected mayors in the East. Police administrators in the West are more likely to be given authority and responsibility for everyday police operations, and "professional" police administration is more apparent. Also in the West, and in the South, the county plays a larger role than elsewhere. In many rural areas the elected county sheriff is the paramount law enforcement officer as well as one of the most prominent politicians. Some counties also have countywide police agencies serving under an appointed chief who is responsible to a county executive or county council. In other areas, however, particularly the Northeast, the county is an insignificant level of government, and frequently the sheriff is responsible only for serving civil court papers and sometimes running a county jail.

The political and governmental environment of police administration, then, varies widely. Whatever the local circumstances, police administration is strongly influenced by these factors. Along with the historical and social contexts, the political context of police administration has important implications for the people, processes, and organization of policing.

THE CHALLENGE OF POLICE ADMINISTRATION
IN A DEMOCRATIC SOCIETY

In discussing the historical, social, and political contexts of police administration, we have skirted the most basic context of all—the democratic nature of our society. This one factor has tremendous implications for the ways in which we police our society, for the role of the police, and for police administration.

George Berkley has best described the difficult position of the police in a democratic society.[12] As he has noted, democracy is based on consensus among the members of the society; the police job starts when that consensus breaks down. Perfect democracy would have perfect consensus and thus have no need for police. Also, in a democracy the government is established to serve the people—to follow their demands and to operate with their consent. Much of policing, however, involves making people behave against their wishes or prohibiting them

from doing what they please. Related to this, a basic element of democracy is freedom, and much of the police job involves limiting or revok-
ing people's freedom. An additional aspect of democracy is equality;
but citizens do not deal with the police on an equal basis. The police
are armed and have the authority to demand cooperation from the
public. So in many ways the exercise of policing is in direct conflict
with the values of our democratic society.

These and other conflicts reflect our continuing pursuit of ordered
liberty. In our society, we basically believe that all people should be
free to do as they please. But we also recognize that the exercise of
total freedom by one person necessarily limits the freedom available to
others. The basic problem, then, becomes one of designing the boundaries on individual freedom. We see that individual freedom must be
limited, but we want to limit it as little as possible. We have not found a
neat equation for determining just how much to limit individual freedom, and so all of us have our own opinions on the matter, and our
opinions also change over time. None of this helps the police, who must
make hard decisions every day about limiting the freedom of individuals. Although we recognize that the police function has to be done,
we basically do not like what the police do. We may accept their role,
but we do not always like it.

Police officers and police administrators quickly become aware of
their less than exalted position in society. Many of them take the dislike personally and become upset and frustrated because they know
that they are trying to do the job the best way they know how. If they
have an understanding of their role in a democratic society, however,
they will understand, and perhaps even appreciate, the dislike and distrust that are inherent factors in the policing process.

Police administrators are in an especially difficult position, because
the public will hold them accountable for crime control, while at the
same time distrusting them for the functions performed by their organizations. This distrust will be reflected in numerous constraints being
placed on the measures available to the police for controlling crime.
The police are required to obtain arrest and search warrants from the
courts; they must advise suspects not to incriminate themselves; their
use of electronic surveillance is severely restricted; and so on. Despite
these stumbling blocks, however, the public still expects the police to
control crime and holds the police administrator accountable for accomplishing that objective.

The police administrator truly is in a difficult position and should
recognize it as such. Society cannot really make up its mind about what
the police are supposed to accomplish or how they are supposed to

accomplish whatever become their defined objectives. A perfect democracy would not need the police, and so society accepts them only as a necessary evil. Society severely restricts the methods available to the police for controlling crime, but still expects crime to be controlled. Somehow the police administrator has to operate and survive in this conflicting environment.

There are no easy answers to be given to police administrators. The job is a very difficult one to perform well. Police administrators must constantly keep in mind that they are operating in a democratic society. They must understand, in fact internalize, the democratic values of the society and their implications for their jobs and their organizations. They must realize that the police are allowed to restrict freedom only so that the freedom of all can be protected and maximized. As Berkley has noted, "the police today are faced with the problem of improving their efficiency while, at the same time, maintaining democratic norms and values."[13] The solution to this difficult and perplexing problem must be democratic, moral, legal, and constitutional. One difficulty for the police administrator is that it must also be effective.

SUMMARY

This chapter helps lay a foundation for the rest of the book. It presents the historical, social, political, and democratic contexts of American policing so that you can gain a better appreciation of where police administration has been and what its present environment is like.

Policing in America, an activity of the executive branch of government, is performed in a democratic, social, and political setting. These various contexts assert important influences on the people, processes, and organization of policing. If in later chapters we do not stress the importance of these external environmental factors often enough, we hope that you will compensate for this omission by keeping this chapter firmly in mind, if for no other reason than to understand that it presents an extraordinarily important perspective on the problems the police face in the modern world.

DISCUSSION QUESTIONS

1. Policing prior to 1829 was informal and personal. What do you think would be the result if we were to return to such a system?

2. Would you categorize policing as demanding or undemanding work? What are the reasons for your choice?

3. Do you agree that in our society there is a lack of agreement about the goals and objectives of policing? What do you think are or should be the goals and objectives of the police? Try listing them in order of importance.

4. How much influence do you think the police have on crime rates? To what extent do you think the police should be held accountable for crime control?

5. What do you think is the proper role of politics with respect to policing?

6. Policing in America is a fragmented, primarily local function. Do you think it should be? Would you alter this arrangement in any way? What purposes does the fragmentation of policing serve?

7. What do you think should be the role of the national government with respect to policing?

8. The text says that in large measure policing conflicts with our democratic values. Do you understand what is meant by that? Do you agree? Is that the way things should be? As a police officer, how would you deal personally with this conflict?

9. Police administrators are held accountable for crime control in their communities even though not all means to attain that objective are available to them. As a police chief, how would you deal with this problem?

REFERENCES

1. A.C. Germann, Frank D. Day, and Robert R.J. Gallati, *Introduction to Law Enforcement and Criminal Justice* (Springfield, Ill.: Charles C Thomas, 1969), p. 54.

2. *Ibid.*, pp. 54–55.

3. See Charles B. Saunders, Jr., *Upgrading the American Police* (Washington, D.C.: Brookings Institution, 1970).

4. August Vollmer, *The Police and Modern Society* (Berkeley: University of California Press, 1936).

5. Bruce Smith, *Police Systems in the United States* (New York: Harper & Brothers, 1940).

6. O.W. Wilson, *Police Administration* (New York: McGraw-Hill, 1950).

7. National Commission on Law Observance and Enforcement, *Report on Police* (Washington, D.C.: U.S. Government Printing Office, 1931).

8. U.S. President's Commission on Law Enforcement and Administration of Justice, *Task Force Report: The Police* (Washington, D.C.: U.S. Government Printing Office, 1967).

9. Larry T. Hoover, *Police Educational Characterisitcs and Curricula* (Washington, D.C.: U.S. Government Printing Office, 1975).

10. For example, for years the Baltimore Police Department was unable to attract enough applicants to reach its authorized personnel strength. That is no longer the case.

11. Victor G. Strecher, *The Environment of Law Enforcement* (Englewood Cliffs, N.J.: Prentice-Hall, 1971).

12. George E. Berkley, *The Democratic Policeman* (Boston: Beacon Press, 1969), pp. 1-5.

13. *Ibid.,* p. 19.

CHAPTER 2
A SYSTEMS APPROACH TO
POLICE ADMINISTRATION

LEARNING OBJECTIVES

1. Identify the two primary goals and objectives of a police department.

2. Identify six secondary goals and objectives of a police department.

3. Cite the finding of studies with respect to the portion of police work specifically directed toward criminal matters.

4. Define the term "system."

5. Compare the likely efficiency of a large and complex system with that of a small and simple system.

6. Identify the three primary characteristics of systems.

7. Define "feedback."

8. Differentiate between open-loop and closed-loop systems.

9. Differentiate between open and closed systems.

10. Characterize living systems as open or closed.

11. Characterize our current understanding of social systems, such as organizations.

12. Identify three different perspectives from which police organizations may be studied.

13. Characterize most police departments in terms of their provision for and use of feedback.

14. Cite several useful purposes of organization charts.

15. Cite two systems of which police departments are primary subsystems.

The consideration of police organization and administration as *systems* will be a recurrent theme of this book. This consideration is what might be generally referred to as a *systems perspective*. This perspective, or viewpoint, has been found to be a very valid way to look at police departments, and it also simplifies the process for students of police administration by providing a framework for study.

The word "systems" has, unfortunately, taken on a connotation of something mystical and forbidding, conjuring up images of highly sophisticated scientists dealing with the most complex of problems. In this book, however, the systems concept is used simply to demonstrate how all aspects of an organization are interrelated and interdependent. The concept will be used not to complicate the subject matter, but rather as a means of simplifying extremely complex relationships.

This chapter will introduce the concept of sytems and show how its application to police administration can set the stage for police departments to meet their goals and objectives.

GOALS AND OBJECTIVES

Every one of us has goals and objectives. Our whole lives are patterned after these. Your goal and objective as a student is to complete your degree requirements. This is extremely important to you, and therefore you spend endless hours working toward that end. Undoubtedly, you have other goals as well. You may want to buy a car, which in your view will facilitate your going back and forth to college. Eventually, you might like to become a police officer. Some of you may even aspire to be a police chief, be married, buy your own home, raise a family, and be happy. Everyone has different goals and objectives in life. All of us regard the achievement of our goals and objectives as a significant part of our lives, and we devote considerable energy toward their achievement. Such factors as background, experiences, values, ambition, talent, and family expectations cause people's goals to differ widely. Two dramatic examples of two different individuals with remarkably different goals and objectives appear in the two true vignettes described on the next page.

STANDARD 2.1

DEVELOPMENT OF GOALS AND OBJECTIVES

Every police agency immediately should develop short- and long-range goals and objectives to guide agency functions. To assist in this development, every unit commander should review and put into writing the principal goals and objectives of his unit.

National Advisory Commission on Criminal Justice Standards and Goals, *Police* (Washington, D.C.: U.S. Government Printing Office, 1973), p. 49.

- A college professor in his fifties applied for a teaching position in a large, urban university. He was asked to fill out an application form and to appear at a scheduled time in the office of the dean for an interview. In response to a question on the application form which asked him to list his major activities in college, he wrote, "Girls." Although this might certainly be considered an unorthodox goal of his younger years, it was, nonetheless, a truthful response to what he evidently considered to be a meaningless question. During the interview with the dean and the dean's assistant, he was asked what his primary goal in life was. He answered very simply, "To go to heaven."

- Seeking advice from a professor of criminal justice on career objectives, a college student still in his teens was questioned closely about his interests and activities. The professor, assuming that the student was interested in a criminal justice career, attempted to narrow down the student's interests in terms of job possibilities in law enforcement, the courts, probation, parole, and institutional corrections. Finally, after much unproductive discussion, the professor asked, "What is your long-range goal? What would you really like to do in life?" Without hesitation, the student answered, "I'd like to be a United States Senator."

Although it is difficult, if not impossible, to isolate the goals and objectives of different individuals, it is a relatively simple task to list the goals and objectives of a police department. Authorities in the field of police administration disagree, sometimes vehemently, over what a police officer should or should not be required to do, but their debate focuses on the role of individual police officers and not on the goals and objectives of the departments for which they work. There is considerable agreement on these.

The two primary goals and objectives of any police department are *to maintain order* and *to protect life and property.* In addition, there are a number of secondary goals and objectives toward which police activities are directed in order to meet primary obligations: *crime prevention, arrest and prosecution of offenders,* * *recovery of stolen and missing property, assistance to the sick and injured, enforcement of noncriminal regulations,* and *the delivery of services not available elsewhere in the community.*

The two primary goals and objectives   Maintaining order and protecting life and property are the two primary police goals and objectives. A

The police have as one of their primary goals and objectives the protection of life and property. (Courtesy of the Cincinnati Police Department)

---

*Prosecution of offenders is a secondary goal and objective in those police departments which are not provided prosecutorial services in the lower courts.

police department exists to guarantee to citizens that order will be maintained in society and that their lives and property will be protected by law. Citizens, unable and unprepared to take the law into their own hands, look to the police for assistance in guarding themselves against unscrupulous elements that would disrupt and disturb their peace, violate their freedoms, threaten their existence, and steal or destroy their property. All citizens have the right to expect that their lives and property will be protected and that the community in which they live will be peaceful.

The right to peace and protection is a responsibility of government. The police department is that branch of government to which this responsibility is assigned. It naturally follows, therefore, that the maintenance of order and the protection of life and property must become the two primary goals and objectives of any police department. This means that police departments must direct all of their energies and activities toward the accomplishment of their primary goals and objectives. To do less than this would be to neglect government's responsibility to the citizens and taxpayers of the community.

Secondary goals and objectives   In order to meet its primary goals and objectives, a police department focuses its efforts on preventing crime, arresting and prosecuting offenders, recovering stolen or missing property, assisting the sick and injured, enforcing noncriminal regulations, and delivering services not available elsewhere in the community.

Studies have shown that better than 80 percent of police work, even in larger cities, is of a service-oriented nature. Less than 20 percent of police activity is specifically directed toward criminal matters. This is a very difficult point for students of police administration to understand. Almost all police shows presented on television would have us believe that 99 percent of police work concentrates on the apprehension of the most violent offenders who are rarely arrested peacefully and who usually give the police a merry chase at speeds of a hundred miles per hour or more through crowded city streets while proceeding to empty their guns of more bullets than they could possibly hold. Police officers are often depicted as tough, hardened, insensitive, unsophisticated products of the criminal milieu in which they work. It is a rarity for them to go through an entire show without killing or rendering unconscious one or more people. At the very least, they can be expected to draw their sidearms on a number of occasions and empty them in the direction of someone who may or may not be a fleeing felon.

Even in the largest cities, most police work is service-oriented. (Courtesy of the Newark Police Department)

Because television is such a strong influence in the transmission of culture, many citizens and, unfortunately, many police officers themselves perceive their goals and objectives to be what the television screen tells them they are. Although most people would agree on the importance of the two primary goals and objectives, many people today, police officers included, would look on secondary goals and objectives as being in no way supportive of primary police obligations. Yet the secondary goals and objectives are of nearly equal importance and bear heavily on the successful performance of police departments.

Let us by way of example examine each of the six secondary goals and objectives by presenting some instances, drawn from actual police cases, which demonstrate the relationship between primary and secondary obligations. Note that the word *obligations* is used synonymously with the phrase *goals and objectives,* inasmuch as the latter implies the former in their implementation.

Television often portrays the police officer, erroneously, as a tough, hardened, insensitive, unsophisticated product of the criminal milieu. (Courtesy of the Metropolitan Police Department, Washington, D.C.)

Crime Prevention. A progressive police chief in a community of 15,000 people realized that his department was making very little effort apart from preventive patrol to impact on crime prevention. Wanting to develop a viable crime-prevention program in his department, he arranged to send one of his best patrol officers to the course on crime prevention theory and practice offered by the University of Louisville. When the officer returned to the department after having completed the course, the chief sent a sergeant to a course on crime prevention administration. Working with the sergeant and the patrol officer, the chief instituted a far-reaching crime-prevention program designed to assist home owners and businesspeople in protecting their property against intrusion. Through the development of a crime-alert effort, the chief was able to make his community more security conscious and thereby reduce the crime rate. Furthermore, he actively sought and received the cooperation of thousands of citizens who otherwise may have been reluctant to report suspicions to the police. Major crime declined 8 percent in one year.

Crime prevention is only one of the police officer's myriad responsibilities. (Courtesy of the Los Angeles Police Department)

Arrest and Prosecution of Offenders. The crime rate in a large city had increased more than 40 percent in the previous year. Realizing that the arrest and successful prosecution of offenders is a crime deterrent, the police chief decided that the detective and patrol divisions alone were incapable of significantly lowering the crime rate in the city. Drawing on his best officers, the chief established a specialized force of crime fighters, which he called his *anticrime unit.* These officers grew beards, wore old clothes, and traveled about the city in vans, trucks, and other nondescript vehicles. They concentrated their efforts in high-crime areas, made many arrests, and successfully prosecuted most of their cases. As a result, crime decreased by 50 percent the following year.

Recovery of Stolen and Missing Property. A detective sergeant in charge of a police department's investigations division was responsible for establishing investigative priorities. Realizing that a large number of merchants in the community were being victimized by an inordinate number of fraudulent-check swindles, he personally took over all check cases. Businesspeople throughout the community, pleased with his results, commended the department for its extraordinarily high rate of recoveries.

The recovery of stolen and missing property is a secondary police objective. (Courtesy of the Jackson Police Department, Jackson, Mississippi)

In a small police department serving a community of 13,000 people, a police management consultant noticed that missing property was never logged and that no effort was ever made to locate or to contact owners. If owners of missing property happened to inquire at the police station, they were shown a drawer full of eyeglasses, wallets, jewelry, pocketbooks, and other items that had been turned into the department by good samaritans. Even if the missing property contained the names and addresses of owners, no attempt was made to reach them. In one case, a lost pocketbook contained not only the owner's name and address, but also a doctor's prescription for a life-saving drug, but no attempt was made to contact the owner. The consultant recommended that all missing property be logged and that an effort be made to contact all owners of missing property.

Assistance to the Sick and Injured. A doctor advised the parents of an 11-year-old boy terminally ill with leukemia that within a few days the youngster should be taken to a medical facility some 60 miles away for specialized treatment. Although the police department in the town where the family lived provided ambulance service, the parents decided to transport their son to the distant city themselves, because it was not imperative that he be taken there immediately.

They changed their minds, however, when the boy started having difficulty breathing. Concerned about their son's worsening condition, the parents decided to go to the police station to get the ambulance. While the mother, father, and son remained outside the police station in their station wagon, two neighbors who had accompanied them entered the station to request ambulance service. They spoke with the shift commander, who was reluctant to have the ambulance make such a long run late at night and during such a busy time. He suggested that they either make the trip themselves or hire a private ambulance.

It was finally agreed that the police department would provide oxygen for the trip. However, there was no oxygen available at the station. A patrol car with an oxygen tank was called to the station, and the two neighbors were given instructions on the use of the oxygen tank. After some time had passed, the mother, father, son, and two neighbors started off in the station wagon for the distant city. They had traveled less than two miles when they realized that the tank had run out of oxygen. The boy's breathing problem was becoming more severe. Out of desperation, the group returned to the police station.

Making no attempt to examine the boy in the station wagon, the police dispatcher called another patrol car to the station to furnish another oxygen tank; the shift commander was still unwilling to use the ambulance. Meanwhile, an off-duty patrol officer arrived in the parking lot of the police station and asked the mother and father what was wrong. They explained the situation and told the police officer that

The police spend much of their time protecting the sick and injured. (Courtesy of the Los Angeles County Sheriff's Department)

they had been unable to get an ambulance. The officer immediately volunteered to take the child in the ambulance to the medical facility. The father carried his son to the ambulance, and the mother and father got into the rear of the ambulance with their son.

By this time, the boy was having extreme difficulty breathing. The officer explained how the oxygen tank worked, informed the station that he was taking the boy to the city, instructed the neighbors to follow the ambulance in the station wagon, and took off at a high speed.

At approximately the same time that the ambulance arrived in the outskirts of the city, the ambulance tank ran out of oxygen. Not knowing how to switch over to the emergency tank, the parents were helpless. The officer drove toward the nearest hospital. When they arrived, minutes later, the boy was dead.

Enforcement of Noncriminal Regulations. Liquor establishments in many communities are regulated by both state and local boards which have the power to establish closing times. In one city, the local liquor control board set the Saturday night closing time at 2 A.M. Last call for all alcoholic beverages was at 1:15 A.M., with patrons being informed at 1:45 A.M. that the establishment was closing. All customers were expected to be outside the premises at 2 A.M. One of the authors, then serving as a consultant to the city, was invited by a uniformed officer at 2:45 A.M. to accompany him on patrol. At 3 A.M., they arrived at a night club which appeared to be closed. The officer knocked on the back door of the club and received no answer. Much to the consultant's amazement, the officer, a big, burly man with the strength of an ox, broke down the door.

Even though the officer's actions were procedurally incorrect and in violation of the club owner's constitutional rights, a passerby might simply have thought the officer to be overzealous in enforcing the liquor board's regulations. Once inside the establishment, it became apparent that his efforts had been directed elsewhere. Paying little heed to the club's numerous patrons, he joked with the owner, had two drinks, and left, fortified for the night ahead. Obviously, the regulations that the liquor board had established were not enforced in this city.

The Delivery of Services Not Available Elsewhere in the Community. In a quiet, residential city of 40,000 people, the police department's six patrol cars patrolled the city's six sectors on the 4 P.M. to midnight tour. An elderly couple lived in a second-floor flat in one of the quietest sectors of the city. The man's operation for a spinal fusion had locked his back into a totally rigid position. He was forced to lie straight, motionless, in a chair all day and into the evening, propped up by pillows. At 9 P.M. each night, his wife called the police department for assistance in lifting him from the chair, for he was unable to get out of the chair himself and she was too feeble to lift him. One officer assigned to the patrol car which covered this sector regularly refused to take the call. He saw himself as a crime fighter exclusively and expressed the opinion vociferously that performing services of this nature was not within the realm of police work.

This officer's feelings were shared by several others on his shift, and they too refused to take the call. Several times the radio dispatcher, unable to find an officer who would respond to the request for assistance, was forced to leave the station, drive in his private car to the man's apartment, and personally service the call.

Delivering services not available elsewhere in the community is an important part of the police officer's job. (Courtesy of the Los Angeles County Sheriff's Department)

The police officer's role is, by and large, a helping role. It is the clear-cut obligation of the police department to help all people who need assistance when that assistance is not otherwise available either privately or from another city department. All police departments must meet their primary and secondary goals and objectives. It is their obligation to do so. It is the only reason for their existence. Application of the systems approach to police administration is by far the best method yet conceived to ensure that goals and objectives will be met.

THE SYSTEMS CONCEPT

As defined by Koontz and O'Donnell, a system is "an assemblage of objects or functions united by some interaction or interdependence." [1] Inasmuch as all factors within a system relate to one another, the action of one factor results in the reaction of another. Your family, for example, is a system. If you as a member of that family borrow your father's car and total it in an accident, you could logically expect that your father would react in some way to the incident. He might be angry; he might express a feeling of relief that you were not hurt; or he might express no feelings at all and simply put a call in to the insurance company. Of one thing you can be certain; he will react in some way. That is, he will do something as a result of what you did. It is also likely that others within the family will react. Your mother, your brothers and sisters, and even your aunts and uncles may do or say something as a result of your initial action. If your family were studied in terms of its actions and reactions, we would say that it was being studied from a *systems perspective.*

All things are systems. The more parts and functions they have, the more complicated they are. For example, a Toyota engine is a system. Because it has more parts that interact and are interdependent, an engine in a Pontiac is a more complicated system. Similarly, a jet engine is more complicated than an automobile engine.

Almost anything you can think of is a system. The human body, a whooping crane, General Motors, American Airlines, the government of South Korea, Indiana University, the Hilton Hotel chain, the National Broadcasting Company, Howard Johnson restaurants, the Knights of Columbus, the Kentucky Derby, the Oshkosh Public Library, the Methodist church, and the New York City Police Department are all systems. There are records systems, thoroughbred handicapping systems, and systems by which people cook food (recipes).

Anything—whether human or nonhuman—with interrelated parts or functions may be thought of as a system. (Courtesy of the Metropolitan Police Department, Washington, D.C.)

Because systems imply interaction or interdependence between or among two or more objects or functions, all systems have subsystems. The sun, moon, stars, Mercury, Venus, Mars, Jupiter, Saturn, Uranus, Neptune, Pluto, and Earth are all subsystems of the solar system. Each one of these subsystems may also be regarded as a system itself, comprising any number of subsystems which in turn may be individually studied as systems themselves. Thus earth, a subsystem of the solar system, is a system made up of the atmosphere, oceans, and land masses. As a country, the United States is a subsystem of the North American continent. The United States is also a system made up of 50 subsystems, i.e., states. Each of the 50 subsystems is also an individual system made up of subsystems—counties, cities, towns, and villages— which too may be viewed as separate systems. Each of these units of government has subsystems—the legislative, executive, and judicial branches. The executive branch, when looked on as a system, has several subsystems, e.g., the public works department, the water department, the sewer department, the recreation department, the school department, the health department, the fire department, and the police department. Each of these subsystems can also be studied as individual systems. The police department, for example, is a system made up of subsystems which, depending on the department and its size, are called bureaus, divisions, units, squads, teams, and shifts. These various subsystems interact and are interdependent. They are established to help the department meet its goals and objectives, just as the department is established to meet the goals and objectives of the executive branch of government.

This explanation of the systems concept is perhaps an oversimplification. When one considers that the subsystems of a police department are themselves systems made up of both human and inanimate factors (people, rules, regulations, policies, desks, chairs, radios, telephones, police cars, chemical sprays, jail cells, weapons, records, electronic data-processing equipment, typewriters, breathalyzers, laboratories, booking desks, radar guns, first aid kits, cutting tools, cameras, helicopters, resuscitators, and much more), it becomes clear that police systems are extremely complex and involved. A single change in any one factor of the system will bring about changes in other factors. An action taken by a single individual in the system will inevitably result in reactions by other individuals. Systems, therefore, are always changing. It is vital to the stability of any system that any changes within it contribute to its capabilities of meeting its goals and objectives. The system must be designed to turn *actions* and *reactions* into *improvements.*

If a system is large and complex, it is much more likely to be less efficient than one that is small and simple. The larger a system is, the more energy and, hence, efficiency it loses. An engine in a jet plane loses more energy than the engine in a compact car. The jet engine uses more fuel and is less efficient because it has more parts which create more friction. In organizations, such as police departments, in which people are major subsystem factors, it is the frictional effects of communication rather than the frictional effects of energy transfer that contribute to the loss of efficiency. The larger the police department, the less efficient it is likely to be because of increased difficulties caused by communications problems. Wherever there are people, there is friction. Wherever there are large numbers of people, there is increased friction.

If one fully understands all of the ramifications of the systems concept, it becomes possible, through the application of the concept, to better manipulate, manage, and control any system with which an individual becomes familiar. The more that jet engine mechanics know about jet engines as systems, the better able they are to manipulate, manage, and control jet engines. They learn their trade by studying and working with jet engines, recognizing that all subsystems of a jet engine are interdependent, that they interact, and that they contribute to the overall goals and objectives of the engine itself. Similarly, the more that police chiefs know about police departments as systems, the better able they are to manipulate, manage, and control their police departments. They learn their profession by studying and working as police administrators, recognizing that all subsystems of a police department are interdependent, that they interact, and that they contribute to their departments' overall goals and objectives.

The better a jet engine and a police department are understood from a systems perspective, the greater the possibility of their becoming more efficient and more productive. One of the greatest problems confronting police administrators today is a lack of understanding of how the systems concept can be applied to the design and development of police departments.

In any system, such as a police department, in which people are assigned to tasks within subsystems of the parent system, it must be recognized that these people as individuals are themselves also subsystems of the parent system. This complicates matters somewhat, because people must be dealt with not only as workers in subsystems, such as operations bureaus, detective divisions, and drug units, but also as individuals having different backgrounds, ideals, religious beliefs, values, philosophies, viewpoints, tolerances, and educations. Each individual must therefore be looked on as a system.

For example, think of yourself as a system. Your nervous system, skeletal system, digestive system, circulatory system, and respiratory system are all subsystems of the total system—you as an individual. You are also part of numerous parent systems—your family, your church, the organization for which you work, the college or university you attend, your government, and your neighborhood. Whatever you do impacts in some way on one or more of your subsystems or parent systems.

Consider the chain reaction of processes that take place in your body when you eat food, have three drinks, or run a mile. Consider the impact on your family if you should be arrested, break your back in an automobile accident, or flunk out of college. What you do personally as a system has a tremendous effect on one or more of your parent systems and on one or more of your subsystems.

As a system, you have goals and objectives. These are many and varied. Only you know what they are, but you can be sure that most of them will vary somewhat from the goals and objectives of people you know. However, some of them may be exactly the same. For instance, most people have an overriding desire to survive. Chances are good that you have geared all of your various subsystems to meet this primary goal; subsystems exist to meet the primary goals and objectives of the parent system. Should you decide to stop eating food, you would impede the normal functioning of your digestive subsystem and not survive. If you sever an artery, you would impede the normal functioning of your circulatory system and not survive. If you are caught in a fire and the oxygen supply is reduced to nothing, you would impede the normal functioning of your respiratory system and not survive. Your subsystems, in other words, are vital to your survival. In this sense, you as a system are no different from any other system. All systems are dependent on the proper functioning of their subsystems for survival.

But you as a system are much more complicated than your stomach, brain, heart, veins, and lungs might suggest. You are a human being with many more goals and objectives than simple survival. If your ultimate aim in life is to become a police chief, you attempt to gear your subsystems to meet that objective. If you are a member of a police department in which there are several other police officers who have this same aim in life, your goals and objectives will conflict with those of many of your fellow workers. You might expect that this conflict could cause friction, alienate associates, and perhaps even reduce effective communications within your police department.

You must remember, however, that becoming police chief is likely to be only one of many goals and objectives that you and your fellow officers have in life. Depending on the relative importance of these aims and depending on the intensity with which different people are willing to use their various subsystems in pursuit of what they want to achieve, people will be either successful or unsuccessful in meeting their goals and objectives. They may be successful in meeting some goals but not others. You may want to get married, buy a home, and raise a family. Some of your fellow officers may place little importance on achieving these goals and objectives and instead make conscious decisions to devote all of their energies toward becoming chief of police. If all of you have equal amounts of intelligence and stamina, the others' chances of becoming police chief should, everything else being equal, be much better than yours. But everything else is not equal.

Your subsystems are significantly different in many respects and will impact in many different ways on your individual goals and objectives. Although you may have to devote large amounts of time and money to your family obligations while they devote the same amount of time and money to education, other aspects of your individual subsystems might make you a more attractive candidate for the chief's job. You might have a better personality or a better disposition. Some of them may have poor temperaments or lack leadership qualities. You might be able to better relate to the community. The mayor responsible for making the chief's appointment, might see in you preferable qualities of character. If you are able to direct all of your subsystems toward making you as a person (system) more attractive and more acceptable than your competitors, you may very well receive the appointment. Remember, however, that all officers in competition for the chief's job are using their own subsystems to best advantage in attempting to achieve that goal at which all of you are aiming. Each competitor is a different person with different goals and objectives and different capabilities (subsystems). All competitors interact with one another and are interdependent. All interact with one another differently and all are interdependent in varying degrees. People are unpredictable. They therefore tend to complicate systems in ways that are difficult to predict. In systems where people as well as things are system factors, the job of systems management is a demanding, difficult, and challenging task.

The mix of all system and subsystem factors in the building of an organization designed to meet goals and objectives cannot be achieved by following any established blueprint or book of rules. The process of systems building is too dynamic to describe in an exact or precise way.

Even the best systems builders make mistakes. Consider the case of Montana ranchers who, having been convinced that coyotes were menacing their grazing livestock, set out to destroy the animals through wholesale poisoning. The coyotes, which were subsystems of the ranch operations, were preventing the ranchers from achieving system goals and objectives: raising livestock and earning a living. But aside from destroying cattle and sheep, the coyotes were making contributions to the balance of nature, unbeknownst to the ranchers, by keeping down the gopher population. Once the coyotes were destroyed, the number of gophers on the ranches increased astronomically. Herds of gophers burrowed all through the ranchers' grazing land, which then became overgrown with sagebrush. Since grazing livestock do not eat sagebrush, their food supply was diminished significantly and they suffered accordingly, as did the ranchers.[2]

Because system factors that are interdependent can be so sensitive to even the slightest change, it is important not to make mistakes in designing systems. Had the Montana ranchers sought advice from an agricultural consultant on the impact of destroying the coyote population, which was for them a system factor relating to the interdependence of subsystems, they might have decided to destroy both the coyote and gopher populations. Had they done this, however, their ranches might very well have been overrun by rodents spreading disease and pestilence among their grazing flocks. By not approaching their problem from a systems perspective, the ranchers impeded progress toward the achievement of their primary goals and objectives.

We may conclude that systems have three primary characteristics:

1. they comprise subsystems which may be looked on as systems in and of themselves;

2. they are made up of factors which interact and/or are interdependent; and

3. they are established for the purpose of meeting specific goals and objectives.

Inputs, processes, outputs and feedback   In addition to their primary characteristics, systems can also be described in terms of what they do. For example, many green plants take sunlight and water (inputs), perform photosynthesis (process), and produce oxygen and food (outputs). Similarly, a construction company takes various inputs (labor, lumber, bricks, cement, and nails), processes them (carpentry and masonry), and produces an output (a house).

Besides inputs, processes, and outputs, most systems are also characterized by feedback. Feedback may be described as an input about how the output is doing. A foreman who criticizes a mason for bricking over a window space is delivering feedback (input) about how well the mason did the job (output). Similarly, when a professor grades an examination and passes it back to a student, the professor is providing the student with information or feedback (input) about the quality of the student's work (output).

This process of feedback is essential to the proper functioning of any system. Without feedback, the system cannot know whether its outputs are good or bad, satisfactory or unsatisfactory, productive or unproductive. When a system continues to perform poorly, it must be assumed that feedback is not being provided to those in control or, from a systems standpoint, to those who have the power to change inputs and processes for output improvements.

Feedback is what differentiates a *closed-loop system* from an *open-loop system.* In an open-loop system, no provision is made for feedback. The system functions in terms of a one-way cause-and-effect relationship,[3] as shown in Fig. 2.1. In a closed-loop system, by contrast, provision is made for feedback (see Fig. 2.2). In other words, a closed-loop system provides for the introduction of information about how well or how poorly the system is working.

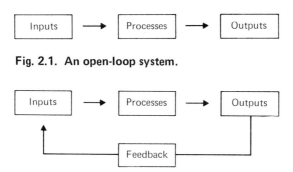

Fig. 2.1. An open-loop system.

Fig. 2.2. A closed-loop system.

Types of systems Any system can be described in terms of the interdependence and interrelatedness of its subsystems; its functions of inputs, processes, and output; and whether it provides for feedback (closed-loop system) or does not (open-loop system). In addition to varying in these characteristics, systems may be described as being either *open* or *closed.*

Open and *closed systems* are distinctly different from *open-loop* and *closed-loop systems.* An *open system* is in contact with its environment; input and output are not restricted to factors directly related to the process involved. For example, in the construction illustration cited above, the weather is an input into the process of building the house. The weather can either help or hinder the process, but it cannot be easily controlled. An environment output of the construction process not directly related to the house might be the forced relocation of the animals that once lived on or around the building site.

A *closed system,* by contrast, is not influenced by its environment. The solar system, which is a static structure in an ordered universe, is a good example of a *closed system.* Typhoons, atomic explosions, and intrusions by humans will not change its processes and outputs.

In this book we will be concerned with police organizations as systems. Because these systems are in part made up of people who are responsive to and influenced by their environments, they may be considered to be *living systems*. All living systems are open systems.[4]

ORGANIZATIONS AS SYSTEMS

In 1956 Boulding identified nine different levels of systems.[5] As adapted from Boulding's research, the nine levels, in order of their increasing complexity, are:

1. static systems—frameworks;

2. simple dynamic systems—machines;

3. cybernetic systems—thermostats;

4. self-perpetuating systems—cells;

5. genetic-societal systems—plants;

6. animal systems—animals;

7. human systems—people;

8. social systems—organizations; and

9. transcendental systems—unknowns.

Boulding maintained that beyond the second level, we have very little understanding of what really goes on in systems. Since 1956, however, much has been learned about the third and fourth levels. But our knowledge is insufficient, even today, to build theoretical system models beyond level four. Cancer research, for example, is at the fourth level. Because they do not fully understand the cell as a system, researchers remain stymied as to how to control the growth of cancer cells.

Our efforts, then, to study organizations as systems (level eight) will be incomplete. Studying the control of organizations from a systems standpoint is four levels more complex than studying the control of cancer. This is not to say, however, that we should not attempt the effort. But we must understand at the outset that we simply do not understand all of the interrelationships and factors that govern organizations as systems. The best we can do is to learn what is known and apply it as effectively as possible. We will therefore proceed to study police organizations as open systems and depend on the confidence expressed by Nigro that open-systems theory "represents an analytical framework believed to be the most effective for adequately describing what an organization is, how it functions, and how it should function."[6]

THE POLICE ORGANIZATION AS A SYSTEM

Police organizations are systems no more or no less complex than any others. Police organizations consist of numerous involved, interdependent subsystems. The investigations division, or subsystem, for example, is dependent on the records division for arrest records, the patrol division for backup, the intelligence division for information on organized crime, the laboratory for scientific investigative assistance, the property unit for the storage of evidence, the detention unit for the holding of prisoners, the maintenance division for servicing its vehicles, the communications division for radio contact, the supply unit for weapons and ammunition, the training division to keep up with the latest investigative techniques, the planning division to isolate high-crime areas, and the pay roll unit to receive weekly paychecks. The work of the detectives who are assigned to the investigations division is made much more difficult, and sometimes impossible, when one or more of these divisions or units performs poorly or works in a way which is inconsistent with the goals and objectives of the organization.

The subsystems of police organizations may be studied from three different perspectives. These are the *human perspective*, the *structural-design perspective*, and the *work-flow perspective.*[7]

The human perspective views the organization from the bottom, looking up. Some subsystems involved in this perspective are leadership, individual police officers, and groups of officers.

The structural-design perspective sees the organization from the top, looking down. The subsystems in this perspective are those found on the traditional organization chart—e.g., the patrol division, the investigations division, the traffic division, the communications division, and all other component parts of the organization.

The work-flow perspective observes the organization from the side, looking across. Its subsystems are the flow of information, the flow of orders, and the flow of communications.

All three perspectives are important. They are, in effect, vantage points from which to examine the organization.

As with other systems, police organizations can be discussed in terms of inputs, processes, and outputs. Inputs include police officers; civilian personnel; mode of dress; equipment, such as patrol cars and two-way radios; budgetary support; rules and regulations; the law; and community values.

Outputs consist largely of primary and secondary goals and objectives. These, of course, include maintaining order, protecting life and property, preventing crime, arresting and prosecuting offenders, recovering stolen and missing property, assisting the sick and injured, enforcing noncriminal regulations, and delivering services not available elsewhere in the community.

The processes involved in police organizations are numerous and relate directly to particular inputs, inasmuch as each input must be processed. Consider, if you will, the single input of police officers. Processing includes such activities as recruiting, selecting, training, equipping, assigning, supervising, paying, and evaluating.

Many police departments fail to recognize as essential one of the most important aspects of the systems approach to police organization—feedback. For example, police chiefs occasionally initiate a new procedure. If they make no effort to determine whether or not their officers understand the new procedure and if they fail to ascertain whether or not their officers are following it as a guideline in their work, they will lack feedback as to how their input (the new procedure) is actually being carried out (output). Lack of feedback within an organization means lack of organizational control. If chiefs fail to make provision for feedback on all outputs, they will soon lose control over their entire organizations. Feedback is that important.

Police management consultants have found that most police departments are open-loop systems characterized by a one-way cause-and-effect relationship. The effective delivery of police services (outputs) demands, however, that police organizations be administered on a closed-loop basis.

A specific example of input, process, output, and feedback may help to illustrate these points. Suppose that a police communications division receives a call from a citizen that a fight is in progress at Joe's Hot Dog and Hamburger Emporium. The call from the citizen is the input. The process is the communications division's receiving and evaluating the call and assigning one or more cars to service the complaint. The output is the arrival of the officer or officers at the scene and the actions they take to break up the fight. The feedback is the information the communications division receives about the disposition of the matter, e.g., there is no fight in progress at Joe's, there never was a fight, more help is needed in order to break up the fight, the fight has been broken up, or an arrest has been made. Figure 2.3 shows this sequence of events from a systems perspective.

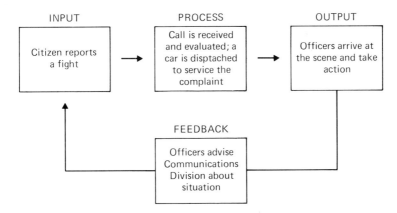

INPUT

Citizen reports a fight

PROCESS

Call is received and evaluated; a car is disptached to service the complaint

OUTPUT

Officers arrive at the scene and take action

FEEDBACK

Officers advise Communications Division about situation

Fig. 2.3. A police action as input, process, output, and feedback.

This one illustration emphasizes the importance of feedback. Without feedback, the communications division would have no way of knowing if the processing of the call was correct, and no information would be available as to whether or not the output was appropriate. If many people had been injured in the fight and if the communications division sent only one car to service the call, the process involved in evaluating calls of this nature should perhaps be modified through the introduction of new or different inputs into the system.

It is essential that the output (what happens at the scene) be described to the communications division (feedback) for consideration and study. It might be determined that the communications division failed to get sufficient information from the person who reported the fight. An effort could then be made to develop procedures by which better information could be taken from people who register complaints over the telephone, thus improving input. It is through feedback that corrective action is taken, thus providing for more effective outputs in the future.

In summary, police organizations are open systems in constant contact with their environment. They can be studied from the human, structural-design, and work-flow perspectives, and they have inputs, processes, and outputs that can be identified. Like many other organizations serving the public, police organizations have a disturbing tendency to disregard the importance of feedback. In order to deliver services effectively, they must be constructed as closed-loop systems. Police organizations also have numerous subsystems which interact and are interdependent. Because of their importance, an entire chapter (Chapter 3) has been set aside to discuss them.

THE ORGANIZATION CHART IN SYSTEMS BUILDING

Some scholars specializing in organization theory and management have been severely critical of organization charts, arguing that they create within the organization process excessive red tape and formality. It has also been pointed out that such charts cannot possibly show all of the relationships that exist, especially in some of the more complex organizations.[8] Figure 2.4 shows an organization chart of the Newark, New Jersey, Police Department. One can readily see how difficult it would be to understand every single relationship that exists within that department.

There is some validity in the arguments against the use of organization charts as a means of showing internal relationships. Many police departments in this country, however, have neither organization charts nor any other means by which internal relationships can be conceptualized. Many police organizations are in much more need of standardization today than they are in danger of succumbing to the potential ills of the organization chart. As Wilson and McLaren have observed, "the police service is in no immediate danger of overmanagement."[9]

Organization charts have many advantages. Koontz and O'Donnell suggest that organization charts can delineate the lines leading to decision-making authority, depict organizational inconsistencies, and demonstrate to personnel how they as individuals relate to the organization.[10] Dale believes that charts can help indicate major functions, principal positions, and primary channels of communication and command within organizations.[11] He notes that "nothing else makes it so easy to grasp the general outlines of an organization structure almost at a glance."[12]

A survey of private organizations conducted by the American Management Association found that 94 of 100 large companies surveyed had organization charts and that 60 of 66 medium-size companies had them.[13] Conversely, of 12 municipal police departments studied in depth by one of the authors during a recent eight-year period, only 3 departments had organization charts.

Although charts may be faulted for not showing *all* relationships that exist within organizations, especially large ones, they do depict major relationships and reveal the important elements in organizational structure. Koontz and O'Donnell concluded that "those firms which have comprehensive organization charts appear to have sound organizational structures."[14]

Why is an organization chart important? What does it do? An organization chart is a diagram of a system, its subsystems, and its subsystems' subsystems. It shows how all subsystems are expected to relate formally within an organization, and it assigns each subsystem a specific task to perform. It improves understanding in that it shows at a glance how information is formally communicated within an organization and who reports to whom within an organization. It prescribes relationships and thereby facilitates communications. It says, "Here I am. This is what I look like as an organization." It is, then, a *picture* of the organization. It is important because it facilitates conceptualization of what an organization consists of. It is as helpful to a chief as it is to a police officer assigned to patrol duties. It shows all organization members, from patrol officer to chief, where they fit in the organization as well as what work they are expected to perform. Of course, an organization chart does not necessarily show *exactly* where everybody fits, nor does it show *precisely* what work everybody is expected to perform. Rather, it provides a general structure of subsystems in which assignments can be made and work can be accomplished. As such, it is an invaluable tool to the police administrator.

Organization charts can introduce a sense of orderliness to any police system. Too often, police organizations have developed haphazardly, with relationships among various subsystems reflecting this. Meeting goals and objectives through system outputs has been hampered because of lack of organization. Just as a carpenter builds a house by using blueprints and a chef prepares a dinner by using recipes, a police administrator organizes a police department by using a chart as a foundation on which to build the organization.

Once an organization is charted, the administrator's job is by no means finished, however. In much the same way that a carpenter will disregard blueprints to turn wasted space into a closet or a chef will deviate from a recipe by adding a sprinkle of salt or a pinch of pepper to make a dish more palatable, the police administrator must always be sensitive to feedback and be willing to change organizational inputs to make the department more viable in terms of meeting overall goals and objectives. This may mean reorganization and therefore one or more changes in the organization chart. In order to meet the changing needs of the police service and to make outputs more effective and productive, it should be expected that an organization will be undergoing changes continually. If these changes are not reflected in its organization chart, a department will very quickly lose its sense of orderliness. The organization chart, therefore, must be an accurate picture of what the organization actually is.

One example of the importance of a good organization chart can be drawn from the experience of a police management consultant who was called in to study a department because of internal problems caused by

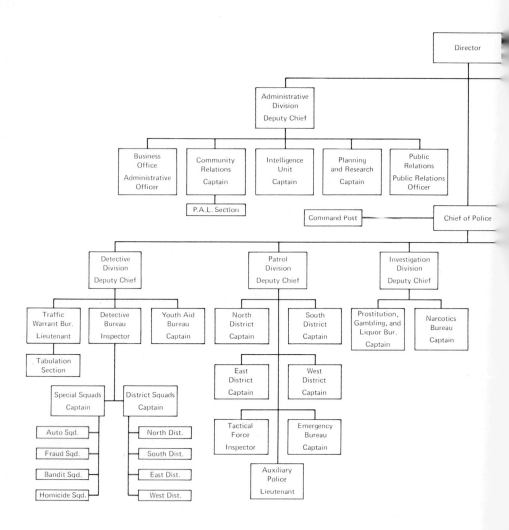

Fig. 2.4. Organization chart of the police department in Newark, New Jersey.

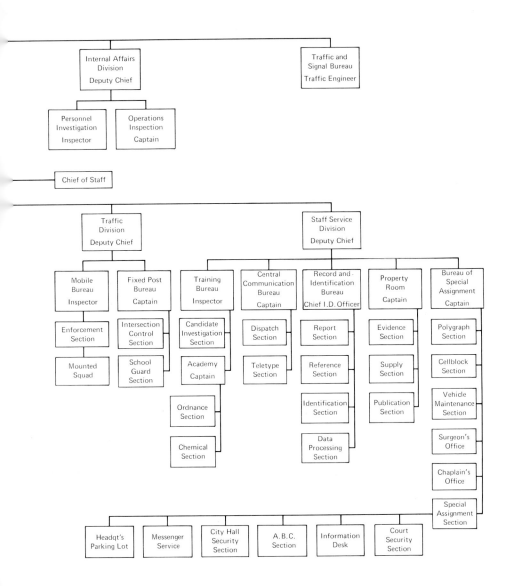

improper organization. The department's original organization chart is shown in Fig. 2.5. Except for the unusual placement of some auxiliary services within the operations component of the organization, a matter which later proved to be justified in terms of how the department met its goals and objectives, the department appeared to be properly organized. By asking questions and by observing departmental functions, however, the consultant soon realized that the organization chart was a misrepresentation of the department's actual organization. After much effort, the consultant was finally able to construct a new organization chart (Fig. 2.6, pp. 48–49) which represented the actual organization of the department.

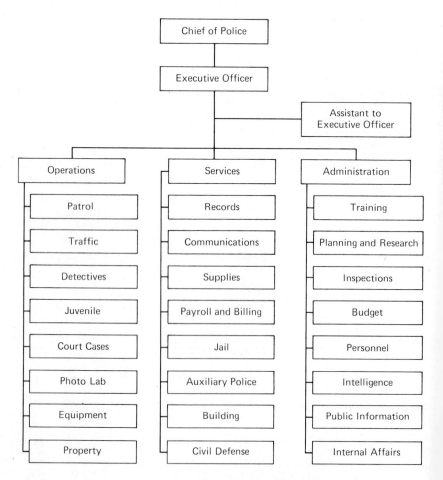

Fig. 2.5. A police department's formal organization chart.

Because 100 police officers were serving a community of over 60,000 people, it was important that the department be reorganized for the proper delivery of services. The problem with the department's formal organization chart was that it did not reflect changes that had occurred in the organization. The problem with its actual organization was that no one in the department had primary responsibility for a number of extremely important functions. Reorganization, therefore, was essential if the department was to be expected to meet its goals and objectives.

The first task in the reorganization was to develop a sound organization chart (see Fig. 2.7). Next, it was essential to devise a personnel table which would show specific assignments (see Fig. 2.8). These steps were absolutely necessary to bring a degree of stability back to the department and to reconstruct it in a form that would be responsive to the systems approach to management.

THE POLICE IN THE LARGER SYSTEM

Earlier in this chapter we mentioned that police systems are subsystems of the executive branch of government. Equally important is the fact that police systems are also subsystems of the criminal justice system, which also has two other major subsystems: the courts and corrections. The fact that these three subsystems have often failed to consider their interdependence has been widely noted, even though each impacts on the other in a profound way.

STANDARD 4.1

COOPERATION AND COORDINATION

Every police agency immediately should act to insure understanding and cooperation between the agency and all other elements of the criminal justice system, and should immediately plan and implement appropriate coordination of its efforts with those of other elements of the criminal justice system.

National Advisory Commission on Criminal Justice Standards and Goals, *Police* (Washington, D.C.: U.S. Government Printing Office, 1973), p. 73.

Backup of cases in the courts contributes significantly to increased crime and increased case loads for the police. Prison overpopulation forces the courts to resort more readily to the use of probation, a rehabilitative technique which has not achieved a remarkable degree of

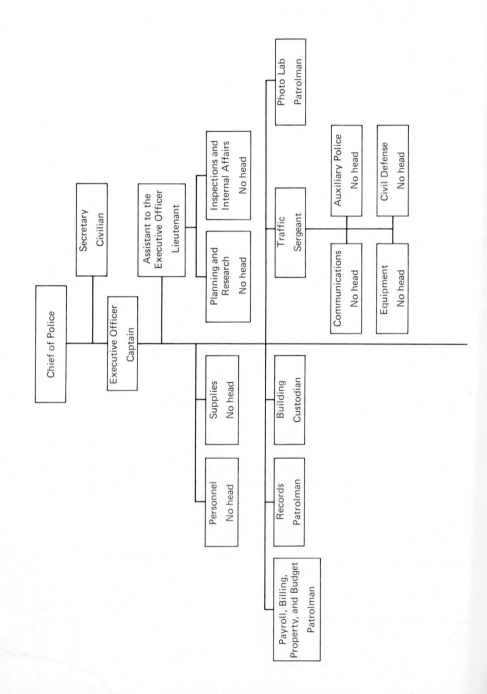

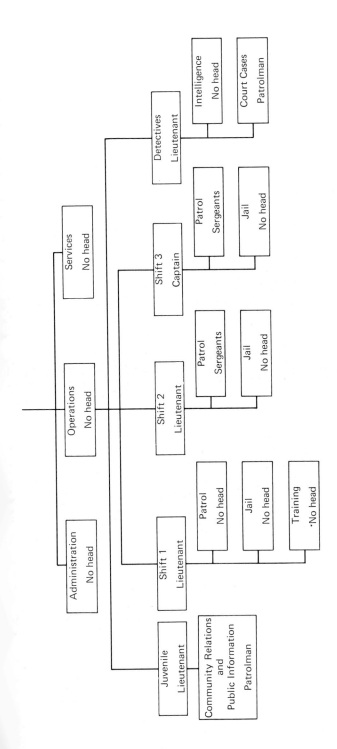

Fig. 2.6. A police department's actual organization.

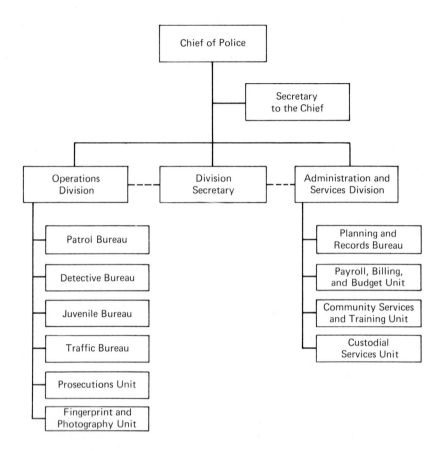

Fig. 2.7. Organization of the reorganized department (compare with Fig. 2.5).

success and which serves, in some cases, to hamper the crime-prevention efforts of police departments. Similarly, police departments that are successful in clearing crimes by arrest are likely to overburden the courts and place severe strains on correctional systems, which are already bulging at the seams with clientele they are incapable of servicing properly. The courts respond by further delaying cases, and the correctional systems respond by increasing the use of parole as a release device.

The results throughout society have been chaotic, contributing to a crime problem which would appear to be, both statistically and actually, very much out of control. Until social scientists, who currently

	Chief	Captain	Lieutenant	Sergeant	Patrolman	Civilian	Coordinators	Crossing Guards	Total
Office of the Chief	1					1			2
Operations Division		1				½			1½
Patrol Bureau									
8-4			1	3	21				25
4-midnight			1	3	23				27
Midnight-8			1	3	15				19
Detective Bureau									
8-4			1		4				5
4-midnight					1				1
6-2					1				1
Juvenile Bureau									
8-4			1		2				3
6-2					1				1
Traffic Bureau									
8-4				1	3		2	57	63
4-midnight					3				3
Midnight-8					2				2
Prosecutions Unit					2				2
Fingerprint and Photography Unit				None full time					0
Administration and Services Division		1	1			½			2½
Planning and Records Bureau					1	2			3
Payroll, Billing, and Budget Unit					1				1
Community Services and Training Unit					2				2
Custodial Services						1			1
Total	1	2	6	10	82	5	2	57	165

Fig. 2.8. Specific personnel assignments in reorganized department.

dominate the fields of applied and theoretical criminology, begin to look at criminal justice problems from a systems perspective, taking into consideration the goals and objectives of all three systems and recognizing the importance of their interdependence, very little progress will be made in combatting the staggering problem of crime. When the police or, for that matter, any systems factors are strained beyond their capabilities, a byproduct of not having all criminal justice subsystems working in concert with one another, it is ludicrous to assume that the application of criminological and sociological theory will solve the crime problem. Theory without viable, well-constructed, interdependent organizations to apply and implement it is, from a realistic standpoint, worthless.

STANDARD 8.1

RELATIONSHIP OF THE CRIMINAL JUSTICE AND OTHER SYSTEMS TO THE QUALITY OF POLICE SERVICE

(a) To the extent that police interact with other governmental systems such as the criminal justice, juvenile justice, and public and mental health systems, police effectiveness should be recognized as often largely dependent upon the performance of other agencies within these systems.

American Bar Association Project on Standards for Criminal Justice, *The Urban Police Function* Approved Draft (New York: A.B.A., 1973), p. 17.

The systems approach to management is, by and large, an approach that has been used until recent years almost exclusively by business and industry. The possibilities that exist for its application to other types of organizations are almost limitless. As applied to police organizations, the systems approach to management offers a genuine and pertinent hope for the future.

SUMMARY

This chapter has introduced the concept of systems and has demonstrated how the concept applies to police organization and management. The application of the systems concept will be a recurring theme throughout this book.

The overriding theme of the systems concept is subsystem interdependence. Input, process, output, and feedback have been stressed as being essential to system design. Finally, all police organizations are open systems because they react to environmental inputs.

DISCUSSION QUESTIONS

1. We note in the text that the police role is primarily a helping role and that most police work is related to service rather than to crime. Does this match your perception of police work? What has been the basis for your perception of police work?

2. Feedback is a key concept in the study of systems. What forms of feedback are utilized in the classroom? On the job? In your personal relationships?

3. Why do you think that many systems, including organizations, fail to provide for and utilize feedback?

4. Are you familiar with police departments or other organizations that do not possess organization charts? What influence does the absence of a chart seem to have on the organizations' operations?

5. Are you familiar with police departments or other organizations whose organization charts do not accurately reflect the way that things are really done? How would you explain the difference between the charts and reality?

6. How is a police department influenced by the larger systems of which it is a part? How are those larger systems influenced by the police department? Would you say that police departments are more or less interdependent on other systems than most organizations?

REFERENCES

1. Harold Koontz and Cyril O'Donnell, *Principles of Management: An Analysis of Managerial Functions,* 4th ed. (New York: McGraw-Hill, 1968), p. 43.

2. Paul B. Sears, "Ecology, the Intricate Web of Life," in *As We Live and Breathe: The Challenge of Our Environment* (Washington, D.C.: National Geographic Society, 1971), as adapted in Ned Greenwood and J.M.B. Edwards, *Human Environments and Natural Systems: A Conflict of Dominion* (North Scituate, Mass.: Duxbury Press, 1973), pp. 62-63.

3. Koontz and O'Donnell, *op. cit.,* p. 43.

4. Robert Chin, "The Utility of System Models and Developmental Models for Practitioners," in *The Planning of Change,* Warren G. Bennis, Kenneth D. Benne, and Robert Chin (New York: Holt, Rinehart and Winston, 1961), pp. 201-214.

5. Kenneth E. Boulding, "General Systems Theory—The Skeleton of Science," in *Management Science* **2,** 3 (April 1956): 197-208.

6. Felix A. Nigro, *Modern Public Administration,* 2d ed. (New York: Harper & Row, 1965), p. 100.

7. Adapted from Edgar F. Huse and James L. Bowditch, *Behavior in Organizations: A Systems Approach to Managing,* 2d ed. (Reading, Mass.: Addison-Wesley, 1977), pp. 57-60.

8. Ernest Dale, *Organization* (New York: American Management Association, 1967), pp. 238-243.

9. O.W. Wilson and Roy C. McLaren, *Police Administration,* 3rd ed. (New York: McGraw-Hill, 1972), p. 51.

10. Koontz and O'Donnell, *op. cit.,* p. 418.

11. Dale, *op cit.,* p. 233.

12. *Ibid.,* p. 243.

13. *Ibid.,* p. 233.

14. Koontz and O'Donnell, *op. cit.,* p. 418.

PART II
THE TRADITIONAL
PERSPECTIVE

The four chapters in Part II address topics that have traditionally been considered central to police administration. The discussions rely heavily on such matters as tasks, structures, principles, and functions. Although in some senses modern management has gone "beyond" these concerns (as Parts III, IV, and V will demonstrate), we feel strongly that the elements of traditional police administration are the building blocks for more "advanced" practices. To use a football analogy, they are fundamentals much like blocking and tackling. The most sophisticated football offenses and defenses are dependent on sound blocking and tackling. Similarly, police departments utilizing the most up-to-date organizational and managerial practices are still dependent in large measure on the sound application of traditional concepts of police administration.

Chapter 3 discusses 30 basic police subsystem tasks within the framework of operations, administration, and auxiliary services. The treatment of these numerous subsystem tasks is necessarily brief. Our intent is to impress on you the number and variety of tasks that *must* be performed in a police organization if the attainment of goals and objectives is to be a realistic possibility.

Chapter 4 presents the basic principles of police organization. These principles are useful guidelines for organizing police work and police personnel. Although the applicability of the principles varies somewhat by size of organization (consider the extremes of the many one-person agencies and the New York Police Department, with more than 30,000 employees), all police managers need a working familiarity with them.

Chapter 5 considers the basic functions of police management. Two of the key things that police managers do, or at least should do, in their jobs are system building and organizing; these were introduced in earlier chapters. The four additional management functions discussed are planning, staffing, directing, and controlling.

Chapter 6 focuses on the chief of police, who has more authority and responsibility than do the other managers in the police organization. The chief's functions differ in some respects from those of other police management positions, as noted in the chapter. Also discussed are a number of important considerations pertaining to the recruitment and selection of chiefs of police.

CHAPTER 3
BASIC POLICE SUBSYSTEM
TASKS

LEARNING OBJECTIVES

1. Characterize police operational tasks.

2. Identify the relationship among operations, administration, and auxiliary services.

3. Identify some of the functions of police patrol.

4. Cite a proper basis for assigning patrol personnel.

5. Identify the five traffic subtasks.

6. Identify selective enforcement with respect to traffic.

7. Cite a rule of thumb with respect to the portion of police personnel committed to investigative functions.

8. Cite some reasons why vice regulation is at the heart of much of the public animosity toward the police and at the heart of much police corruption.

9. Identify the strike-force approach to organized-crime suppression.

10. Explain why police work with juveniles may be considered a separate task.

11. Identify three varieties of police–community service roles.

12. Identify the most dangerous and most common type of service request handled by the police.

13. Identify the target-hardening approach to crime prevention.

14. Cite the reason for the formation of many police-community relations units.

15. Explain why the community relations unit approach came to be viewed as not totally satisfactory.

16. Characterize police administrative tasks.

17. Identify seven personnel subtasks.

18. Identify the crucial role of the field training officer.

19. Differentiate between traditional budgeting methods and PPBS.

20. Identify some of the possible functions of legal assistance.

21. Identify the aim of the inspections function.

22. Identify the function of internal affairs.

23. Cite the recommendation of the Knapp Commission with respect to internal affairs personnel.

24. Identify the intelligence function.

25. Characterize police auxiliary services tasks.

26. Identify the foundation of the records task.

27. Explain why the communications subtask is closely related to both operations and auxiliary services.

28. Explain the relationship between the property subtask and the chain of custody.

29. Identify the police detention function.

30. Identify the police identification task.

31. Cite the reason why some police agencies contract out for maintenance service.

Based on impressions gleaned from movies, television, novels, and occasional encounters, most people believe that they know what police work is all about. Most dramatic presentations centering on police activity are totally unrealistic, yet fiction is the cornerstone of people's opinions and assumptions about law enforcement. Real police officers are more often than not evaluated on the basis of fictional works. Why are local detectives not as successful as Columbo in solving the crime? And if the police on television always dust for fingerprints at crime scenes, why don't the local police follow suit? Every layperson has his or her opinion and offers it freely.

If you were asked to list the basic police tasks as they are portrayed in the media, you would probably think only of those that are closely related to the apprehension of criminal offenders. These are the tasks that television and the movies focus on. They are certainly the most exciting and interesting tasks that police officers perform, yet they represent only a small percentage of what police officers actually do. Who would want to watch a movie about directing traffic, planning, or maintaining police vehicles? Despite the relatively uninteresting nature of these and many other kinds of tasks, any police organization is dependent on them for the accomplishment of goals and objectives.

This chapter will briefly discuss 30 basic police subsystem tasks. The exact number of tasks that the police perform is really not that important; it could easily be argued that there are only 20 such tasks or, for that matter, that there are 40 or 50—the specific number of tasks performed by the police depends on the observer's perspective. We have identified 30 that we believe are important and should be discussed. The number is significant in that it suggests that there is a proliferation of tasks that must be performed in any police organization.

Some police departments are so large that separate units have been established to perform each task; others are so small that all tasks are performed by one person. The remaining police organizations fall somewhere in the middle; for them, the major problem is developing a logical and effective approach for grouping similar or like functions into operating units.

The three major subsystems of the police organization are operations, administration, and auxiliary services. These three subsystems provide the framework for our discussion of the basic police tasks. The list below shows the tasks arranged within the subsystems of the police organization.

Operations	*Administration*	*Auxiliary Services*
Patrol	Personnel	Records
Traffic	Training	Communications
Criminal investigations	Planning	Property
Vice	Budget and finance	Laboratory
Organized crime	Legal assistance	Detention
Juvenile services	Public information	Identification
Community services	Secretarial	Alcohol testing
Crime prevention	Inspections	Facilities
Community relations	Internal affairs	Equipment
	Intelligence	Supply
		Maintenance

THE OPERATIONS SUBSYSTEM

Operations are those activities performed in direct assistance to the public. The operations subsystem is that part of police work with which most people are familiar. Through the operations subsystem, police officers are deployed to take action, to fight crime, and to provide services to the public. It is by far the most interesting of the three major subsystems and is always the largest of the three subsystems.

The other two subsystems—administration and auxiliary service—exist to provide day-to-day and long-term services to personnel working with the operations subsystem. The operations subsystem is their *raison d'être.*

The goals and objectives of the operations subsystem are identical to those of the entire police agency. All work in which operations personnel are involved is directed toward the accomplishment of organizational goals and objectives. The tasks included within the operations subsystem are aimed directly at achieving one or more of these goals and objectives. These tasks are patrol, traffic, criminal investigations, vice, organized crime, juvenile services, crime prevention, and community relations.

Patrol   Patrol is commonly referred to as the backbone of the police service.[1] Patrol officers are normally the first to respond to crime scenes, accidents, and calls for service. In some instances, patrol officers handle the entire matter with which they are confonted; in others, they conduct the preliminary investigation before turning the matter over to specialized personnel. Patrol officers are expected to be ever alert for

---

STANDARD 9.1

SPECIALIZED ASSIGNMENT

Every police agency should use generalists (patrol officers) wherever possible and, before establishing any specialization necessary to improve the delivery of police service, specifically define the problem that may require specialization, determine precisely what forms of specialization are required to cope with this problem, and implement only those forms in a manner consistent with available resources and agency priorities.

National Advisory Commission on Criminal Justice Standards and Goals, *Police* (Washington, D.C.: U.S. Government Printing Office, 1973), p. 210.

---

crimes in progress, traffic violations, suspicious persons and circumstances, public property in need of repair, and anything else out of the ordinary. Patrol is also intended to prevent crime through its omnipresence, to keep in touch with the community, and to be responsive to citizen needs and problems. One of the most important aims of patrol is to provide law-abiding citizens with a feeling of security so that they can conduct their affairs without fear of criminal interference. The patrol function maintains order and protects life and property on a continuing basis.

Patrol is commonly referred to as the backbone of the police service. (Courtesy of the Metropolitan Police Department, Washington, D.C.)

Webster defines patrol as "the action of traversing a district or beat or of going the rounds along a chain of guards for observation or the maintenance of security."[2] The police use several methods of *traversing a district or beat*—foot patrol, car patrol, motorcycle patrol, wagon patrol, bicycle patrol, horse patrol, aircraft patrol, marine patrol, canine patrol, and tactical patrol. Circumstances in each situation should dictate the means employed, and none should be used simply because of tradition or common practice.

The patrol task must be organized by time and location; that is, patrol personnel work shifts on a 24-hour basis and are assigned to beats so that the entire jurisdiction receives patrol coverage. Unfortunately, many police administrators assign personnel to patrol times and locations on the basis of tradition and/or whim; as a consequence, patrol personnel in many communities are not allocated so as to maximize their effectiveness.

Patrol personnel should be assigned according to the patterns of crime and requests for service in the community they serve. This is their *business*, and they should work when and where their business occurs. To do otherwise is to waste tax dollars and reduce the effectiveness of the police.

STANDARD 8.1

ESTABLISHING THE ROLE OF THE PATROL OFFICER

Every police chief executive immediately should develop written policy that defines the role of the patrol officer, and should establish operational objectives and priorities that reflect the most effective use of the patrol officer in reducing crime.

1. Every police chief executive should acknowledge that the patrol officer is the agency's primary element for the deliverance of police services and prevention of criminal activity.
2. Every police chief executive should insure maximum efficiency in the deliverance of patrol services by setting out in written policy the objectives and priorities governing these services.

National Advisory Commission on Criminal Justice Standards and Goals, *Police* (Washington, D.C.: U.S. Government Printing Office, 1973), p. 191.

A recent experiment conducted in Kansas City, Missouri, raised some serious questions concerning the true value of police patrol.[3] Although most observers consider the findings of the experiment to be inconclusive, they are nonetheless important as challenges to traditional assumptions. The experiment, conducted by the Police Foundation and the Kansas City Police Department, could find no real evidence that routine patrol deters crime, improves the delivery of services, or affects citizen feelings of security. These findings, although highly controversial, will undoubtedly spur further research into the effectiveness of police patrol as we know it and could result in a rethinking about the patrol function, leading to significant improvement.

Traffic   The traffic task includes several subtasks relating to different police activities vis à vis motor vehicles. These subtasks include intersection control (traffic direction), traffic law enforcement, radar operation, parking law enforcement, and traffic accident investigation.

Except for unusual situations at accident scenes or large gatherings, the task of intersection control is ordinarily a major concern only in urban or in highly congested suburban areas. In such situations, the demands of intersection control can cause severe drains on police personnel. To combat this drain on police resources, the city of London utilizes 2000 civilians as traffic wardens, thus freeing the police for more important tasks.[4] In the United States, the use of civilians for intersection control work has been much more limited. However, several police departments, e.g., New York, Los Angeles, San Francisco, and Dallas, are now employing civilian traffic controllers for intersection work.

STANDARD 9.6

TRAFFIC OPERATIONS

Every police agency and every local government responsible for highway traffic safety should perform the basic functions of traffic law enforcement, traffic accident management and traffic direction and control.

4. Every police agency should develop and implement written policies governing the investigation of traffic accidents, enforcement of State and local traffic laws and regulations, and traffic direction. Police chief executives should insure that these policies are regularly communicated to all supervisors and line personnel.

National Advisory Commission on Criminal Justice Standards and Goals, *Police* (Washington, D.C.; U.S. Government Printing Office, 1973), p. 225.

The traffic law enforcement subtask involves issuing citations for various motor vehicle violations; this activity is directed toward the reduction of accidents and injuries and fatalities caused by accidents. Because the average citizen usually comes in contact with the police

Investigating accidents is an important aspect of enforcing traffic laws. (Courtesy of the Savannah Police Department, Savannah, Georgia)

only as a result of having violated a traffic law, this activity has serious implications for the relationship between the police and the community; consequently, it must be performed with considerable care and courtesy. Traffic law enforcement should be based on careful analysis of traffic accident patterns so that the kinds of violations that cause accidents in certain locations at certain times are suppressed. This approach, which should be the basis for every police department's traffic law enforcement activities, is called *selective enforcement.*

The use of radar by the police has proved to be an extremely effective deterrent to speeding. Radar gives the police a scientific tool for the strict enforcement of speed laws. Unfortunately, even those departments equipped with radar devices use them all too infrequently. Any community anxious to reduce its accident rate should use radar on a 24-hour basis. There is no more effective way to slow down an entire community than through the consistent use of radar.

The enforcement of parking laws is designed to keep the traffic moving, to keep fire hydrants clear of obstructions, to keep intersections unclogged, and to keep parking spaces free at meters and in front of businesses. In some large jurisdictions, this activity is performed primarily by civilians assigned exclusively to the task; in other jurisdictions, police officers perform the task as a part of their generalist function.

The subtask of traffic accident investigation serves to determine the causes of motor vehicle accidents. In cases where fault can be established, traffic accident investigators issue citations; accident investigation, therefore, is an enforcement task. The task also provides input to the process of insurance claim settlement in jurisdictions where insurance claims are based on fault. Traffic accident investigation can, in addition, focus on criminal law violations ranging from assault to manslaughter to murder. It is an extremely important, specialized task that requires considerable training and insight.

In a small police department, intersection control, traffic law enforcement, radar operation, parking law enforcement, and traffic accident investigation may all be performed by officers serving as generalist patrol officers. In a large department, each of these subtasks may be handled by a separate subunit of a traffic division. Some of these tasks can easily be performed by civilians; indeed, some of them can be performed better by civilians and at a much lower cost. A decision to create a specialized traffic division and to employ specialized civilian personnel should be based on the size of the organization and on the volume and patterns of traffic-related business.

Criminal investigations Criminal investigations, the actions taken by the police to identify and apprehend perpetrators of crimes, include such activities as crime-scene investigations, interviewing, and interrogation. Ideally, they culminate in the criminal conviction of suspects, but most often they do not. The American police are successful in clearing by arrest (not conviction) only 21 percent of the serious crimes called to their attention.[5]

Detectives are the specialists in criminal investigations; they are not, however, its only practitioners. As a rule, officers assigned to the patrol function conduct all preliminary and minor investigations. Because all police departments have more officers assigned to the patrol subtask than to the criminal investigations subtask, patrol officers routinely shoulder a major part of investigative activity. Many police departments have adopted a policy stipulating that uniformed patrol officers should conduct investigations of all minor crimes, referring them to detectives

This team of police officers is preparing to investigate a crime scene. (Courtesy of the Los Angeles Police Department)

only when they have reached a dead end in their efforts. This policy, which embodies the generalist patrol theory, allows detectives to concentrate on more serious crimes and at the same time provides for the handling of investigations of less serious offenses for which most criminal investigation divisions have little time.

STANDARD 9.7

CRIMINAL INVESTIGATION

Every police agency immediately should direct patrol officers to conduct thorough preliminary investigations and should establish in writing priorities to insure that investigative efforts are spent in a manner that will best achieve organizational goals.

1. Every police agency should recognize that patrol officers are preliminary investigators and that they should conduct thorough preliminary investigations. However, investigative specialists should be assigned to very serious or complex preliminary investigations when delay will not hamper the investigation.

National Advisory Commission on Criminal Justice Standards and Goals, *Police* (Washington, D.C.: U.S. Government Printing Office, 1973), p. 233.

Most police departments, no matter how committed to the generalist theory, find it necessary to assign some personnel solely to criminal investigations. The number of officers to assign to investigative activities is a common point of contention in many municipal police agencies. The Police Foundation has found that "in major police departments, 10 per cent or more of available police manpower is committed to investigative functions."[6] Although this may be a useful rule of thumb, the extent of investigations handled by patrol officers and by investigative specialists varies according to circumstances and activity from place to place. Each department must analyze its own activity and its own needs before determining the ideal size of its criminal investigations division.

Another common point of controversy is the degree of specialization needed in the criminal investigations division. Departments with the least specialization might use the generalist assignment approach, with all detectives handling all types of investigations; highly specialized departments might have a Crimes Against the Person Unit, with separate squads handling homicides, assaults, sex offenses, and robberies. A Crimes Against Property Unit might have specialized squads handling

Police officers investigating a stolen auto. (Courtesy of the Jackson Police Department, Jackson, Mississippi)

burglaries, auto thefts, and larcenies. Some departments have auto squads, hotel squads, arson squads, fraud squads, bandit squads, and many others. The degree of specialization in any police agency must be based on local circumstances, taking into consideration such factors as the size of the department, the skills of its personnel, the patterns and amounts of its activities, and prevailing policies.

Another important consideration is that the position of detective almost always carries greater status than the position of patrol officer. Detectives work in plain clothes; they are not confined to small patrol areas; they do not handle minor matters; they receive a significant amount of public recognition; they usually make large numbers of arrests; and their work is often exciting and interesting. Detectives' elevated status may also be reflected in better pay and grade classification, but whether these status differences *should* be so is highly questionable.

Detectives are concerned with only a small part of the police function. They have very little to do with the discovery or prevention of crime and little to do with the maintenance of order and the protection of life and property. Detectives are afforded the luxury of concerning themselves with only the most glamorous aspects of police work and are rewarded for their good fortune with higher status and sometimes with higher pay.

Vice The responsibility for vice regulation has caused the police innumerable problems, largely because vice laws declare illegal a host of goods and services desired by a great number of citizens. The rationale for laws that forbid people to do much of what they might like to do is not that some unsuspecting stranger might be victimized, but rather that people must be protected from their own sometimes questionable wants and desires.

Vice regulation has to do with enforcement of laws relating to so-called crimes without victims; this, however, is a gross oversimplification of such crimes and is not totally accurate. Many people argue, although it is not entirely fashionable today to do so, that gambling, prostitution, narcotics, pornography, and illegal liquor sales undermine the very foundations of civilized society. Others argue, with considerable justification, that vice breeds more serious crime which does have victims.

Because there is no consensus about the desirability of vice laws, the enforcement of those laws places the police in a difficult position. The police understand that many people desire the goods and services curtailed by vice laws; they see that society in general is frequently

A vice raid in progress. (Courtesy of the Wilmington Police Department, Wilmington, Delaware)

indifferent to violations of vice laws. The police are not often hounded by aggrieved victims, as they are in the cases of rapes, robberies, and burglaries. They observe that the courts usually deal very leniently with vice offenders. And they further observe that vice generates fantastic sums of money.

It is for these reasons that vice regulation is at the heart of much of the public animosity toward the police and at the heart of much police corruption. If the police strictly enforce all vice laws, the public as well as the purveyors of illegal goods and services become upset. If the police are lenient toward vice, the public assumes that they have been corrupted. In many cases this suspicion has proved to be well founded; whether well founded or not, however, the damage in terms of public support and respect is the same.

As long as vice laws remain on the books and as long as vice regulation remains the responsibility of the police, the police administrator will have to deal with these problems. Even in police circles, there is

STANDARD 9.9

VICE OPERATIONS

Every police agency should immediately insure its capability to conduct effective vice operations against illegal gambling, traffic in liquor, prostitution, pandering, pornography, and obscene conduct. These operations should be capable of reducing the incidence of vice crimes and related criminal activity.

1. Every chief executive should establish written policies governing vice operations. These policies, consistent with existing statutes:
   a. Should reflect community attitudes toward vice crimes, the severity of the local vice problem, and the effect of the vice problem on other local crime problems.
   b. Should acknowledge that the patrol force is responsible for taking enforcement action against all vice violations they see.
3. Every chief executive should insure close coordination and continual exchange of information between vice, narcotic and drug, patrol, and intelligence operations, and close liaison with other agencies conducting similar operations.
5. Every chief executive should insure that every field commander reports in writing every 30 days to the chief executive, or his designee, the form and extent of the current vice problem in his area and the effort of vice operations on that problem.

National Advisory Commission on Criminal Justice Standards and Goals, *Police* (Washington, D.C.: U.S. Government Printing Office, 1973), p. 242.

considerable confusion over the best methods to use in dealing with vice problems. Most police officials would agree that vice enforcement should be prioritized with other enforcement activities; this is not to say, however, that vice enforcement should be disregarded. The police administrator should not ignore vice offenses, but instead should make it clear through policy that crimes against persons and property generally have a greater impact on society and thus demand priority in investigation. Former New York City Police Commissioner Patrick V. Murphy took this step and prioritized vice investigations. He decreased the personnel involved in gambling investigations and ordered those still assigned to that function to concentrate less on street activities and more on those who bankroll and profiteer from gambling. He then had precinct stations remove prominently displayed photographs of known gamblers and replace them with photographs of more serious criminal offenders. In this way, he let every member of the department know what the new priorities were.[7]

Organized Crime Organized crime has always caused difficult organizational problems for the police, in part because of the extent of organized crime. Gambling, prostitution, pornography, narcotics, hijacking, and loan sharking are the bread and butter of organized crime, but the need to control the marketplace also gets organized crime involved with such crimes as murder, assault, robbery, theft, and extortion. Also, the process of laundering dirty profits involves various kinds of frauds and swindles, some of which impact on legitimate business. Because each kind of criminal offense committed by organized crime may be investigated by a separate police subunit, the police very often fail to see the big picture of organized crime at work.

In addition to the wide variety of offenses involved, the structure of organized crime acts to thwart traditional police efforts. The people who collect the bulk of the profits and who direct the operations of organized crime rarely commit observable offenses. Usually, they order someone who orders someone else who orders someone else to commit a crime. Everything is done covertly through layers of organization designed to protect the leadership. These layers are reinforced by money, legal services, loyalty, and force. Despite numerous arrests of organized-crime figures, the police are rarely able to bring syndicate bosses to the bar of justice.

In recent years the strike-force approach has had some success in combatting organized crime's upper echelons. This approach is usually multijurisdictional, often taking in metropolitan areas, states, and regions. It involves investigators and prosecutors from local, state, and federal agencies. The approach is usually very sophisticated and often makes use of financial and tax records, on the valid assumption that profits from organized crime are not usually reported to the Internal Revenue Service. Increased use has also been made of grand juries and of immunity, two techniques which when used in concert can force syndicate leaders and their underlings to choose between telling what they know or going to jail. Also, the resources of the combined agencies at different levels of government make more credible the assurances of protection offered informants and prosecution witnesses.

The strike-force approach, or one closely allied to it, seems to be the only effective and feasible police response to organized crime. To be successful, a strike force has to cut across traditional organizational and jurisdictional boundaries. These conditions for success sometimes cause tensions and interagency jealousies. Therefore, the police administrator's task is to provide the strike force with the authority and flexibility it needs while at the same time convincing the police and the community that such an approach is a good one.

Juvenile services Police services for juveniles constitute a separate task because of the special legal and practical aspects of dealing with children. Juveniles are a clear and distinct subgroup of society, and their offenses are ordinarily handled more informally and with more leniency. In addition, juveniles are usually dealt with by the criminal justice system as parts of family units rather than as free and responsible citizens. They are often tried in juvenile courts by special judges; when incarcerated, juveniles are placed in special institutions apart from adult offenders.

Most large police departments have separate juvenile divisions, which are essential because of the factors outlined above and because of the enormity of the juvenile crime problem. In addition to getting referrals from other departmental divisions and units, the juvenile division may take a special interest in matters of child abuse and neglect, children in need of supervision, runaways, and truants. The juvenile division will also ordinarily coordinate relations among the police department, the juvenile court, juvenile detention centers, and social service programs for juveniles.

The focus of the juvenile division is decidedly more on social welfare than on crime; for this reason, the juvenile division is often denigrated by police officers who fail to understand the importance of having some police officers involved in social welfare activities, especially as these relate to children. Social workers also tend to denigrate the work of juvenile divisions, claiming that the inexperience of the police and their general lack of educational background should disqualify them from participation in social service activities. Yet if the police fail to become involved in helping children in trouble, even if only referring them to appropriate social welfare agencies, the children will probably receive no help whatsoever. Police officers assigned to juvenile divisions, therefore, should be well grounded in social work theory and should work from a social welfare orientation. As this aspect of police work with juveniles becomes more accepted, the status of juvenile service units should improve.

Because of the legal and practical differences in dealing with children and adults, police services for juveniles are considered as a separate task. (Courtesy of the Los Angeles County Sheriff's Department)

Community services There is a general recognition today that the police have a key role to play in the delivery of a variety of services to the community. By default, social service agencies have given to the

---

STANDARD 9.5

JUVENILE OPERATIONS

The chief executive of every police agency immediately should develop written policy governing his agency's involvement in the detection, deterrence, and prevention of delinquent behavior and juvenile crime.

1. Every police agency should provide all its police officers with specific training in preventing delinquent behavior and juvenile crime.

2. Every police agency should cooperate actively with other agencies and organizations, public and private, in order to employ all available resources to detect and deter delinquent behavior and combat juvenile crime.

3. Every police agency should establish in cooperation with courts written policies and procedures governing agency action in juvenile matters. These policies and procedures should stipulate at least:

   a. The specific form of agency cooperation with other governmental agencies concerned with delinquent behavior, abandonment, neglect, and juvenile crime;

   b. The specific form of agency cooperation with nongovernmental agencies and organizations where assistance in juvenile matters may be obtained;

   c. The procedures for release of juveniles into parental custody; and

   d. The procedures for the detention of juveniles.

National Advisory Commission on Criminal Justice Standards and Goals, *Police* (Washington, D.C.: U.S. Government Printing Office, 1973), p. 221.

---

police much of the routine, day-to-day responsibilities that were once considered solely within their province. What traditional social service agency operates 24 hours a day, 7 days a week, 52 weeks a year? The police department is the only such agency in the community. And unlike many other social service agencies, the police still make house calls.

Depending on the nature of the service needed, the skills of individual police officers, and the policies of the departments in which they serve, the role of the police may be to: (1) provide the service themselves; (2) assist others in providing the service; or (3) refer the matter to another agency. If the appropriate social service agency is not open, it becomes the responsibility of the police to handle such matters. Police officers' qualifications to handle the wide variety of situations which come to their attention is secondary to the need to handle all matters that cannot be immediately referred to a social service agency.

The police play a key role in the delivery of a variety of services to the community. (Courtesy of the Los Angeles Police Department)

People who would completely divorce the police from all social welfare activities often fail to recognize that if such activities are not handled by the police, they will not be handled at all. Whether they like it or not, social workers who work 40 hours a week leave the other 128 hours for the police to service. At the very minimum, then, police probably handle two-thirds of all threshold social work in this country; when one considers that human trauma occurs more frequently at night, and often on weekends, that percentage figure undoubtedly rises. When people need immediate help, regardless of the circumstances, they call the police. Furthermore, they expect the police to respond right away and to alleviate the immediate problem.

The degree to which police officers should become directly involved in social service work is open to debate. The work of family crisis–intervention teams, which exist in many cities, has shown that the police can be extremely effective in handling family problems if they are properly trained. Because of their availability, the police must have the capability for primary-level counseling. In situations in which people are threatening to kill themselves and others, there is usually no time to call on the psychiatric social worker to intervene. Such life-and-death situations are completely in the hands of the police, who must respond intelligently, persuasively, and professionally.

The police deal on a continuing basis with delicate situations involving human trauma and need. How they respond to such situations impacts significantly on the lives of human beings. The primary role of the police officer is to maintain order and protect lives and property. If the police were to turn their backs on people in need, they would not be fulfilling their primary obligations. To say that the police should not perform social welfare and social service functions because they are not trained social workers is like saying that the general practitioner should not perform surgery in a life-or-death emergency situation when a surgeon is not available. By the very nature of their jobs, police officers are in part social workers. People who suggest otherwise are naive to the realities of the police task.

Domestic disputes are undoubtedly the most common and most dangerous types of service requests handled by the police. These disputes may be handled in a variety of ways. Some departments do little more than determine if anyone has been injured or killed. Others, looking at the dispute only from a legalistic standpoint, seek to determine whether or not the aggrieved party is willing to sign a complaint. But some police agencies, notably those in New York City and Dayton, Ohio, have forged a larger role for themselves by giving their officers specialized training in applied psychology, family sociology, and crisis-intervention theory and practice. In response to domestic complaints, their officers take an active part in settling disputes and offering primary-level counseling services. They fully recognize that they cannot solve the problems that precipitated the disputes. Rather, they seek truces between and among combatants, an important social service skill that should not be underestimated, and they endeavor to refer the parties involved to professional social service agencies, which then attempt more lasting solutions.

Referral is a practice that even the smallest police department can adopt. All departments come in contact with various kinds of social problems that do not require arrest, but which cry out for help and treatment. If police officers know what social services are available in their communities and the kinds of assistance programs they offer, they have a viable and productive alternative to arrest. They do not, of course, have the authority to require participation in treatment programs, but their recommendations can be critical to those troubled individuals who need help but do not know where to find it.

A case drawn from the files of one of the authors demonstrates how a police department not oriented to social service can, through omission, negatively affect a family in trouble. The police received a call early one holiday evening to go to a local hospital emergency room. There they were requested to take an older, drunk woman to a mental institution for ten days of observation. The woman's husband, a victim of several strokes, had sought medical assistance for his wife, who had been drinking heavily all afternoon. The husband was unable to work, and his wife was the sole support for them and their preteenage daughter. The husband, a mild-mannered and feeble person, accompanied the two police officers who transported his wife to the institution. During the trip the wife heaped oral abuse on the husband, swore at him frequently, and flicked ashes from her cigarette on his coat. The husband took all this patiently and refused to react. While the police officers were leading her by the arms to the door of the institution, she went limp and passed out. She looked as if she were about to die; she was suffering from acute alcoholism. The two police officers carried her into the institution and placed her on an examining table. While she was being treated, the husband was asked to furnish information for her admission—her name, address, age, church affiliation, and the like. He even named the church his wife attended. The police were very courteous to the husband and drove him back to the hospital where his car was parked. After filing a short report on the incident, the case was closed.

The police could have provided much more help than they did in this situation. They could have brought into the case the minister of the church the woman attended. Both the visiting nurse and the director of public welfare should have been contacted; it was obvious that the man needed continuing medical assistance and that he was not well off financially. The police also missed an opportunity to involve the local chapter of Alcoholics Anonymous. A police department that was more oriented to community service might have also made referrals to a family counseling service, the daughter's school guidance department, the woman's doctor, and perhaps even the local veterans' agent. Certainly the police could have done much more to help the family than they did.

One positive step that police departments can take in attempting to develop referral services is to establish police-community councils. These councils attempt to relate the police to the community in a positive way and serve to bring together all those members of the community who play helping roles. Such a council might include the following people and organizations, as listed on the next page.

1. school guidance counselors;

2. school principals;

3. local clergy;

4. probation personnel;

5. senior citizens' organizations;

6. local judges;

7. multi–health service centers;

8. alcohol and drug treatment facilities;

9. local youth resource bureaus;

10. juvenile court personnel;

11. public welfare departments;

12. employment security officials;

13. homemaker services;

14. local doctors, dentists, and hospital officials;

15. nursing home representatives;

16. church-affiliated charitable bureaus;

17. park and recreation personnel;

18. tenant councils;

19. neighborhood youth programs;

20. neighborhood councils and improvement organizations;

21. YMCA and YWCA leaders;

22. officials from boys' and girls' clubs;

23. Boy Scout and Girl Scout leaders; and

24. health department officials.

These police-community councils would meet frequently, giving all helping agencies in the community, the police included, an opportunity to familiarize themselves with the various kinds of services currently being offered. The councils should by no means be limited to those people and organizations listed above. If a community has a visiting nurse, a veterans' agent, an ombudsman, or anyone else in a position to be of help to people, that person should most certainly be included in the council's membership. Such a council facilitates communication between the police and the people and serves as an important resource for talent the police can take advantage of in their efforts to help people.

Crime prevention   Crime prevention, as mentioned in Chapter 1, is one of the secondary goals and objectives of the police service, especially for those officers assigned to the patrol function. Crime prevention is accomplished by having uniformed police officers in marked vehicles moving about the community to give the impression of police omnipresence. This kind of effort has long been thought sufficient to deter crime. Statistics, however, would seem to prove otherwise. Traditional police methods have not been very successful in preventing crime.

STANDARD 3.2

CRIME PREVENTION

Every police agency should immediately establish programs that encourage members of the public to take an active role in preventing crime, that provide information leading to the arrest and conviction of criminal offenders, that facilitate the identification and recovery of stolen property, and that increase liaison with private industry in security efforts.

National Advisory Commission on Criminal Justice Standards and Goals, *Police* (Washington, D.C.: U.S. Government Printing Office, 1973), p. 66.

Techniques developed in recent years mandate that the police concentrate on high-crime risks in attempts to either remove or nullify them. In many instances dramatic decreases in crime rates can result. These techniques, referred to as *target-hardening* activities, simply seek to make crimes more difficult to commit. Some of these techniques are improving security, locking devices, and construction; screening or barring doors and windows; providing more and better alarm systems and better lighting; and teaching citizens and businesspeople how to secure their premises more effectively. Through Project Identification programs, many police departments loan marking tools to the general public so that citizens can mark valuable property in their homes and businesses; such programs increase the chances of recovering stolen property. Some police departments even provide special officers as security consultants to business and industry in an effort to prevent or reduce crime. In addition, two specialized courses—Crime Prevention

Theory and Practice and Crime Prevention Administration—are offered by the University of Louisville; police officers from cities across the nation attend these courses and return home to serve as crime-prevention specialists in their police departments.

The idea of crime prevention as a specialized activity is new in police circles. The police have traditionally been prosecution-oriented, not prevention-oriented. They have gauged their success on clearances by arrest and successful prosecutions and, except for preventive patrol, have placed little emphasis on preventing crimes. Learning from the successful experiences of security administrators whose private-sector companies are much more interested in preventing thefts than in prosecuting offenders, the police have slowly come to realize that prosecutions alone are not an adequate measurement of police success. Controlling, reducing, and preventing crime are more viable yardsticks for measuring police effectiveness in dealing with crime. Citizens are far less interested in numbers of prosecutions than in rising crime rates. Police success in crime-related activities, therefore, should be predicated on crime reduction and not, as has been the traditional practice, on numbers of crime clearances and prosecutions.

It should be pointed out that the police are limited in what they can do to control crime. Not everyone understands this, and there are many who think that the police should be able to control all crime. Such is not the case. The police are not responsible for social conditions which breed crime. They have no control over poverty, bad housing, poor health care, discrimination, child neglect, and inadequate education. The bitter fruit of these social conditions is crime. It is generally recognized that crime will not disappear, regardless of what the police do to prevent it, until the social conditions that cause it disappear. Given this reality, the most that the police can do is attempt to reduce crime, not eliminate it. Theirs is a never-ending battle against a crime problem that cannot be won until the problem of poverty in this country is beaten. Even if this should occur, a highly unlikely possibility, other forces and factors which cause crime can always be expected to be present in a democratic society which cherishes freedom and individual rights. Indeed, some say that crime is the price we pay for democracy, and they are probably right. The responsibility of the police is to prevent crime to the degree that they reasonably can and to refine their techniques for preventing crime in a social milieu that breeds it.

Community relations Confrontations between the police and minority communities and between the police and students in the mid- and late-1960s drove home the point that relations between the police and the

Good community relations bring the police and community together. (Courtesy of the Newark Police Department)

community were not all they should be. Although most of these protests were directed at the white establishment, politicians, and school administrators, the police were perceived as representatives of these and all other elements of the power structure. The police were the arm of government most visible on the scene, and they had the power to put down the protests and the protesters. In the beginning the police, not used to such confrontations, saw force as the only workable solution for dealing with trouble on the streets. Too often, they tended to characterize all protesters as rabble-rousers and revolutionaries, denying the legitimacy of their complaints and their right to dissent. In numerous riots it was the police who triggered the situations which ultimately caused the riots. Police handling of street disturbances precipitated the escalation of tensions and brought them into considerable disfavor with large segments of the public.

In response to the breakdown in the relations between police and community, police–community relations units were formed in many police departments. Initially these units were staffed by officers who called for the development of programs designed to acquaint school children with the police, provide speakers for community groups, assemble police and community spokespeople for dialogue about police-community problems, and publicize positive police accomplishments. But other than to emphasize the need for better relations between the police and the community, these initial programs met with very little success. The worst of them were quickly exposed as shams or as mere publicity organs for police-image improvement; they had no impact on the actual relationships that existed between the police and the people. The best of these programs served as an embryonic impetus for the development of more meaningful programs which actually brought the police and the community together for fruitful discussion of roles, motives, and needs; these programs promoted mutual understanding and an appreciation of both police and community problems.

Soon it became apparent that this approach was not completely satisfactory. Because the community relations unit was not directly involved in what was going on in the streets and neighborhoods, it had a low status position in the eyes of patrol officers who were personally involved in dealing with citizens. Although rapping with dissidents might sometimes be a productive endeavor, it does not go to the heart of police-community problems. Additionally, the existence of community relations units tended to relieve operational personnel of the responsibility of nurturing their relations with the community. The community, seeing that the community relations unit served only as an apologist for the status quo, remained dissatisfied.

Gradually, police administrators came to realize that community relations is the task of each and every police officer. Although a police-community relations unit can assist in refining the obligations of this task, it cannot replace the combined efforts of each departmental member toward the development of good relations with the community. The Police Foundation points out that "it is imperative that every . . . officer sees a great deal of community relations as part of his daily patrol or investigative assignment."[8] The officer who treats the police job as a public trust, who sees the police role as including the provision of a variety of social services, who treats all people with respect, and who works hard to reduce crime and increase safety in the community does more for good police-community relations than any 40 institutionalized programs.

Police-community relations is a two-way street. It involves the police attempting to determine how they can best serve the community as well as an honest effort by the police to provide quality service. It also involves community participation in the development of police policy. This requires an understanding of both the requirements of the law and the necessities of certain police practices, e.g., the use of force, the need to make arrests under certain circumstances, and the procedural tactics necessary to maintain order and keep the peace in volatile situations. Further, it requires a realization on everyone's part of the fact that we are all human and subject to human frailty, that we often conflict in our ideas and attitudes, that invariably we are never satisfied with the way things are, and that consequently we will inevitably and always be in conflict. The containment of that conflict, the ideal of ordered liberty, is inseparably associated with police-community relations. We have come a long way; we have a long way to go.

Community relations involves community participation. (Courtesy of the Newark Police Department)

THE ADMINISTRATION SUBSYSTEM

The tasks that constitute the administration subsystem—personnel, training, planning, budget and finance, legal assistance, public information, secretarial, inspections, internal affairs, and intelligence—are performed not in direct assistance to the public, but for the benefit of the organization as a whole. The tasks of the administration subsystem have a more long-term application than do those of the auxiliary services subsystem. One way to differentiate administration tasks from auxiliary services tasks is to ask: "Does this task need to be performed continually around the clock?" Tasks that do not, such as planning and budget preparation, are generally considered administrative tasks; tasks that need to be performed continually, such as communications and identification, are usually categorized as auxiliary service tasks. Both types of tasks are of benefit for or service to the department as a whole; both types of tasks are performed internally. Operational tasks, on the other hand, are performed externally not for the department, but for the public.

Personnel The personnel task—recruitment, selection, assignment, transfer, promotion, termination, and labor relations—has to do with who gets what jobs when and, very often, who gets what pay. It is, therefore, an extremely important task. Janger has noted that personnel units have not been content in confining themselves to these activities and that they are also becoming involved with management development, organization planning, personnel development, benefits, and personnel research.[9]

In recent years police personnel practices have come under close scrutiny with respect to minority recruitment, selection, assignment, and promotion. In numerous instances the federal courts have found entrance-level tests and job qualifications to be discriminatory against blacks, women, and Spanish-speaking Americans. Patterns of discrimination have also been identified in promotion and transfer practices. In some cases the courts have required that eligibility lists based on old tests be voided, that certain percentages of newly hired recruits be from a particular minority group, and that certain numbers of promotions be given to minority-group members.

Such decisions have thrown the police service into some turmoil and have angered many white male police officers, who charge reverse discrimination. Our society is a society of laws, however, and court orders, regardless of whether they are liked or disliked, must be followed. The police service is undergoing the affirmative action process in an effort to meet a court order to equalize service opportunities, a matter which is impossible to challenge under our form of government. That police administrators have been forced to hire and promote minority-group members rather than attempting to do this on their own is looked on by many to be a sad reflection on the administrators' real commitment to justice. The personnel task has been complicated significantly by this turn of events.

STANDARD 13.3

MINORITY RECRUITING

Every police agency immediately should insure that it presents no artificial or arbitrary barriers—cultural or institutional—to discourage qualified individuals from seeking employment or from being employed as police officers.

1. Every police agency should engage in positive efforts to employ ethnic minority group members. When a substantial ethnic minority population resides within the jursidiction, the police agency should take affirmative action to achieve a ratio of minority group employees in approximate proportion to the makeup of the population.

National Advisory Commission on Criminal Justice Standards and Goals, *Police* (Washington, D.C.: U.S. Government Printing Office, 1973), p. 329.

STANDARD 13.6

EMPLOYMENT OF WOMEN

Every police agency should immediately insure that there exists no agency policy that discourages qualified women from seeking employment as sworn or civilian personnel or prevents them from realizing their full employment potential.

National Advisory Commission on Criminal Justice Standards and Goals, *Police* (Washington, D.C.: U.S. Government Printing Office, 1973), p. 342.

Another recent trend that has caused personnel administrators new problems is the increase of college graduates joining police departments. These new officers bring with them high expectations in terms of salary and advancement which are difficult to satisfy within the traditional police structure. When they fail to succeed as quickly as they expected to, they tend to leave, thus increasing turnover rates. Some departments have attempted to alleviate this problem by offering college graduates

more money to do the same job being performed by noncollege graduates; this has tended to anger noncollege grads, who believe that they
work just as hard and just as well. One solution has been to increase the
number of ranks or job classifications, making education a factor for
promotion.

Training   The police training task can be broken down into a number
of different approaches—in-class and on-the-job training, physical and
mental training, formal and informal training, theoretical and practical
training, recruit and in-service training, and specific and general training. The instructors can be police personnel assigned to a training unit,
general police personnel, supervisory personnel, command-level personnel, professional trainers, or college professors. The training can be conducted at a departmental training academy, a regional training
academy, roll-call sessions, on the street, in patrol cars, or at a college
or university. The training might be for newly hired recruits, newly
promoted officers, experienced officers, or even for a police chief.

Training has become very sophisticated in order to meet the professional needs
of the police service. (Courtesy of the Los Angeles Police Department)

STANDARD 16.3

PREPARATORY TRAINING

Every police agency should take immediate steps to provide training for every police employee prior to his first assignment within the agency, prior to his assignment to any specialized function requiring additional training, and prior to his promotion.

1. Every state should require that every sworn police employee satisfactorily complete a minimum of 400 hours of basic police training. In addition to traditional basic police subjects, this training should include:

   a. Instruction in law, psychology, and sociology specifically related to interpersonal communication, the police role, and the community the police employee will serve;

   b. Assigned activities away from the training academy to enable the employee to gain specific insight in the community, criminal justice system, and local government;

   c. Remedial training for individuals who are deficient in their training performance but who, in the opinion of the training staff and employing agency, demonstrate potential for satisfactory performance; and

   d. Additional training by the employing agency in its policies and procedures, if basic police training is not administered by that agency.

2. During the first year of employment with a police agency, and in addition to the minimum basic police training, every police agency should provide full-time sworn police employees with additional formal training, coached field training, and supervised field experience through methods that include at least:

   a. A minimum of 4 months of field training with a sworn police employee who has been certified as a training coach;

   b. Rotation in field assignments to expose the employee to varying operational and community experiences;

   c. Documentation of employee performance in specific field experiences to assist in evaluating the employee and to provide feedback on training program effectiveness;

   d. Self-paced training material, such as correspondence courses, to assist the employee in acquiring additional job knowledge and in preparing for subsequent formal training;

   e. Periodic meetings between the coach, the employee, and the training academy staff to identify additional training needs and to provide feedback on training program effectiveness; and

   f. A minimum of 2 weeks' additional training at the basic academy 6 months after completion of basic training and again after 1 year's employment in field duties.

3. Every police agency should provide every un-sworn police employee with sufficient training to enable him to perform satisfactorily his specific assignment and to provide him with a general knowledge of the police role and the organization of the police agency.
4. Every police agency should provide every police employee newly assigned to a specialized task the specific training he needs to enable him to perform the task acceptably.
5. Every police agency should provide sufficient training to enable every newly promoted employee to perform the intended assignment satisfactorily.

National Advisory Commission on Criminal Justice Standards and Goals, *Police* (Washington, D.C.: U.S. Government Printing Office, 1973), pp. 392–393.

Most small departments depend on the services of nearby larger departments or regional or state training academies. Many states require by law that recruits and newly appointed officers receive minimum amounts of training either before assuming their duties or during the first several months they are on the job. Such requirements, and the training commissions developed to satisfy them, have contributed significantly to upgrading police services in small communities.

Unless new police officers are thoroughly trained before they are on the job for any considerable length of time, they will develop rigid habits and attitudes that training will be hard-pressed to alter. After recruit training, officers should be assigned to field training officers, who will break them in on the job, showing recruits how their training is related to their work on the street. Field training officers should be carefully chosen from among the best officers in the department. The early days of a new officer's career are crucial; they should be devoted to internalizing what he or she has learned from recruit training and reinforcing principles of good police practice.

When patrol officers are promoted to supervisory positions, they are ordinarily unprepared for their new responsibilities. Just because they are capable police officers with considerable street experience and are well trained for the work they do doesn't necessarily mean that they will make good supervisors. The same holds true for administrative and management positions; a good supervisor does not automatically become a good administrator. The higher a police officer ascends in the hierarchical structure of the police department, the more training he or she needs to meet increased responsibilities. The training at each level must necessarily be different and must be designed to prepare officers for the work they will be expected to do on the level on which they happen to be.

In-service personnel—whether generalists or specialists—need regular refresher training. Some police departments conduct daily roll-call training sessions. Others insist that their officers undergo one week of in-service training every year. Some departments do both. Regardless of how in-service training is accomplished, it is a must in a field as complex and involved as police work. How well or how poorly a police officer is trained relates directly to the success or failure of the entire organization to meet its goals and objectives.

Planning   Planning is preparing for the future in the hope that anticipation and preparation will lead to more effective coping with whatever comes along. Planning is a much underrated function in most police departments. Many police departments do no planning whatever; others, through their budgets, plan only for the coming year. The philosophy of *we'll cross that bridge when we get to it* is prevalent throughout the police field.

It is essential, however, that police organizations plan for such eventualities as civil disorder, natural disasters, and rises in the crime and accident rates. They must also plan for change and the effects of such trends as energy depletion, rapid technological advancement, and population shifts. Everyday planning for personnel requirements, police officer deployment, and patrol concentration is important in the planning process.

Budget and finance   This task involves the administration and handling of departmental money matters. It includes such activities as payroll, purchasing, budgeting, billing, accounting, and auditing.

Depending on the size of the department and local governmental practice, some of these activities are handled by the parent system. In all cases, however, the police are involved, to a greater or lesser degree, in all of these functions. In the case of budgeting, the police department usually has full responsibility for the development of its budget. The budget is very important in that it prescribes police activities and programs for a given period of time, usually a year.

Many police administrators have little understanding of the budgeting process; their yearly budgets tend to be the same, with minor increases or decreases depending on the state of the treasury. This kind of copy-cat budgeting provides for no evaluation of the actual desirability of various programs and budget categories and leaves no room for innovation. No effort is made to determine what kinds of expenditures might bring the organization closer to achieving its goals and objectives. As a rule, only incremental changes are made.

STANDARD 5.7

FISCAL MANAGEMENT PROCEDURES

Every police chief executive should use the most effective and appropriate fiscal management techniques available. He should establish policy and procedures so budgeting is a fundamental part of the management planning process.

1. Every police chief executive should initiate annual budget planning with a detailed statement on budget preparation. This statement should reflect fiscal direction received from the fiscal affairs officer of the jurisdiction.

4. Every police agency should study and experiment with various forms of systems budgeting: budgeting based on the consolidation of functionally unrelated tasks and corresponding resources form a system that will achieve an identified objective. If the value of systems budgeting will offset the simplicity and convenience of line item or other modified budgeting methods already in use, the agency should adopt such a system.

National Advisory Commission on Criminal Justice Standards and Goals, *Police* (Washington, D.C.: U.S. Government Printing Office, 1973), p. 135.

In recent years enlightened police administrators, recognizing that traditional budgeting practices tend to stunt the growth of their departments, have increasingly relied on a new approach to budgeting—Planning-Programming Budgeting System, or PPBS. This new system, or method, seeks to force administrators to identify the goals and objectives of their organizations and then to move toward these goals and objectives on the basis of intelligently allotting available funding resources. PPBS is a means by which administrators weed out ineffective or superfluous programs and practices and then emphasize activities that lead their organizations toward their goals and objectives in better ways. PPBS is an ongoing process which mandates the continuing evaluation of programs to determine their effectiveness and usefulness.

PPBS is not a panacea; most administrators find it difficult to evaluate their own programs objectively and resist change even in the face of facts. The true relevance of programs to departmental goals and objectives is often difficult to determine. In addition, budget review and appropriation committees of the parent governmental system, accustomed to working with traditional budgets, are frequently unimpressed with what they often look on as the hocus-pocus of PPBS. Despite all these shortcomings, however, the Planning-Programming Budgeting System is helpful in that it forces police administrators to ask themselves whether or not they are making the best possible use of the public's tax dollars. PPBS forces them to consider financial requests in light of actual goals and objectives and allows them to manage their organizations systematically through their budgets.

Legal assistance In some jurisdictions the police prosecute their own cases in the lower courts without any assistance from a district attorney or a state's attorney. In such instances legal assistance is of the utmost importance and is concerned primarily with aiding officers in the prosecution of criminal cases.

A police legal advisor researching the law. (Courtesy of the Jackson Police Department, Jackson, Mississippi)

STANDARD 11.2

LEGAL ASSISTANCE

Every police agency should immediately acquire the legal assistance necessary to insure maximum effectiveness and efficiency in all its operations.

1. Every policy agency should make maximum use of the offices of its city attorney or county attorney, the county prosecutor, and the State attorney general, to acquire the legal assistance it needs. If it is necessary to provide legal assistance supplementary to these sources, a police legal advisor should be employed.

National Advisory Commission on Criminal Justice Standards and Goals, *Police* (Washington, D.C.: U.S. Government Printing Office, 1973), p. 280.

A police department may designate a police officer who has had legal training as its prosecutor and legal advisor. Or, it may hire an attorney specifically for this purpose.

Legal assistance includes, depending on the jurisdiction, training in legal matters, legal advice in policy formulation and planning, liaison with legislatures and the courts, departmental representation in civil proceedings, advice and direction for internal administrative hearings, and counsel on specific problems arising out of criminal cases.[10]

Since most police departments are not large enough to employ a full-time attorney, many small departments may band together on a regional basis to hire a legal advisor who is available to all of them on a full-time basis. Other departments have retained counsel on a part-time basis.

Public information Both public relations and press relations come under the subtask of public information. Keeping the public informed about police activities includes news about crime, media relations, features on police officers and programs, information on crime prevention and how to avoid being victimized by crime, public lectures on policing, and explanations of policies and procedures which affect the public. The public information function is important to the police because it gives them the opportunity to tell their story, to explain their position on controversial issues, and to respond in a meaningful way to public concerns.

Unfortunately, many police officials find it difficult to relate to the media. Because of poor experiences with newspapers and television stations, some police officials see the media as enemies or, at the very least, antagonists. As a result, they make it difficult for reporters to get the news and exhibit open hostility toward the press. This creates a negative attitude on the part of media representatives toward the police and contributes to the development of what can easily become a vicious cycle of open warfare between the police and the press. Needless to say, such a relationship works to the detriment of everyone concerned and impacts negatively on the image of the police.

STANDARD 1.7

NEWS MEDIA RELATIONS

Every police chief executive immediately should acknowledge in written policy statements the important role of the news media and the need for the police agency to be open in its relations with the media. The agency should promote an aggressive policy of presenting public information rather than merely responding to occasional inquiries.

National Advisory Commission on Criminal Justice Standards and Goals, *Police* (Washington, D.C.: U.S. Government Printing Office, 1973), p. 44.

It is essential for police administrators to cultivate good relations with the working press. Whether this is done through the formal establishment of a public information division, as in large departments, or through the careful handling of media relationships by the chief or a designated officer of rank, as in small departments, it is important to understand that a positive policy needs to be developed within every police department for the handling of public information. Whoever is responsible for public information should make every possible effort to provide news on police activities as accurately and as quickly as possible. The designated public information officer should encourage feature stories about the police department and cooperate in every way in their development.

The police administrator must resist the temptation, albeit strong on occasion, to manipulate reporters and the news. The responsible police administrator cultivates healthy media relations not only because they enhance the flow of news and information, but also because the media provide a line of communication between the police and the public that the police cannot afford to jeopardize. Media institutions are essential to the democratic process and serve as adversaries to governmental abuse. In the United States they are as much a part of the system of checks and balances as are any of the branches of government; as such, they must be respected and treated fairly. Thomas

Jefferson once said that he would prefer the press with no government to the government with no press. The responsible police administrator is acutely aware that one of the most important objectives of the police organization is to safeguard rights and constitutional guarantees; the First Amendment of the Constitution guarantees freedom of the press.

Few police agencies are large enough to employ full-time public information officers. Regardless of the size of the agency, however, it is important that someone be designated as public information officer. Whether the position is a full-time or part-time job, the person assigned to it should be fully responsible for dealing with the media.

Secretarial   Very little needs to be said about the secretarial task. Secretaries perform a support service and, in a sense, might be looked on as assistant administrators or, perhaps more accurately, assistant to administrators. Their work is largely clerical, although in some cases they also become involved in scheduling, greeting visitors, and controlling access to their employers. Secretaries are typists, file clerks, and stenographers, providing the logistical support needed to maintain communications in any organization. In addition, they also keep track of appointments and keep the offices over which they have responsibility bright and pleasant. In short, they perform many important but somewhat routine and mundane tasks, relieving their employers of much work that must be done on a regular, continuing basis but which, if performed by administrators, would hinder them from meeting their major responsibilities.

Secretaries can either make or break their employers. Good secretaries can assist their employers immeasurably in the performance of their duties; ineffective or inefficient ones can significantly hinder organizational goals and objectives. In short, secretaries are vital to the success of organizations. It is important that they be chosen well and that their work be evaluated continually.

Inspections   The aim of the inspections function is to ascertain adherence to direction. Persons delegated this task systematically check the organization to determine how well policies, procedures, rules, and regulations are being followed.

Although larger departments need to establish specialized inspections units, it should be understood that in all police departments, regardless of size, every administrator and supervisory officer has inspections responsibilities. Each must attempt to learn how well subordinates are adhering to directives and to control subordinates in their adherence to directives.

STANDARD 2.3

INSPECTIONS

Every police agency should immediately establish a formal inspection system to provide the police chief executive with the information he needs to evaluate the efficiency and effectiveness of agency operations.

National Advisory Commission on Criminal Justice Standards and Goals, *Police* (Washington, D.C.: U.S. Government Printing Office, 1973), p. 57.

In departments large enough to have a specialized inspections unit, the persons responsible for this function are not directly involved in the controlling process. They merely inspect the organization and report their findings, both good and bad, to the chief. If they discover any lack of adherence to directives, it is the chief who exercises the controlling function, not they. It is important to understand that in large departments the inspections function and the controlling function are different functions performed by different people. In departments not large enough to have an inspections unit, both the inspections and controlling functions are usually performed by the chief or by someone designated to do this on a part-time basis.

It is essential that the inspections function be administered on a totally professional, objective, and impartial basis. Under no circumstances should those assigned to inspections go about their work in clandestine fashion. Officers should be advised that inspections is an ongoing function within the department and that all operational, administrative, and service subsystems will be examined to determine adherence to directives. It should also be understood that all positive as well as negative findings will be reported.

The inspections function will serve the chief as a secondary source of information to supplement information received through the regular chain of command. Many important matters about which the chief should be aware will either purposely or inadvertently never come to the attention of anyone at the command level. Some of these problems will be of such significance that they will impact negatively on the entire organization if they are not identified and solved. A good inspections program will identify them. A good chief will solve them.

Officers who perform the inspections function are in a sense the chief's internal patrol unit. Whereas the regular patrol unit becomes involved with violations of the criminal law as committed by the general public, the inspections unit is interested in the enforcement of the department's internal laws, policies, procedures, rules, and regulations—violations of internal edicts as committed by police officers. Just as the personnel of the regular patrol unit must be regarded as fair and honest to be successful at their jobs and respected by the public, so too must inspections personnel have a reputation for fairness and integrity if they are to perform their function effectively and without creating excessive internal strife.

Internal affairs Internal affairs personnel investigate allegations of police misconduct and criminality. These investigations emanate from information received from the public, the police, and independently developed sources.

STANDARD 19.1

FOUNDATION FOR INTERNAL DISCIPLINE

Every police agency immediately should formalize policies, procedures, and rules in written form for the administration of internal discipline. The internal discipline system should be based on essential fairness, but not bound by formal procedures or proceedings such as are used in criminal trials.

National Advisory Commission on Criminal Justice Standards and Goals, *Police* (Washington, D.C.: U.S. Government Printing Office, 1973), p. 474.

The internal affairs function should always be a specialized function in large departments. In small departments the chief should be responsible for internal affairs.

STANDARD 19.3

INVESTIGATIVE RESPONSIBILITY

The chief executive of every police agency immediately should insure that the investigation of all complaints from the public, and all allegations of criminal conduct and serious internal misconduct, are conducted by a specialized individual or unit of the involved police agency. This person or unit should be responsible directly to the agency's chief executive or the assistant chief executive. Minor internal misconduct may be investigated by first line supervisors, and these investigations should be subject to internal review.

National Advisory Commission on Criminal Justice Standards and Goals, *Police* (Washington, D.C.: U.S. Government Printing Office, 1973), p. 480.

The Knapp Commission, which investigated police corruption in New York City in 1972, recommended that internal affairs personnel be assigned that task for their entire careers.[11] The underlying rationale is that officers assigned to the internal affairs task will inevitably make many enemies among their police colleagues and consequently should never have to anticipate working directly with or for these colleagues at some later date. It is easy to understand why internal affairs officers who expect to return to a regular duty assignment at some later date might be hesitant to pursue internal investigations with that amount of enthusiasm, honesty, and vigor that the task requires.

The need to have the internal affairs function performed by the chief of police in small departments should be obvious. In such departments the chief is, as a general rule, the only sworn officer in the department who will not be reduced in rank and reassigned. The chief, therefore, is the only logical candidate; only the chief can handle such an assignment without having to fear its consequences at a later date. In highly political police departments, in which police chiefs change with the election of a new mayor or with the appointment of a new city manager, it is virtually impossible to establish viable internal affairs programs. This is especially so if police chiefs are recycled back into the organization with every change in political administration.

Several years ago, a presidential commission noted that "if the police are to maintain the respect and support of the public, they must deal openly and forcefully with misconduct within their own ranks whenever it occurs."[12] This can be accomplished only through the establishment of an internal affairs component which is designed to fully meet its obligations. The people who *guard the guards* must be skilled investigators of unquestionable integrity.

Intelligence   The gathering and analyzing of information comprise the intelligence function within a police department. For the most part, it involves collecting and analyzing information which relates to the existence, scope, and impact of organized crime. In recent years this function has been expanded to include analysis of information about radical and terrorist groups, which are inherent threats to individuals and to society as a whole.

Most intelligence units operate through the extensive use of informants and undercover employees. Officers assigned to the intelligence function usually serve in a staff capacity and rarely become involved operationally. In most departments intelligence personnel report directly to the chief, who makes tactical and strategic decisions based on the information and analyses provided.

STANDARD 9.11

INTELLIGENCE OPERATIONS

Every police agency and every State immediately should establish and maintain the capability to gather and evaluate information and to disseminate intelligence in a manner which protects every individual's right to privacy while it curtails organized crime and public disorder.

National Advisory Commission on Criminal Justice Standards and Goals, *Police* (Washington, D.C.: U.S. Government Printing Office, 1973), p. 250.

Officers assigned to the intelligence function should be selected very carefully and should possess qualities of integrity which are completely above reproach. They should be experienced police officers who have served their apprenticeships as departmental investigators.

With the emergence of terrorist, extremist and militant groups openly dedicated to the violent overthrow of the government and to the destruction of the democratic process, the police intelligence function has become increasingly important and controversial. That the government and the society have a right and an obligation to defend themselves from such groups is not usually questioned. But of great and legitimate concern are decisions about which groups to investigate and what means of investigation should be used.

Many police agencies apparently closely monitored totally law-abiding groups during the past decade. The suspected "crimes" of these groups seem to have been nothing more than opposition to prevailing government policies, such as escalation of the Vietnam War. These groups were spied on (and in some instances had their mail illegally opened and their homes and offices burglarized) because they were political dissenters. But the efforts of earlier political dissenters—John Adams, Thomas Paine, and George Washington—made political dissent legal and indeed important in our system of government. Police administrators must have a very strong appreciation of this. They must be careful to differentiate between dissenters and truly violent opponents of the democratic process. The latter, but not the former, are worthy targets of police intelligence activity.

THE AUXILIARY SERVICES SUBSYSTEM

We have described *operations* as including those activities performed in direct assistance to the public and *administration* as including those activities which are likely to be of long-term benefit to all units of the organization. The remaining activities constitute the *auxiliary services* subsystem. It should be noted that these activities also benefit other units within the department, but on a more regular and frequent basis than administrative activities. Auxiliary services functions are usually available to assist the police officer on a 24-hour-a-day, 365-day-a-year basis; administrative functions are usually available 8 hours a day, 5 days a week. Although it is sometimes difficult to distinguish between the two types of activities, it is useful to think of administrative services as long-range services available on a limited basis and of auxiliary services as direct services available on a continuing basis. The tasks included within the auxiliary services subsystem are records, communications, property, laboratory, detention, identification, alcohol testing, facilities, equipment, supplies, and maintenance.

Records   The records task, a vitally important one for the police organization, furnishes the agency with a memory, enabling it to retrieve information long forgotten. It can provide information on wanted persons, unpaid parking tickets, last year's traffic accidents, crime patterns, and activity statistics.

STANDARD 24.1

POLICE REPORTING

Every police agency should establish procedures that will insure simple and efficient reporting of criminal activity, assist in criminal investigations, and provide complete information to other components of the criminal justice system.

1. Every police agency should immediately publish the circumstances which require an officer to complete a report, and should provide printed forms for crime, arrest, and other reports.

National Advisory Commission on Criminal Justice Standards and Goals, *Police* (Washington, D.C.: U.S. Government Printing Office, 1973), p. 570.

The foundation of the records task is the reporting system. Some departments use one report form for all types of complaints (see Fig. 3.1); others have separate forms for each type of complaint.[13] Regardless of the system used, each complaint should be assigned a unique *complaint number* for use in case control. All initial and follow-up reports on a given complaint should bear this number, enabling the records unit to maintain individual files on all investigations.

In addition to files of complaint reports, the records unit should ordinarily maintain files on arrests, warrants, traffic tickets, summonses, method of operation, aliases, and mug shots. The records unit should also maintain cross-index files for the quick retrieval of information.

In recent years most large police departments have found it helpful to computerize their records sytems, thereby giving them a capability of instant record retrieval. A few departments have refined this process to the point of installing computer terminals in patrol cars, thus giving individual officers the opportunity to check immediately on such matters as suspicious persons and stolen vehicles they might come across in the course of their duties. The computerization of records has made police work more effective and efficient.

Access to departmental records must be available 24 hours a day. For the small department with limited personnel, this sometimes poses a severe problem, especially from a security standpoint. Because of the necessity to control access, records cannot be made available on a one-to-one basis to anyone in the department who happens to need them. Therefore, small departments must assign records officers who will be responsible for records for control purposes during given shifts. A strict system of accountability should be enforced in all such instances.

Communications   The communications function is peripheral to both operations and auxiliary services, but is generally categorized as an auxiliary service. Although the lack of personnel in smaller departments usually necessitates the use of operational personnel for communications, the function itself is an internal task which services police personnel on a continuing basis. It is therefore a service function. There are, however, some operational aspects to it. In many instances communications personnel handling incoming telephone calls are able to satisfy callers' needs directly, without having to refer matters further. When such services are provided to the public directly in this way, they are operational rather than auxiliary services. But for the most part, communications personnel provide internal services that benefit police officers and assist them in their work. The bulk of their work is directed toward helping officers perform their tasks, and therefore they are generally looked on as being auxiliary service personnel.

As a vitally important police function, communications provides the link between the police and the public for the delivery of all police services to the community at large. It should go without saying that people assigned to the communications task should be effective communicators who are receptive to and concerned about the public

COMPLAINT SHEET

HOW RECEIVED: Complaint Number _____

Phone _____ Person _____
                                                 Complainants Name _____
Letter _____ Radio _____

Alarm _____ T.T. _____   Street _____

Received by: _____   Town _____

Invest. by: _____   Telephone: _____ D.O.B. _____

                    NATURE OF COMPLAINT

_____

_____

_____

_____

_____

_____

_____

_____

_____

_____

_____

_____

_____

_____

_____

_____

_____

_____

_____

_____

_____

Status _____ _____   _____
                    Signature of C. O.   Signature of Officer

Fig. 3.1. Example of a complaint sheet: (a) front; (b) back.

QUANTITY	ARTICLE Name Only	Description of property missing	Value

Description of person wanted

Name Alias and Address	Nativity	AGE Year	AGE Months	HEIGHT Feet	HEIGHT Inches	WEIGHT Pounds	EYES Color	HAIR Color

Teletype message sent by _____ Date _____ Time _____ No _____

QUANTITY	ARTICLE Name Only	Description of property recovered	Value

Property returned to signature _____ by officer _____ date _____ time _____

ARRESTS AND DISPOSITIONS

Name and Address	Arrest Number	DISPOSITION	SENTENCE Years	SENTENCE Months	SENTENCE Days	SENTENCE Fine

Commanding Officer _____   Records Clerk _____

interest. When answering telephones, communications officers must obtain as much accurate information as possible about complaints so that responding personnel can be prepared for what is likely to await them. As dispatching officers, communications officers must be aware of the seriousness of all calls and assign appropriate numbers of officers and vehicles to accommodate needs and ensure officer safety. The communications unit is the heart of every police department; it receives information, processes it, and pumps it out into the system to be acted on.

Communications is a vitally important police function. (Courtesy of the Metropolitan Police Department, Washington, D.C.)

STANDARD 23.1

POLICE USE OF THE TELEPHONE SYSTEM

Every police agency should develop as a subsystem of its overall communications system a telephone communications component designed to reduce crime through rapid and accurate communication with the public. This design may require an upgraded physical plant and supportive equipment, and procedures to shorten the time of the internal message handling.

National Advisory Commission on Criminal Justice Standards and Goals, *Police* (Washington, D.C.: U.S. Government Printing Office, 1973), p. 546.

STANDARD 23.2

COMMAND AND CONTROL OPERATIONS

Every police agency should acknowledge that the speed with which it can communicate with field units is critical; that it affects the success of agency efforts to preserve life and property; and that it increases the potential for immediate apprehension of criminal suspects. Therefore, a rapid and accurate communications capability should be developed.

National Advisory Commission on Criminal Justice Standards and Goals, *Police* (Washington, D.C.: U.S. Government Printing Office, 1973), p. 551.

Property   This task encompasses the handling of all property for which the police are responsible, e.g., prisoners' property, recovered stolen property, lost property, confiscated property, departmental property, abandoned and towed vehicles, and evidence.

The handling of property, thought by some to be a simple warehouse operation, can be complicated and burdensome for the police administrator. In all cases, property must be protected in a systematic way. Although some items need to be stored for only short periods of time, others, such as perishable goods or narcotics evidence, need special care and continuing surveillance. Honest attempts must be made to find owners of lost property; departmental property and equipment must be accounted for and maintained.

Special procedures must be devised for the control of all property, and records must be maintained so that any single piece of property can be located at a moment's notice.

Handling evidence is an especially difficult and important task. In order for evidence to be admissible in court, it must be maintained within a chain of custody that guarantees it to be in the same condition as when it was seized by the police. Each time a piece of evidence is passed, for whatever reason, from one person to another, the person taking possession becomes a link in the chain of custody. Officers responsible for property within a given police department must maintain records indicating the chain of custody and describing the purposes for which evidence has been passed from one to another. Property officers must establish a system to maintain the integrity of evidence, always exerting caution that it is not altered or contaminated. A rigid system of security for the property-storage area is essential for the protection of all property, and great pains must be taken to control property in the possession of the police.

STANDARD 12.3

THE PROPERTY SYSTEM

Every police agency immediately should establish a system for the secure and efficient storage, classification, retrieval, and disposition of items of evidentiary or other value that come into the custody of the agency.

1. Every police agency should establish a filing system that includes, but is not limited to:
   a. A chronological record of each occasion when property is taken into police custody;
   b. A separate itemized list of all items of property that are taken into custody;
   c. A record that indicates the continuity of the property from its entry into the system to its final disposition. This record should include the name of each person accountable for each item of property at any given time.
2. Every police agency should conduct regular property inventories and property record audits to insure the integrity of the system. Such measures should be performed by personnel who are not charged with the care and custody of the property, and the results should be reported to the police chief executive.

National Advisory Commission on Criminal Justice Standards and Goals, *Police* (Washington, D.C.: U.S. Government Printing Office, 1973), p. 309.

Laboratory The police laboratory has grown in importance in direct proportion to the number of procedural constraints imposed on the police by the courts. Court-imposed restrictions on operational activities require that the police conduct investigations in a much more

A criminalist examines evidence in the laboratory. (Courtesy of the Los Angeles Police Department)

sophisticated fashion. Sophistication in investigative activities requires the use of technology and science. Instead of relying on confessions to get convictions, which had always been the traditional approach, the police now rely on the development of scientific evidence. Physical evidence such as fibers, tool marks, tire tracks, blood stains, and fingerprints are considered the most reliable of all forms of evidence; the examination and classification of such evidence rests with the laboratory.

Few police departments have the financial resources to maintain their own laboratories, although in recent years even the smallest police organizations have been able to train evidence technicians to perform some of the more routine scientific tasks. Most police departments rely on the facilities of regional or state laboratories, and many send evidence to the Federal Bureau of Investigation Laboratory in Washington, D.C., certainly one of the best police laboratories in the world.

Because physical evidence has come to play such an important role in the successful prosecution of cases, it is imperative for all police departments to rely on the laboratory for processing evidence. This requires all departments to either establish their own laboratories or develop working relations with other laboratories that have the capabilities of examining every conceivable type of evidence. In departments that do not have their own laboratories, one person should be designated as *laboratory coordinating officer,* and this person should be given the responsibility for coordinating physical evidence examinations.

Detention   For most police departments the detention task usually involves the temporary confinement of arrested persons for short periods of time after their arrest. If the accused person is not released by the court after his or her arraignment or cannot raise the necessary bail for release, he or she is usually taken to a holding facility, often administered by the county, until trial. Incarceration in police lock-ups, therefore, is usually for short periods of time, and police jail populations are generally very transient.

Because our system of justice presumes the innocence of all persons charged and because our Judeo-Christian ethic dictates that all human beings be treated with dignity, arrested persons in the custody of the police deserve fair and just treatment. Detention areas should be clean and should give prisoners the opportunity to rest, wash, and use toilet facilities. Prisoners should be fed and housed in accordance with their needs and should be protected from other prisoners and sometimes from themselves. All personal property, including belts, shoelaces, neckties, matches, and cigarettes, should be temporarily confiscated. Prisoners should also be checked periodically to prevent them from doing bodily harm to themselves. If they need medical attention, it should be immediately provided. In short, in attempting to meet their responsibilities to prisoners, the police should act responsibly.

STANDARD 12.4

THE DETENTION SYSTEM

Every police agency currently operating a detention facility should immediately insure professionalism in its jail management and provide adequate detention services. Every municipal police agency should, by 1982, turn over all its detention and correctional facilities to an appropriate county, regional, or State agency, and should continue to maintain only those facilities necessary for short term processing of prisoners immediately following arrest.

National Advisory Commission on Criminal Justice Standards and Goals, *Police* (Washington, D.C.: U.S. Government Printing Office, 1973), p. 313.

Detention facilities should be secure and should be designed to prevent escape as well as any danger to police personnel. One officer should be placed in charge of all prisoners and should be held accountable for their care while in custody.

Although there is no requirement that detention facilities must rival the luxury of a Holiday Inn or a Hilton Hotel, they should be habitable and should take into consideration the needs of the prisoners they house.

Identification The identification task, which usually entails fingerprinting and photography, relates most notably to detention, records, and criminal investigation. Prisoners should be both fingerprinted and photographed immediately following arrest. Fingerprints are maintained as permanent records in local, state, and federal files. Photographs are usually maintained locally for future reference. Both are extremely useful in criminal investigation for identification purposes. Photographs are used to identify suspects and to record crime scenes in vivid detail; they are often useful in the prosecution of cases. Fingerprints also serve to identify suspects and sometimes provide the only link between a crime and a criminal.

Large police departments usually have identification experts who are skilled in all aspects of fingerprinting and photography. Small departments, recognizing the importance of the identification function, rely on evidence technicians and crime scene search specialists, who generally do fingerprinting and photography work as an adjunct to their major operational responsibilities. Some departments equip all of their police vehicles with inexpensive cameras and require their patrol officers and detectives to do their own photographing. Some small departments also train one or more officers on each shift to handle fingerprinting as a part of their normal patrol or investigative activities as the need arises.

For the proper investigation of major crimes, it is essential for all police departments to have available to them the resources of a truly professional police photographer and identifications expert. If such an expert is not locally available, the department should depend on the services of personnel available from regional identification facilities or from state police organizations.

Alcohol testing   Because drunk driving causes so many personal injuries and fatal automobile accidents, many police departments consider the apprehension and conviction of intoxicated drivers to be one of their highest priorities. In addition to an officer's observations of a defendant's driving behavior and condition, the results of an alcohol test can be compelling evidence of intoxication.

Several different methods can be used to test for the degree of intoxication, including the examination of the breath, blood, and urine. Because the breath test can be administered by a police officer trained in the operation of the testing equipment, it is the test most commonly used by police departments. Blood and urine tests involve laboratory analysis and have proved to be difficult methods for the police to use.

It is the policy of most police departments, both small and large, to train a number of officers on each shift to administer breath tests. The process is simple and can be learned in a short period of time. All police departments should be equipped for alcohol testing or should have the facilities for such testing available to them immediately.

Facilities   The police facilities task involves all aspects of the building or buildings in which a police department is housed. It encompasses the allocation and efficient use of space. The facilities task is designed to make the best possible use of available space, with full consideration given to the goals and objectives of the organization.

Not until 1973 was any serious attention given to the development of police facilities. Although much had been written prior to 1973 regarding the locations of bureaus, divisions, and units structurally within police buildings, very little research had been conducted on the subject. In its *Guidelines for the Planning and Design of Police Programs and*

Facilities, the National Clearinghouse for Criminal Justice Planning and Architecture at the University of Illinois, under a 1972 Law Enforcement Assistance Administration grant, published the results of the only truly definitive research project ever conducted on the design of police facilities. Aside from focusing attention on the problem, this research effort set forth numerous innovative recommendations for police departments to follow in designing their facilities to more adequately meet needs.

Because most police chiefs are not qualified as building superintendents or architects, the police facilities task has been poorly handled over the years. Yet the way space is used is of supreme importance in the implementation of police programs and in getting the work done. To this day many police departments are cramped in abandoned city halls or in station houses built in the early 1900s. These ancient edifices often lack proper security, sanitary facilities, and rooms for lockers, roll calls, and interviews. Very often their layouts expose communications rooms to the public and necessitate the location of cell blocks down flights of stairs in basements which lack ventilation and which over the years have become moldy and dirty.

With an increase in police station bombings and sieges by dissident groups, it has been discovered, sometimes sadly, that ancient police facilities are defenseless and vulnerable to attack. This has resulted in a new awareness about police buildings and how they should be constructed and renovated.

The structural grouping of related police functions is one of the most important aspects of the facilities task. Subsystem components that depend on each other or are similar in nature should be located in close physical proximity. The communications and records sections, for example, should be close together, with consideration given to the necessity to locate records in an area accommodating public access while at the same time sealing off communications from the range of public view and hearing. Similarly, offices used for operational purposes, such as patrol and investigations, should be separated but at the same time near each other. Detention facilities should be located in or near an area staffed 24 hours a day, in an effort to enhance prisoner safety.

Equipment   As one might imagine, there is an almost endless variety of police equipment. Anything the police use to do their work should be considered police equipment—vehicles, typewriters, bullhorns, search lights, first aid kits, computers, firearms, cameras, uniforms, riot gear, radios, report forms, tear gas, dogs, horses, microscopes, chemicals, aircraft, boats, motorcycles, scooters, and even bicycles. The list of the various kinds of equipment the police use would fill a book.

STANDARD 22.1

TRANSPORTATION EQUIPMENT UTILITY

Every police agency should annually evaluate the tasks performed within the agency and the transportation equipment which may be utilized by the agency to determine how the proper application of transportation equipment can improve the agency's ability to accomplish its objectives.

National Advisory Commission on Criminal Justice Standards and Goals, *Police* (Washington, D.C.: U.S. Government Printing Office, 1973), p. 526.

A police officer without proper equipment is like a sailboat without a sail. (Courtesy of the Los Angeles County Sheriff's Department)

Personnel responsible for the equipment task are involved with all equipment the police use, from acquisition to disposal. In some instances they may even be involved in purchasing and installation. They monitor equipment performance and evaluate departmental needs for new equipment. One of their more important functions is to develop an inventory system by which equipment can be controlled and not lost or stolen. Because good equipment is an essential element in the operation of every police department, the equipment function must be performed expertly and must be looked on, as it oftentimes is not, as a specialized function requiring the constant concern of specialists.

Supply   Personnel responsible for the supply function are involved, as the word *supply* suggests, with ensuring that the department has everything it needs to function as a modern-day police agency. In addition to obtaining the types of equipment mentioned in our discussion of the equipment function, the supply function is responsible for maintaining adequate supplies of gasoline, flashlight batteries, tires, bullets, insignia, pencils, and myriad other necessities.

The supply function includes the actual purchase of supplies as well as the maintenance of supply inventories. Every police department should calculate the rate of usage of each kind of supply item and flag items for repurchase when stocks have dwindled.

The officer or officers in charge of this responsibility should attempt to purchase supplies at the lowest possible cost. It is their obligation to establish bidding procedures, to put items out for bid, and to supervise the bidding process. Also, to the degree possible, they should be required to enter into regional purchasing compacts with other police departments in their area in order to purchase supplies in quantity and therefore obtain the lowest possible unit cost.

Maintenance   Keeping police facilities clean and equipment repaired and functioning properly has a positive impact on the effectiveness of every police agency. Those who perform the maintenance task have this responsibility.

There is nothing more frustrating for a police officer than to be forced to work out of a dirty police facility with equipment that works only occasionally. In departments where maintenance of facilities and equipment holds a low priority, the morale of police officers is likely to be low. In fact, one of the most frequent complaints voiced by police officers concerns the poor maintenance of the vehicles they drive.

Because most police chiefs do not regard maintenance as a police function per se, they rarely use good judgment in ensuring its performance at an acceptable level. Thus in city after city, police cars chug about at less than full spark plug capacity and have dented fenders, broken mirrors, and nonfunctioning lights. Very often one finds oxygen tanks without oxygen, fire extinguishers without contents, and first aid kits without bandages.

Many police chiefs find that it is more cost effective to have maintenance service performed by outsiders on a contract basis. Some departments, for example, hire custodial services to maintain their buildings and private auto repair shops to maintain their vehicles. Because such services are provided on a competitive basis, outside service agencies are often found to perform them significantly better than departmental personnel so assigned. Most departments cannot afford full-time radio technicians, computer repairers, mechanics, and custodians. They can afford, however, to assign the responsibility for maintenance to someone within the department and hold that person accountable for the performance of the function. Although the maintenance function is not at all glamorous, it is nonetheless vital to the functioning of the organization.

INTERDEPENDENCE OF SUBSYSTEM TASKS

The 30 basic police subsystem tasks discussed in this chapter must be performed in every police agency. If any one of these tasks is neglected or not performed, the job of providing good police services to the community will be impaired, often to a great degree. Inasmuch as each task is an integral part of the police system as a whole, the system itself as well as component subsystems will be affected adversely if any one of the subsystem tasks is performed poorly or not performed at all.

From an organizational standpoint, because all subsystem tasks are interrelated, all subsystem tasks are interdependent. Each relies on all of the others being performed well. When an organization fails to meet its goals and objectives, the failure can always be attributed to a breakdown in one or more subsystem tasks. Understanding the importance of these tasks is the first step in understanding the organization itself—the system. All of the organization's subsystem tasks are parts of the machinery that make the system run. Just as a worn tire, a faulty spark plug, or a sticky carburetor reduces the efficiency of an engine, an inept patrol supervisor, an inadequately equipped laboratory, or a poorly planned budget reduces the efficiency of a police department. When all component parts of a system are working together in good order, the total system works in good order. Take away or damage one component part of the system, however, and you damage the whole system—it begins to break down. Systems that are put together poorly to begin with or which lack the necessary parts to function stand little or no chance of achieving their goals and objectives—the reason for their being.

Bearing in mind what the police system is and what comprises its subsystems is essential in understanding police administration. The systems concept is basic to the administrative process, and all students of police administration should study the subject, continually being aware of what it comprises.

SUMMARY

In this chapter we have examined the most important basic police subsystem tasks, those tasks that must be performed if police departments are to be viable. To suggest that these subsystem tasks are the only ones that police perform would be naive. Each subsystem task could, in fact, be looked on as an individual system in and of itself, with each task comprising numerous additional subsystems.

You should be aware that operations, administration, and auxiliary services are the three major subsystems of the police organization and that each comprises several additional important subsystem tasks that are essential to the system as a whole if it is to function properly. We have examined 30 of these subsystem tasks and have attempted to explain their importance and interdependence.

DISCUSSION QUESTIONS

1. When the subject of police work comes up, what kinds of activities do you think of? What are the implications for police work of the glamorized, fictional presentations seen by the public on television, in the movies, and in novels?

2. How much crime do you think patrolling prevents? Do you think that random, routine patrolling is an efficient utilization by the police department of its limited resources? If not, how would you use those resources differently?

3. Do you think that detectives should be paid more than patrol officers? Should one or the other be a higher rank?

4. What do you think should be the police response to crimes such as gambling, prostitution, narcotics, and other vice offenses?

5. Juvenile services, community services, crime prevention, and community relations are often looked down on by police officers as not

being "real police work." What is real police work? As a police manager, how would you go about elevating the status of such tasks?

6. When police recruits leave the training academy and hit the streets, they are frequently advised by more experienced officers to forget everything they were taught, as it isn't applicable to the real world. The recruits then learn from the "old salts" such things as sleeping on the job, accepting gratuities, quickly getting rid of service calls, and putting in reports many activities not actually performed. How can this cycle be broken? How can the department guarantee that proper procedures taught in training classes are actually implemented?

7. An age-old problem concerns the responsibility for police abuses. If the investigation of police corruption and brutality is left to the police themselves, how can the public be sure that proper action is taken? If the responsibility is placed elsewhere, such as with a civilian review board, how can the police be convinced that they will be dealt with justly?

8. The police must collect intelligence about certain groups. Experience suggests that the police often exceed their proper role and use illegal means or collect intelligence on legal and nonviolent groups. How can these problems be resolved? Who should decide what means are proper and what groups should be investigated?

REFERENCES

1. G.D. Eastman and E.M. Eastman, eds., *Municipal Police Administration,* 7th ed. (Washington, D.C.: International City Management Association, Institute for Training in Muncipal Administration, 1971), p. 77.

2. By permission. From *Webster's New Collegiate Dictionary* © 1977 by G. & C. Merriam Co., Publishers of the Merriam-Webster Dictionaries.

3. George L. Kelling, Tony Pate, Duane Dieckman, and Charles E. Brown, *The Kansas City Preventive Patrol Experiment: A Summary Report* (Washington, D.C.: Police Foundation, 1974).

4. Stanley P. Friedman, "Civilians Who Keep Traffic Moving," *Parade* (March 31, 1974).

5. Clarence M. Kelley, *Crime in the United States, 1976, Uniform Crime Reports* (Washington, D.C.: U.S. Government Printing Office, 1977), p. 160.

6. *Experiments in Police Improvement: A Progress Report* (Washington, D.C.: Police Foundation, 1972), p. 28.

7. Robert Daley, *Target Blue* (New York: Delacorte, 1971), p. 28.

8. *Experiments in Police Improvement, op. cit.,* p. 28.

9. Allen R. Janger, "The Expanded Personnel Function," in Dale S. Beach, ed., *Managing People at Work: Readings in Personnel* (New York: Macmillan, 1971), p. 34.

10. President's Commission on Law Enforcement and Administration of Justice, *Task Force Report: The Police* (Washington, D.C.: Government Printing Office, 1967), pp. 63–65.

11. Knapp Commission, *The Knapp Commission Report on Police Corruption* (New York: George Braziller, 1972), pp. 16-17.

12. President's Commission on Campus Unrest, *Report of the President's Commission on Campus Unrest* (Chicago: Commerce Clearing House, 1970), p. 5/8.

13. Robert Sheehan, *Police Management Study, Bellingham, Massachusetts: A Survey Report* (Medway, Mass.: Robert Sheehan Associates, 1974), pp. 146-147.

CHAPTER 4
BASIC PRINCIPLES OF
POLICE ORGANIZATION

1. Define hierarchy.

2. Define authority.

3. Differentiate between authority delegation and authority recovery.

4. Define the principle of accountability.

5. Define the principle of functional definition.

6. Cite three criteria by which functions may be examined for similarity.

7. Differentiate between line and staff duties.

8. Define the scalar principle.

9. Cite the three levels of management.

10. Cite several undesirable by-products of specialization.

11. Define the authority-level principle.

12. Identify the most difficult principle of organization to put into effect.

13. Define the principle of unity of command.

14. Define the principle of span of control.

15. Cite the most effective size for a span of control.

In Chapter 5 we will see that *organizing* is one of the basic functions of the police manager. The application of the systems concept can help the police manager develop orderliness in the process of organizing and hence in the development of the police organization. Chapter 4 will lay the foundation for that effort by presenting the basic principles of police organization.

ELEMENTS OF HIERARCHY

Any organization in which someone has authority over someone else is a *hierarchy*. Governments, corporations, families, fraternities, universities, and police departments are all hierarchies. Not generally regarded as hierarchies are communes, food cooperatives, and religious denominations that encourage total flexibility in dogma or belief. Even these organizations, however, may have some hierarchical aspects, some members either assuming or being voted into certain leadership roles. A member of the clergy, for example, may not have any authority over parishioners per se, but may have the authority to establish times for services.

Most organizations are hierarchical in some respects; some are more hierarchical than others. The larger the number of supervisors or administrators an organization has, the more hierarchical the organization is. For example, Fig. 4.1 shows that organization B is more hierarchical than organization A, even though both employ the same number of workers.

When we say that someone is a person's *boss,* we generally mean that he or she has the authority to give the person orders. In terms of authority, the boss is the *superior* and has the power to command the *subordinate.* If the boss has the power to command the subordinate, it follows that the boss has the right, as well as the responsibility, to command the subordinate.

Besides bestowing on the boss the right and the responsibility to command, authority also gives the boss the right to make decisions and take actions. A police sergeant, for example, has the right as supervisor to approve a patrol officer's request to leave an assigned patrol area. The sergeant makes such a decision and takes such an action based on the responsibility to exercise delegated authority to make the decision and take the action. The patrol officer, who by departmental policy is mandated to remain within a designated patrol area, has no authority to leave it without permission.

In one municipal police agency with which we are familiar, the authority for a patrol officer to leave a patrol area was vested in both the shift commander and the radio dispatcher. One patrol officer left an assigned patrol area to attend an auction elsewhere. Upon arriving at the auction, the officer left his patrol vehicle unlocked and unattended, with the keys in the ignition. When he returned from the auction, the car was gone. A number of days later, the car was found burned in an isolated sand pit deep in the woods.

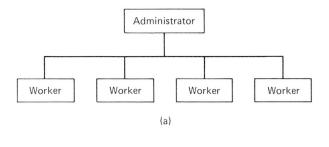

(a)

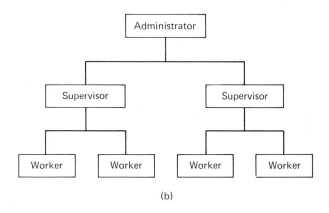

(b)

Fig. 4.1. Of these two hierarchical organizations, organization A (a) is less hierarchical than organization B (b).

An internal investigation was initiated to determine whether the officer had received permission to leave his patrol area to attend the auction. The officer claimed that he had received permission from the radio dispatcher, who denied that he had given permission. Inasmuch as the department did not monitor its radio calls with tape recording equipment, there was no way of determining who was telling the truth. Because the department had no written policy prohibiting patrol officers from leaving their vehicles unlocked, no action could legitimately be taken against the patrol officer. Had the department had sound-monitoring equipment, it would have been possible to determine whether or not the patrol officer had taken authority into his own hands. If the facts in the case had supported the radio dispatcher, action could have been taken against the patrol officer for using authority he had not been delegated. If the facts had supported the patrol officer, action could have been taken against the dispatcher for using his authority irresponsibly.

THE DELEGATION OF AUTHORITY

In a properly organized police department, the chief delegates authority for decision making to people at all levels within the organization. Authority is the power to make decisions or to perform tasks. The ultimate authority in a police department lies with the chief, who must wisely and widely delegate authority to others so that decisions can be made and tasks performed. Those to whom authority is delegated should be expected to use their authority responsibly.

Although authority may be delegated, responsibility may not. Responsibility is the obligation to make decisions, to perform tasks, and to use authority prudently. Responsibility is often defined improperly to mean duty or activity. It is neither of these; rather, responsibility is an unwritten understanding or acknowledgment by workers at all levels within an organization that they are expected to make wise decisions, to do their jobs as well as they possibly can, and to exercise whatever authority they have in the best possible manner.

Every person within an organization who is expected to perform a specific task should be delegated the necessary amount of authority to perform it well. In police departments where chiefs do not understand this necessity, there will be very few operational decisions made and very little work accomplished. For example, when the chief of a small department had been appointed in 1938, there was only one other member of the department. Thirty years later, when one of the authors conducted a study, the department had more than 20 members. Although the chief was well intentioned and had the best interests of the department and the town at heart, the department had grown so rapidly that he was not able to adjust to the fact he could no longer retain all authority and make all decisions in the department. He gave the one lieutenant and three sergeants very little authority to make decisions and to assume command and supervisory responsibilities. As a result, the patrol officers' work was totally unsupervised. The sergeants were little more than patrol officers with three stripes on their sleeves and greatly resented the fact that the chief would not give them the authority to do their jobs. Both the department and the town suffered because of the chief's unwillingness to delegate his authority to others who needed it in order to do their work and meet their responsibilities.

The failure to delegate authority is not at all uncommon in police organizations. In many instances police chiefs simply do not understand the mechanics of the delegation process. In other cases chiefs are unwilling to delegate authority, fearing that it will be abused by subordinates and reflect negatively on both the department and themselves. Many chiefs are aware that most citizens will attribute success or failure to their efforts and accordingly are extremely cautious about allowing others within their organizations the opportunity to make mistakes that could be embarrassing. Yet police chiefs are oftentimes the least qualified people within their organizations to make decisions, because they are generally furthest removed from the people and situations on which most decisions will directly impact.

Police chiefs will recognize the need to delegate authority only when they realize that they cannot be everywhere at once all the time. Only by delegating authority can they be assured that their organizations will continue to function when they are not physically present.

In delegating authority, chiefs should make absolutely certain that everyone within their departments has a precisely defined understanding of not only the authority he or she has been delegated, but also the circumstances under which the authority may be used. In order to be sure that the person receiving delegated authority thoroughly understands it, it must be delegated *in writing*. Except for emergency situations, a chief of police should never delegate authority using only the spoken word. Confusion, forgetfulness, and misunderstandings can quickly dissipate authority that is not in writing.

Even when the written word is used to delegate authority, great care must be taken to spell out exactly what authority is being delegated to whom for use in which situations. The delegation of authority must also be consistent with the policies and procedures of the department. If officers assigned to the patrol function, for example, are expected to work a full eight hours, shift commanders should not be allowed to authorize officers to go home early except in cases of illness or injury. Such an authorization would be in direct violation of policy.

Just as the chief has total authority over the entire police department, officers in high-ranking positions within the hierarchy have more authority than do those in lower ranks. Captains generally would have more authority than lieutenants; lieutenants, more authority than sergeants. A captain in charge of an operations bureau, for example, should have the authority to decide what priorities will be assigned to various types of investigations. The captain exercises authority by establishing these priorities responsibly in terms of a number of factors, which might include work load, seriousness of offense, current crime problems, and availability of personnel. The captain might choose to either delegate the authority to establish the priorities to the lieutenant in charge of the investigations division or retain the authority and establish the priorities personally. As a good administrator, the captain should delegate the authority to the lieutenant, spelling out *in writing* specifically what the lieutenant is to do. The lieutenant, in turn, might further delegate the authority to establish the priorities to the sergeants in charge of investigative shifts. To do so, however, would be irresponsible, and the lieutenant could be accused of having the sergeants perform work that the lieutenant should be doing personally. The lieutenant, with an overview of the entire investigations division, is in a much better position than the sergeants are to establish the investigative priorities. The only certain way to avoid problems in this situation is to word the original delegation of authority from the captain to the lieutenant so precisely that the lieutenant understands fully that under no circumstances is the authority to establish the priorities to be delegated to anyone else in the command structure.

There should be room, however, for some flexibility in the delegation process. The lieutenant should have the authority, for example, to allow the sergeants in charge of investigative shifts to amend the priorities occasionally whenever they judge that for some good reason a low-priority investigation should have priority over what would normally be looked on as a high-priority investigation. For instance, if the lieutenant has established that homicide investigations should have priority over rape investigations, generally homicides should be investigated first. However, if it is apparent to an investigative sergeant that a reversal of priorities would be likely to result in an immediate clearance of a rape case whereas a homicide would be unlikely to result in a clearance if given prompter attention, the sergeant should have the authority to switch priorities and either investigate the rape first or assign more officers to the rape investigation.

In delegating to the lieutenant the authority to establish priorities, the captain is in effect telling the lieutenant that priorities must be established. By specifying through the delegation process that the authority for this task is not to be further delegated, the captain makes it clear that the lieutenant is to do the job personally. And by building into the delegation process the flexibility to allow investigative sergeants to amend priorities if under certain circumstances to do so would better meet organizational goals and objectives, the captain is acting responsibly in using authority as a tool for task accomplishment.

Whenever feedback within a police system indicates that authority is being abused or that officers to whom authority has been delegated are not using it responsibly, that authority must be recovered, or taken back. When they delegate authority, police chiefs must be fully aware that the delegation is never permanent. This must also be understood by everyone to whom authority is delegated. When a department is reorganized, when duties are rearranged or reassigned, and when departmental objectives, policies, and programs are modified, authority will inevitably be *recovered*.[1] The delegation of authority and the recovery of authority are continuing processes by which the organization is made more responsive to the interests of its clientele (citizens, in the case of a police department) and more productive in terms of its output (services).

If the concepts of authority and responsibility are fully understood by everyone within a police department and if the chief follows some simple principles of organization in administering the agency, there should be no difficulty in using authority delegation as an organizational device to increase departmental efficiency and effectiveness. These basic principles of police organization are discussed in the remainder of this chapter.

THE PRINCIPLE OF ACCOUNTABILITY

Police chiefs should never make the mistake of assuming that those to whom they have delegated authority will use it wisely. In order to minimize the ever-present possibility that delegated authority will be misused or abused, chiefs must institute some formal system for monitoring the activities of all officers who have been delegated authority. Such a system is based on the *principle of accountability*.

Very simply, the principle of accountability means that all individuals to whom authority has been delegated must be held accountable for its use. It demands that some action be taken if and when individuals are exercising their authority improperly or irresponsibly. Further, it requires that a conscious effort be made to identify organization members who fail to use their authority, use too much authority, or use their authority improperly. In a police department the action taken is a judgmental matter which should be designed primarily to burn into the minds of everyone in the organization that delegation and use of authority are to be taken seriously. A person misusing authority might be transferred, suspended, or, in extreme cases, fired. For an initial minor violation, a friendly warning or a mild reprimand might suffice. But under no circumstances can police chiefs allow anyone in their departments to misuse authority in any way on a continuing basis or to otherwise fail to do an assigned task without taking some action.

The principle of accountability is put into effect through swift and certain action uniformly and fairly administered. All individuals should be treated alike regardless of rank or position, and no favoritism should be shown in implementing the principle. An action must be taken, therefore, in every single instance in which authority is misused or when it becomes apparent that an individual is shirking responsibility or not doing the job as assigned.

If a chief does not use the principle of accountability as a control device and takes no action, everyone tacitly understands that the department will condone certain improprieties under certain circumstances. When officers realize that they *can* misuse their authority or neglect their responsibilities with impunity, authority *will* be misused and responsibilities not met on a consistent basis throughout the organization.

In departments where functions are poorly defined and little or no authority is delegated, it is impossible to put the principle of accountability into effect. In such organizations authority, which is the glue that holds an organization together, becomes an administrative tool by which friends are rewarded and enemies punished. Personalities rather than organizational principles take over the department and become the focal point around which the organization is administered. In such departments an officer gets ahead by siding with the right people politically, not by doing the job. The job becomes incidental to personality priorities and prerogatives. The department becomes self-centered rather than community-centered.

THE PRINCIPLE OF FUNCTIONAL DEFINITION

Police officers have many basic responsibilities and work in a variety of ways. They direct traffic, intercede in family disputes, counsel youth, make arrests, drive patrol vehicles, conduct surveillances, enforce laws, write reports, maintain records, interrogate suspects, interview complainants and victims, testify in court, enforce parking regulations, investigate accidents, supervise subordinates, prepare budgets, provide for the safety of school children, render first aid, inspect liquor establishments, book prisoners, check doors and premises at night, collect and preserve evidence, perform breathalyzer tests, deliver babies, and engage in myriad other functions that come within the purview of their mission. Their duties are many and are often conflicting.

Because a police organization cannot have a separate unit to perform each of the tasks listed above, it becomes necessary to combine them in some systematic way. The most useful way of grouping functions is through application of the *principle of functional definition,* which in police circles is usually referred to as *grouping like functions.* Very simply, this principle holds that functions that are similar should be grouped together organizationally. Functions are similar when:

1. The same level of authority is required for their execution;

2. responsibility for them is executed at the same time or in the same place; and

3. they require the same amount of training and/or degree of skill to be performed.

It is through the grouping of similar functions that the various units within a police organization are formed (see Chapters 2 and 3). Suffice it to say here that a chief of police should make a concerted effort to group similar tasks together logically within the organizational framework.

The chief should be guided not only by similarities in functions, but also by the size of the department. In a department with one chief and four patrol officers, the chief would in all likelihood perform all administrative and auxiliary service functions as well as numerous operational tasks. The patrol officers would probably be assigned exclusively to operational responsibilities. The chief would have no alternative but to organize the department as depicted in Fig. 4.2. In departments having more personnel available to perform specialized functions, any number of possibilities exist for grouping like functions. Figure 4.3, for example, depicts a police department of 21 sworn personnel and 1 civilian secretary. Figure 4.4 shows a department of 30 sworn personnel and 1 clerk-matron.

As a department grows, so too do the opportunities to put similar functions together. In the 22-member department (Fig. 4.3), there are nine separate groupings of similar tasks—five more groupings than in the 5-member department (Fig. 4.2) and four fewer groupings than in the 31-member department (Fig. 4.4). A 200-member department (see Figs. 4.5 through 4.9) offers many additional opportunities to put like functions together. The larger the department, the more possibilities for specialization. In other words, the larger a department is, the more organized it can be.

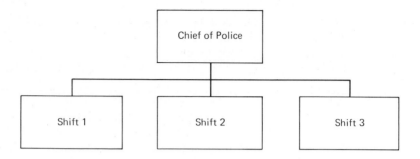

Fig. 4.2. Organization chart for a five-member police department.

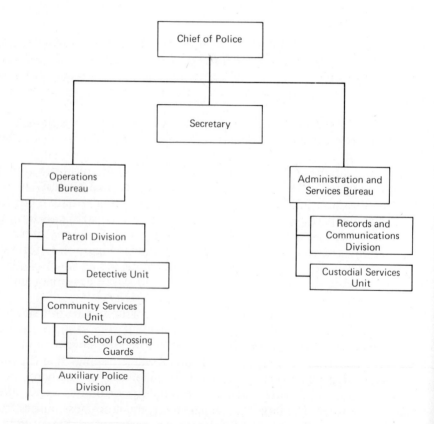

Fig. 4.3. Organization chart for a 22-member police department.

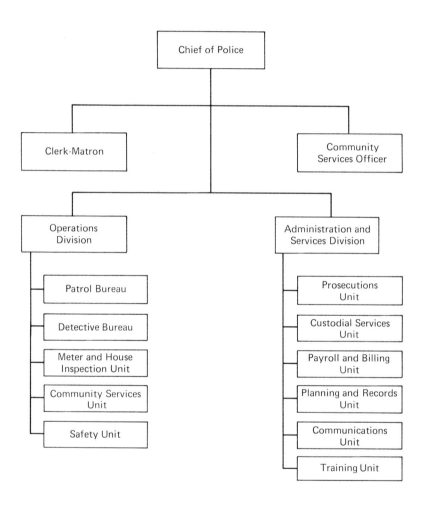

Fig. 4.4. Organization chart for a 31-member police department.

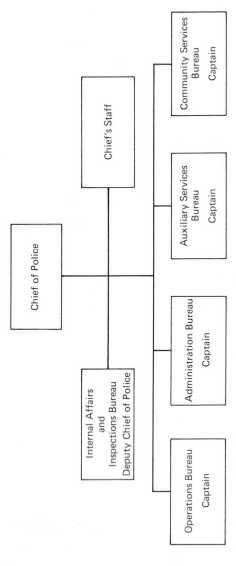

Fig. 4.5. High-level organization for a 200-member police department.

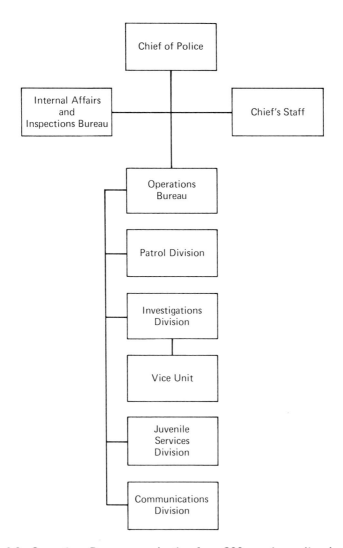

Fig. 4.6. Operations Bureau organization for a 200-member police department.

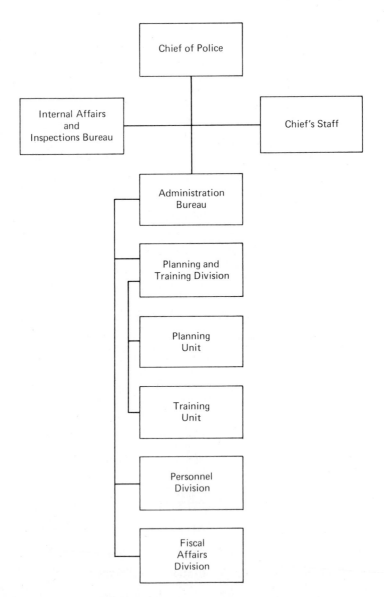

Fig. 4.7. Administration Bureau organization for a 200-member police department.

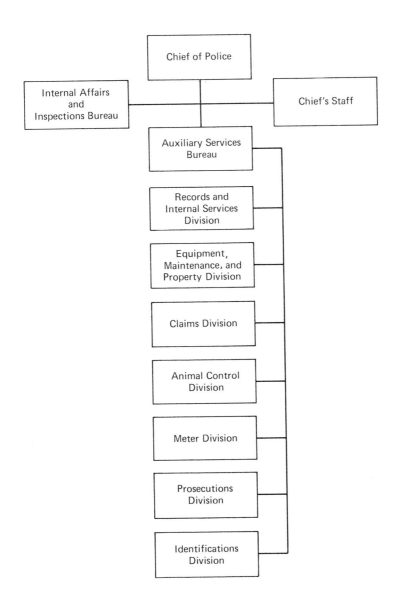

Fig. 4.8. Auxiliary Services Bureau organization for a 200-member police department.

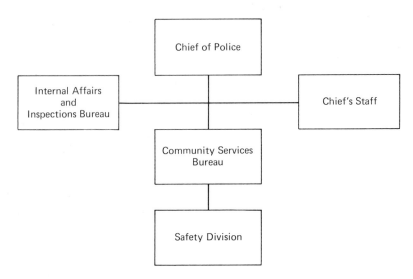

Fig. 4.9. Community Services Bureau organization for a 200-member police department.

Unless a conscious effort is made to group like functions in some systematic, logical way, officers within the department will eventually become confused over how they should perform assigned tasks. In one department, a sergeant assigned to the day shift was given responsibility for the safety of children as they traveled to and from school. In this position, the sergeant served as supervisor for more than 50 school crossing guards who assisted youngsters across busy city streets. That the sergeant and the school crossing guards were placed organizationally in the same division was an appropriate grouping of similar functions.

The sergeant, however, was also assigned the additional task of inspecting the operations division's police vehicles at 8:00 A.M., Monday through Friday. These inspections usually lasted between 15 and 30 minutes. With schools opening at 8:30 A.M., the half hour between 8:00 and 8:30 was critical in terms of the sergeant's major responsibilities. His assignment to vehicle inspection at that time meant that he had to neglect his primary functions in order to perform a task very different from his major responsibilities.

In assigning the sergeant dissimilar functions, the chief was violating the principle of functional definition; it was a serious violation because it was made at the peril of youngsters walking to school. Although important, the vehicle inspection function should have been performed by someone else, logically by someone assigned to the operations division.

School safety and vehicle inspections are dissimilar functions and should not, unless the department is a very small one, be performed by the same person or by the same group of persons. Although, depending on circumstances, the same level of authority may be required for their execution, the two tasks are not executed in the same place and do not require the same degree of skill or training to be performed.

This department consisted of 100 police officers. The one sergeant assigned to the operations division during the day shift was not assigned to vehicle inspection duties, largely because no one had ever thought of it and because traditionally vehicle inspections had always been a duty of the school safety division. It never occurred to anyone except the sergeant assigned to the two dissimilar tasks that the two responsibilities were mutually exclusive.

A good rule of thumb in organizing a department is to group all operational duties, all administrative duties, and all auxiliary service duties separately. If a department is not large enough to accommodate these groupings, a distinction should be made organizationally between *line* and *staff* duties. Line duties are departmental functions that are operational in nature; staff duties are those performed within the administrative and auxiliary service components of the organization.

Police chiefs who understand the principle of functional definition and who use it as a guideline in organizing their departments will avoid many problems that need never arise and that could prove extremely difficult to solve.

THE SCALAR PRINCIPLE

The *scalar principle,* taken from the military model and often referred to as the *chain of command,* is an organizational mechanism which establishes formal lines of communication within a police department. It is founded on the premise that the clearer the line of authority from the ultimate authority to every subordinate, the more effective will be decision making and organizational communication. It is, in effect, a schematic design used as a conceptual framework through which there is a vertical flow of information, directives, and orders downward through an organization. The scalar principle establishes a direct path between every person in the department and the chief. The path may also be looked on as a two-way street whereby information may flow upward through the organization from subordinates through superiors and ultimately to the chief.

The schematic design that establishes the chain of command is the organization chart. As we saw earlier in this chapter, organization charts may be very simple or very complex, depending on departmental size. Regardless of their simplicity or complexity, however, they all show the relative positions of all subsystems within the police department. The organization chart in Fig. 4.10, for example, shows the chain of command from chief to operations captain to patrol lieutenant to patrol sergeant to patrol officer. (The subsystems not involved in this single chain have been left out to avoid confusion.) A slightly different chain is clearly defined schematically in the organization chart presented in

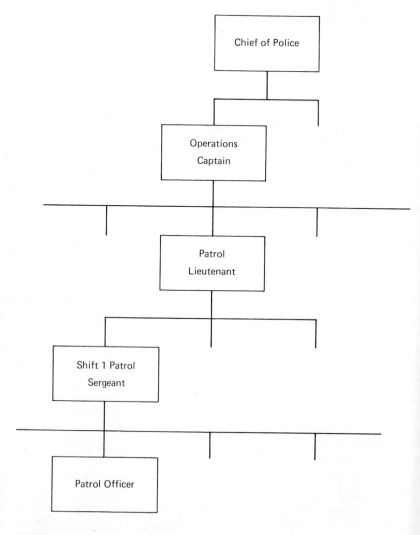

Fig. 4.10. Chain of command from chief to patrol officer.

Fig. 4.11, which shows the chain of command from the chief to the captain in charge of administration and services to the lieutenant in charge of communications to the shift 1 communications sergeant to one of several radio dispatchers.

The organization chart is the diagrammatic means by which all subordinates throughout an organization can see at a glance where they fit in an organization and from whom within the organization they receive their authority. Additionally, the organization chart establishes in a very rigid sense the structural design for all formal reporting and communicating in the organization.

The scalar principle is an invaluable organizational tool because it establishes formal communication links. If a department is to be properly organized, these communication links must be used by everyone within the organization to communicate formally in any way. If the chain of command is not used for *all* formal communicating, serious organizational difficulties can be anticipated. For example, a chief of police who disregards the chain of command by issuing an order directly to a patrol officer is breaking the chain and dissipating the authority of all those within the chain who have varying degrees of authority over what the patrol officer does. If the chief makes a habit of issuing orders directly to patrol officers, they quickly learn that the chain of command is inconsequential in internal communications and that they too may disregard it in their efforts to communicate upward in the organization.

An organization chart, therefore, is useless if it is not used consistently on a day-to-day basis as a communications device. The scalar principle is established visually through the organization chart and provides the foundation for the distribution of authority within the organization.

In applying the scalar principle to the organizing of a police department, a chief should consider the fact that there are various levels of management, each with somewhat different functions. For our purposes, we can group these levels of management into three categories:

1. chief administrative level;

2. command level; and

3. supervisory level.

The chief administrative level, always the top level within the organization, consists of the chief and the chief's staff. The command level comprises all officers of the rank of lieutenant and above who have authority and overall responsibility for line or staff functions. The supervisory level consists of ranking officers below the rank of lieutenant who are assigned to supervisory duties. Most departments have sergeants, and many have corporals who fall into this category.

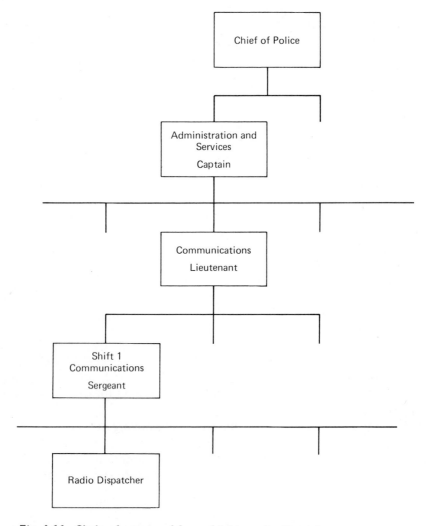

Fig. 4.11. Chain of command from chief to radio dispatcher.

Ranking officers who neither command nor supervise line or operational functions are generally referred to as *staff personnel.* Although they hold rank and often perform important functions, they do not have any command or supervisory authority over anyone. Most often staff personnel are assigned to the higher levels of management. A lieutenant, for example, who is assigned to the operations bureau as legal advisor is in a staff position, not a command-level position, even though the work is performed at the command level. Another lieutenant assigned to the operations bureau might have the overall responsibility for running a patrol shift. Because the assignment would involve command responsibilities, the lieutenant would be considered to be in a command-level position.

Bearing in mind that most police departments have three levels of management in their structure will give a chief better organizational perspective in constructing an organization chart and in assigning tasks according to their various levels of importance.

The final element in designing a chain of command is the impact that *specialization* at the various levels within the department will have on meeting the department's overall goals and objectives. Specialization impacts directly on the application of both the scalar principle and the principle of functional definition as these are used in the organizing of a police department. Specialization must be carefully considered when the chief makes initial efforts in grouping like functions and in establishing a chain of command.

In a small police department, officers should be assigned to duties as *generalists* rather than as *specialists.* Large departments lend themselves to specialization much more readily than do small departments.

The authority delegated through the chain of command for the performance of tasks will differ greatly, therefore, depending on the size of the department. In a 20-member police agency, for example, the patrol and investigative functions might be grouped together as similar functions and performed by the same people. A 30-member department, on the other hand, might lend itself to the establishment of both a patrol division and an investigations division, with the performance of patrol and investigative tasks assigned to two different groups of people. In a much larger department, where the availability of personnel would suggest further specialization, the patrol division might be subdivided into a number of subsystems to include a tactical unit, an emergency unit, a family crisis intervention unit, a helicopter unit, a scuba unit, a mounted unit, a canine unit, and a bomb unit. Similarly, the investigations division in the larger department could be subdivided into a vice unit, a narcotics unit, a shoplifting unit, a hotel unit, a stolen auto unit, a fraud unit, a homicide unit, a burglary unit, a robbery unit, and a liquor-violations unit.

Care should be taken in determining the degree of specialization that should be introduced in any police department. Although traditional organization theorists tend to believe that effectiveness increases with specialization, this is not necessarily so. It was originally believed that the more concentrated the talents and energies of a worker, the greater the worker's productivity. The assembly line, the logical manifestation of this belief, revolutionized the manufacture of goods. In time, however, problems arose. Many workers became bored with the sameness of their routine. As boredom increased, so too did absenteeism and labor problems.

In police departments specialization tends to deflect efforts away from meeting total organizational objectives and to concentrate efforts on attaining the more narrow goals of the specialist's subunit. If a narcotics detective, for example, is both paying and protecting an addict informant from arrest, a very real possibility exists that the informant may be committing burglaries to support his or her drug habit. Although the objectives of the narcotics detective may be satisfied, the overall goal of the department to decrease burglaries is not. The narcotics detective is in fact working against the overall goals and objectives of the department because the goals and objectives of the specialization seem to demand it.

Decisions about how much specialization there should be in organizing a police department are vitally important because they will directly influence the department's overall effectiveness. Wilson and McLaren observed that "specialization has a direct bearing on relationships of members in their performance of police duties; it also complicates direction, coordination, and control."[2] In departments having many specialized subunits, the chain of command becomes a less effective communications device. These units tend to work independently of one another. Information tends to be guarded on a unit proprietary basis and not shared with the rest of the department. Detectives in some departments have been known to pocket arrest warrants in anticipation of making a major arrest themselves. Specialization tends to increase unit competition and negate departmental cohesiveness.

The problem of specialization versus generalization does not lend itself to an easy solution. The President's Crime Commission wrestled with the problem and offered a compromise solution, calling for the establishment of three classifications of patrol personnel: *community service officers, police officers,* and *police agents.*[3] Although generalists, the patrol officers would deal with different types of situations depending on their complexities. By contrast, former Attorney General Ramsey Clark wrote that "the nature of police work . . . so interweave the easy and the difficult that an officer today must be prepared for both . . . ."[4]

Perhaps the best advice on the use of specialization in police organizations came from Thomas Reddin, former Chief of the Los Angeles Police Department. Reddin suggested that when specialization was considered to be absolutely necessary, personnel should be frequently rotated through specialized positions: "a good general rule to follow is to specialize if you must, generalize if you can."[5] This proposal seems to be an excellent rule to follow in organizing any police department.

In designing a 20-member police department, therefore, it would seem much more logical to group patrol and investigative functions together within an operations bureau than to establish separate patrol and investigative divisions. By having both functions performed within a single subunit of the department, the scalar principle can be used as a device for much more effective departmental communications. Rather than having two people coordinating patrol and investigative activities individually, thereby complicating communications within the chain of command, it would make much more sense and provide for a much clearer path of communication if the two functions could be combined into one. Even in large departments, there is considerable organizational justification from the standpoint of coordination to put one command-level officer in charge of both functions. Having a bird's eye perspective of both operational subunits, the single officer would be in a far better position to make judgments about each, thereby enhancing communications within the chain of command.

In one 200-member department in which the investigative and patrol functions operated autonomously, a frequent complaint from investigative personnel was that patrol officers, intent on preventing crime in their sectors, often interfered with stakeouts and investigations. They did this unknowingly, never having been informed about investigative activities. The problem was organizational in nature and was finally resolved by placing one captain in charge of both functions. The original organization chart (see Fig. 4.12) had the captains in charge of patrol and investigations reporting directly to the chief. In the reorganization (see Fig. 4.13) one captain was in charge of operations and reported to the chief, with two lieutenants in charge of patrol and investigations, respectively, reporting to the captain in charge of operations. This served to better coordinate both operational functions and to promote better communications between the two. This example illustrates the importance of organizing a department properly and demonstrates the practical application of the principle of functional definition and the scalar principle in the process.

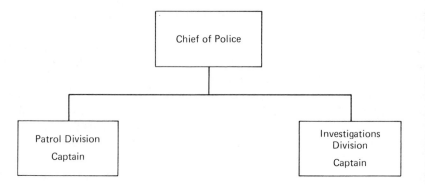

Fig. 4.12. Organization chart of separate patrol and investigations divisions, with captains reporting directly to the chief.

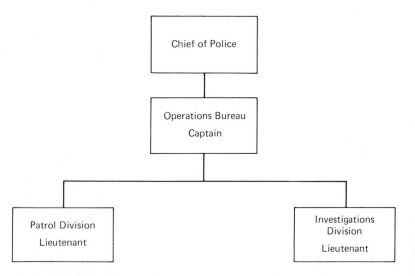

Fig. 4.13. Organization chart of an operations bureau consisting of a patrol division and an investigations division.

THE AUTHORITY–LEVEL PRINCIPLE

The authority-level principle is based on the premise that authority exists within organizations at all levels and that only those decisions that cannot be made at a given level because of lack of authority should be referred upward for resolution. The authority-level principle cannot be put into effect until after the principle of functional definition and the scalar principle have been instituted within an organization; it is totally dependent on the previous implementation of these two principles and provides a theoretical basis by which authority may be used at all organizational levels for problem solving. The authority-level principle may therefore be regarded as a problem-solving device. It is based on the valid assumption that there will be problems everywhere within an organization that must be solved continually if the organization is to meet its goals and objectives. Further, it dictates that "all decisions should be made as low as possible in an organization."[6]

In police departments where functions have been improperly grouped, the scalar principle is not in effect, and individuals at various rank levels lack the authority to do their jobs, departmental personnel tend to either sweep problems under the rug or rely on the chief to make most decisions. Sweeping problems under the rug is the easier of the two alternatives; the chief, lacking a viable chain of command, will in all likelihood never be advised that the problems exist.

If, on the other hand, the chief has made the effort to group like functions and to establish a chain of command, it naturally follows that the department is organized to the point where it is relatively easy to put the authority-level principle into effect. Problems are solved because the organization has a built-in mechanism for delegating authority to specific individuals and insisting that those individuals use that authority to solve problems at their own levels.

Authority is delegated to individuals through the scalar principle. The responsible use of authority is demanded through application of the principle of accountability. Therefore, everyone in an organization who has authority to solve problems will be held accountable for their solution. The authority-level principle provides a safety valve for solving all problems by allowing those that cannot be solved at a given level to be referred upward to a level where the authority exists to solve them.

The principle of functional definition, the scalar principle, the principle of accountability, and the authority-level principle are thus interrelated to the extent that they must operate in concert to be effective. There is no sense in instituting one of the principles to the exclusion of the other three. When the four are operating at the same time, the organizational cohesiveness that develops stabilizes the system as a whole.

The authority-level principle is perhaps the most difficult principle of organization to put into effect. Weak command-level personnel and inept supervisors can be expected to avoid their problem-solving responsibilities and allow problems to fester into open sores. An insistence that problems which cannot be solved at lower levels be communicated upward is therefore essential. In police departments this insistence should be procedurally formalized, with departmental officers at all levels mandated to write weekly reports on problems that have surfaced which they lack the authority to solve themselves. This procedure was developed as a result of the work of Hrand Saxenian, a management consultant and former Harvard Business School professor, who has successfully applied it in working with business and industry. By writing down their problems and by passing along their reports to the person within the organization to whom they report and from whom they receive their authority through the chain of command, they are in fact referring the problems upward for solution. When superiors receive reports outlining problems from subordinates, it is incumbent on them, if they have the necessary authority, to solve the problems themselves. If they lack the necessary authority to solve the problems, they too are obliged in their weekly reports to their superiors to list the problems that they lack the authority to solve personally. If such a system is put into effect and if reports are kept by the department for one year, accountability can be fixed on those officers who are shirking their problem-solving responsibilities.

Most problems in most departments will probably be solved more informally. A patrol officer, for example, who is having mechanical difficulties with a patrol vehicle should only need to mention this to the sergeant in order to have arrangements made for the vehicle's repair. If this problem is then solved, it would not be listed among the problems the sergeant outlined in his or her weekly report. If, on the other hand, the sergeant refuses to make arrangements to have the vehicle repaired, thereby refusing to make a decision on the matter, it would be the patrol officer's responsibility to list this as a problem in his or her weekly report. By insisting that the patrol officer reduce this problem to writing and by keeping the reports for a year, it will be a relatively easy matter for the lieutenant in charge of the shift or for the captain in charge of operations to fix accountability on the sergeant for not dealing with a problem for which authority had been delegated to solve. Both the captain and the lieutenant should, by departmental policy, be required to make periodic spot checks on weekly reports in an effort to find problems that their subordinates may be attempting to keep from them.

Although this example may seem to be a rather inconsequential matter, it should be understood that when combined with a number of other little problems, this problem can seriously impede the effectiveness of the patrol division. In one large police department studied by one of the authors, minor problems similar to the one above seriously affected the morale of patrol officers and stood in the way of achieving departmental goals and objectives. Almost no problems were solved at the operating level, and no system existed for referring problems upward. Although the department consisted of almost 200 police officers, it had a very loosely knit chain of command and no organization chart. If the chief was aware of the principle of accountability or of the authority-level principle, he was certainly not applying them to the management of the department. As a result, portable radios were in varying stages of disrepair, and many were missing. Police vehicles were poorly equipped and maintained. Several would have had difficulty passing state inspection; one had a nonfunctioning front headlight, another had a blown muffler. Once a police car ran out of gas while on an emergency run to the local hospital. In another instance, a patrol vehicle was out of service for five days because no one assumed the responsibility of cleaning vomit from its rear floor rug. One car with a broken inside dome light and a broken rear-view mirror had no accelerator pedal. Cars badly in need of tune-ups chugged about the city. They carried no mechanical resuscitation equipment and no oxygen. None had fire extinguishers or first aid kits. Vehicle interiors were filthy, and stretchers used to transport the sick and injured were rarely, if ever, sanitized. These problems remained unsolved because no one had the authority to solve them and because the chief was either unaware of or chose to ignore their existence. He simply did not know how to apply the basic principles of police organization to his department. He, the officers in his department, and the citizens in his community all suffered as a result of his inability to manage.

It should be pointed out that problem solving is not always as simple a matter as it might seem to be. If a police department has degenerated so that it is only barely functioning and meeting very few of its goals and objectives, total reorganization is necessary. Also, highly complex problems will not easily lend themselves to solution. For instance, if a department policy stipulates that all gambling investigations be handled by the investigations division, it is not an easy matter to resolve problems that might arise among patrol officers who might feel, sometimes legitimately, that they should be allowed to exercise their arrest powers whenever they come across a situation which might warrant an arrest or arrests for gambling. If they find that no action is taken by the investigations division on cases that they themselves initiate, these patrol officers may be inclined to take a devil-may-care attitude toward their responsibilities in other matters.

To solve this kind of problem is a much more delicate and complicated task than solving simple problems such as those that relate to vehicular maintenance. First, the problem may never surface at the patrol officer's level. A patrol officer, disenchanted by lack of action by the investigations division, may choose not to list the problem in the weekly report. The officer's patrol sergeant, however, should be sensitive enough to recognize some problems that are never identified as such and report them upward through the chain of command. If gambling poses a significant problem in a given sector, the sergeant will lack authority to solve the problem personally and should refer it to the lieutenant who, lacking authority to address the issue personally, should mention it in the weekly report to the captain in charge of operations. The captain should have the authority to act on the problem. However, the lieutenant in charge of the investigations division may have decided to wait on the evidence with the hope that the investigations division can make a stronger case, with more arrests, that will have a better chance of being successfully prosecuted in court. If the case has organized-crime overtones, the lieutenant may have made a conscious decision to hold off on arrests in an effort to involve some of the higher-ups in the operation. There may be, in fact, very good reasons for the investigations division not acting on the evidence presented by the patrol officer or by the patrol sergeant. The fact remains, however, that the patrol officer perceives this situation to be a problem. Not having the authority to solve it personally and realizing that its solution is not within the purview of the patrol sergeant or the lieutenant to whom the sergeant reports, the officer only naturally would tend to feel frustrated that the gambling is being allowed to continue.

The easiest and best way to solve the problem, of course, is informally. If the patrol lieutenant, once having become aware that the problem existed, were to discuss its ramifications immediately with the lieutenant in charge of the investigations division, a decision might be made to allay the patrol officer's fears by explaining the rationale behind the reluctance of the investigations division to move immediately on the problem. If it is impossible to solve the problem informally, the patrol lieutenant must then list it as a problem in the weekly report to the operations captain, who has been delegated the authority to manage and to coordinate patrol and investigative activities. The captain would be required to make a decision in the matter and to resolve the problem. Needless to say, this is a very involved procedure, but it is one that must be followed if the department is to function smoothly and if problems are to be solved.

The authority-level principle, if it is applied consistently throughout the organization, will serve to solve many problems that would otherwise go unsolved. It is a device that all police chiefs should utilize to the fullest extent if they are to expect realistically that their departments will meet their goals and objectives.

THE PRINCIPLE OF UNITY OF COMMAND

The *principle of unity of command* insists that the reporting relationship between subordinate and superior be on a one-to-one basis. A subordinate should not be expected to report to more than one superior or to take orders from more than one superior.[7]

Expecting a person to take orders from more than one superior can result in tremendous confusion. (Courtesy of the Los Angeles Sheriff's Department)

If a person is expected to take orders from more than one superior, tremendous confusion can result. A young boy whose father tells him to mow the lawn and whose mother tells him to wash the dishes instead will be wrong regardless of what he does. His parents have violated the *principle of unity of command.* They have both given the youngster orders, and they both expect him to follow through.

The consequences of this situation in a family setting are not disastrous. But consider the case of a patrol officer who receives three different patrol assignments from the sergeant, lieutenant and chief, respectively. Both the sergeant and the lieutenant will be upset by the chief's action, the patrol officer will be totally frustrated: which of the three superiors' orders should be followed?

This kind of problem must be taken into consideration when a police department is organized; departmental policy must stipulate that each officer take orders from and report directly to only one person—his or her immediate superior within the chain of command. If the chief wants to issue an order to a patrol officer, it must be understood by everyone that this can be done only through the chain. In this instance the chief would tell the lieutenant what area to assign the patrol officer to, the lieutenant would tell the sergeant, and the sergeant, as the patrol officer's immediate superior, would issue the order to the officer.

The principle of unity of command is a simple device which helps to avoid confusion in the issuance of orders. It makes all personnel within the organization more comfortable in their roles and more secure in terms of reporting relationships.

THE PRINCIPLE OF SPAN OF CONTROL

The total number of subordinates reporting to a single superior is referred to as that supervisor's *span of control.* The chief who commands three captains has a span of control of three. The patrol sergeant who supervises the activities of nine patrol officers has a span of control of nine. The captain who heads the operations bureau in the organization chart presented in Fig. 4.14 has a span of control of seven.

Early theorists believed that the number of persons within a span of control could be precisely established. Formulas were developed to "prove" that six or seven or some other number of people was the optimum number that could be supervised with ease. Over the years, however, it became apparent that the complexities of tasks and responsibilities, the skills of subordinates, and the talents of supervisors make it impossible to establish an ideal span of control. Rather, determining a given span of control is based on a subjective evaluation of the number of people a given supervisor can supervise effectively. Drucker even suggests that a supervisor's span include a few more persons than he or she can closely supervise, thus making it impossible for a supervisor to do subordinates' work.[8]

It is useful to think of a span of control as narrowing progressively toward the top of the organization. Thus a police chief has the smallest span of control. A good rule of thumb is that the span should be devised according to the degree of responsibility and authority that exists at a particular level in the hierarchy. The greater the degree of authority and responsibility that exists, the narrower the span of control.

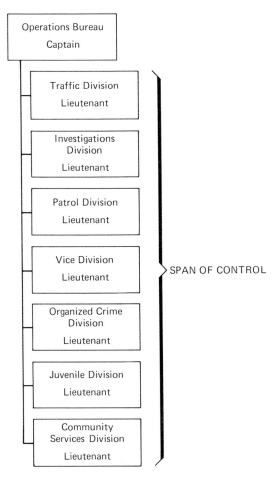

Fig. 4.14. Organization chart showing a span of control of seven.

Depending on circumstances, however, this general guideline need not always be followed. It is possible, for example, that a chief might have a span of control consisting of four captains, whereas a lieutenant who is in charge of a patrol shift in that department has responsibility over only three sergeants. As Pfiffner and Presthus point out, "there is no constant number applicable to every situation."[9] In short, span of control is an organizational supervisory tool which, if used with care and revised through experience, can contribute significantly to organizational solidarity.

SUMMARY

This chapter has presented the basic principles of police organization. These principles are means to ends (meeting departmental goals and objectives) and not ends in and of themselves. These principles can help to provide a sense of orderliness to any organization. Their purpose is not to create absolutes or to fit people rigidly into predesigned hierarchies. Rather, it is to bring some degree of order to what otherwise would surely be organizational chaos. Just as builders need blueprints to build houses, so too police chiefs need organizational principles to build police departments. If they neglect to apply any one of the principles in their organizing efforts, they can anticipate problems. If, on the other hand, they use these basic principles in organizing their departments, they can be certain that their organizations will be constructed in solid fashion, capable of meeting their responsibilities and achieving their goals and objectives.

DISCUSSION QUESTIONS

1. Think of the organizations to which you belong—for example, family, school, church, employment, voluntary, and others. Are any of them not hierarchical? Which are the most, and the least, hierarchical?

2. Many managers never learn how to delegate authority. Because they have no confidence in their subordinates, they try to do everything themselves and of course get worn out in the process. Do you know managers like this? How do their subordinates react to the unwillingness to delegate? How would you explain such managerial behavior? How would you change it?

3. The principle of accountability might be characterized as a strict but fair system for organizational discipline. Do you know of many

organizations that have disciplinary systems considered fair by their employees? Without the principle of accountability, personalities and personal contacts rule the disciplinary system. Under which approach do the organizations to which you belong operate? Which method seems preferable to you?

4. Many organizations use specialization to create units and positions through which they can rotate personnel. This is thought to be pleasing to employees, as they can transfer from one position to another whenever they get bored. On the other hand, specialized jobs may become boring more quickly than generalist jobs, because they are so narrowly defined. So in one respect specialization contributes to boredom, and in another respect it seems to combat it. How do you explain this apparent contradiction? How would you resolve it as chief of police?

5. The authority-level principle seeks problem resolution at that organizational level where authority exists for such resolution. It is a principle that attempts to overcome both buck passing and problem hiding. It seems simple, and yet is very difficult to implement. Why?

REFERENCES

1. Harold Koontz and Cyril O'Donnell, *Principles of Management: An Analysis of Managerial Functions,* 4th ed. (New York: McGraw-Hill, 1968), pp. 69-70.

2. O.W. Wilson and Roy C. McLaren, *Police Administration* (New York: McGraw-Hill, 1972), pp. 63-64.

3. President's Commission on Law Enforcement and Administration of Justice, *The Challenge of Crime in a Free Society* (New York: Avon, 1968), pp. 275-277.

4. Ramsey Clark, *Crime in America* (New York: Simon & Schuster, 1970), p. 145.

5. Thomas Reddin, "Are You Oriented to Hold Them?: A Searching Look at Police Management," *Police Chief* **33**, 3 (March 1966): 12-20.

6. Robert Townsend, *Up the Organization* (New York: Knopf, 1970), p. 45.

7. Wilson and McLaren, *op. cit.,* p. 67.

8. Peter F. Drucker, *The Practice of Management* (New York: Harper & Brothers, 1954), p. 139.

9. John M. Pfiffner and Robert Presthus, *Public Administration* (New York: Ronald Press, 1967), p. 190.

CHAPTER 5
THE BASIC FUNCTIONS OF
POLICE MANAGEMENT

LEARNING OBJECTIVES

1. Cite the six basic functions of police management.

2. Describe planning in systems terms.

3. Define the concept of completed staff work.

4. Cite the five classifications of police plans.

5. Describe the role of evaluation in the planning system.

6. Define organizing in systems terms.

7. Characterize the variety in police organizational arrangements caused by situational factors.

8. Describe staffing in systems terms.

9. Identify six basic aspects of staffing.

10. Identify two forms of feedback in the staffing system.

11. Describe directing in systems terms.

12. Identify the four activities that comprise the directing process.

13. Identify several means of obtaining feedback about the directing system.

14. Differentiate between directing and controlling.

15. Define controlling in systems terms.

16. Identify two important behavior-modification methods that are easily developed and implemented.

17. Cite a basic reason why the activities of police officers are difficult to control.

18. Identify the desired output of the controlling process.

19. Identify several means of obtaining feedback about the controlling system.

20. Describe system building in systems terms.

What do people who are called *managers* do? What are their primary responsibilities? A review of the literature of management functions shows that everybody has different answers to these questions. There is very little agreement as to what managers do and what their primary responsibilities are. We can be sure, however, that managers have hundreds of different functions and responsibilities. Unfortunately, the functions of management do not easily lend themselves to categorization.

Acronyms such as PODSCORB (Planning, Organizing, Directing, Staffing, Coordinating, Reporting, Budgeting)[1] and POSTBECPIRD (Planning, Organizing, Staffing, Training, Budgeting, Equipment, Coordination, Public Information, Reporting, Directing)[2] have been proposed by management theorists in order to define management functions. Other theorists completely reject traditional groupings. Sayles, for example, identifies three basic managerial functions: participation in external work flows through lateral interaction, leading, and monitoring.[3] Eastman and Eastman see the functions of management as planning, organizing, assembling resources, directing, and controlling.[4] Koontz and O'Donnell agree, but substitute the word *staffing* for the term *assembling resources.*[5]

It would be possible to go on and on, presenting endless conceptualizations of management functions as perceived by various authorities. Suffice it to say that the ordering of management functions is a subjective process and that there is considerable disagreement among the experts as to exactly what managers do and precisely what their responsibilities are.

With some trepidation and a large measure of humility, we set about the task of identifying the most basic management functions common to all police administrators. Throughout the remainder of this chapter, we will discuss six basic police management functions:

1. planning;

2. organizing;

3. staffing;

4. directing;

5. controlling; and

6. system building.

PLANNING

Planning is the most basic management function. All of the other five functions are totally dependent on planning for their implementation. Without planning, none of the other functions can be viable.

Planning is future-oriented. One plans in order to prepare for the future. The future may be the next minute, the next hour, the next day, the next week, the next month, the next year, the next decade, or the next century. Planning is a process that everyone participates in. A person may plan for the future by buying a life insurance policy, opening a bank account, investing in stocks, or planning meals, vacations, and shopping excursions. Children plan to do homework, watch television, and play baseball.

Much of our future activity is planned either by us or by someone else. Your course in police administration was planned by your instructor. It was planned or scheduled to meet at a certain time on certain days of the week by the dean of your college. You are probably reading this book in accordance with your instructor's plan to have you read it. You probably plan to finish reading it. The fact that you are in college is evidence of considerable planning on someone's part. It is not unlikely that your parents may have begun planning on the day that you were born to have you go to college. It is probably within your plans to graduate from college and to be successful in your career. Perhaps you plan to be married and plan to have a family. One day you may plan to buy a home. You may even plan for your own children to go to college. Plans are preparations for future expectations. They are the means by which you will meet your goals and objectives.

Planning, then, is an extremely important function in which all of us are involved. If we plan unwisely, we may never achieve our goals and objectives, or at the very best we may make them difficult to achieve. Poor planning can result in catastrophic consequences, even in death. For example, a police patrol officer was assigned to a one-officer car in a large city. At 2 A.M., he received a radio call to go to a convenience store where a silent burglar alarm had been tripped. When he arrived at the scene, he saw two men in the store rifling the cash register. He drew his gun and entered the open front door of the store. On seeing the patrol officer, the two men ran to a window at the side of the store. The patrol officer ordered them to freeze and threatened to shoot. In the meantime, another officer who was on patrol in a contiguous sector and who heard the radio call arrived at the scene and jumped out of his car. As he did so, he saw one of the two men climbing out of the side window of the store and running off into the darkness. The second officer ran toward the store where the other man was crouched on the window sill, preparing to jump. As he approached the store, the patrol officer inside the store fired two shots. One hit the burglar in the leg, and the other deflected off the window sill and came one-quarter of an inch from hitting the other officer in the head.

STANDARD 5.3

COMMITMENT TO PLANNING

Every police agency should develop planning processes which will anticipate short- and long-term problems and suggest alternative solutions to them. Policy should be written to guide all employees toward effective administrative and operational planning decisions. Every police agency should adopt procedures immediately to assure the planning competency of its personnel through the establishment of qualifications for selection and training.

1. Every police agency should establish written policy setting out specific goals and objectives of the planning effort, quantified and measurable where possible, which at least include the following:
   a. To develop and suggest plans that will improve police service in furthering the goals of the agency;
   b. To review existing agency plans to ascertain their suitability, to determine any weaknesses, to update or devise improvement when needed, and to assure they are suitably recorded;
   c. To gather and organize into usable format information needed for agency planning.
2. Every police agency should stress the necessity for continual planning in all areas throughout the agency, to include at least;
   a. Within administrative planning: long range, fiscal and management plans;
   b. Within operational planning: specific operational, procedural, and tactical plans;
   c. Extradepartmental plans; and
   d. Research and development.

National Advisory Commission on Criminal Justice Standards and Goals, *Police* (Washington, D.C.: U.S. Government Printing Office, 1973), p. 117.

An examination of departmental policies and procedures showed that the department had no plans for handling such an incident. The fact that no plans existed had almost cost an officer his life. Had police administrators in the department had the foresight to understand the importance of planning and had they developed a contingency plan for handling burglars in buildings, this incident would have been dealt with much differently. All cars in contiguous sectors would have been dispatched to the scene immediately to provide backup for the officer taking the call. Policy would have dictated that a patrol supervisor also proceed immediately to the scene. No officers would have been allowed inside the store. The store should have been surrounded, with all officers instructed to wait for the patrol supervisor before taking any other action. On arriving at the scene, the patrol supervisor would have assessed the situation before making a decision on what to do. Among the supervisor's alternatives would have been to talk the burglars out of the store, to call for the canine unit or the tactical team, or to gas the burglars out of the store. Any of these decisions would have been better than the one the patrol officer made.

Although the officer made what he considered to be the best decision possible given the circumstances, it had to be made solely on split-second thinking rather than on a well-thought-out plan. That unfortunate decision almost had disastrous results. Planning could have averted this potential tragedy.

So planning is important. Everybody does it all the time. Football teams have game plans; armies have battle plans; communities have master growth plans; and corporations have production plans. Planning is going on all the time, all around us.

Planning may be good, mediocre, or ineffective. Not all people and organizations plan equally well. Examples of poor planning are everywhere: children left unprovided for after the death of a parent; a laid-off specialist who has no alternative plans for employment; a motorist who runs out of gas on the freeway; a student who fails an examination; a teacher who comes to class unprepared. Poor planning depletes forests, puts corporations out of business, pollutes rivers, wastes food, causes bankruptcy, creates wars, loses games, contributes to the suicide rate, and produces Edsels. Good planning, on the other hand, has output success as its only hallmark.

All too often people and organizations confront problems only when they have become crises. The old adage "I'll cross that bridge when I come to it" is the attitude of those who place a low priority on planning. The good planner arrives at the bridge and crosses with no difficulty. The poor planner finds that the bridge has been washed away.

Planning is a problem-solving device. Inasmuch as all people and all organizations have problems, it is essential that they also have a capability for planning.

Effective planning is especially crucial for the police. The protection of lives and property and the maintenance of order in the community depend on the police being in the right place at the right time, taking proper actions. In our complex and rapidly changing society, only careful planning can make this possible. If a police administrator, for example, has not properly staffed patrol shifts, there is a distinct possiblity that all calls for service cannot be handled. In one Eastern city with a population of 360,000 people, 15,000 calls for service per year went unanswered because of lack of available personnel. This was a serious matter that reflected poor planning; it had serious consequences for the citizens of the city.

Planning is an exercise by which information, resources, goals, and objectives (input) may be processed in an effort to develop plans and programs (output). Consider Fig. 5.1, which shows the planning function from a systems perspective, in terms of the burglary of the convenience store mentioned earlier. The information input would include the number of burglars in the building, whether or not they were armed, when the burglary took place, the floor plan of the store, the number and location of exits from the store, the geography around the store, and any additional known information about the burglars' methods of operation. The resources input would include the officers on the scene, additional officers who might be available for backup, the availability of special equipment such as tear gas, gas guns, shotguns, and bullhorns, and any special units such as canine, tactical, or S.W.A.T. that might be needed. The objectives input would be the goal of the operation: capturing the burglars without loss of life or injuries.

Although a general plan stipulating certain prohibitions and providing a general guideline for meeting objectives might be available, each situation is unique because inputs change from situation to situation. Therefore, even if the situation has been preplanned by the department's planning division, considerable planning, based on the uniqueness of the inputs, will have to be done at the scene by the patrol supervisor. What the patrol supervisor finally decides to do and what is actually done must then be evaluated (feedback) in order to determine the degree to which objectives have been met. In Fig. 5.1 this evaluation would become information input for the planning division to consider should it subsequently wish to modify its own plan as a basis for departmental policy change. If both the planning division's plan and the patrol supervisor's on-the-scene plan were successful in meeting objectives, in all probability there would be no need for any modifications. This information about the success of the operation would be an input which would reinforce the validity and viability of the department's contingency plan for burglars in buildings.

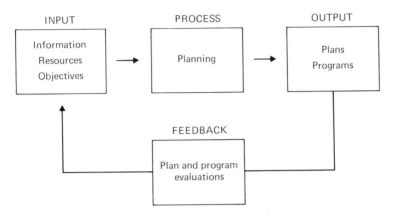

Fig. 5.1. The planning function from a systems perspective.

Because planning is a problem-solving device, it begins with the identification of a problem. The problem may be identified by a patrol officer, the chief, the planning division itself, a clerk in the records division, a citizen, or by anyone else either inside or outside the organization. If the authority-level principle has been applied to the department, the planning involved in solving many problems will be relatively simple and will not require the attention of the planning division. Only those problems that require research and that cannot be solved at any working level within the police department should be referred to the planning division for study.

The planning division should be responsible for studying specific problems that are not easily solved and presenting solutions to these problems in the form of plans that can be either accepted or rejected by the chief.

The planning division should work in accord with the concept of *completed staff work;* that is, *completed* plans, not *partial* plans, are presented to the chief for evaluation. Any plan presented to the chief should be so thorough that it can be used as a basis for the development of new policies and procedures. Whenever a complex problem arises or whenever an alternative method of doing something surfaces, a full solution or a fully completed alternative should be presented.

Except in small departments, chiefs should not be involved in day-to-day planning activities. In all departments, large and small, they should direct all phases of the planning function and review completed plans for acceptance or rejection.

The planning division itself should have very broad responsibilities and should be involved in studying every aspect of the department. Specifically, it should perform the following functions:

1. staff supervision of all planning activities;

2. development of long-range planning capabilities;

3. analysis of all departmental subsystems, policies, and procedures;

4. analysis of crime and accident patterns, service needs, and personnel deployment;

5. development of contingency plans for operational activities, natural disasters, crowd control, and riots;

6. liaison with police departments in contiguous areas to coordinate regionalized planning;

7. establishment of intracity and intercity road-block plans to intercept fleeing felons;

8. study of the feasibility of developing regionalized police services;

9. selection of electronic data-processing systems to streamline records keeping;

10. development of a fiscal planning capability for future support of police services;

11. analysis of the changing demographic characteristics of the community in order to provide for future services according to changing needs;

12. periodic analysis of existing plans;

13. periodic review of the planning division's needs and capabilities; and

14. liaison with departmental commanders to provide assistance in improving operational procedures.

In addition, the police planning division should periodically examine every procedure and every operation within the department to determine if these are operating effectively and efficiently. The planning division should be self-starting, proceeding on its own without necessarily taking any direction from the chief, but in no way precluding such involvement should the chief wish to provide guidance.

The planning division should begin its work by identifying and isolating *every* departmental procedure and operation. Matters that had never even been considered for study should be examined. Depending on the department's level of sophistication, these might include roll-call procedures, training, high-speed chases, use of firearms, use of chemical sprays, transportation of prisoners, maintenance of vehicles, dispatching activities, assignments, transportation of the sick and injured, answering telephones, arrest reports, feeding of prisoners, use of sirens and roof lights, quality of equipment, utilization of one- and two-officer cars, feasibility of foot beats, canine activities, use of portable radios, testifying in court, searching of prisoners, traffic enforcement, school safety programs, report forms, internal communications, and myriad other matters that in many police departments are routinely taken for granted.

Questions such as the following might be asked when examining procedures and operations:

1. Is this really necessary?

2. Should this be eliminated?

3. How could this be done better?

4. Could this be done less expensively?

5. If a change were made, what would the result be? and

6. Has another police department found a way of doing this better?

When a procedure or operation is determined to be faulty or to have weaknesses, alternatives must be explored and studied. Every aspect of a matter must be thoroughly researched and considered before a final plan is devised. This must then be presented to the chief for acceptance or rejection. The final plan should consist of the following parts:

1. a brief narrative stating the problem;

2. background information necessary for understanding the problem;

3. a full presentation and complete analysis of facts which relate to the problem;

4. a statement of conclusions drawn from the information obtained and the analysis made;

5. an outline of the research conducted substantiating the conclusions drawn; and

6. a final proposal outlining what actions are recommended.

As previously indicated, the outputs of the planning process are plans and programs. As might be expected, these are many and varied. Wilson has presented five classifications of police plans:

1. procedural plans;

2. tactical plans;

3. operational plans;

4. extradepartmental plans; and

5. management plans.[6]

Procedural plans may be either general or specific. They are looked on as the standard operating procedures of the department. They describe what a police officer should do under certain circumstances. Some general procedural plans might be walking a beat, patrolling a sector, writing reports, and checking doors at night. Some specific procedural plans might dictate exactly what actions a police officer should take in making an arrest, booking a prisoner, searching a building, and questioning a suspect.

Tactical plans are even more specific than procedural plans. A tactical plan might, for example, indicate exactly what action should be taken when conducting a bomb search of a high school or of a department store. The action prescribed for dealing with union pickets who refuse to let through their picket lines nonunion workers would be considered a tactical plan. Tactical plans generally deal with matters that are not generally considered to be routine, whereas procedural plans deal with matters with which police officers deal as a regular part of their everyday activity.

Operational plans involve personnel and equipment allocation. They indicate where beat boundaries should be drawn, when and where officers should be scheduled for patrol, the number of officers who should be assigned to specific functions, the equipment that should be used by the officers, and where special units can best be utilized.

Extradepartmental plans are developed in conjunction with people, agencies, or organizations outside the police department. A disaster plan, for example, might be worked out with the community's civil defense agency; a patrol plan for an elderly-housing project, with the city's housing authority.

Management plans, the most comprehensive and complex of the five categories, deal with the overall administration of the police department and with general societal trends that impact on the total organization. A management plan, for example, might deal with all of the implications that a foreign oil embargo might have on departmental gasoline supplies. Another management plan might be developed to concentrate on problems that can be anticipated as the result of the formation of a citizens' vigilante police patrol.

STANDARD 7.1

COMMAND AND CONTROL PLANNING

The chief executive of every municipality should have ultimate responsibility for developing plans for coordination of all government and private agencies involved in unusual occurrence control activities. Every police chief executive should develop plans immediately for the effective command and control of police resources during mass disorders and natural disasters. These plans should be developed and applied in cooperation with allied local, State, and Federal agencies and should be directed toward restoring normal conditions as rapidly as possible.

National Advisory Commission on Criminal Justice Standards and Goals, *Police* (Washington, D.C.: U.S. Government Printing Office, 1973), p. 166.

The role of *evaluation* in the planning process cannot be overemphasized. An absolutely essential component of all planning, evaluation is the feedback which closes the loop of the planning system. Planning cannot be effective unless it has as input evaluative information about the success or failure of past plans (old outputs). The planning function, then, is in and of itself a subsystem of the police organization and can therefore be examined from a systems standpoint, as can all police management functions.

Returning once again to our example of the burglars in the convenience store, the planning problem can be defined as how to get the burglars out of the building. One alternative for forcing the burglars out would be to set fire to the building. But the building might burn to the ground in the process, or the burglars might die in the fire; this solution would not be considered consonant with the goals and objectives of the police department. This points up the necessity for studying all alternatives in terms of goals and objectives. Evaluation of output (the success of the plan to get the burglars out of the building while at the same time preserving their lives and protecting the property involved) becomes feedback or information which is reintroduced into the system as input to be used in improving future plans.

Because planning is the most basic of all management functions, the police administrator who fails in the planning function will also fail in organizing, staffing, directing, controlling, and system building. Planning is the one management function on which all of the others depend. Planning makes effective management possible.

ORGANIZING

Organizing is the process involved in putting together the subsystems of an organization in order to achieve maximum efficiency, effectiveness, and productivity in meeting organizational goals and objectives. The subsystems of any organization must be arranged so that they can work well with one another. It is the organizer's job to do this; or, because organizing is a basic function of management, it is the manager's job to do this. In police organizations the key organizer *is* the chief of police. A chief who is unable to organize the police department properly, using the systems approach as a basis for organizational efforts, will achieve little success in meeting goals and objectives. As Mooney and Reilly have pointed out, "it is inconceivable that a poor organizer can make a good manager . . . ." [7]

The kind of organizing that must be done in systems comprising a multitude of subsystems is totally different from and much more complex than the kind of organizing with which we are most familiar, the organizing of our own personal lives. We organize our homes into different rooms that will be used to greater or lesser degrees by different people for different purposes; we organize our finances to guard against being overdrawn in the bank; we organize our incomes in order to pay our bills; and we organize our time in order to provide for work, school, and leisure activities. Even at this personal level of organization, some people are good organizers and others are not. The student who is unable to find enough time to study and the home owner who finds it difficult to keep up with housework are good examples of poor organizers. In order to maintain ordered lives, it is vitally important to each of us to recognize the importance of organizing all of our activities properly to accomplish our purposes.

The organizing effort that went into writing this book is a good case in point. Once we had agreed to collaborate on the effort, we had to meet several times to discuss the book's content and to arrange by mutual agreement exactly what the input of each of us would be. Once these details were worked out, the publishing company was contacted to determine whether or not it might be interested in publishing the book. This contact resulted in our meeting with the publisher. As a result of the meeting, we prepared an outline and submitted it to the publisher. On the basis of the outline, the publisher issued a contract for the book.

Once the book was under contract, our work efforts were directed toward researching the literature available in the fields of management practice and theory. In the meantime, we redrafted the outline for the book and then redrafted it in order to more properly organize the material to be presented. Our copious notes, taken on $3'' \times 5''$ cards were organized according to chapter, then according to chapter subheadings. Once the research had been completed, a first-draft manuscript was written in longhand. The first draft went into a second draft, this time on the typewriter. A review of the second draft resulted in our rewriting the entire manuscript. It also became apparent that the third outline for the book should be redrafted, and a fourth outline was prepared. Work proceeded on the third manuscript. Part way through this effort, one of the authors felt that some further revisions should be made in the outline. A fifth and final outline was devised. We both agreed that this fifth outline provided the best possible organization for the presentation of the material. The book was completed a full four years after our initial organizational efforts had begun.

Organizing, then, is not a simple process. It takes time, effort, and energy. It also takes skill and considerable patience. In addition, it takes knowledge and understanding of the basic principles of police organization as described in Chapter 4 and a willingness and ability to apply these organizational principles to the process of organizing.

As pointed out earlier, it is important to use the systems approach in any organizing effort. Figure 5.2 shows the organizing function from the systems perspective.

The inputs of people, jobs, and objectives emphasize that to be effective, an organizer cannot simply go to a textbook, choose an organization chart at random, and apply it *carte blanche* to organizing a police department. Instead, the organizer must take into consideration the people to be organized. Are they highly motivated and interested in their work, or are they clock watchers? Are some of them sickly? Are there people in the group to be organized who have personality clashes so strong that they will not be able to get along with one another? Are there older workers who might resent being supervised by younger people? Are there alcoholics who might need extremely close supervision? Are there people who have great difficulty in relating to the public? These kinds of questions are critical to the organizer. The interactions and interdependence of people as organizational sub-systems will either make or break a police department in terms of its obligations to meet goals and objectives. These inputs, therefore, are very delicate considerations.

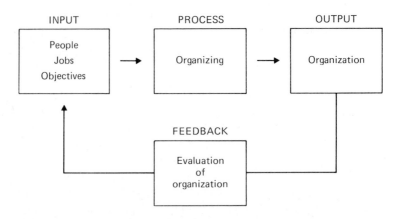

Fig. 5.2. The organizing function from a systems perspective.

Unless one fully understands the people, jobs, and objectives (in-puts) of the police department being organized (process), it can be anticipated that the organization (output) will be far less productive than one in which the inputs are known and given full consideration in the organizing effort. Although rarely expressed in system terms, one major complaint of police chiefs who have relied on police management consultants to assist them in organizing their department is that the consultants are not at all familiar with the unique inputs peculiar to their particular departments and make faulty organizational judgments based on lack of understanding of system inputs. There is considerable justification for these complaints. Organizing must be done by people who fully understand what the organizing inputs are. In one classic example, a small New England town of 12,000 people retained a police management consulting organization to study its police department. The organization assigned one of its most competent consultants to the job, a former police chief whose experience had been concentrated in Midwestern and Western cities. Never having worked in New England before, the consultant was unaware of New Englanders' pride in their town meeting form of government, which makes every voter a member of the legislative branch of town government. Unlike cities in which legislative power is vested in a city council, New England towns were founded on the premise that *everyone* should have a say in local government. This prerogative is something not to be trifled with. Looking at the police department as a subsystem of local government, the consultant reasoned, based on his previous experience in government, that the organization of the police department could not be improved until improvements were made in local government, which he perceived to be about as inefficient as any government he had ever seen. One of his major recommendations, therefore, was that the town be turned into a city, and he pointed out the advantages of the city form of government. In his efforts to organize the police department, his lack of knowledge of New Englanders as a people input in the organizing process made him a laughing stock throughout the town and seriously impeded efforts to organize the police department properly.

The nature of jobs to be performed is also an important input to the organizing process. Each job must be carefully assessed and placed into a position within the organization where, grouped together with other similar functions, it can be performed most effectively. Specific jobs are the basis for the establishment of bureaus, divisions, units, squads, teams, and other subgroupings.

In organizing a police department, the objectives of the organization must be kept clearly in mind by the organizer. The primary and secondary goals and objectives that all police departments have in common are the threads that must be woven into the fabric of all police organizations. The process of organizing is directed solely to facilitate the accomplishment of the organization's goals and objectives. They are therefore an important input into the process.

Because the inputs to the organizing process are peculiar to each given situation, the organizing process is necessarily situational. Because the people, jobs, and objectives encountered by every organizer are different, the organization developed in each situation will be different. Even in police organizations having nearly identical goals and objectives, an examination of different departments would show that they could be vastly different.

Although all police departments have the maintenance of order and the protection of life and property as primary goals and objectives, any number of their secondary goals and objectives might differ. For example, noncriminal regulations enforced by the police might differ greatly from community to community. In those cities and towns having private ambulance services or ambulance services provided by the fire department, the police are relieved considerably of responsibility in serving the needs of the sick and injured. In those jurisdictions where numerous social services are available to citizens, the services that need be supplied by the police are drastically reduced. Organizing, therefore, is a situational process which depends on the accurate identification of varying organizing inputs. The process depends on the application of the basic principles of police organization (see Chapter 4). This involves providing for the grouping of like functions, assigning functions to appropriate subsystems, delegating authority, and coordinating the overall effort.[8]

The output of the organizing process is the organization itself. It is grouped functions, delegated authority, assigned activities, and overall coordination. Mooney and Reilly call organization "the form of every human association for the attainment of a common purpose, relating duties and functions in a coordinated scheme."[9]

Feedback on the organization itself can vary considerably. In the broadest sense, the effectiveness of the organization can be measured in terms of its accomplishment of goals and objectives. In a more narrow sense, its effectiveness can be gauged in terms of whether or not workers have the necessary authority to do their jobs, whether or not they exhibit confusion over the identity of their immediate superiors, or whether or not each worker's tasks are relatively similar.

Where does the radio dispatcher in the following example fit into the organization? As a worker within the police department's communications division, the radio dispatcher's immediate superior is the sergeant in charge of that division. But in actuality the radio dispatcher takes orders from patrol sergeants and sometimes even from patrol officers. The radio dispatcher obviously works in a disorganized organization, the result of a failure in the organizing process.

This information must be available as feedback to the organizer so that it can be used as an additional input in the organizing process. A police chief must know what kinds of organizational problems exist if this information is to be used as input into what must become a continuing reorganizing effort. As organizational problems arise, they must be identified, fed back to the chief as feedback, and used as inputs in the continuing reorganizing process. One can readily see that organizational problems cannot be solved unless a systems approach is taken in the effort to solve them. Once understood, the systems approach is an excellent device for organizational problem solving.

In order for continuous feedback to be made available to the organizer, or the chief, it must be understood by everyone, from the chief on down, that the organization in its present form is not sacred. Even if everyone believes the unlikely assumption that the organization is functioning perfectly today, the possibility of its malfunctioning tomorrow is entirely likely. System inputs (people, jobs, and goals and objectives change. Furthermore, they change frequently. In order to accommo-date these changes in input, the organization must be regularly scruti-nized for signs that it is no longer suitable for the accomplishment of its objectives. And the process of scrutinization must be designed so that the results (feedback) are introduced as input to the organizer.

It must also be understood that the organization is much more than a chart on the wall. Organizations should not be thought of as simple, unchanging groups of homogeneous people working together with computerlike efficiency. Rather, as Leavitt suggests, organizations are "rich, volatile, complicated but understandable systems of tasks, struc-tures, tools, and people in states of continuous change."[10]

STAFFING

Staffing involves the functions of recruiting, selecting, training, assign-ing, promoting and terminating. These functions are often performed by a police department's personnel division; they are of such extreme importance, however, that they come within the purview of the police chief's major duties.

As with all other basic functions of police management, staffing should be examined from a systems standpoint. Figure 5.3 shows the staffing function from a systems perspective.

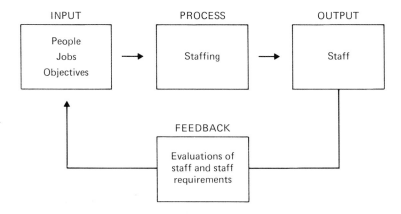

Fig. 5.3. The staffing function from a systems perspective.

Inputs to the staffing function are of three types. The *people input* includes both present employees as well as candidates for job openings. The *jobs input* involves the positions presently held by employees plus job openings. The *objectives input* is the standard or standards used to measure the performance expected from present and prospective employees.

Recruitment The first stage of the staffing process is recruitment. Somehow a police department must induce individuals to apply for position openings. Generally, there are three categories of people who seek employment with a given organization:

1. people who are very interested in the position and who are anxious to obtain it;

2. people who are not very interested in the position and who see it as one employment alternative among many; and

3. people who have no real interest in the position and who, because of their limited marketability, see it as their only employment alternative.[11]

Although one might assume that people in the first category would tend to perform better on the job than those in the other two groups, research fails to support such a contention. There is no simple correlation between reasons for seeking employment and applicants' subsequent performance. It is clear, however, that the image of an organization is one important factor in attracting numerous applicants. An organization can select employees only from those who apply. A police chief may feel fortunate to be able to choose from a hundred applicants for a single position; in not applying, however, literally millions of people will have been bypassed in the process. Perhaps the most qualified person for the job was among those who did not apply.

Indeed, some police departments seem to discourage applicants from applying. The low esteem in which police are held in some communities and the fictitious image of the TV cop are also factors in keeping qualified applicants away. Gellerman refers to this phenomenon as a "prevailing mythology"[12] and suggests to the organization that it "prevents much of the available labor pool from passing through its evaluation process and compels it to make its selections from a much narrower segment of the population."[13]

The critical nature of this "prevailing mythology" for police recruiting should be a matter of concern to every police administrator. The arbitrary establishment of height, weight, eyesight, and other physical requirements is but one example of how the police service has effectively eliminated from consideration countless prospective candidates. Physical requirements in many police jurisdictions have been established at a level much higher than requirements for entrance into West Point, Annapolis, and the Air Force Academy. Physical requirements to become a career military officer, then, are much lower than physical standards required to become a police officer in numerous police departments.

Recruitment is the first element in the staffing function. (Courtesy of the Metropolitan Police Department, Washington, D.C.)

The ludicrousness of this situation is evidenced by the experience of a young college student who was one of more than 1000 applicants who applied for 100 openings in a state police organization. The young man successfully passed written, oral, and physical-strength tests. He had only a physical examination to pass in order to be accepted into the service. In looking over the organization's physical requirements, he noticed that it was necessary to have 28 teeth in order to pass the physical examination. In counting his teeth, he discovered, much to his amazement, that he had only 27. Panic-stricken, he discussed his problem with one of his police science instructors, a retired state police captain. The instructor called the state police physician who would be conducting the physical examination and asked whether a waiver could be obtained. The physician said no, but suggested that the man's dentist make a one-tooth plate for him. The young man followed the suggestion and wore the plate on the day of the examination. He passed the physical with no difficulty and was appointed as a state trooper. The twenty-eighth tooth was never worn again and to this day remains in a bureau drawer, a reminder of the one ridiculous physical requirement that could have cost him his job and the state police an otherwise highly acceptable candidate.

One can easily see from this true story that the generally held belief that police recruiting methods are effective is a myth. Rigid requirements eliminate many good people from consideration and significantly narrow a police administrator's choices.

In order to be successful as a recruiter, a police administrator must design requirements to meet objectives. Objectives, after all, are inputs to the staffing process. If the administrator loses sight of this fact, the output of the staffing process (staff) will be negatively affected. This raises some interesting questions. Is a height requirement of 5'9" equally as important as a requirement that applicants be college graduates? Would applicants who meet the height requirement but do not have college degrees be as desirable as applicants who have college degrees but who are only 5'8½" tall? Everything else being equal, the latter applicants would ordinarily be considered preferable to high school graduates who are 5'9" tall. Yet rigid requirements might preclude the former group from consideration. The police service is attempting to address these problems, but progress is slow. Until meaningful decisions can be made on such matters and requirements adjusted accordingly, police departments will continue to have staffing problems

Having mentioned the college degree as a requirement for police entrance, it might be well to explore how the ramifications of such a requirement might impact on the staffing function. Education is very often seen as a vehicle for professionalization. If used as an entrance level required input to the staffing process, it can be presumed that staff (output) should be improved. A person who poses as a doctor but has had no education beyond high school would be less likely to succeed as a brain surgeon than someone who has successfully completed medical school and is a member in good standing of the American College of Surgeons.

Educational background is one characteristic of the professional person. Yet a demand that all police applicants be college graduates necessarily narrows the field from which the applicants may be drawn. By establishing the college degree as an entrance-level required input, the police administrator precludes thousands of capable prospective applicants from applying for entrance-level positions. Is the college degree, then, a desirable systems input? This, of course, is a much more difficult question to answer than whether or not the height requirement is a desirable systems input.

Both requirements eliminate many thousands of people from consideration, thereby narrowing the possibilities of finding the best people available. The applicant who cannot meet the height requirement might very well be able to outperform taller applicants. However, *depending on situations in which applicants might be required to perform,* the applicant who is 5'9'' tall might outperform one who is 5'2''. But the reverse might also hold true. A 5'2'' applicant who holds a black belt in karate and is from Puerto Rico would probably be able to outperform someone taller in breaking up a fight in a Spanish-speaking neighborhood.

Proper staffing implies the assignment of officers to tasks they are best able to perform. Should the 5'2'' applicant from Puerto Rico be precluded from consideration for not having a college degree or being too short? The answer is obviously *no.* Considering input objectives, the Puerto Rican's language abilities, ethnic background, and self-defense talents would tend to single out that applicant as much more desirable than a tall college graduate lacking those abilities.

From this discussion, it would seem obvious that police entrance requirements should be flexible, with staffing judgments being made in terms of service needs. Because staffing includes the assignment of officers to specific jobs, the process necessarily involves consideration of an individual officer's talents *and* weaknesses. All officers should be assigned to positions where their talents are maximized and their weaknesses minimized. There are so many functions performed by police officers that a wide variety of people should be considered for police positions at the entrance level. College degrees and height should, of course, be considerations, but they should be established as guidelines rather than as requirements. Police departments operate in a pluralistic society; their police officers, therefore, should reflect that pluralism.

It should be noted that what we suggest is contrary to much current police thinking. Many police administrators today tend to equate successful police performance with the successful completion of college courses. Although there is some evidence of such a correlation, there is no evidence to indicate that a requirement of *preservice* higher education is a positive or beneficial input to the staffing process. Because the absolute requirement of preservice higher education, the college degree, precludes so many otherwise excellent candidates from consideration as staffing inputs, it is undesirable as an absolute requirement. It is not undesirable as a guideline if the chief exercises discretion in its use.

You should not imply from this discussion that we are opposed to college education as a means of professionalizing police departments. We are opposed only to *rigid* higher-education requirements at the entrance level. We suggest that higher education be used only as one of many guidelines for the screening of police applicants.

When the staffing function involves promoting officers into supervisory and command-level positions within police departments, college education should be established as an absolute requirement. Although the B.A. degree should not be looked on as a panacea in police management or even as an instrument for solving all police problems, it will expose the department's future leaders to a wide range of thinking and theory that *might* broaden their outlooks and expand their parochial inclinations. Eventually, within the next hundred years or so, such a requirement will professionalize the police service. This certainly should be a paramount objective of the staffing function.

Selection The process of choosing from among applicants is called *selection.* One theory of the selection process emphasizes the person; accordingly, the most mature, intelligent, stable applicant should be selected, without particular regard for the position to be filled. Hrand Saxenian, a former professor at the Harvard Business School and a prominent management consultant, is one outstanding advocate of this theory. To Saxenian, maturity is the single most important criterion in the selection process. He has attempted, with some success, to measure maturity by determining "the extent to which a man expresses his own feelings and convictions, with consideration for the thoughts and feelings of others."[14]

In an experiment conducted with one large state police organization, Saxenian, using his own unique system for determining maturity interviewed all 50 recruits undergoing 12 weeks of training at the police academy. Each recruit was interviewed for less than 30 minutes. The recruits were then ranked for maturity from 1 to 50 according to Saxenian's system of measurement. At the end of the 12-week training period, the academy staff ranked the recruits from 1 to 50 on the basis of their overall performance while in training. The two sets of ranking were remarkably similar and statistically showed a very high degree of correlation.

Follow-up studies several years later verified the statistical validity of Saxenian's original findings. Those recruits singled out by Saxenian as being the most mature were by far the best performers. The rationale behind the theory of emphasizing the person in the selection process is that the right individual can be trained for the job easily enough once the right person has been selected.

Another theory of the selection process emphasizes the job to be filled rather than the person selected to fill it. The advocates of this theory believe that some jobs require particular skills and abilities that cannot be easily learned. The major problem with this approach is the difficulty of testing for these skills and abilities. One could say without qualification, for example, that order maintenance (one of the police department's two major goals and objectives) is dependent on an innate ability to manage conflict. Some officers are much more naturally inclined toward peace-keeping responsibilities than others are. The problem arises in the development of a testing instrument to predetermine which applicants have ability in this sensitive area of concern. Very little significant effort has been made in the police field to validate entrance-level testing. Until this is done to the satisfaction of police administrators everywhere, problems will persist in the attempt to find applicants who can be neatly fitted into specialized job slots.

Both of these selection-process theories have merit. However, the wide variety of duties that police officers perform, coupled with the innumerable talents and abilities needed to perform them, suggest that the entrance-level selection process must necessarily focus primarily on the person and not on the job. The fact that the focus has traditionally been on the job has led to staffing problems of an enormous magnitude. Only in recent years has the police service introduced psychological testing into the selection process on a wide scale. The results have been more than satisfactory when combined with the development of more sophisticated police training programs. Police administrators in recent years have begun to place emphasis on selecting personnel on personal qualities such as common sense, intelligence, ability to verbalize, good judgment, and maturity. It is assumed, with considerable justification, that an applicant with these basic skills can be trained to perform the endless number of tasks that a police officer is expected to perform. Job skills are learned *after* an applicant is accepted as a police officer, not *before*.

Besides the particular mix of skills and qualities on which police departments base their selection decisions, there are important considerations that transcend traditional police practices. Numerous police departments have been required by the federal courts to develop affirmative action programs and to hire more minority-group members and women. The courts found that some selection criteria, including some physical requirements and entrance-level testing, were discriminatory when not clearly job-related. It is important for police administrators to understand that regardless of their own predispositions with respect to hiring practices, federally established selection guidelines must be followed and their own selection processes adjusted accordingly. There is every reason to believe that personnel carefully selected on the basis of affirmative action programs will significantly strengthen police staffs, giving the police a better capability of dealing with all segments of the population. The best way for a police department to avoid discriminatory hiring practices is to adopt fully the philosophy of the Police Foundation, which contends that "it is clearly desirable, consistent with America's democratic principles, that police agencies have a healthy balance of people representing the range of citizenry in the communities those agencies serve."[15]

Training   Once selected, a new employee enters the training stage of the staffing process. Loen has identified four major activities:

1. a basic orientation, outlining organizational goals and objectives;

2. a planned, scheduled training program aimed at teaching new personnel how to perform tasks expected of them;

3. an organized in-service training effort directed toward upgrading personnel; and

4. a self-development training program designed to encourage personnel to develop themselves professionally.[16]

The first two of these activities are generally referred to as *recruit training* and typically involve both in-class and on-the-job training. In the police service the latter is often called *field training.* In-service training is provided to a greater or lesser degree by many departments and not at all by some departments. More progressive police agencies provide at least one week of in-service training a year for each police officer. Some departments take advantage of excellent in-service training courses offered by organizations such as the International Association of Chiefs of Police, the Federal Bureau of Investigation, the Traffic Institute of Northwestern University, the General Management Training Institute of the United States Civil Service Commission, and the National Highway Traffic Safety Administration of the United States Department of Transportation. Since the passage of the Safe Streets Act in June 1968, millions of dollars of federal funds have been made available to the states for the development of many state and regional in-service training academies. In-service police training is available extensively everywhere. A department need only take advantage of the wide range of training opportunities.

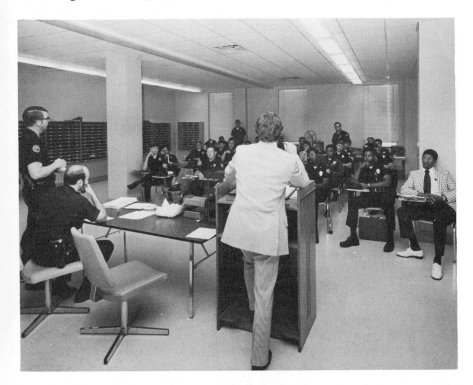

Officers receive roll-call training before going on patrol. (Courtesy of the Jackson Police Department, Jackson, Mississippi)

The fourth training activity, self-development, has been encouraged in recent years through the establishment of the Law Enforcement Education Program (LEEP) of the Law Enforcement Assistance Administration, a federally funded effort which has paid the tuitions of more than 100,000 in-service police officers who have attended colleges and universities throughout the nation. As these federal funds become less available, however, the police administrator will be challenged to devise new programs to encourage employees to further develop themselves.

Assignment Once trained at the orientation and recruit levels, the new employee must be assigned to a job within the organization. The nature of the job in which the trained recruit is placed ordinarily requires little choice for most police departments, because most new police employees usually begin their careers as patrol officers. This tradition has changed very little since Sir Robert Peel established the first metropolitan police department in London in 1829. However, in larger police departments, the assignment of rookies may involve some choice as to the locations of their assignment. Some departments assign officers to districts in which they live; others intentionally assign officers away from their places of residence. Some assignments are made on the basis of race and ethnicity. For example, black and Spanish-speaking officers may be assigned to predominantly black and Spanish-speaking

STANDARD 16.5

INSERVICE TRAINING

Every police agency should, by 1975, provide for annual and routine training to maintain effective performance throughout every sworn employee's career.

1. Every police agency should provide 40 hours of formal inservice training annually to sworn police employees up to and including captain or its equivalent. This training should be designed to maintain, update, and improve necessary knowledge and skills. Where practicable and beneficial, employees should receive training with persons employed in other parts of the criminal justice system, local government, and private business when there is a common interest and need.

2. Every police agency should recognize that formal training cannot satisfy all training needs and should provide for decentralized training. To meet these day-to-day training needs, every police agency should provide each police station with:

   a. As soon as practicable, but in no event later than 1978, a minimum of one police employee who is a State certified training instructor;

   b. Audio-visual equipment compatible with training material available to the police agency;

   c. Home study materials available to all police employees; and

   d. Periodic 1-day on-duty training programs directed at the specific needs of the police employees.

3. Every police agency should insure that the information presented during annual and routine training is included, in part, in promotion examinations and that satisfactory completion of training programs is recorded in the police employee's personnel folder in order to encourage active participation in these training programs.

National Advisory Commission on Criminal Justice Standards and Goals, *Police* (Washington, D.C.: U.S. Government Printing Office, 1973), p. 404.

neighborhoods, respectively. Occasionally, some new officers are assigned to work in undercover capacities or, if a department has a police agent program, as police agents.

Although there are vastly conflicting philosophies regarding assignments, the placing of individuals within any organization is an extremely important staffing function. Individuals improperly assigned can impact negatively on the organization's effort to meet its goals and objectives.

Assignment should be regarded as a continuing staffing process. Those responsible for the staffing function should continually assess assignment output through feedback in order to make staffing adjustments, or personnel transfers. Very few police officers spend their entire careers in the positions to which they were assigned as rookies. Although many may remain as patrol officers throughout their careers, most will probably be transferred from district to district within the community or to specialized duties within the organization. The transfer of personnel should be looked on as a healthy application of the systems concept to the police management function. It should never be anticipated that everyone placed in every position will always be best suited to perform in that position. Just the opposite, in fact, should be assumed. Those responsible for staffing should be fully aware that transferring personnel can have a decided effect on the organization's capabilities to meet its goals and objectives. Where feedback indicates that individuals have been inappropriately assigned, a staffer would be neglecting a major responsibility in not taking the information being fed back through the system, reinserting it as a new staffing input, and transferring personnel accordingly.

There is much to be said for regular, periodic shifting of personnel. It not only develops more well-rounded employees, but by rechallenging them to learn new and more interesting jobs also lessens the likelihood that they will stagnate in one position. Transfers also become necessary in problem situations. Some employees simply may not be able to perform satisfactorily in a particular area of the community or in a particular job. Disputes between co-workers or between subordinates and superiors may be insoluble except through transfers. However, when personality problems impede an organization from meeting its goals and objectives, great care should be taken in using transfer as a staffing process. In such cases transfers should be used only as a last resort, especially when feedback indicates that transfers would only transfer problems from one subsystem of the organization to another. Transfers should be made, therefore, only if it appears likely that they will impact positively on system output.

Promotion Promotion as a staffing activity is a transfer upward in rank. The methods used by police departments to determine who will be promoted vary tremendously; there is no consistent police promotion pattern anywhere in the United States. At one extreme are departments that base promotions purely on political considerations. At the other extreme are departments that promote solely on the basis of merit. Because merit is an elusive evaluative factor to isolate and because political considerations have proved to be so unfair and discriminatory, staffing decisions to promote certain individuals and not others almost inevitably lead to organizational conflict.

STANDARD 17.1

PERSONNEL DEVELOPMENT FOR PROMOTION AND ADVANCEMENT

Every police agency should adopt a policy of promoting to higher ranks and advancing to higher paygrades only those personnel who successfully demonstrate their ability to assume the responsibilities and perform the duties of the position to which they will be promoted or advanced. Personnel who have the potential to assume increased responsibility should be identified and placed in a program that will lead to full development of that potential.

National Advisory Commission on Criminal Justice Standards and Goals, *Police* (Washington, D.C.: U.S. Government Printing Office, 1973), p. 423.

Another consideration that the police service has failed to come to grips with, except in a few isolated instances, is the development of career ladders for police officers working at the lower operational levels within police departments. The delivery of police services to the public is at the lower operational levels. To promote police officers to higher levels in police departments and to pay them accordingly is to place a relatively low priority on the services rendered by those officers in the lower ranks who actually service the public's needs. The work performed by patrol officers, for example, is often much more sensitive and therefore much more important to society than the work performed by some high-ranking supervisory and command-level personnel. The patrol officer is on the street dealing every day with departmental goals and objectives. Therefore, the patrol officer is the key factor in the delivery of services. Yet in the vast majority of police departments, patrol officers are paid the lowest salaries and given the least amount of authority. Should they happen to like their work and should they be good at it, there is absolutely no way to satisfy their own personal ambition for promotion and its accompanying raise in salary other than leaving the job of patrol officer. There are many, many cases that could be cited in the history of American policing where extraordinarily capable people at the lowest operational level have been promoted into supervisory and command-level positions where they performed poorly.

One progressive municipal police agency, the Los Angeles Police Department, has developed a comprehensive *career path* program which accommodates police officers at the lower-ranking levels and is designed to encourage personnel to pursue police careers below the rank of lieutenant. Table 5.1 outlines the career path that an officer may follow, stipulating the requirements needed for promotion from one level to the next. There are five pay steps at each of the nine career path levels. Maximum pay increases from level to level, thereby giving officers at the lower-ranking levels an opportunity to achieve career success within the department even if they should choose not to aspire to command-level positions. Although it would be difficult to adapt this specific plan to small police department promotion requirements, police administrators everywhere should give serious consideration to the possibility of developing similar and, in some instances, less elaborate programs.

Traditional police promotion criteria usually include one or more of the following evaluative criteria:

1. written examination;

2. oral interview;

3. experience (sometimes called *longevity*); and

4. evaluation of past performance.

As a rule, various percentage weights are assigned to each evaluative criterion. These will vary from department to department, depending on which criteria the department's administrator regards as the more important ones.

Police departments that use only one or two of the evaluative criteria in their promotional systems can anticipate having many problems in the administration of the promotional process. It is inconceivable, for example, that promotions would be based solely on the outcome of a written examination. Yet this is the case in many police departments. And this is why so many police departments have problems with their promotional systems. Departments that fail to use all four of the evaluative criteria, with published weighted values assigned to each criterion, are impeding the successful output of the staffing process, which in

Table 5.1 Los Angeles Police Department career path program

Career Path	Requirements
Policeman—Recruit	● High school graduate or equivalent
Policeman II—Radio car officer, foot-beat, communications, desk	● 18 months as Policeman I
Policeman III—Crime Task Force, Divisional Vice, Intelligence and Training Officer, Instructor, Dispatcher, Investigator Trainee	● 18 months as Policeman I or II plus successful completion of Policeman III written and oral evaluation
Policeman III + 1—Crime Task Force Squad Leader, Accident Investigation Follow-up Investigator, Vice Coord., Sr. Lead Officer	● Same as Policeman III plus selection by Division Commander and approval by Bureau Chief
Investigator I—Specialized Detectives, Geographic Detectives, Administrative Vice, Administrative Narcotics, Intelligence	● 3½ years as a Policeman I, II, III, or III + 1 and successful completion of Civil Service written and oral exam
Sergeant I—Uniformed Field Supervisor: Patrol/Traffic	● Same as Investigator I
Investigator II—Sr. Investigator, Narcotics, Juvenile, Administrative Vice, Bunco/Forgery, Robbery/Homicide	● One year as Investigator I or Sergeant I and successful completion of Investigator II evaluation
Sergeant II—Instructor: Training Academy, Assistant Patrol Watch Commander, Captain's Adjutant, Labor Relations Investigator	● One year as Sergeant I and successful completion of evaluation process
Investigator III—Investigator Expert, Supervisory Investigator	● One year as an Investigator II and successful completion of evaluation process

turn hinders their efforts to meet goals and objectives. Problems arising from the promoting process that are not being fed back into the staffing process as new inputs provide proof that most police departments do not look on staffing from a systems perspective. The value of the systems approach to any process of police management, including promoting and staffing, is that problems will be identified through feedback and that systems will be improved through new input.

The four evaluative criteria for promotion mentioned here are merely tools for promotional improvements. They are, however, the *basic* tools. Their success or failure will be dependent on the ways in which they are applied to the promoting process.

Termination The final staffing activity, terminating, may occur on the employee's own initiative through either early but voluntary retirement or resignation. It may also occur at the department's direction through forced retirements, forced resignations, or firings. An employee may also be terminated as the result of mandatory retirement requirements based on age. Finally, terminations may be based on sickness, injury, or death. Table 5.2 shows the various kinds of special and routine decisions made in the termination process by both the police department and the employee. When the department makes termination decisions, regardless of whether they are special or routine decisions, the department is engaging in the terminating process.

Table 5.2 Special and routine decisions made in the termination process

Source of Decisions	Special Decisions	Routine Decisions
Department	Forced retirements Forced resignations Firings	Mandatory retirements due to age Retirements due to sickness or injury Terminations due to death
Employee	Voluntary resignations	Early but voluntary retirements

An employee's voluntary retirement is usually the cause of much rejoicing and is regarded as the happy ending to many years of productive employment. By reaching retirement age or by choosing to retire early, the employee leaves the police department with the realization that he or she performed adequately for a considerable period of time.

When a police department fires employees or forces them to resign or retire, it is telling them, in effect, that they are no longer useful to the organization in its attempts to meet its goals and objectives. Such actions may have serious adverse effects on employees' self-esteem and sense of personal worth as well as on the department's relations with its remaining employees. Much consideration, therefore, should be given to firing or to forcing the resignation or retirement of an employee. Such an action will necessarily impact on the entire system and cause severe subsystem reactions. These reactions may be either positive or negative. When an employee is fired or forced to resign or retire as the result of an internal investigation which uncovered corruption or incompetence, the effect on the system should be positive. When an employee is forced out of a department based on inconclusive evidence of corruption or incompetence, it should be anticipated that the effect on the system will be negative. In the former instance, the action taken by the department serves notice on all other employees that corruption or incompetence will not be tolerated by the department. In the latter instance, action against the employee serves notice on all other employees that the same rules of evidence that are applied generally throughout the criminal justice system are not applicable to them, thus creating a morale problem that the department could very well do without in its efforts to meet its goals and objectives.

The voluntary resignation of an employee short of retirement age is usually regarded as a setback for the department. When a police officer quits, the department loses not only its investment in the individual, but also an experienced employee. Although many employees terminate voluntarily for personal reasons beyond the control of the police department, such as sickness, injury, or a better-paying position, others terminate voluntarily because of dissatisfaction with their jobs or because of departmental organizational problems with which they cannot cope. Still others quit because they are disinterested in their jobs, cannot get along with people, or are job-hopping nomads who find it difficult to adjust to the status quo. Voluntary terminations should be expected. Massive numbers of voluntary terminations, however, should be a signal to people involved in the staffing function that something is seriously wrong with the department.

A classic example of the voluntary termination being used as an indicator of departmental instability was observed by one of the authors, who was called in as a police management consultant to a Midwestern police department of 54 employees. A study of the department's staffing function revealed that in the 13 months immediately prior to the consultant's arrival in the city, there had been a personnel turnover of 40 employees. In the 15 months prior to the consultant's arrival, there had been two chiefs; one lasted nine months, the other six. The department's third chief in less than two years was due to arrive on the scene in time to use the consultant's findings for departmental reorganization.

This tremendous turnover of personnel at a time when unemployment rates were skyrocketing throughout the nation was a clear indicator that something was drastically wrong. As might be expected from the rapid turnover in police chiefs, the problem was systemic in nature and originated largely from the parent system, city government, which was totally unaware of its impact on the police subsystem. Although staffing the police department was the problem, it was largely a problem of city government and coincidentally a problem for the police department. Although neither the city government nor the police department operated from a systems perspective, it was impossible for anyone involved to avoid noticing the feedback provided by the figures: 40 of the department's 54 employees had resigned within one 13-month period. That a problem existed was obvious. But most staffing problems are not so easily identified and require considerable study of output through feedback.

The involuntary termination of an employee, besides being a waste for both the department and the individual concerned, may in all likelihood also be substantial proof of a breakdown somewhere in the staffing function, most probably in selection, training, or placement. Those responsible for staffing should therefore be required to examine carefully all aspects and all ramifications of involuntary terminations in an effort to improve staffing input with respect to the terminating process. Application of the systems approach is the only way to get at and to solve organizational problems that stem from management deficiencies. If an organization's selection, training, and assignment processes can be refined so that most problems are eliminated through the adjustment and change of system inputs, a department can most likely avoid most involuntary terminations.

The output of all staffing function activities (recruitment, selection, training, placement, promotion, and termination) is the staff itself. The staff does the work of the organization. Through its efforts, the organization either fails or succeeds. The importance of staffing should be apparent; it may very well be the most important aspect of the police administrative process.

Feedback in the staffing function is the evaluative tool by which the performance of people within an organization is measured. In recent years the methods used to achieve such feedback have become the subject of considerable controversy. In police departments not administered from a systems perspective, little or no effort is made to evaluate performance. Departments managed with a high degree of systems emphasis use some extremely complex and sophisticated performance evaluation procedures and various kinds of quantitative and qualitative evaluative methods. One system requires supervisors to rank subordinates from best to worst. Another requires employees to rate fellow employees. One frequently used method of performance evaluation is to have supervisors categorize the performance of each employee as good, fair, or poor either generally or specifically in terms of certain specified activities they perform.[17]

The variety of evaluative techniques is endless. The choice of the right technique is important, because it impacts heavily on employee morale and organizational stability. An unfair or unrealistic performance evaluation system complicates the staffing process by providing false and worthless feedback which is then analyzed and fed back into the staffing process as improper new input. It is therefore essential to take great care in designing a performance evaluation procedure which not only is fully accepted by employees themselves but also works to the department's benefit in meeting goals and objectives. A performance evaluation program which places great emphasis on numbers of arrests, for example, might very well encourage police officers to use their arrest powers indiscriminately in performing their order-maintenance function and hence impede the department's interest in mediating conflict without creating more conflict.

By emphasizing those factors of performance that are relevant to the department's goals and objectives, the police administrator is indirectly exerting a degree of control over the organization. In effect, the administrator is saying, "These are the activities that I consider to be important; if you perform these activities well, you will be rewarded." A well-designed performance evaluation system, therefore, will be built around the department's goals and objectives. If it is to be a viable system, it must isolate criteria that can be *objectively* evaluated. Furthermore, everyone within the department should be fully apprised of exactly what these criteria are and precisely how they will be applied and weighted in the evaluating process.

There is an inherent inequity in having supervisors rate personnel from a variety of different perspectives applied subjectively in terms of their own individual value judgments. Because the people who do the rating are key factors in the success of the rating system, it is important that they be *trained* to rate and that their rating abilities be given a high weighted value in their own performance evaluations.

It is not a well-kept secret that supervisors generally dislike performance evaluation.[18] Most of them abhor this task, which they consider the single most difficult part of their work. Most people do not enjoy being critical of their fellow workers on a regular basis. Those criticized may and often do harbor resentments for the rest of their lives. The job of the performance evaluator, therefore, is not an easy one. To sit in judgment of another person's worth and to discuss that judgment meaningfully and productively with the person is without question the most sensitive task the supervisor performs. It may also be the most important task, for it goes to the very heart of organizational viability and survival. The police department that places little emphasis on performance evaluation and that provides no guidance to its performance evaluators cannot help but have severe staffing problems.

Finally, in this discussion of feedback as an important element in the staffing function, some consideration should be given to the need that police departments have to evaluate personnel strength requirements. All too often in the past, the number of police officers needed in particular assignments or in specified geographical areas has been predicated on political and sometimes even emotional factors. By conducting a personnel requirements survey, based on actual activity and the time needed to service it, a department will be armed with information that can be fed back into the staffing process as new input so that assignment adjustments can be made in terms of the department's actual needs.

The loop of the staffing system is now closed. The inputs of people, jobs, and objectives are processed through recruitment, selection, training, placement, promotion, and termination to produce staff. Feedback is provided through performance evaluation of staff members and analysis of staff requirements. Although many aspects of the staffing function legitimately belong to the department's personnel division, others are either the direct or indirect responsibility of each and every supervisor and manager.

DIRECTING

Directing is perhaps the most difficult management function to describe accurately. Think for a moment of motion picture directors and what they do. Their job is directing; they tell the actors and actresses in their employ how to speak their lines, what movements to make before the cameras, and what emotions to display. They show their camera crews what angles, lenses, and filters to use. They establish filming schedules. They direct the activities of people involved in casting, costumes, and makeup. Their job involves telling people what to do, when to do it, and how to do it. Put more succinctly, they *call the shots.* They do this by bringing together all of the talents they have at their disposal and orchestrating them as best they can into what will become the final production, a motion picture.

Their job may seem to be a simple process. It is not. Consider some of its complications. Actors and actresses are professionals in their own right, and some of them may be more highly paid than the director. They may refuse to comply with shooting schedules or refuse to take direction. Other members of the crew may have technical disagreements with the directors, or they may simply misunderstand their directions. In other instances, personality conflicts between the directors and their employees may impede progress. Problems involving sickness, injury, alcoholism, family, and just plain irresponsibility will contribute to holding up production and are likely to be costly.

All of these *variables,* as well as many others, affect the directing process. Variables are factors that change from situation to situation. Their impact on the directing process is either positive or negative, and they must be dealt with expeditiously whenever they appear in whatever form on the scene. A variable that impacts negatively on the directing process is a *constraint.* When the union to which the camera crew members belong, for example, restricts its activities in any way, this restriction is a constraint on the directing process and must be dealt with by the director. The union itself is a variable. When it acts to limit the activities of a director, it becomes a constraint.

Directing, then, may be looked on as a system of interrelated variables and constraints. Figure 5.4 shows the directing function from a systems perspective.

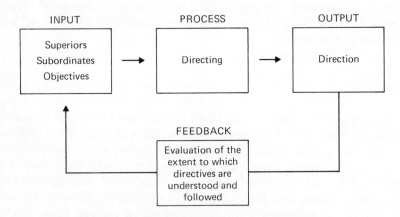

Fig. 5.4. The directing function from a systems perspective.

In the directing function the input of superiors is the directing. Superiors develop and disseminate directives. The input of subordinates is the receiving of and acting on those directives. The input of objectives is the purposefulness of the process. If directives fail to point an organization toward the accomplishment of its goals and objectives, they serve no useful purpose.

The process of directing involves the following activities:

1. development;

2. dissemination;

3. reception; and

4. action.

These are the activities which, when impacted on by variables and constraints, make directing such a complex task.

Development The development of directives involves considerable planning and a careful analysis of organizational goals and objectives. Because directives tell people what to do, they must be designed in accordance with what the organization itself wants to accomplish through the people it employs. People are the instrumentality by which the organization functions. It is only through the direction of people that the organization accomplishes what it sets out to do. Deciding what directives should be developed, therefore, is an important part of the directing process.

Dissemination Directives are disseminated, or communicated from superiors to subordinates. The process of communicating directives to those who are expected to follow them and act on them is an involved and complex procedure. Literally millions of people in the world earn their living by either communicating with people or telling people how to communicate with one another. Communication is an art practiced by many but mastered by few. It is the primary vehicle for the dissemination of directives.

Reception The reception of directives involves individual perception, a matter as difficult to analyze as it is to predict. Nations have gone to war, businesses have gone bankrupt, and people have committed suicide because of faulty perception. Huge bureaucracies such as the Central Intelligence Agency and the Russian KGB exist almost solely to provide their respective governments with accurate perceptions of foreign powers. Political candidates and large corporations expend tremendous energy and sometimes substantial sums of money in efforts to perceive accurately what people are thinking and what they want. Pollsters such as Gallup and Harris are widely read and generally relied on to provide perceptions of various trends that are occurring and always changing in society.

Yet even the most astute professionals frequently perceive incorrectly. The Ford Motor Company was guilty of inaccurate perception when it conceived the Edsel. Neville Chamberlain was guilty of inaccurate perception when he chose to trust Adolf Hitler. Every financial expert in the United States, except for Roger Babson, was guilty of inaccurate perception in failing to predict the stock market crash of 1929. How often have you personally made an innocent remark to someone that was taken the wrong way?

Everyone is guilty of inaccurate perception. Unfortunately, the results can be catastrophic. The reception of directives within organizations is a matter of perception. It is well for that person within the organization who is doing the directing to understand that inaccurate perception of directives can result in horrendous consequences and might even result in the dissolution of the organization. Directors of organizations should never assume that their directives are perceived as they intend them to be. Many organization directors have gone right down the professional tube for making such a naive assumption.

Action The action taken as a result of directives depends on a number of factors, including the effectiveness of the dissemination and reception processes, group dynamics, leadership, values, attitudes, and motivation. Taken as a whole, the process of directing is all tied up with the psychology of human behavior, which itself is an academic discipline. The better one understands the pragmatics of human behavior, human relationships, and human interaction, the better director one becomes. If one cannot understand and deal with the behavior of human beings pragmatically and without illusions, one should not be involved in the directing process.

The output of the directing process, in general terms, is direction. In more specific terms, the outputs are policies, procedures, rules, regulations, general orders, special orders, and personal orders. Policies are guides to thinking, whereas procedures are guides to action. They serve as general guidelines for officers to follow in conducting their duties.

There is no distinction, on the other hand, between the word *rule* and the word *regulation;* they are one and the same. Unlike policies and procedures, rules and regulations are binding mandates that all officers *must* follow in the conduct of their duties. They are usually published in permanent, printed form and are distributed to all department members. General orders, a form of rules and regulations, are equally as binding; they are usually published and distributed to all personnel as additions or amendments to rules and regulations.

Special orders are generally nonpermanent and are issued only in special circumstances not covered by policies, procedures, rules, regulations, or general orders. The roster of officers expected to represent the department in the Fourth of July parade or at a funeral detail, for example, would be issued as a special order. Unlike general orders, special orders are self-terminating. When the parade is over and the funeral finished, the special order governing officer participation would be automatically cancelled and would no longer exist.

Personal orders are given to subordinates by supervisory or command-level personnel. Personal orders are usually given orally.

All orders, rules, regulations, policies, and procedures are direction, the output of the directing process. The feedback to the directing function is the evaluation of the extent to which directives (orders, rules, regulations, policies, and procedures) are understood and followed. Because dissemination and reception of directives involve the intricate processes of communication and perception, it is essential that the output of the directing process (direction) be very carefully evaluated on a continuing basis so that any directives that are improperly communicated or misunderstood can be redesigned as new input and redisseminated through the directing process.

Some types of directives lend themselves to immediate feedback. For example, in issuing a personal order to a patrol officer to leave the police station immediately to answer a burglary in progress call, a sergeant will learn within a matter of seconds whether or not the patrol officer understands the order. Similarly, in discussing a newly disseminated general order with patrol officers at roll call, a sergeant can learn from their responses whether or not they understand the content of the order.

Most feedback to the directing process, however, is not such a simple matter. Several months might go by before officers encounter a situation in which a new directive should be applied. If they have forgotten the directive, they will improvise as best they can under the circumstances but not necessarily perform according to the method prescribed by the department through the directive. If they misunderstood the intent of the directive when it was issued, chances are good that they will perform in a manner not consonant with departmental procedure. Supervisors must be alert to such possibilities and advise their superiors when directives, for whatever reason, are not being followed. Supervisors, therefore, are key people in providing feedback to keep the loop closed in the directing process. If supervisors fail to provide information for evaluation and new input, the department will in all likelihood be unaware that its directives are not being followed and will be lulled into a false sense of security about the activities of its officers.

There is no quicker way for a police department to degenerate organizationally than to allow the directing process to function in open-loop fashion. Departments that fail to approach the directing process from a closed-loop systems perspective actually encourage their police officers to defy directives and to handle all situations through a process that the President's Crime Commission has referred to as "unarticulated improvisation."[19] This means, in effect, that police officers will handle situations according to their own individual judgments and whims and not according to the articulated policies of their departments. This results in laws being enforced indiscriminately and services provided haphazardly. The resultant inconsistencies in levels of enforcement and levels of services impact negatively on the police generally and on the individual department particularly. Although this may be a "comfortable approach,"[20] as the Commission put it, for the officers involved, it is organizationally chaotic and flies in the face of the systems approach to good management. As an alternative, the Commission recommended a different process, which is "systematic, intelligent, articulate and responsive to external controls appropriate in a democratic society. . . ."[21] The *only* way to achieve this is to keep the loop closed in the directing process.

Although feedback from supervisors is probably the single most important factor in keeping the loop closed in the directing process, other methods should also be used. One such method is the test. When a directive is issued, all employees governed by the directive should be tested on their understanding of its specifics. The test can be either written or oral; the written test, however, is more advantageous because it affords a better opportunity to examine in depth the individual's reception and perception of the directive. Also, an individual forced to describe the directive in written form is more likely to remember it than if the description is given orally. In addition, the answers on a written test can be reviewed by a number of people, thereby reducing the possibility of perception errors on the part of the reviewers. If the test indicates that the directive is generally misunderstood, it can be used as an evaluative criterion which can be fed back into the directing process as new input, which would probably result in having the directive rewritten and redisseminated. If the directive is misunderstood only slightly or by only a few officers, it might be more prudent to design a roll-call training session or even a series of such training sessions to explain the directive. Testing should be an ongoing feedback mechanism and should be discontinued only when management is assured that a given directive is fully understood.

Another feedback mechanism which has proved to be extremely useful is *Post Office Box 911.* The department rents the post office box and mounts a public information campaign designed to encourage people to report anonymously their concerns over police misfeasance and malfeasance. This further closes the loop in the directing process by allowing citizens who deal with the police to become involved in providing feedback which, if proved to be reliable through evaluation, can be introduced as new input.

Informal conversations with police officers themselves can also be very helpful. One former chief of police in a large West Coast city devoted one-half day per week to informal interviews with individual officers. This proved to be a very effective feedback device and gave the chief an opportunity he would not otherwise have had to learn in what ways his own direction output was ineffective.

By closing the loop of the directing process through feedback and by introducing corrective input into the system, police administrators can exercise their prerogatives and meet their responsibilities as the *directors* of their organizations. One of the most successful directors in law enforcement history was the late J. Edgar Hoover, Director of the Federal Bureau of Investigation. Although many of Mr. Hoover's system outputs have come under fire by critics since his death, no one can cast aspersions on his ability to direct and on his capability to maintain a closed-loop directing process. From a systems standpoint, it is an outstanding model for police chiefs to follow in their own efforts to direct their own organizations.

CONTROLLING

The management function of controlling is closely related to directing. Whereas directing is involved in communicating what should be done, controlling is involved with ensuring that what should be done *is* done. If directing is the making and the communicating of rules, controlling is the *enforcing* of rules.

Controlling as a management function is somewhat broader, however, than simple rule enforcement. It includes functions which might not generally be looked on as control devices. Budgeting, for example, is one way in which an organization uses the allocation of money to control its subsystems. Another control mechanism is the gathering and evaluation of statistics, a means by which an organization learns about the effectiveness of its operations and thereby controls its activities. Controlling is designed essentially to make certain that an organization and its component parts are adhering to established directives (see Fig. 5.5).

The directives input concerns all aspects of the way functions are supposed to be performed in the organization. By contrast, the information input involves the way functions are actually being performed.

The objectives input—the goals and objectives of the organization and each of its subsystems—is utilized as a check on the directives input. It is important that directives be carefully examined in light of organizational goals and objectives *before* control in the form of adherence to these directives is required. It is entirely possible that some directives may be found to be incompatible with organizational goals and objectives; in such cases they should be discarded or rewritten in terms of organizational needs.

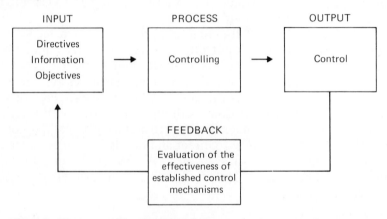

Fig. 5.5. The controlling function from a systems perspective.

A significant gap between the way functions are being performed and the way they are supposed to be performed is an indication that the controlling function is not serving its purpose. It may also indicate a failure of the directing function; in such instances it can be assumed that employees simply do not understand directives. It may further indicate that prevailing directives are not consonant with organizational goals and objectives, presenting employees with a choice between doing what they have been told to do and what they personally may feel is best for the organization. Each of these possibilities must be kept in mind by police chiefs who administer their organizations from a systems perspective and who are responsible for directing and controlling.

The process of controlling is getting employees to do what the organization expects them to do. Directing has informed them what is expected of them. Controlling is the mechanism that will ensure that they will do what is expected of them. As such, controlling involves influencing behavior. Numerous methods are used to influence behavior: rewards, punishments, threats, promises, and cajoling. In general, most police departments make very little effort to influence the behavior of police officers through established techniques designed to effect control. This is probably because it is generally assumed by people who are unfamiliar with behavior-modification techniques that the modification of behavior is an impossible task. Unfortunately for the police service, the major behavior-modification technique used consistently by most police chiefs is punishment, at best a negative technique which usually creates serious morale problems.

The influencing of human behavior is a difficult, complex, and involved process. Most parents are thoroughly familiar with problems inherent in the process. Although they have almost total authority over their children, especially in their younger years, they very often find it impossible to control their behavior and to have them act according to parental expectations. Parents' failures in controlling their children are disruptive to the family and harmful to the children themselves. Testing their parents to see how much they can get away with is not uncommon among children; it is, in fact, a continuing process. Consider how much more difficult it is to control an entire organization. It is a relatively simple matter to control one's children; yet many parents fail at the task. In an organization comprising hundreds of people, the controlling function, by comparison, is much more involved and requires a much more concerted effort. If one is to achieve any degree of success in controlling people within large organizations, it is absolutely essential that a closed-loop systems approach be used in the process.

Behavior-modification techniques must be used intelligently to get people to perform effectively. These techniques are used to motivate people to do what you expect them to do, what they are directed to do. Once a directive is issued, there is no guarantee that an individual will be automatically predisposed to follow it, even if he or she understands it. In most organizations, the tendency is just the opposite; the tendency is called *beating the system.* People must somehow be motivated to follow directives if the organization for which they work is to meet its goals and objectives. Because it is essential for people in organizations to follow directives, the methods used to modify their behavior so that they will be willing to perform their jobs as expected must be carefully designed and implemented.

Of the many behavior-modification methods used, the two most important for police administrators to consider are *reward* and *recognition,* both of which are easy to develop and implement. Reward and recognition might take the form of pay increments for work well done, promotions, public recognition, days off, favorable assignments, and special awards. Even a pat on the back for a job well done should not be underestimated as a motivational factor.

Recognition is perhaps the most compelling behavior modifier of all. People who do good work should be recognized for their contributions. Recognition gives an individual a sense of organizational belongingness. It is nonmonetary pay for a job well done. It says to the officer, "We recognize your worth, and we place great value on your being an important part of the organization." It provides a tremendous incentive for the officer to want to continue to perform effectively. The officer feels a part of the organization team and is therefore motivated to follow directives in an effort to help the organization meet its goals and objectives.

Police departments that fail to realize the importance of reward and recognition as behavior modifiers cannot possibly meet their goals and objectives and will be constantly plagued by large numbers of officers attempting to *beat the system.* The system has to be geared to recognize the need that all people have to feel important and must consciously devise as many methods as possible to make them feel important. Otherwise, they will feel that the system does not recognize their talents and contributions and that regardless of how well they do their work, nobody really cares. This contributes to an "organization be damned" philosophy, a feeling of uselessness, and a commitment to do as little work as possible just to get by.

Police officers' attitudes toward their jobs vary tremendously from department to department. In departments where officers are rewarded and recognized for the good work they perform, attitudes are excellent and morale is high. In departments where officers are not rewarded and recognized, attitudes are almost always poor and morale low.

In one large police department in which one of the authors served as a consultant studying why the department was malfunctioning at almost all levels, no meaningful systems of reward or recognition were evident. As a result, departmental personnel, except for a few conscientious officers who were performing at peak efficiency under the most adverse conditions, had simply given up. Nobody cared about them, they cared about nobody. Once the consultant observed a situation that was almost unbelievable. Riding on patrol with two officers on a cold snowy night, the consultant saw an obviously intoxicated man staggering about on the street in the center of the city. Drunkenness was not a crime in that state and therefore not considered an arrestable offense. Under state law, however, police officers were permitted to hold intoxicated people in what was referred to as *protective custody;* that is, they could transport intoxicated persons to the station lock-up and hold them until they were sober enough to care for themselves. Another option was to transport them or arrange to have them transported to a regional detoxification center.

In this particular city a detoxification center was located less than two miles from where the man was observed at 2:15 A.M. The man was so intoxicated that he could hardly walk. He was coherent enough, however, to request that he be taken to the detoxification center. The officer brushed the man aside, telling him that he was too busy to comply. The man then pleaded that he be taken to the police station for the night; the snow was turning to rain and he was soaking wet. After much cajoling by the man, the officer contacted the radio dispatcher at the station, requesting that the detoxification center be contacted so that arrangements could be made to pick up the man.

With no calls to service and with nothing but preventive patrol to engage them for the moment, the police car drove off into the night to fight crime, leaving the man to fend for himself. At 3:45 A.M. the same patrol team made another swing through the center of the city. The man, still very intoxicated, again pleaded to be taken off the street. One of the officers again contacted the station by radio and inquired whether arrangements had been made with the detoxification center. The radio dispatcher routinely informed the officer that he had forgotten about the request. A few minutes later the dispatcher came back on the air with the information that the detoxification center would be down to pick up the man. The patrol team again drove off, leaving the man staggering about the street. One and one-half hours later, the consultant left the city, driving by the area where the intoxicated man had made his requests. Lonely, forgotten, and a danger to himself, the man was still there waiting for someone to help him.

This is but one pitiful example of the extent to which police officers who go unrewarded and unrecognized for what they do can work in defiance of departmental goals and objectives. The officers' attitudes and their actions accurately reflected their department's attitude toward and disinterest in them. In departments where good work is recognized and rewarded, the unfortunate man on the street would have been immediately picked up by the officers themselves and transported to either the station or the detoxification center, both of which were only minutes away.

In situations such as the one cited above, decisions made by individual officers with respect to actions taken often depend largely, and sometimes solely, on the sense of belongingness that officers have toward their department. If they are comfortable in their positions and feel that their department recognizes what they do, chances are excellent that they will do their jobs to the best of their abilities and be organizationally productive in terms of goals and objectives. Because police officers work alone with very little direct supervision, their activities are extremely difficult to control. An assembly-line worker with a hovering supervisor is much easier to control than a police officer who might see a supervisor only once or twice during an entire tour of duty. It is therefore important to realize that controlling a police officer involves the application of highly refined motivational devices. The mechanisms of reward and recognition as behavior modifiers can, when properly applied, make the difference between meeting or not meeting organizational goals and objectives.

It would be unfair to leave you with the impression that other behavior-modification devices should be discarded in favor of reward and recognition. Punishment, for example, can be very effective as a behavior modifier if used fairly, consistently, and not to the exclusion of other behavior modifiers. Punishment, however, should be used only as a last resort. Realistically, it must be understood that some people are difficult to motivate except through punishment. The effort to motivate people through other means should always be made and punishment used only if everything else fails. Depending on the seriousness of infractions, everyone should probably be given a second chance and perhaps even a third before the administrator resorts to punishment. When an infraction occurs, a subtle threat or even a direct promise to take action should the infraction reoccur might very well serve to motivate the individual sufficiently. The best method for effecting control within any organization is through the sensible application of as many motivational techniques as possible. These techniques, working in concert with one another, can very effectively serve to motivate people to follow directives, to do their jobs, and to meet organizational goals and objectives.

The output of the controlling process is control. If every employee always acted in exact accordance with organizational directives, absolute control would exist. In order for this to happen, perfect communications would have to exist within the organization; every directive would have to be completely understood by every employee; and every employee would have to agree that every directive issued was consonant with organizational as well as with personal goals and objectives. Considering that some people are more motivated, more conscientious, and more talented than others, one should conclude that in an organization of any size, absolute control cannot exist.

The desired output of the controlling process is, very simply, employee behavior that conforms to organizational directives. Control does not involve conformity of opinions and attitudes; it involves conformity of behavior. This behavior is described fully in organizational directives.

The great difficulty in achieving conformity of behavior stems from the inevitable gap in all organizations between what the employee perceives to be acceptable behavior and what the organization has prescribed to be acceptable behavior. In order to understand what control involves, it is essential to understand how individual police officers personally perceive their role, particularly if their perception of their role is different from that of their department.

Police officers work in a wide variety of settings, confronting large numbers of different, changing, and volatile situations and circumstances. Their activity centers on delicate, interpersonal relationships. When they arrive on a scene, they are expected to take some action, which is usually based on their immediate assessment of the situation. Many situations require a cool head and a considerable amount of maturity. Police officers must resolve the sometimes bitter conflicts that erupt when tempers flare, when injustice is alleged, when people are injured or dying, and when emotion has replaced rational judgment. When an anticipated element of danger or of potential violence involving one's personal safety and that of others is added, a police officer's demeanor, bearing, appearance, and choice of alternatives depend largely on how he or she perceives self, others, and the police role in the situation. If the department has prescribed what the officer's behavior should be in the situation through the issuance of a directive, the officer may choose to behave in accordance with the directive. Or, the police officer may choose to disregard the directive and behave on the basis of gut feeling. In choosing the latter course and disregarding the directive, the officer's personal perception of the total situation would govern his or her response, and herein lies the danger.

Because everybody perceives differently, everybody acts differently, in accord with the personal variables of personality, values, predispositions, and prejudices. Officers who perceive themselves as crime fighters will act differently from officers who see themselves as mediators of conflict; the former are more likely to use arrest as a tool of conflict resolution, whereas the latter are more likely to resolve the situation through mediation. Officers who are militaristically oriented will act differently from officers who are service-oriented. Secure officers will act differently from insecure officers. Officers who easily lose control of their emotions will act differently from officers who are emotionally stable. Officers who possess leadership qualities will act differently from officers who are not innately leaders. Officers who perceive themselves as helpers will act differently from officers who place little value on the helping role. Officers who are prejudiced toward certain groups of people will act differently from officers who are relatively prejudice-free.

If departmental directives governing behavior are not followed, officers will handle situations in whatever manner they might be predisposed to behave as human beings and not necessarily as police officers. Where departmental goals and objectives are contrary to their own or when they perceive their roles to be different from what their department perceives them to be, police officers very often work counterproductively to departmental interests. Control over the activities of police officers is therefore extremely important if a department is to meet its goals and objectives. Police departments cannot afford to have officers impeding departmental progress by following their own feelings.

The evaluation of the effectiveness of established control mechanisms provides feedback for the controlling function. It is essential to evaluate the degree of adherence to organizational directives if the anticipated output of the controlling function is to be effective.

Activities that yield information on how well employees are conforming to the official behavior expected of them provide feedback for new input into the controlling function. The feedback of supervisors who observe their officers at work and who review their reports is critical to the controlling process. Informal feedback from officers themselves and from the public can also be very helpful.

Large departments have specialized inspection divisions which make periodic checks throughout their organizations in an effort to determine the degree to which directives are being followed. Inspection divisions exist primarily to provide feedback in the controlling process. Their very existence, however, is a control mechanism in and of itself which ensures a certain degree of compliance with departmental directives. Even in the smallest police departments, the inspection function can be performed by the chief or a trusted associate. It is an excellent feedback device.

The departmental audit is another mechanism frequently used to provide feedback on control output. Audits can be performed to determine conformity to almost any type of organizational directive. Some departments rely on independent, outside consultants to study all aspects of the degree to which control over all activities is exercised. Such organizations as the Westinghouse Justice Institute, the International Association of Chiefs of Police, Robert Sheehan Associates, and the Public Administration Service have been widely used for this purpose.

The establishment of an internal affairs division is another useful feedback device. These divisions investigate internally such matters as police impropriety, brutality, corruption, and malfeasance. Aside from being a response to citizen interest in having the police police themselves, internal affairs divisions provide a strong incentive for police officers to comply with organizational directives, particularly to directives relating to behavior that borders on being improper or criminal. The results of internal affairs investigations should always be fed back into the controlling function as new input.

As with all management functions, the importance of feedback cannot be stressed too strongly. No chief of police, especially one several levels removed from operational components, can assume that directives are being followed; if the job of management is not approached from a systems perspective, the chief can be almost certain that they are not.

The controlling function of management, much like the directing function, is concerned largely with the psychology of human behavior, a subject which will be treated more fully in subsequent chapters.

SYSTEM BUILDING

System building is not generally thought of as a separate management function. Most management theorists contend that system building is so fundamental to other primary management functions that there is no need to identify it as a primary function and to isolate it for study. In the *ideal* organizational setting, where the systems approach to management has traditionally been applied, this might be so; however, in the police field, where so little attention has been given to managing from the systems perspective, it is essential for administrators to realize that many police problems have evolved solely because police administrators by the thousands have developed their organizations without paying any attention whatever to systems concepts.

The systems theory is so foreign to police administrators generally and so basic to the development of sound organizations universally that special emphasis needs to be placed on system building, what it is, and how it can be used. Although good police administrators build good systems instinctively, few really have understood all of the ramifications of what they have been doing. Therefore, system building has been isolated in this chapter as one of the six primary management functions, because the other five primary functions are totally dependent on it for their implementation. Figure 5.6 shows the system-building function from a systems perspective.

The inputs of the system-building function are people, information, jobs, directives, resources, and objectives. All of these inputs have been discussed throughout this chapter. Inputs for specific primary management functions have been identified in our discussion of each primary function. Note, however, that these identified inputs were the *dominant* inputs in the respective functions, not the *only* inputs. The dominant inputs of the controlling function, for example, are *directives, information,* and *objectives.* It is important to understand that these are not the *only* inputs to controlling. *People* are certainly inputs, for they are the controllers and the controllees and as such are extremely important to the managing of good output. Jobs and resources are also inputs to the controlling function, but to a much lesser degree than the *dominant* inputs.

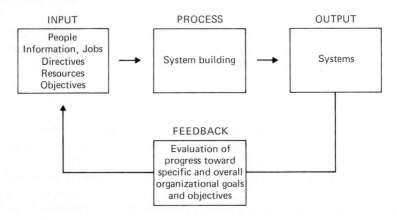

Fig. 5.6. The system-building function from a systems perspective.

Almost any situational variable that you can think of could conceivably be considered a system input to the controlling function if it in any way relates to controlling. Morale, for example, which has been mentioned only peripherally as one of many factors relating to control, is certainly an input to the controlling function. Therefore, anything affecting morale is an input. Thus the condition of police vehicles, the cleanliness of the police station, the degree of fairness with which employees are treated, the attitude of the public toward the administration of the police department, the availability of equipment, and police pay should all be looked on as system inputs in the controlling process.

Minor, relatively insignificant changes made by a police chief in order to increase efficiency, even if they impact on the morale of a single employee, could be construed to be extraordinarily important inputs to the controlling process. One competent police chief who managed his department from a systems perspective learned very quickly the importance of seemingly insignificant factors when he decided that it would be in the best interests of departmental efficiency if he moved the office of one civilian employee from one area of the police station to another. His decision was made purely on the basis of a need to utilize space more effectively; the decision was made in keeping with the goals and objectives he had established for his department. The civilian employee, a 55-year-old woman, was a very responsible person who had complete authority over the department's fiscal affairs. When the chief announced that her office was to be changed, she construed the move as a personal affront, a reflection on her abilities, and an attempt to downgrade her status. She became extremely emotional, cried, and expressed her outrage to family and friends. Her husband became so concerned over her condition that he came to the police station and personally registered a complaint with the chief. The woman's work suffered as a result, and she sought employment elsewhere.

Was the chief's decision to move the woman's office a system input in the controlling process? In retrospect, definitely yes. Did the chief's decision affect control output? It most certainly did. Did the chief consider the ramifications of his decision in terms of the controlling function? The answer, of course, is that he did not. He acted in good faith, perceiving the move to be a positive input to the organizing process, never realizing that it could be a negative input to the controlling process. Did the chief receive negative feedback on the control output? The reactions of the woman employee and her husband provided enough feedback for the chief to realize that he had inadvertently made a wrong decision. Realizing this, he considered what to do. Should he allow a faithful, valued employee to resign after many years of productive service, an action which would imperil the fiscal management of his department and open the loop in what otherwise was a closed-loop system of control? Or should he not allow the employee to resign and instead reverse his original decision? His dilemma was very real. Whichever decision he made would have a negative influence on organizational goals and objectives.

After much deliberation, the chief finally decided to reverse the original order to move the woman's office and made every conceivable effort to explain a mistake for which he took total blame. The woman is now happy, her work output better than ever, and her feelings toward the chief warm and friendly. Although the chief succeeded in closing the loop in the controlling process, the loop in the organizing process remained slightly open, a future challenge to the chief's ingenuity as a system manager.

This little vignette, taken from a real-life situation, illustrates the sensitivity a manager must have in dealing with *all* system inputs. It also demonstrates how one very minor, seemingly insignificant system input to which little or no consideration was given and that probably was never even considered to be an input in the first place can impact on an organization.

The number and kinds of inputs the system builder should consider are so numerous, diverse, and closely related to individual human perception that they defy description. Suffice it to say that extreme care should be exercised in isolating and defining inputs. Taken in their totality, they are the variables that influence organizational decision making. A manager should be aware that the introduction of any new input into a system will cause some reaction in interdependent subsystems; where there is an action, there is always a reaction.

Skillful managers are able to predict accurately the reaction that will result from the introduction of new inputs and always plan organizational changes in terms of reactions they forecast. Successful managers must, therefore, be discriminating in their efforts to identify system inputs to which there will be positive reactions. In order to do this, they must have a good understanding of the intricacies of human behavior and a pragmatic ability to apply their understanding to making changes in their organizations through the introduction of new inputs that will meet with the approval of their employees and contribute in a productive way toward the meeting of organizational goals and objectives.

Skillful managers are always walking tightropes in dealing with the delicate balance between what they perceive to be valuable new input to their organizations and what their employees will accept gracefully as new input. This is particularly so in public service organizations, such as police departments, where tenure provisions, civil service protection, and union contracts tend to encourage employees to challenge management decisions. These factors serve as constraints on management and must, in and of themselves, be considered as inputs to the managing process.

In studying the six primary police management functions, you should realize that we have identified only what we consider to be the *dominant* inputs to each function. That thousands of other inputs exist for each primary function should be taken into consideration by the system builder, who should carefully isolate and evaluate each input before introducing it into any given system.

Under no circumstances should you assume that all inputs into a system must necessarily meet with total employee acceptance. All new inputs represent change, and change is never universally accepted in any organization. Managers should be aware that there will always be some negative reaction to almost every new system input. They must weigh their evaluation of anticipated negative reaction against the new input in terms of its relative importance in meeting goals and objectives. If the new input is essential to organizational stability, they have no choice but to introduce it and take the consequences of negative reactions.

If, for example, a new chief of police becomes aware through feedback that officers are accepting gratuities, that this practice is traditional within the department, and that no policy exists to govern such matters, the chief may decide to develop a policy forbidding officers to accept gratuities and introduce the policy as a new input in the controlling process. If the practice of accepting gratuities is widespread, the input of the new policy will be received by many officers with no degree of enthusiasm and, indeed, may produce a negative reaction with far-reaching implications. The officers might react by calling in sick, slowing down in their work, responding to calls in haphazard fashion, or issuing large numbers of parking tickets. Angered by a change that significantly affects them financially, some officers may even decide to ignore the policy and continue to accept gratuities. Regardless of the negative reaction that assuredly could be predicted by the introduction of the new input, the chief would be remiss in meeting organizational goals and objectives by not introducing the new policy. By forecasting negative reaction on necessary new inputs, the chief can anticipate subsystem problems and deal with them accordingly.

Whenever a new system input is introduced, especially one likely to be controversial and result in negative reaction, a chief must be ready to respond vigorously by strengthening controlling processes and by being particularly receptive to feedback on control output. To do the job properly and meet organizational goals and objectives consistently, a chief must be ready and willing to introduce controversial system input and deal firmly with negative reactions whenever they occur.

Problems in dealing with negative reactions to new system input is what makes the chief's job difficult and challenging. A chief who is intelligent enough to exercise care in the introduction of new inputs, to prepare the necessary groundwork for their introduction, to forecast reactions accurately, to strengthen controlling processes in terms of predictions, and to refine feedback mechanisms for the introduction of essential new inputs should be right on top of any problems that might develop. Without a comprehensive understanding of the systems approach to managing and an ability to apply the approach realistically in building a system, the chief will fail as a manager, and the organization will fail in its efforts to meet even its most elementary goals and objectives.

The introduction of new input is a delicate but necessary task in the process of system building. The actual process of system building involves taking all system inputs and combining them in the best possible way to develop the total system. The complexity of the process is mind-boggling. It involves the juggling of thousands of input variables that are as difficult to isolate and understand as they are to amalgamate. The process is perhaps best understood through simple illustration.

Suppose that you as chief of police wish to develop and administer a departmental training program. You would first examine the dominant inputs that relate to system building—people, information, jobs, directives, resources, and objectives. In processing these inputs, you would consider the relative importance of each in the development of your program. You would want to know as much as possible about the officers to be trained, information that is available about training, jobs or tasks that officers will be trained to perform, money and equipment resources available to you, and the goals and objectives of the training program itself. You would also attempt to identify and examine myriad other inputs that you believe might impact in any way on the program. With all this in mind, you would design your program and put it into operation.

The output of the process would be personnel trained to meet the goals and objectives of the department. Through examinations, you would determine whether or not officers were learning to meet these goals and objectives. Through student evaluations, you would ascertain whether or not the program was perceived by the officers to be of value and what inputs they might have for improvements. Through follow-up studies and supervisors' reports, you would attempt to discover the extent to which officers retained and applied material covered in the program. Examinations, evaluations, follow-up studies, and supervisors' reports would all provide feedback on output and give you an opportunity to reintroduce this feedback as new input. The process itself would therefore always be changing. As personnel are replaced, learned skills forgotten, accepted practices modified, and objectives adjusted, the training process must change to meet these changing needs.

This example of the development of a training program is, of course, an oversimplification. The process itself is much more involved than it might appear. The use of judgment, discretion, and intelligence in the development of a process cannot be underestimated. Those charged with the development of processes must have a good, comprehensive grasp of systems theory and system building if their output is to be productive in terms of meeting organizational goals and objectives. Furthermore, the meeting of organizational goals and objectives is the primary purpose of the processing function. Unless directed toward this end, processing will be a useless tool in the attempt to achieve organizational success. All organizations are purposeful. The processes they devise to be purposeful are the only methods they have to achieve their goals and objectives. It is therefore important to understand that the processing function is fundamental to their success. It is *the major function* on which viable systems are built. The function is absolutely dependent on continuing feedback being translated into new inputs for system improvement.

The output of the system-building process is the system itself, the *total* system. The output of the system-building process in police organizations is the police department in its totality.

Feedback on the system-building process results from the evaluation of the department's progress in meeting specific and overall organizational goals and objectives. Feedback is imperative because it provides information for the development of new inputs which can be used in changing processes that are discovered to be counterproductive to the organization's purpose.

Goals and objectives assume great importance in system building. They must be identified and articulated; they must be regularly reevaluated; and the progress of the organization in meeting them must somehow be measured. These are extremely difficult and complicated tasks for the system builder. But they are essential to the effective functioning of the system as a whole.

The system-building function is not easy to conceptualize. As one of the six primary functions of management, it encompasses all of the other five; thus it serves to integrate planning, organizing, staffing, directing, and controlling. Johnson, Kast, and Rosenzweig see it almost as a *frame of mind.* In speaking of the systems concept, they believe that managers "must be receptive to this approach and develop a philosophy in which planning, organizing, controlling, and communication are accomplished in terms of subsystems integrated into a composite whole."[22]

SUMMARY

This chapter has discussed the six basic, or primary, functions of management. Each function is extremely intricate, and each could be the subject of a separate volume. We have discussed all six functions within the framework of systems theory. Although later discussions involving primary functions will be conducted from somewhat different perspectives, we urge you to retain the systems concept as a *frame of mind* and as an important point of reference. By regularly searching for the inputs, processes, outputs, and feedback in management activities, you will become more adept at analyzing and building systems. Or, to put it another way, you will become more adept at managing.

DISCUSSION QUESTIONS

1. Some people argue that planning is a wasteful activity because they believe that the future is either preordained or too unpredictable to prepare for. Do you agree with these people? Does planning serve any useful purpose?

2. In Chapter 4 we presented several principles of organization. In this chapter we said that organizing must be based on the characteristics of each particular situation. Have we contradicted ourselves? Explain.

3. How would you describe the ideal police officer? How would you translate your description into staffing criteria for the recruitment and selection of police officers?

4. Blacks, women, and other groups have traditionally been underrepresented in police organizations. Why do you think this has been the case? How would you correct this situation?

5. Some authorities have proposed that police officers should be chosen only from among those people possessing college degrees. Do you agree with this position? If you do, how would you answer the criticism that many otherwise well-qualified people have been excluded from consideration? Also, what about the argument that college is not as available to poor people and thus that they would be unfairly discriminated against by a college-degree requirement? On the other side of the coin, if you do not favor the requirement, what consideration would you give to those people who do have the degree? Would you offer promotional advantages, extra money, or special positions?

6. Given the reality that police officers perform widely varying duties in diverse situations with little direct supervision, how would you as a police chief direct and control your organization?

REFERENCES

1. L. Gulick, "The Theory of Organization," in *Papers on the Science of Administration*, ed. L. Gulick and L. Urwick (New York, Institute of Public Administration, 1937), p. 13.

2. R. L. Holcomb, ed., *Municipal Police Administration* (Chicago: International City Management Association, 1961), p. 77.

3. L. R. Sayles, *Managerial Behavior: Administration in Complex Organizations* (New York: McGraw-Hill, 1964), pp. 49-54.

4. G. D. Eastman, "Police Management," in *Municipal Police Administration*, 6th ed., ed. G. D. Eastman and E. M. Eastman (Washington, D.C.: International City Management Association, 1969), p. 37.

5. H. Koontz and C. O'Donnell, *Principles of Management: An Analysis of Managerial Functions* (New York: McGraw-Hill, 1964),

6. O. W. Wilson, *Police Planning*, 2d ed. (Springfield, Ill.: Charles C Thomas, 1957), pp. 4-7.

7. J. D. Mooney and A. C. Reilly, *Onward Industry: The Principles of Organization and Their Significance to Modern Industry* (New York: Harper & Row, 1931), pp. 9-11, 12-17, as quoted in E. Dale, ed., *Readings in Management: Landmarks and New Frontiers* (New York: McGraw-Hill, 1965), p. 155.

8. H. Koontz and C. O'Donnell, *op. cit.*, p. 227.

9. J. D. Mooney and A. C. Reilly, in Dale, *op cit.*, p. 155.

10. H. J. Leavitt, *Managerial Psychology* (Chicago: University of Chicago Press, 1972), p. 259.

11. S. W. Gellerman, *Motivation and Productivity* (New York: American Management Association, 1963), p. 238.

12. *Ibid.*, p. 240.

13. *Ibid.*

14. H. Saxenian, "To Select a Leader," in *M.I.T. Technology Review* 72, 7 (May 1970): 55-61.

15. *Experiments in Police Improvement: A Progress Report* (Washington, D.C.: Police Foundation, 1972), p. 13.

16. R. O. Loen, *Manage More by Doing Less* (New York: McGraw-Hill, 1971), pp. 126-131.

17. D. E. Balch, "Performance Rating Systems—Suggestions for the Police," *Journal of Police Science and Administration* 2, 1 (March 1974): 40-49.

18. D. McGregor, "An Uneasy Look at Performance Appraisal," *Harvard Business Review* (May-June 1957): 134-135.

19. President's Commission on Law Enforcement and Administration of Justice, *Task Force Report: The Police,* Report by the Task Force on the Police (Washington, D.C.: U.S. Government Printing Office, 1967), p. 18.

20. *Ibid.*

21. *Ibid.*

22. R. A. Johnson, F. E. Kast, and J. E. Rosenzweig, "Designing Management Systems," in *Business Quarterly* (Summer 1964): 59–65, as reprinted in P. P. Schoderbek, ed., *Management Systems* (New York: Wiley, 1967), p. 120.

CHAPTER 6
THE CHIEF OF POLICE

LEARNING OBJECTIVES

1. Explain why the chief is one person who can be held accountable for everything that happens in a police department.

2. Cite the police chief's seven preliminary organizing tasks.

3. Differentiate between the police chief's seven preliminary organizing tasks and the six basic police management functions.

4. Describe why it is essential that a police chief be educated at or above the level of the officers within the department.

5. Define organization sense.

6. Cite the six primary components of organization sense.

7. Describe the educational and experiential background of the ideal police chief.

8. Describe the work habits, personality, and value system of the ideal police chief.

9. Describe the intelligence input to organization sense.

10. Define ability as it applies to organization sense.

11. Write an advertisement for a police chief's position.

12. Describe the various processes by which a police chief is selected.

13. Identify the elements of a background investigation.

14. Outline the initial responsibilities of a new chief.

15. State the three day-to-day functions of a police chief.

16. Differentiate between direction and control as day-to-day functions performed by the police chief and directing and controlling as basic police management functions.

A police chief is by far the most important input to the planning, organizing, staffing, directing, controlling, and system-building functions within a department. Background, education, experience, value system, personality, intelligence, work habits, and ability are the dominant inputs a chief brings to the six basic police management functions. The chief is the apex of the traditional triangular police hierarchy. All authority within the organization comes from the police chief. The chief is the one individual who can be held accountable for everything that happens in the department. The chief is a leader, innovator, motivator, and boss. If the mayor or city manager is dissatisfied with the performance of the police department, the chief may be fired. The chief is expendable; one who is not functioning properly can be replaced. It is the chief and the chief alone who is responsible for the way the department is managed. A good chief-manager can contribute greatly to the public safety of the community and provide excellent police services for its citizens. A chief who brings viable inputs to the management function will probably succeed; one whose inputs are poor will probably fail.

Because the position of chief of police is so precarious, many chiefs try to do everything themselves, attempting to become personally involved in *all* aspects of administration, services, and operations. Many chiefs perceive their careers as being totally dependent on the successful execution of every police task at every organizational level. Although this is so in one sense, career success is not achieved through interference in activities for which other people have been delegated authority. If chiefs feel fully responsible, as they should, for the accomplishment of organizational goals and objectives, they should recognize the necessity of applying all of the principles of police organization toward that end.

Initially, all chiefs *must* successfully perform the following seven preliminary organizing tasks:

1. delegate the necessary authority for the successful performance of all police functions;

2. hold those to whom authority has been delegated fully accountable for their actions;

3. group like functions within their organizations to facilitate task accomplishment;

4. establish a meaningful chain of command to enhance organizational communication;

5. insist that decision making and problem solving take place at all organizational levels;

6. develop good working relationships between superiors and subordinates through application of the principle of unity of command; and

7. construct sensible and relevant spans of control designed to strengthen supervisory processes.

Police chiefs' organizing responsibilities are, of course, by no means limited to these preliminary tasks. Chiefs must organize and continually reorganize their departments if they are to meet their management responsibilities. Their preliminary organizing tasks, however, are important *first steps* in the overall organizing effort.

Additionally, police chiefs must staff, direct, control, build, and plan for the total police system, constantly assessing feedback from their preliminary organizing efforts in order to improve system inputs. In short, chiefs must manage their departments in accordance with the six basic police management functions described in Chapter 5.

Police chiefs should have no illusions about their positions. The job is difficult and demanding. Few, if any, chiefs will ever be so competent as to command universal respect and admiration. Although this should be the unqualified goal of every chief, the variables and constraints with which they must contend make the accomplishment of the goal almost an impossibility. Early in their careers chiefs must adjust to the foregone conclusion that they will never be fully successful in terms of goal accomplishment. They must realize that oftentimes they will be called on to make necessary decisions that will affect people in negative ways. It is incumbent on the chief, for example, to terminate incompetent or corrupt employees in order, from a systems standpoint, to close the loop in the controlling process. The discharged employees and the members of their families can be expected to be highly critical of the chief and harbor resentments.

Some chiefs find it difficult, if not impossible, to handle criticism and personal resentment and shy away from making hard decisions that they know will affect them emotionally. Such chiefs should never have been selected for their positions in the first place. The old adage "Nice guys don't win ball games" can be aptly applied to the negative aspects of the chief's function. The job of police chief is a tough, demanding one and requires the talents of a sensitive, demanding person who is dedicated to police work and whose *every* action is directed toward the accomplishment of organizational goals and objectives.

QUALIFICATIONS FOR THE POLICE CHIEF'S POSITION

It perhaps goes without saying that police chiefs should be highly qualified for their jobs. But what does this mean? What qualifications should an individual have to meet the demanding responsibilities of the job?

The single most important requisite is that police chiefs be good administrators who are well grounded in the principles of organization and management. This implies that they should be well-educated persons who have spent a number of years in the academic environment acquiring skills, knowledge, and understanding. Because so many police officers either are going or have gone to college, it is essential that police chiefs be educated at least to the level of most of the officers in their commands. Educationally and intellectually, chiefs should at least be on a par with people within their organizations. If they are educated at or above the level of most of the officers within their commands, they will stand a greater chance of being looked on as professionals than if they brought lesser qualifications to the position.

Educational background is important, but exactly what it should be is a matter of conjecture. The person who holds a degree in public administration or criminal justice administration would very likely be ideal; that person certainly would be preferable, all else being equal, to someone whose degree is in music or physics. Because police administration is indeed a professional task requiring learned skills, the chief's educational background should be professionally oriented, based on theoretical knowledge that can be applied to real-world situations. Education should give the chief a conceptual framework to use in a pragmatic sense for system building.

It is not unlikely that in the not too distant future many chiefs of police will be required to hold a master's degree in either public administration or criminal justice administration. As police problems become more complex in the dynamic societal milieu, it will become essential that police chiefs be selected on the basis of their capabilities to solve problems that impact on government in general and police departments in particular.

One need only observe the changing educational requirements in school systems over the last half century to realize the inevitability of higher police educational requirements. The police service is bound to professionalize in much the same way that public education has professionalized. Few school superintendents today have less than a master's degree; many have their doctorates. Large numbers of teachers have master's and doctor's degrees; in the 1920s, by contrast, teachers were not required to have even a baccalaureate degree, and many of them became school principals and superintendents.

Educational requirements in public school systems rose largely because of public demand for better education. Exactly the same situation prevails in the police service today; the public is demanding more and better police service. As a result of the rapid rise in crime over the last several years, the public has become keenly aware of and extremely sensitive to police inadequacies. As a result the public is demanding more for the higher tax dollar it is paying for police services. Through the Law Enforcement Education Program of the Law Enforcement Assistance Administration, the public has, in effect, said to the police, "We are so concerned about crime and about problems within our police departments that we are willing to spend millions upon millions of dollars to help you get an education and to professionalize yourselves; now we want something in return for our investment in you, and that something is improved police services." This demand for improvement cannot be realized, as it ultimately must be realized in a political sense, without the insertion of professional police administrators into police systems. The public is supporting police services to a much greater degree than it ever has before. Police professionalization is right around the corner. It will not be accomplished, however, until there is an improvement in police leadership.

The single most important element for such improvement is that education be used as a basic criterion for selecting police chiefs. Although the use of such a criterion will inevitably narrow the field of choice and eliminate many capable people from consideration, the hard fact remains that the police chief's job is the single most important, and by far the most difficult, job in the department. To deal successfully with the myriad problems a police chief faces and to understand the nuances of the many system variables a police chief confronts is a truly professional task requiring considerable skill and know-how not ordinarily the by-product of experience and innate ability alone.

In order to be successful, police chiefs must learn how to be successful through the use of refined management techniques which academic programs are designed to teach. Without such an academic background, it is virtually impossible for any person, regardless of intelligence and organizational dedication, to succeed totally as a police chief. The college degree is basic. It is a must, and all police chiefs should have it.

By no means is education the only selection criterion, however. The baccalaureate degree serves only as evidence that a person has successfully completed an educational apprenticeship and has been exposed for a certain period of time to new ideas and innovative systems of thinking. Many college graduates lack the common sense to come in out of the rain; despite their well-rounded academic backgrounds, they lack the ability to apply what they have learned in the professional environments in which they work. This is true in all fields of endeavor, even in academic institutions, which are charged with the responsibility of teaching students and transmitting culture.

As one former police official, a Ph.D. who retired from police service to become a full professor at a prestigious Midwestern university, once remarked, "If half the Ph.D.'s at the university stepped off campus, they'd be killed." What he was saying, in effect, was that there is no positive correlation between a person's knowledge and ability. What the police service today needs is police chiefs who know *what to do* and *how to do it*. Being able to work effectively with the realities of life is what police officers often refer to as *having street sense*. Police chiefs need something more; they need an education to know *what to do* from a theoretical perspective and *organization sense* to know *how to do it* from a pragmatic perspective. If they hold seven degrees and lack organization sense, they are destined for failure.

Organization sense is a nebulous quality, but basically it has five primary components:

1. value system;

2. personality;

3. intelligence;

4. work habits; and

5. ability.

Because all candidates for police chief positions must possess organization sense in addition to education in order to be actively considered for appointment, we shall consider briefly each of these five primary components.

Value system   The value system a chief brings to the job is very important because it provides relevant inputs to the chief's organization sense. The chief must be honest and have a firm moral and ethical base, using morality and ethics as tools fundamental to the process of managing. The chief's value system must include a full commitment to the principles and processes of democracy. In addition, the chief must be willing to administer the police organization in keeping with the governmental doctrine of separation of powers, recognizing that the police department is a subsystem of the executive branch of government and demonstrating responsiveness to the community by maintaining a close relationship with elected and appointed officials.

No longer can police chiefs isolate themselves and their departments from public scrutiny. Today's police chiefs must work within the parameters of the law and the procedural guidelines established by the courts. They must do this by nature and through an almost innate sense of responsibility. They must be able to work naturally within the confines of ethical, moral, and legal constraints. In short, police chiefs must be good persons to begin with.

Personality   The chief's personality, the outward manifestation of inner self, is another essential input to organization sense. A chief must be able to get along well with people both socially and officially. The chief's demeanor, bearing, and outward appearance should command immediate respect and even admiration. In short, a police chief should have charismatic qualities of leadership which are readily identifiable and which are consistently demonstrated in all interpersonal dealings.

Intelligence   Intelligence is the capacity for understanding. All police chiefs must have this fundamental quality if they are to be successful in managing the many thousands of variables that constantly impact on the police system. A chief who lacks the capacity for understanding these variables and their relative significance in the management process will be unable to deal realistically and productively with the dynamic forces that come into play in organization development. There is no better way to throw a system into chaos than to appoint a chief administrator who is unable to understand how to best bring all subsystems of an organization together for the purpose of meeting goals and objectives.

Work habits   Because the position of chief of police is so complex and demanding and because system management is so dependent on intensive and continuing system supervision, chiefs must have good work habits as a part of their organization sense—a strong motivational predisposition to work every day in relentless fashion toward system improvement. Too many chiefs retire into their jobs and envision their appointments as being little more than ceremonial in nature; nothing could be further from the reality of their responsibilities. A complete dedication to the department and an unceasing willingness to work hard to improve it are essential ingredients that all chiefs must bring to the job.

Ability The fifth component of organization sense is ability. Whereas intelligence is the capacity for understanding, ability is the capacity for putting understanding to work. If a chief has a highly refined value system, a cordial personality, keen innate intelligence, and good work habits, but lacks the ability to put these to work in administering the department, the chief's failure in developing a sound organization is predictable. Ability is an elusive quality that is difficult to define, but it is of paramount importance in selecting a chief.

SELECTING A NEW POLICE CHIEF

Any community looking for a new police chief should look for a person who possesses organization sense, and its national search and selection processes should be geared toward that end. Although it is a relatively easy matter to conduct a national search, the actual selection process is somewhat more complicated. How does a city or town go about selecting a chief? What steps must be taken to find the right person?

Nationwide search The nationwide search for a chief is, of course, the first step. Initially, candidates should be requested to submit their personal resumes to the appointing authority. The advertisement itself should provide as much detail as possible about the job and its requirements. A sample advertisement appears in Fig. 6.1.

The advertisement sets the stage for attracting large numbers of candidates who meet minimum standards. It also serves to eliminate unqualified candidates from consideration, i.e., those persons who have no police experience. Unless legal requirements specifically stipulate that a prospective chief must be selected from among officers who have achieved a certain rank level, the advertisement should not precisely define what police experience is required.

The personal resumes and cover letters requested in the advertisement provide an excellent opportunity for the appointing authority to determine the candidates' abilities to express themselves in writing. Because written communication is so vital to the directing process, the candidates' writing ability is a primary qualifying factor.

It can therefore be anticipated that any number of candidates will be disqualified from consideration on the basis of their resumes and cover letters. Candidates who fail to provide five personal and five credit references as requested in the advertisement should also be disqualified; police chiefs must be able to take directions as well as give them. Candidates who fail to meet other requirements specified in the advertisement will also be eliminated at this stage in the selection process.

CHIEF OF POLICE
Central City, Idaho

Central City, Idaho, an urban community of 55,000 located close to the geographical center of the state, is seeking a professional police administrator to fill a vacancy created by the retirement of its present chief of police. The department consists of 87 sworn officers and 16 civilian personnel and works from a budget base of $1,850,000. Minimum qualifications include: working experience as a police officer; baccalaureate degree from an accredited college or university in business, public, police, or criminal justice administration; an unblemished record of integrity; and excellent health. All applicants must agree to have their backgrounds thoroughly scrutinized through investigation. Annual salary ranges from $24,700 to $33,400, depending on qualifications. Send resume, cover letter describing your experience, and five personal and five credit references no later than August 15th to D. Ignatius Driscoll, City Manager, Central City.

Central City is an Equal Opportunity Employer

Fig. 6.1. Model advertisement for police chief's position.

Evaluate applications The next step in the selection process is to thoroughly review and evaluate all remaining resumes. These remaining resumes should then be ranked from 1 to an arbitrary number established by the appointing authority. All disqualified candidates should be written letters which express appreciation for their interest in the position and which inform them as tactfully as possible that they have been disqualified from consideration. All remaining candidates should be contacted by letter and informed that they are among those being actively considered for the position.

Narrow the field At this stage in the selection process, the appointing authority has a number of alternatives. These are, in descending order of viability:

1. Hire a nationally recognized police management consulting organization, such as the International Association of Chiefs of Police or McCann Associates, to conduct written and oral board examinations to all remaining candidates, with results given to the appointing authority and candidates ranked first to last in order of preference. This procedure should be followed by personal interviews with each candidate not disqualified by the written and oral board examinations; these interviews should be conducted by the appointing authority, who will have the final say in the selection process. After these interviews have been completed, the appointing authority should choose and rank in order of qualifications three individuals for final consideration.

2. Administer a written examination devised and corrected by a local police management consulting firm, a local police management consultant, a professor recognized as an authority in the field of police personnel administration, a personnel management consulting firm, or a personnel management consultant. Oral board examinations should be given to all candidates not disqualified by the written examination; these may be administered by either the same person or firm that conducted the written examination or locally available professional law enforcement and personnel experts. All candidates not disqualified by the oral board examination should be personally interviewed by the appointing authority, who should choose and rank in order of qualifications three individuals for final consideration.

3. Conduct a written examination devised and corrected by the appointing authority. Administer oral board examinations for all candidates not disqualified by the written examination, using the services of local professional law enforcement and personnel experts. All candidates who pass both written and oral examining procedures should be personally interviewed by the appointing authority, who should select and rank in order of qualifications the top three for final consideration.

4. Use an oral board consisting of local professional police and personnel authorities as the only qualifying examining procedure and provide personal interviews conducted by the appointing authority for all candidates passing the oral board examinations, with the top three candidates ranked in order of qualifications for final consideration.

5. Make provisions for the appointing authority to interview all candidates who have been chosen as a result of resume review and evaluation,

singling out the three most qualified candidates for final consideration in order of best to least qualified.

In cities and towns constrained by civil service regulations and examining procedures affecting the selection of a chief, one of the processes described above should be chosen, if possible, and adjusted to local regulations and procedures. In Massachusetts, for example, many cities and towns are forced by law to select their police chiefs on the basis of a written examination conducted by the state. The results of a given examination are published and presented to the appointing authority, who *must* select a police chief from among the top three qualifiers. Many appointing authorities, to avoid political complications and community criticism, feel obliged to appoint the top person on the list. Therefore, many Massachusetts chiefs are chosen solely on the basis of a paper-and-pencil test. Nonetheless, the appointing authority could re-examine the three candidates and interview them as suggested above, selecting the best of the three for the job.

Conduct background investigations   Once three candidates have been selected through interview with the appointing authority and ranked from best to least qualified, thorough and complete background investigations should be conducted on each. Aside from the fact that most police departments lack the personnel resources to conduct such investigations, it is important to understand that these investigations should not be conducted by the department for which a chief is being sought. Other than to take the candidates' fingerprints and routinely process them through the FBI to determine whether criminal records exist, the local police department should not be involved.

Because the three candidates will probably reside in different areas of the country, the investigation of their backgrounds poses some real problems. Although some large police departments are equipped to conduct background investigations and are willing to do so on request, consideration must be given to the possibility that a background investigation on a local candidate being considered for a chief's position elsewhere might be influenced either for or against the candidate.

In order to ensure absolute objectivity, background investigations must be conducted by one of many private, independent investigative agencies. The process is complicated by the fact that because a candidate may have lived in a number of communities, the person's activities in each of these communities must be checked. In addition, a national company such as the Retail Credit Corporation should be engaged to run credit checks in all communities in which a candidate lived after age 21. The credit company chosen should be furnished with the credit references supplied by the three candidates and requested to conduct *full* credit investigations.

Additionally, a national private investigative organization, such as Burns or Pinkerton, should be retained locally to coordinate all aspects of the investigations to be conducted nationally. The private investigative agency selected should be given copies of the candidates' resumes. Application forms devised by the appointing authority and filled out by each candidate prior to interview should also be forwarded to the agency coordinating the investigations.

The investigative agency should be charged with the specific responsibilities listed below and requested to submit reports to the appointing authority on each aspect of its investigation.

1. Interview three of the candidate's five personal references, focusing on the applicant's personal integrity, intelligence, mental maturity, emotional stability, personality, values, work habits, background, education, experience, drinking habits, family relationships, known weaknesses, personal problems, financial status, questionable associates, ability to get along well with people, and performance as a police officer. Questions should be asked about each of these traits or characteristics. Each person interviewed should be asked whether or not he or she would recommend the candidate for a police chief's position. In addition, each reference should be requested to name two people who know the candidate well. These references are called *throw-offs.*

2. Interview at least four of the throw-off references obtained, asking the same questions asked listed references. Each throw-off reference should be asked to name two people who know the candidate well.

3. Interview four of the eight people named by the throw-off references, with the same questions asked.

4. Interview the registrar of the college or university from which the candidate graduated to determine if the candidate has a baccalaureate degree as required and to get a photostatic copy of the candidate's academic record, if this is available. If the investigator is unable to get this information or this record, the candidate should be requested to ask the registrar to forward to the appointing authority a copy of the transcript, stamped with the college or university seal.

5. Follow the procedure above for all colleges or universities or postgraduate institutions the candidate may have attended.

6. If possible, conduct interviews with the candidate's immediate supervisor and at least three fellow employees at the last two places the candidate was employed. All of the questions covered in the interviews with listed and throw-off references should be asked.

7. Interview at least three people from the neighborhood in which the candidate resides, asking each to name two people who know the candidate well.

8. Interview thoroughly three of the six throw-off references obtained from the neighbors.

9. Check police and court records in each community in which the candidate has resided since the age of 17 to determine if the candidate has a criminal record and, if so, what it consists of. State records should also be checked.

Once this procedure has been completed, the investigative agency should file its reports with the appointing authority. If the agency develops what would appear to be negative information on a candidate, it should be permitted to expand the investigation beyond the limits described above in order to either confirm or disprove negative allegations. Such an expanded investigation might consist of several more interviews with throw-offs as well as the accumulation of additional documentary information about the candidate.

When all three background investigations have been completed and all reports are in, the appointing authority will have sufficient information with which to make a final decision in the selection process and appoint the new chief.

A word of caution, however, is in order. The appointing authority should be aware that many police officers make numerous enemies during their careers. Investigations of police chief candidates, therefore, are particularly sensitive and must be conducted by senior investigative personnel thoroughly experienced in conducting background investigations. People's negative opinions about a given candidate should be included in the reports submitted to the appointing authority. This procedure is not ordinarily followed in most investigations, which are usually designed to uncover only information of evidentiary value. All negative opinions should be considered by the appointing authority in light of their source and weighed according to their seriousness. If, for example, a neighbor refuses to recommend a candidate solely on the basis of the latter's noisy children, this type of input should not be considered.

A candidate should be disqualified from consideration only if a general pattern of negative reaction is reported. If 10 of 21 people interviewed indicate that the candidate has a drinking problem, this should be considered a pattern. If, on the other hand, 1 of the 21 provides what would seem to be positive proof that a married candidate is unfaithful to his or her spouse, this single input, if substantiated by further investigation, should be considered a disqualifying factor. Although a community can adjust to a police chief's noisy children, if in fact they are, it does not need to invite the kind of problem that could be created by family difficulties to which the chief has been unable to adjust in the past. The appointing authority must use a considerable degree of discretion in evaluating all background investigative reports and weigh carefully all factors relating to each candidate before making a final decision.

Announce the appointment Once the final decision is made, all unsuccessful candidates who were examined and/or interviewed for the job should be informed by personal letter that they have been disqualified. The letters should be carefully constructed and express thanks for the applicants' interest, time, and effort. These letters should be mailed *after* the successful candidate has provided written acceptance of the position, but *before* a public announcement has been made. The importance of following this procedure exactly cannot be overemphasized. Should the successful candidate later decide not to take the position after all, the appointing authority will want to select one of the previously disqualified candidates.

INITIAL RESPONSIBILITIES OF THE NEW POLICE CHIEF

Once appointed and sworn in, the new police chief must immediately become familiar with the department and its personnel. To do this, the chief must be available on an informal basis to as many people within the organization as possible. The appointing authority can pave the way by initially introducing the chief to command-level personnel, who in turn can introduce the chief to supervisory, operational, and civilian personnel.

Although all this may seem unimportant to you, the first impression the new chief makes is very likely to be a lasting impression. All new chiefs should therefore be cordial and friendly, making every possible effort to create an honest impression of being open, receptive, and concerned about the people within their commands. This should be a genuine effort inspired by a real interest in the personnel of their departments.

New chiefs should make no changes in their organizations for at least six months, after having had the opportunity to examine fully every aspect of the way their departments function. They should also make it known that there will be no immediate changes in their organizations, thereby not immediately providing any input to which there could be any negative reaction. Everything they do during their first six months should be directed toward creating a positive impression on everyone with whom they come in contact. Thus they will make no attempt to engage in planning, organizing, staffing, and system building and will exercise their directing and controlling functions only minimally. However, they should attempt to evaluate their personnel, particularly at the command and supervisory levels, in terms of their capabilities to work within a systems-oriented organization. Changes that they inevitably and ultimately make should be made very gradually after they have had an opportunity to review all departmental problems.

During the first six months, new chiefs should make large blocks of time available for scrutinizing all facets of departmental operational and staff functions. In doing so, they must be observers, but never participants. They must ask many questions and become interested listeners. They should spend a great amount of time accompanying operational personnel on their assignments and at the same time exercise considerable caution not to interfere with or criticize their work. This will give new police chiefs a chance to not only identify problems, but also get to know their police officers on a personal basis and demonstrate an interest in them and in the difficulties they face in their work. They can also dispel any concerns their officers might have about them and about the new administration. This groundwork will greatly facilitate later communications within the department and will provide initial feedback on organizational weaknesses that can eventually be translated into new inputs for system change.

New police chiefs should, as soon as possible after their appointments, familiarize themselves with their communities—the geographical layout, streets, demographic characteristics, and people. New chiefs should respond willingly to invitations to speak to local service clubs, fraternal organizations, business clubs, and church groups. They should make the effort to introduce themselves to all city or town officials and department heads, expressing eagerness to cooperate with them and to assist them in every way possible. In short, new chiefs should become a part of their new communities as soon as they can and work diligently to become accepted and to gain community support. By their manner and demeanor, they should attempt to foster a professional police image and should seek to be recognized as competent police leaders who are concerned about their communities and who want to provide them with the best possible police services.

After the first six months have passed and the new chiefs have had a chance to examine their organizations fully, they should take approximately one month to devise a working plan for their efforts to develop their organizations into viable systems. The plan should provide for *very gradual change* and should be developed on the premise that *all* initial inputs *must* be designed to create positive reactions among departmental personnel. When change comes, as it inevitably must, it should come slowly and should be initially well received. System inputs that are expected to create negative reactions must be very carefully and gradually inserted only after the chief has achieved full acceptance by the community and by the department.

However, in departments with severe problems and ineffective police output, a new police chief must move on problems much more quickly and must introduce a large amount of new input to effect change almost immediately. It can be anticipated that personnel in a department that has long been functioning very poorly will react negatively to *any* attempt, regardless of when it comes, to effect positive change. In such departments new chiefs must be willing to make massive changes right away and to deal with the consequences of such actions.

They will not be successful in this effort, however, if they do not have the full backing of the appointing authority and the political leadership of the community. In many communities the political leadership is so poor and so unreceptive to the public interest that a new police chief, no matter how well intentioned and highly skilled, could never succeed in developing a police organization capable of delivering high levels of police service. This is an unfortunate fact of life which bears heavily on police problems and which precludes the development of viable police agencies. The only advice for a new police chief forced to work under such circumstances would be to look for another job with all due speed and deliberation.

There is no way that a poor police department can be improved if the political leadership of the community is not fully supportive of the effort. There are many highly skilled but unsuccessful chiefs of police today working within the confines of poor political systems. But if the political system of the community is a good one and the police department is functioning properly, or nearly properly, at the time of the new chief's arrival, there is no way that a professional police administrator, working from a systems perspective, cannot be successful in developing a finely honed, totally responsive organization.

If a police department is relatively large and serves a population of 25,000 people or more, some consideration should be given to employing a police management consulting organization to conduct a full management study of the department, with on-site work to be completed prior to the new chief's appointment. Many police management consultants finish on-site work in approximately three months and furnish a comprehensive, written report six months later. This report provides an objective evaluation of the department at about the time the new chief will be ready to devise a plan for departmental improvement. Such an objective report provides additional feedback on the success of departmental output and concrete recommendations for improving departmental input. The consultant's report can be used as a rationale for actions that might precipitate negative reaction and significantly reduce the effects of the personal blame the new chief might otherwise have to take for making such changes. The chief can simply point to the consulting organization and say, "I am making this change because it was recommended by impartial, objective police management experts who believed that such action is necessary."

If a police department, regardless of its size, is functioning poorly, a management study conducted prior to the time a new chief takes office is an absolute must. It will provide not only feedback that the new chief might never become aware of, but also an organizational framework for departmental improvement that otherwise might take months to conceive. The management study should be looked on as an aid to assist in turning a poor situation into a good one. The expense of the study will be more than returned to the community in the form of improved police services.

A CHIEF'S DAY-TO-DAY TASKS

So far we have outlined the police chief's seven preliminary organizing tasks, stressed the importance of the six basic management functions, described the personal and professional qualities and characteristics the chief brings to the job, outlined the selection procedures used in finding a new chief, and defined a new chief's initial responsibilities in taking over the administrative reins of a police department. The only consideration left to discuss is what a police chief does in meeting everyday responsibilities.

The chief's main job on a day-to-day basis is managing the police department through other people. The chief's major day-to-day functions are *direction, coordination,* and *control. Direction* and *control* differ significantly from the chief's management functions of *directing*

and *controlling.* The former are activities that all chiefs personally perform in dealing with departmental staff and with command-level officers within their spans of control. The latter are two of six basic police
management functions used throughout the organization to manage the
entire department in closed-loop fashion from a systems perspective.
The direction and coordination functions performed by the chief on a
day-to-day basis are merely two of many inputs to the directing process. Likewise, the chief's control function as performed on a day-to-
day basis is but one of many inputs to the controlling process. Although
day-to-day *direction, coordination,* and *control* are only three of many
inputs to the directing and controlling processes, they are three extremely important inputs and are essential to good management.

Chiefs' major day-to-day functions, therefore, are the *direction*
of staff and command-level personnel within their spans of control, the
coordination of their efforts for organizational productivity, and the
continuing *control* over their activities to ensure quality work output.
Figure 6.2, an upper-level organization chart, shows the people with
whom and the functions with which the chief must deal on an everyday
basis. As shown in Fig. 6.2, the chief's span of control encompasses the
captain in charge of Inspections, the captain in charge of Internal Affairs, the lieutenant in charge of Special Staff, the captain in charge of
the Administration Bureau, the captain in charge of the Operations
Bureau, and the captain in charge of the Auxiliary Services Bureau.

The chief, then, is responsible for *directing, coordinating,* and *controlling* the activities of only six people. By delegating to them the authority to perform the six basic police management functions and by
insisting that they use their authority wisely and perform their functions well, the chief can be assured that the organization will work
effectively toward the accomplishment of its goals and objectives.

A chief's ultimate success may be measured in terms of effectiveness in performing the major day-to-day functions. If a police chief
concentrates on performing these functions well and if the people in
the chief's span of control carry out their responsibilities fully from a
systems standpoint, a chief should have very little else to do in managing the department. If, on the other hand, the chief should wander from
these major day-to-day functions and become personally involved in
activities at lower organizational levels, the department will soon be in
turmoil and the chief will discover that involvement at lower levels is
counterproductive. For purposes of command, a police chief must remain at the upper level of the organization and delegate authority for
the accomplishment of tasks. Those in the chief's span of control will
in turn delegate their authority to people in lower departmental levels

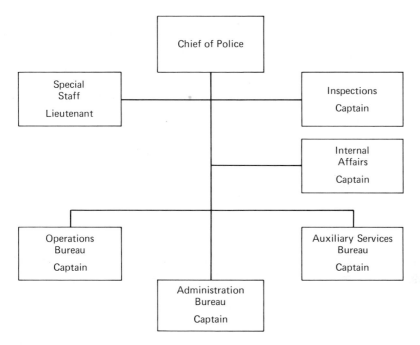

Fig. 6.2. Upper-level organization chart.

Aside from issuing directives which are forwarded downward through the chain of command, chiefs should never become involved in giving orders or in providing personal direction to personnel other than those who report directly to them. This does not mean that chiefs should not informally establish a continuing relationship with personnel at lower levels. Such informal relationships are essential for purposes of communication and feedback and provide them with information that they need in order to be fully apprised of organizational problems. Under no circumstances should police chiefs ever go outside of the chain of command to issue direct orders to personnel at lower levels; those command-level officers within their spans of control exist for this purpose, and they must make full use of them to accomplish their goals and objectives.

Police chiefs do this on a day-to-day basis by *directing, coordinating,* and *controlling* their efforts, being ever mindful that subordinates need the authority, delegated by the police chief, to make decisions and to solve problems within their respective, specialized areas of command. By holding subordinates accountable for their actions and by providing continual supervision over their activities, chiefs should have very little difficulty in managing their organizations.

This presupposes, of course, that officers assigned to staff and command-level functions are capable of meeting their responsibilities. Such is not always the case. Police chiefs are severely constrained in their efforts to meet goals and objectives if the officers who report to them are incapable of doing their jobs, if they have no loyalty to them personally, or if they have difficulties in meeting their responsibilities. Unfortunately, many capable police chiefs are saddled with staff and command-level officers who are products of police departments never administered from the systems perspective. In such cases police chiefs must make every effort to train their top-level officers to not only understand the systems approach, but also apply systems methods to their own managerial responsibilities. They must also attempt to gain their respect and loyalty by working closely with them, by helping them in whatever way possible to meet their obligations, and by being sensitive to and concerned with their own personal and professional problems.

The development of close ties between police chiefs and the people who work directly for them is essential to organizational stability. These top-level administrators are, in a very real sense, the most useful tools a police chief has to work with in developing a viable organization. It is they who take the authority the chief gives them and redistribute it throughout the police department. It is they who provide the direction and solve the problems within their respective commands and staff-components. It is they who evaluate feedback and provide new input for organizational improvement. They are, therefore, the most essential elements in the management process; management cannot exist without them. The chief cannot be successful if they are not successful. The chief is totally dependent on them. It behooves the chief, therefore, to develop them professionally and provide them with guidance and encouragement in their work. Even in departments that are professionally staffed at high levels, this is necessary. In fact, this *is* the chief's job.

Because chiefs have only a few people reporting directly to them, it is a relatively easy matter to maintain a relationship with them. Chiefs should meet with them individually on a frequent, periodic basis to provide them with *direction;* they should also meet with them frequently and periodically as a group for purposes of organizational *coordination;* and finally, they should require frequent and periodic written reports from each of them so as to review their accomplishments and thereby more closely *control* their activities. These meetings and reports will serve as vehicles for communication between the chief and the chief's top-level administrators. They will provide an appreciation of departmental problems and give the chief an opportunity to work with staff and command-level personnel toward problem solutions.

As police chiefs go about performing their day-to-day functions of *direction, coordination,* and *control,* they must be ever cognizant that they are fully responsible for the implementation of their seven preliminary organizing tasks and their six basic police management functions. Although the importance of these tasks and functions demands that chiefs be involved personally in their implementation, they should be aware of the necessity not to neglect their day-to-day functions. Chiefs can, of course, delegate authority for the performance of preliminary organizing tasks and basic police management functions. Chiefs cannot delegate authority, except when ill and during vacation periods, for the performance of their day-to-day functions of *direction, coordination,* and *control.* These functions are uniquely the chiefs' and are the only devices they have with which to meet their total responsibilities.

Extreme caution should therefore be exercised in not delegating the authority for the performance of day-to-day functions. The temptation to bring in an assistant at a command-level rank to whom the authority for day-to-day functions can be delegated will be great. If police chiefs succumb to such a temptation, they will discover to their regret that there is no better way to lose control of their organization. In theory the assistant's position might appear to be useful; in practice, it will prove to be counterproductive to organizational cohesiveness at the top level of the organization and will very likely create a morale problem throughout the department. An assistant such as the one described here can rise to a level of great power within any organization and subjectively filter information intended for the chief administrator, greatly distorting it. The assistant may also be able to control access to a chief of police, thereby angering subordinates and isolating the chief.

Assistants with power create a superficial layer in the organizational hierarchy and can assume an unhealthy amount of authority. One need only examine the power roles played by presidential assistants John Erlichmann and H.R. Haldeman in the demise of the administration of Richard M. Nixon to appreciate the extent to which powerful assistants can contribute to the ruination of a system. Police chiefs must guard against being placed in positions of weakness by not appointing assistants to perform their day-to-day functions. Those chiefs who do not follow this basic tenet of good management must be ready to accept the consequences of their actions and assume full responsibility for the chaos they will assuredly create. The assistant who is given power cannot be totally blamed for abusing it. Appointed to an assistantship by a chief who was either insecure or felt overworked, the assistant grows in power and authority. As Townsend notes, "Instead of giving pieces of his job to other line officers, or carving out a whole job and giving it to someone to run with, he hired an assistant-to, and immediately became much less effective than he was when he was just overworked."[1]

Finally, in carrying out day-to-day functions, the chief of police must be a decision maker. McGregor points out that "it is a major function of the top executive to take on his own shoulders the responsibility for resolving the uncertainties that are always involved in important decisions."[2] The chief who procrastinates on tough decisions will always be plagued with problems both internally and externally. Chiefs who fail to make decisions will find that their support from their police officers and the public will quickly dissipate and that their controlling function will be severely impaired. Failure to make decisions can have far-reaching ramifications and ultimately result in total loss of control manifested by police misconduct and departmental corruption. The President's Commission on Campus Unrest noted that "if the police are to maintain the respect and support of the public, they must deal openly and forcefully with misconduct within their own ranks whenever it occurs."[3] This observation would appear to be a gross oversimplification that is symptomatic of management problems that run very deep and that reflect patterns of indecisive police leadership. When a police system has degenerated to that point where corruption and misconduct become accepted system outputs, the chief of police must accept full responsibility for not having made hard decisions with respect to the controlling process. Being decisive and making difficult decisions on every problem that surfaces is an extremely important part of a police chief's job.

SUMMARY

The police chief's job is the most important job in the police department. This difficult and trying job requires tremendous skill, understanding, and background. To be successful, police chiefs must *know* what they are about in theoretical terms and understand how to *deal* with what they are about in pragmatic terms. They must know how to apply the principles of organization and management by using the talents of their immediate subordinates, whose activities they must direct, coordinate, and control. Chiefs must be richly endowed with personal characteristics and traits that make them truly *professional* in every respect. In addition, they must be carefully selected and fully supported. Their organizations will reflect them, their ideals, and their commitment to excellence. The goals and objectives of their police departments will be realized only if all of their efforts are directed toward that realization.

DISCUSSION QUESTIONS

1. What qualities do you think the ideal police chief should have?

2. Should a police chief be held accountable for everything that happens within the police department?

3. Do you think that it is necessary for a police chief to have a specialized degree in police administration, public administration, or criminal justice? Why?

4. Which is the most important of the six primary components of *organization sense*? Which is the least important?

5. Do you agree with us that a police chief should not be chosen from within the department? Why?

6. Why is a police chief's value system so important?

7. Why should background investigations be conducted on prospective police chief candidates?

8. If you were a newly appointed police chief, what ten things would you do first on beginning your new job? What would you be careful *not* to do?

9. Discuss a police chief's major day-to-day functions. How do these differ from the six basic police management functions?

10. What consequences might result from a police chief's delegating authority to an assistant to perform the chief's day-to-day functions?

REFERENCES

1. R. Townsend, *Up the Organization* (New York: Knopf, 1970), p. 23.

2. D. McGregor, *Leadership and Motivation* (Cambridge, Mass.: MIT Press, 1966), p. 67.

3. President's Commission on Campus Unrest, *Report of the President's Commission on Campus Unrest* (Chicago: Commerce Clearing House, 1970), p. 5/8.

PART III
THE HUMAN PERSPECTIVE

The three chapters in Part III discuss the human, or behavioral, perspective of police administration. The importance of this behavioral approach was recognized several decades ago by business and industrial managers who observed that people at work do not always produce with machinelike regularity and efficiency. Since that revelation, management has come increasingly to be viewed as a people-oriented function in terms of both managers and those managed. Management is often now described as the business of getting things done through other people. Certainly this description of management in general closely fits the tasks and purposes of police administration.

In Chapter 7 the behavior of individuals in organizations is discussed. The primary aspects of organizational behavior presented in this chapter are attitudes, roles, self-concept, motivation, perception, and communication. We attempt to provide some clues for understanding why people behave as they do in organized settings. Such understanding can be very helpful to the manager charged with the responsibility for directing and controlling people at work.

Chapter 8 addresses organizational behavior in terms of groups rather than individuals. The approach in this chapter is basically sociological, as compared with the more nearly psychological discussion of individual behavior. The discussion in this chapter supplements that of the previous one, so that taken together Chapters 7 and 8 should provide considerable insight into the behavior of people in organizations.

Chapter 9 discusses leadership, one of the most critical and elusive elements in management. The differences between management and leadership are sketched; although the two concepts are closely related, we stress that they are not identical. A number of functions, styles, and theories of leadership are presented, although it is emphasized that the intangible quality of leadership makes it difficult to analyze and categorize. Unfortunately, clear instructions for developing leadership talents have not yet been, and in fact are unlikely ever to be, discovered.

CHAPTER 7
THE INDIVIDUAL IN THE
POLICE ORGANIZATION

LEARNING OBJECTIVES

1. Explain why an understanding of human behavior is important for the police manager.

2. Characterize human behavior as either an open or a closed system and explain your reasoning.

3. Identify two interdependent subsystems of the individual.

4. Cite the six major aspects of organizational behavior.

5. Define attitudes.

6. Characterize the relationship between attitudes and behavior.

7. Cite several factors influential in the development of attitudes.

8. Explain why attitudes are so difficult to change.

9. Differentiate between behavior modification and sensitivity education.

10. Identify in general terms the number of roles that people play.

11. Characterize the agreement among people about how similar roles are played.

12. Compare the degree of effect on behavior of different roles (for example, the influence on behavior of the sex role as compared to a club membership role).

13. Identify the conforming influences that roles exert on behavior.

14. Cite the relationship among roles, the dominant culture, and subcultures.

15. Identify those officials in our society who have the responsibility for dealing with role conflicts.

16. Explain why the police manager must establish policy that defines the organization's expectations of the police role.

17. Describe the process by which police-role expectations may be established by a subculture.

18. Define self-concept.

19. Describe the relationship between self-concept and ideal self-concept.

20. Characterize the relationship between self-concept and behavior.

21. Describe the effect that inaccurate perception can have on self-concept.

22. Describe the effect that behavior deficiencies can have on self-concept.

23. Differentiate among the three general models of motivational systems.

24. Cite some problems often associated with force and coercion motivation.

25. Cite the findings of the Hawthorne studies.

26. Describe Maslow's hierarchy of needs.

27. Describe the multiple motivational influences of money.

28. Define the nonmodel of human behavior.

29. State the cause of the difference between the way individuals see things and the way things really are.

30. Describe the influence of physiological differences on perception.

31. Describe the influence of learning on perception.

32. Cite the influences of attitudes, roles, self-concepts, and motivation on perception.

33. Describe the influence on perception of the selection process.

34. Describe the role of feedback in perception.

35. Identify the medium through which a police manager conducts day-to-day functions.

36. Define communication.

37. Cite three varieties of communication.

38. Differentiate between one- and two-way communication.

39. Describe the role of feedback in communication.

40. State the only advantage of one-way communication.

41. Compare one- and two-way communication in terms of effectiveness and frequency of use.

42. Cite the advantages and disadvantages of written and oral messages.

43. Cite the portion of a police officer's time spent communicating.

44. Identify the individual the police manager must first come to understand.

This chapter introduces the fundamentals of human behavior in organizational settings. Factors that mold and inspire individual behavior and affect interaction between and among individuals will be discussed.

An understanding of human behavior is extremely important for police managers because every aspect of organization and management involves people. Police managers must understand and successfully deal with the behavior of their clientele (citizens), their subordinates, their peers, their superiors, and most important, themselves. Furthermore, they must influence the behavior of others while at the same time controlling their own.

Human behavior is the most intricate and involved input to the management process. There are innumerable explanations of human behavior. Most people make subjective judgments all the time as to why other people behave in given circumstances as they do. People tend to perceive what others do and say from their own peculiar perspectives, explaining away motivational influences in keeping with their own unique modes of behavior. Unless they are well grounded in behavioral theory, individuals' subjective evaluations of what other people do and say are very likely to be erroneous. Even psychiatrists, who are professionals in the study of human behavior, often have difficulty interpreting it. For nonprofessionals, problems of interpretation become even more difficult.

This chapter, then, is not intended to provide comprehensive understanding of human behavior. Rather, we will provide little more than a *basic* overview of the subject matter. Even we, whose combined experience in observing human behavior in police organizations exceeds 20 years, approach the subject with considerable humility and no small amount of trepidation. Defining human behavior in police organizations is a difficult task that cannot be fully accomplished; human behavior is too dynamic a force to lend itself easily to description. This presentation, therefore, will be limited to what we believe to be the *most important* factors that impact on human behavior in organizations. Discussion of these factors will be based on the premise that behavior, as an open system, is influenced by all kinds of outside environmental forces.

THE INDIVIDUAL AS A SUBSYSTEM

The individual is the basic subsystem of the organization. In structural terms, individuals are grouped to form bureaus, staffs, divisions, units, squads, and teams, which together make up the *formal organization.* In work-flow terms, individuals do the work, pass the information, and do the communicating in the organization. Individuals also create *informal* groups, which combine to form a powerful *informal organization.* It is individuals who provide the leadership and make the decisions.

As pointed out in Chapter 2, an individual consists of numerous interdependent subsystems, each of which may be considered a system in and of itself. In physiological terms, an individual has muscular, skeletal, nervous, sexual, digestive, circulatory, and respiratory systems; in psychological terms, emotional, value, ethical, moral, religious, and motivational systems. Each of these interdependent systems is a subsystem of the whole individual, and each works in concert with the others to influence the individual's behavior.

In addition to internal-subsystem influences, the individual is influenced by external subsystems and systems of which he or she is a part— the governmental system, the political system, the religious system, the family system, and the organizational work system. The dynamic interdependence between human and organizational systems accounts in large part for the complexities of human behavior.

There are so many interdependent variables involved in the process of human behavior that it is virtually impossible to understand them all and to predict accurately how they will impact on one another; voluminous research conducted on this subject by medical and social scientists has failed to reduce human behavior to an exact science. However, the vast resources of the academic disciplines of physiology, psychology, and sociology, when considered in terms of the systems perspective and as applied to the organizational setting, provide some substantial and worthwhile insight to human behavior. Our discussion of human behavior, borrowed from these disciplines, will focus on the following six major aspects of organizational behavior:

1. attitudes;

2. roles;

3. self-concept;

4. motivation;

5. perception; and

6. communication.

Several of these aspects of organizational behavior have been peripherally considered in earlier chapters. Here they will be more fully discussed in terms of the various ways they impact interdependently on individual human behavior within the organizational setting.

ATTITUDES

Maier describes an attitude as a psychological "mental set," which represents "a predisposition to form certain opinions."[1] Attitudes may be ideals, values, sentiments, thoughts, ideas, concepts, feelings, beliefs, and assumptions.

Attitudes affect people's evaluations, behavior, and events. People with different attitudes will form different opinions of the people with whom they associate and different opinions of the behavior of the people with whom they associate. They will also evaluate events and activities in which they are involved differently, depending on their attitudes. They will perceive their fellow workers, their commanding officers, the citizens of their communities, their pay, the way they are treated, and everything they do according to their preconceived opinions, or attitudes. In short, attitudes are what people are predisposed to bring to everything in which they become involved.

The relationship between attitudes and behavior, however, is not a direct one. Some people have the attitude, for example, that their work is boring; yet they work. Some police officers believe that their sergeants are incapable of supervising; yet they follow orders. Others feel that their police chiefs deserve their best efforts each and every day, but nonetheless find themselves coasting in their jobs. How people behave does have a great deal to do with their attitudes. But behavior also has to do with many other inputs, all of which go into the process that has behavior as its output.

The classic example of the indirect relationship between attitude and behavior is the relationship between prejudice (attitude) and discrimination (behavior). All of us have our prejudices, or preconceived notions, about groups of people. People tend to form attitudes about individuals on the basis of the groups they belong to. In terms of racial prejudice, for example, whites' attitudes about individual blacks are based on what they think they know about all black people in general. But for various reasons whites' behavior toward blacks may not flow directly from their prejudices. A white store owner who does not like blacks may still act friendly toward black customers, because he or she needs their business. Similarly, a male businessperson who thinks that all women are lazy or incompetent may still employ some, thinking that it is only fair or because the union or the government requires it.

In his study of police-community contacts in large cities, Albert Reiss found very little evidence of discriminatory behavior on the part of white police toward black people.[2] However, he did find that the white police officers studied had very prejudicial attitudes toward blacks. So again, although attitudes have an important influence on behavior, the relationship is not a simple, one-to-one variety.

Figure 7.1 shows the behaving process as well as its inputs and outputs from a systems perspective. Attitude, it should be noted, is but one of six system inputs that influence behaving. Although extremely important, attitudes make a *relatively* minor contribution to the behaving process when considered in light of the other five inputs. Behaving is a process affected by each input interacting with the others, with no single input having a consistently higher or lower weighted value. Considering the variables associated with each input, behaving must be looked on as an extraordinarily involved process. So the relationship between attitude and behavior is not a direct relationship.

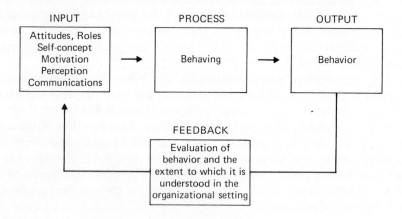

Fig. 7.1. Behavior from a systems perspective.

In fact, when describing behavior in systems terms, Huse and Bowditch do not include attitudes as input.[3] Instead, they classify attitudes as steering mechanisms in the behaving process—factors which influence and direct tasks, problems, relevance, and rewards as each of these bears on eventual behavioral output. They believe that attitudes, which are not perfectly responsive or accurate, impart only general tendencies to behavior. Although this is an oversimplification of their position, it illustrates the differences of opinion that exist with respect to where attitudes belong in the overall scheme of the behaving process. But regardless of the exact function assigned to attitudes and taking into consideration the indirect relationship that exists between attitudes and behavior, the fact remains that attitudes are important inputs to the behaving process.

The development of a person's attitudes is influenced by such factors as family, sex, age, race, ethnicity, economic and social status, education, intelligence, and place of residence. Attitudes are also influenced by myriad other factors that are peculiarly unique to a given person. Each person's set of attitudes, therefore, is different from every other person's. Even in a closely knit family, where one might expect similar attitudes to prevail, the members' differences in attitudes are likely to be remarkable and can usually be easily identified.

Individuals usually have fairly elaborate rationales by which they explain and justify their attitudes to themselves and to others. People even tend to associate with others who have similar attitudes; this is a means by which individuals reinforce their own sets of attitudes. Living becomes a more comfortable experience if a person can be surrounded by people who agree with what he or she thinks. Thus very few conservative Republicans associate socially with liberal Democrats. Proabortionists and antiabortionists find little solace in one another. People with different attitudes are often psychologically threatened by one another; the sacredness of one's own attitudes is a personal domain in which the individual encourages little or no interference. However, behind the "rational" explanations for one's attitudes lie strong emotional reasons. Because a person becomes emotionally attached to his or her attitudes through years of conditioning and experience, they are extremely difficult to change.

The traditional route to behavioral change has been by way of attitudinal change. But because of the strong emotional aspect to attitudes, this route has often failed. By contrast, some of the contemporary methods of behavioral change bypass attitudes altogether and concentrate on the relationship between behavior and reward. This relationship, which was discussed in some detail in Chapter 5, is referred to as *behavior modification;* it assumes that behavior can be changed through reward and punishment. Because behavior modification evades confrontation with attitudes, many behavioral scientists believe it to be tantamount to brainwashing; others see it as the only sensible method available to get around strongly held individual attitudes in moving forward toward the goal of organizational productivity. Individually held attitudes can be major stumbling blocks in attempting to achieve goals and objectives and must somehow be dealt with in the process.

You should not assume that behavior modification achieved through punishment and reward conditioning is the only effective method that can be used in dealing with attitudes. Although the process involved is a prolonged, difficult, and sensitive one, attitudes can be changed. The method most commonly used to change attitudes is *sensitivity training,* which is designed primarily to force an individual to face the irrationality involved in his or her own attitudinal shortcomings. Although it is called *training,* it is much more of an *educational* process than it is a *training* process. Training is designed to teach a person how to do something; education is designed to provide an intellectual base for individual behavior. *Sensitivity education,* then, offers an individual an opportunity to examine his or her own attitudes intellectually.

If a person's attitudes are to change, it is essential that he or she be forced to examine critically and objectively the rationales used to support them. This is indeed a difficult and delicate process. For an individual to come to the realization, for example, that his or her long-held negative attitudes about Catholics, Jews, blacks, foreigners, or slum dwellers are without foundation and based on ignorance can be an extremely traumatic experience. To face the facts about one's own inadequacies, particularly intellectual inadequacies, is no easy matter for anyone. The skilled sensitivity educator, dealing with the dynamics of human behavior in the classroom, can bring about this realization only if there is sufficient time to deal effectively with the natural resistance that is inevitable in getting people to face their own attitudinal inadequacies.

Sensitivity education is directed toward getting people to see themselves as they are and as other people see them. Because attitudes develop over a period of many years and are so strongly reinforced, even if erroneously, they are likely to be rigid and difficult to change. This whole process is complicated by the fact that some attitudes are reasonable and valid and can be supported by facts. Everyone, then, has a mixture of reasonable and unreasonable attitudes.

People find it impossible to confront their own shortcomings because they are unwilling to admit to either themselves or others that they might be wrong. Pride and a misguided sense of self-preservation unconsciously stand in the way of approaching one's own inadequacies, and this hinders people professionally and impedes personal growth. Very few people have the character, understanding, and inner strength to ask of others: "What's wrong with me?" and to be receptive to the answers without being personally threatened.

It is human nature to see oneself not as one is, but as one would like to be. In order to change one's attitudes toward self and others, a person must go through an experience that very carefully and very slowly leads to the realization that many of one's attitudes are based on false reasoning. This is something that cannot be taught directly; in fact, any attempt to intrude on one's attitudes will be looked on as an invasion of privacy.

Sensitivity education stays away from any direct confrontation with attitudinal inadequacies. There is no attempt to teach individuals anything about their shortcomings directly. Rather, the sensitivity educator gradually forces individuals to examine themselves and their attitudes in light of the facts and to come to a personal realization that they have been wrong and that they must change. The sensitivity educational experience provides them with the support and encouragement necessary to confront the fact that they have been wrong and must change. They are never told that their attitudes are faulty; they come to this conclusion themselves. They are never told to change their attitudes; they change them themselves on the basis of having undergone the sensitivity experience. What happens really is that their attitudes change as they become more sensitive to themselves and to their shortcomings.

Sensitivity education, to be effective, takes a great amount of time as well as skillful direction. Classes should be small, and students should be fully committed to the sensitivity concept. Instructors must be experienced in the dynamics of human behavior and have a comprehensive understanding of sensitivity teaching methods.

If this discussion proceeds on the premise that attitudes can be changed, as they can be, it is not at all difficult to understand that attitudes as system inputs can be modified on the basis of feedback. A police officer's attitudes are important only insofar as they negatively affect one's work as a police officer. Officers' social, political, and religious attitudes, for example, will probably have little or no bearing on their behavior as police officers. On the other hand, if they have strongly held negative attitudes toward people of different races, social classes, political views, or religious affiliation, their attitudes may affect their work in a negative sense. From a systems perspective, their behavioral outputs may be damaged. If they are prejudiced against Republicans, Puerto Ricans, and teenage boys with long hair, they may behave negatively and even counterproductively when dealing with those people whom they are predisposed not to like.

Only those attitudes that are likely to precipitate negative behavioral output within the police system should be of concern to the police administrator. Such attitudes are extremely serious and must be dealt with through either behavioral-modification processes or sensitivity education. If a police officer, acting in an official capacity, is allowed to translate negative personal attitudes into negative behavioral output that impacts on police responsibilities, the time has come for the chief administrator of the department to recognize the need to initiate a well-designed behavioral-modification program, based on reward and punishment, or to develop a sensitivity education effort.

In order to close the loop in the behavioral system, strong action is needed. Personal attitudes must be either changed or bypassed. This must be looked on as essential in the achievement of goals and objectives. Police officers must somehow learn to align their behavior with organizational expectations. If this demands a change in attitudes, so be it. The organization cannot be sacrificed to the whims and fancies of a few police officers who behave in unacceptable fashion because they have problems in understanding themselves. No police department needs the kind of problem created by police officers whose behavior is predicated on ignorance. The police task is much too sensitive and important to allow the personal attitudes of a few to interfere in any way with the delivery of police services to the public. Such interference should not be tolerated.

ROLES

In Chapter 5 we briefly touched on how the individual police officer perceives his or her role and suggested that the individual's perception of the police role might be different from that of the department. Here we will offer a much more comprehensive treatment of the police officer's role as it affects the officer's behavior.

In much the same way that actors in a motion picture assume certain characteristics of behavior that conform to the roles they are playing, all human beings are similarly responsive to what they perceive to be the necessity for playing their real-life roles according to accepted behavior.

Everyone is involved in playing many roles at the same time. This presents somewhat of a problem, because the roles played are often very different from one another, with each role demanding a different kind of behavior. For example, a man may be a father, husband, son, brother, uncle, cousin, Mason, police officer, Methodist, Democrat, Texan, fisherman, baseball fan, amateur gardener, stamp collector, and a member of the National Rifle Association. These roles, all of which influence the man's behavior, are all played differently according to the way they are perceived. One man, for example, in attempting to play the male role, might feel it necessary to prove his masculinity by drinking, fighting, swearing, and carousing. Another man, having no need to prove his masculinity, might perceive his role to be sober, non-combative, temperate in language, and chaste.

Similarly, a woman who sees herself as an advocate of the women's liberation movement might play her female role with considerable hostility toward men who play what is generally considered to be the traditional male role. On the other hand, women who do not embrace the basic tenets of women's liberation are likely to play the female role somewhat differently from those who actively support the concept.

Everyone plays his or her role as he or she perceives it. In a free country, everyone has that right just so long as processed role input does not produce behavior which hurts people or which is against the law. Although you might have little affection for a hermit who bathes but twice a year, and then without the advantages of soap, you must respect the hermit's right to play that role so long as no health hazard is created.

The fact is that each person plays his or her own roles much differently from the way other people play their roles. Some fathers become actively involved in their children's activities; others do not. Some husbands outwardly manifest affection for their wives; others do not. Some sons feel a responsibility to visit their aging parents frequently; others feel no such responsibility. Some sisters feel a sense of satisfaction from close association; others rarely see one another. Some cousins get together for family reunions at Thanksgiving and Christmas; others do not. Some Methodists go to church every Sunday; others do not. Some stamp collectors are consumed by their hobby, spending every spare dime on their collections; others only dabble in the hobby. Finally, some police officers see themselves as tough, hard-line crime fighters; others see themselves as professional, service-oriented public servants.

All of these descriptions of the way people play their roles are vast oversimplifications and represent only the most distant points in the *role continuum.* Figure 7.2 shows just a few of the role-continuum variables in husband-wife roles within the family setting. This figure illustrates the extent to which roles can vary according to the way people perceive themselves, as well as the fact that role variables are both interdependent subsystem factors and inputs to the behaving process.

We may therefore conclude that the way people play their roles is dependent not only on the expectations of others as these expectations are individually perceived, but also on the way other people play their own roles. The man who marries a woman who perceives a wife's role differently from the way he perceives it is heading for trouble in terms of role conflict if an adjustment cannot be made to resolve conflicting perceptions. It is important to point out, however, that it is possible to resolve role conflicts through adjustment. Adjustment, or mutually agreed on role change, sometimes involves major changes in attitude and behavior, changes which are extremely difficult to accomplish.

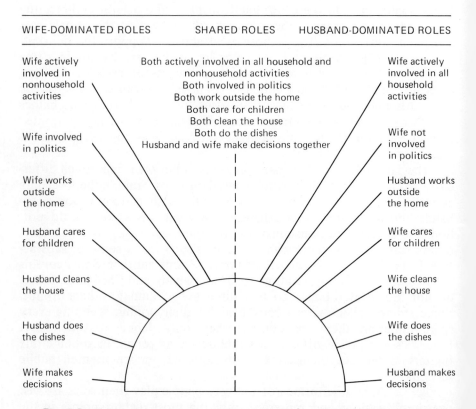

| WIFE-DOMINATED ROLES | SHARED ROLES | HUSBAND-DOMINATED ROLES |

Wife actively involved in nonhousehold activities

Wife involved in politics

Wife works outside the home

Husband cares for children

Husband cleans the house

Husband does the dishes

Wife makes decisions

Both actively involved in all household and nonhousehold activities
Both involved in politics
Both work outside the home
Both care for children
Both clean the house
Both do the dishes
Husband and wife make decisions together

Wife actively involved in all household activities

Wife not involved in politics

Husband works outside the home

Wife cares for children

Wife cleans the house

Wife does the dishes

Husband makes decisions

Fig. 7.2. Role continuum of variables in husband-wife roles within the family setting.

The effect of roles on behavior varies according to the situation. Some roles guide behavior in virtually every situation, whereas others apply only in specific circumstances.[4] Sex roles, for example, influence behavior in a wide range of situations; in most instances, they have a much stronger impact than many of the other roles that people play. The fact that a person is male will probably influence his behavior to a much greater degree than will his membership in the Masons, the Democratic Party, or the National Rifle Association. Although in some cases the man may perceive his membership in these organizations as part of being a man, it is almost impossible to understand exactly how he perceives his role as a man and to identify the variables involved in his perception.

All people play some roles that they perceive to be more important than others. The Trappist monk is a good example of a person whose religious role as a Catholic completely dominates his life; other people are Catholics in name only and neither practice nor subscribe to the basic tenets of their faith.

The relative importance of people's roles are individually determined and therefore extremely difficult to isolate for study. In dealing with roles from a systems perspective as inputs to the behaving process, one must understand that there are literally thousands of intricate variables that impact on each individual's personal role perceptions and therefore influence individual behavior. One of the reasons that social scientists may never be able to explain human behavior in completely realistic terms is the impossibility of identifying *all* behavioral system inputs, as these apply *individually* and *interdependently* to billions of people. In discussing roles, considered from the individual and interdependent perspectives, and in applying role theory to behavior, it is essential that the subject be approached with no small amount of humility and with the realization that they cannot be *fully* understood by mortal beings. Making an effort to apply the variables involved in role theory to behavior becomes a much less frustrating experience if these limitations are kept in mind. There are some generally accepted theories, however, that do apply to roles and that should be considered by anyone aspiring to become an administrator.

Roles exert conforming influences on behavior. Roles stabilize society. Citizens conform generally to society's expectation of obedience to the law. Club members are expected to follow the rules, and most do. The Judeo-Christian ethic requires Jews and Christians to abide by the Ten Commandments; most do. Games are played according to rules; most players follow them. Written and unwritten rules of social conduct require prescribed behavior for students in classrooms, teenagers at dances, judges on the bench, legislators in session, union members picketing their employer, worshipers in church, and so on. Most people play their roles in conformance with what they perceive to be societal norms and expectations.

These societal norms and expectations, however, differ considerably from society to society, from culture to culture, and even from subculture to subculture. Understanding the norms and expectations of the society, culture, or subculture from which an individual comes is therefore an extremely relevant factor in attempting to understand how an individual's behavior is affected by his or her personal and peculiar role perception. The United States is made up of many people from many different cultures and subcultures, all of which impact differently on the way individuals play their roles. There is in the United States, however, what might be considered a *dominant culture* which demands that certain roles be played according to certain expectations; it is the rules established by this dominant culture to which most citizens of the United States conform in playing their roles. People who subscribe to subcultural role expectations that are in conflict with the role expectations of the dominant culture inevitably find it difficult, if not impossible, to adjust to the dominant culture.

If such adjustment is to be made, it must be made in terms of attitudinal change or behavior modification. As we have seen, these two processes are very involved. To change the attitudes or modify the behavior of entire subcultures is virtually impossible. For example, the entire correctional system in the United States is based on the assumption that subcultural attitudes can be changed and subcultural behavior modified *en masse.* The correctional system has failed, in part, because the people who administer it and the theorists who provide them guidance fail to understand fully, from a systems perspective, all of the ramifications of multiple inputs to the behaving process.

Even in the most homogeneous societies, however, role conflicts are inevitable. If a society is to remain stable, these conflicts must be dealt with sensibly and intelligently, with those having the responsibility for dealing with them fully apprised of their origins and their cross-cultural implications. In American society it is the judges, religious leaders, legislators, corrections officials, executive governmental heads, psychiatrists, organizational administrators, marriage counselors, and police officers who have the responsibility for dealing with role conflict. In general, most of them do a rather poor job in meeting this responsibility. Here we focus only on the role of the police officer in conflict resolution.

The police officer's role   The role played by an individual police officer is influenced by all of the other roles he or she plays. Unfortunately, these other roles significantly affect the role played as a police officer. A police officer who is a nondrinker is more likely to enforce drunken-driving laws than is an officer who is a heavy drinker; the latter might tend to empathize with a drunken driver, take the driver's keys, and let the person sleep it off by the side of the road, whereas the former would be more likely to make an arrest and press the case. Similarly, a police officer who has a part-time job driving a truck might overlook overload violations or truckers' exceeding the speed limit; the part-time role as a trucker might influence the full-time role as a police officer. A police officer who is a member of the Rotary Club would not be likely to ticket a fellow Rotarian for a stop-sign violation and would probably be similarly disposed toward his friends, neighbors, children, parents, and wife. All of this officer's other roles impact, in varying degrees, on the role as a police officer.

This officer is playing a traditional police role. (Courtesy of the Jackson Police Department, Jackson, Mississippi)

The police administrator must understand the various relationships that exist between roles and deal with these relationships in determining what the police officer's role should be, realizing that the officer's behavior in a given situation will be strongly influenced, *unless otherwise checked,* by the way he or she perceives these different roles. The police officer is expected to take some action based on an immediate assessment of every situation confronted. An officer who acts on the basis of personal attitudes and role perception rather than on established departmental policy will act in terms of personally perceived role expectations rather than on those role expectations established by the police department. In departments where policy does not dictate role expectations, police officers tend to establish their own dominant subculture, which unofficially dictates role expectations and significantly affects the roles officers play. It is not at all unusual in such a milieu for role expectations to develop which condone and encourage the most outrageous kinds of police behavior that could be imagined.

In instances where a large number of police officers share similarly predisposed negative attitudes and questionable role expectations, these tend to be reinforced through general acceptance and be adopted as unwritten but institutionalized operating procedures and practices. Once police officers accept the role expectations of the dominant police subculture, they are relieved of considerable frustration in having to assess accurately each situation in which they find themselves; they simply follow the established subcultural role expectations and behave accordingly. If the role expectation of the dominant police subculture is to arrest people as the only means of conflict resolution, the officer is left with little choice but to make large numbers of arrests. If the role expectation of the dominant police subculture is to brutalize loud-mouth drunks, officers may feel free to resort to such behavior with impunity. If the role expectation of the dominant police subculture condones and encourages police officers to accept bribes, many will probably do so. If the role expectation of the dominant police subculture allows police officers to be rude and discourteous in dealing with the public, rude and discourteous they will be.

It should be noted that subcultural roles as described here, once accepted as the institutionalized way of behaving, are played unconsciously and accepted as being *normal.* Officers who deviate from the norm and refuse to accept the role expectations of the dominant police subculture become outcasts, much as a criminal becomes an outcast in the dominant culture. A police officer whose self-perception is as a service-oriented professional—refusing to brutalize prisoners or take bribes, refraining from verbalizing indignities aimed at minority-group members, and being courteous toward the public—is very likely to be ostracized by other members of the dominant police subculture.

The influence of dominant police subcultural role expectations can have a devastating effect on a police department. In fact the existence of such unofficially established, negative, institutionalized role expectations is the primary reason that so many police departments are held in such low esteem by the public. Three examples of behavior deriving from these role expectations will illustrate their impact.

Cod Bay. Cod Bay is a summer resort community; its winter population of 19,000 expands to 60,000 in the summer. The Cod Bay Police Department has many problems in controlling summer visitors. One persistent problem is illegal parking. Because there are numerous complaints from year 'round residents about parking, the Cod Bay Police Chief arranged with several towing companies to tow all illegally parked cars to the police station parking lot. The towing companies did a brisk business, particularly over weekends, when the town was inundated with visitors. Part-time police officers, who were not professionally trained, were hired by the department to work weekends and were assigned to the downtown area specifically to enforce parking laws. All violators were towed; no one escaped the watchful eyes of the part-time downtown patrol officers, who were occasionally overzealous in their enforcement activities and who perceived some of the parking violators as wanton criminals. In their desire to carry out departmental policy and to compete for tows with fellow officers assigned to the same task, they occasionally made mistakes and towed cars not illegally parked.

Having one's car towed can be a traumatic experience, particularly if the car is not illegally parked. On one such occasion, an irate young man came to the police station to reclaim his car, a matter which involved paying the towing company $12. Refusing to pay the fee, the young man asked to see the sergeant in charge. The burly sergeant was predisposed to dislike irate young men. At first, the sergeant attempted to determine the facts, and he summoned the part-time patrol officer back to the station to get his side of the story. After listening to the stories of the patrol officer and the young man, the sergeant realized that the young man's car had been legally parked. But even so the sergeant sided with the patrol officer and informed the young man that if he wanted his car back, he would have to pay the $12 towing charge.

The man refused, and a shouting match, precipitated by the sergeant, developed. When the man was told to leave the station, he demanded what he knew were his rights. He was told that if he did not leave the station, he would be arrested. Finally, he was taken bodily from the station by the patrol officer, who pushed him down a flight of steps to the sidewalk. The man regained his equilibrium and quietly walked off into the night, beaten by the system. He returned later, paid the $12, and reclaimed his car.

This situation illustrates two major problems involving the dominant police subculture and role expectations. Departmental policy dictated that the sergeant investigate the citizen's complaint, in this case the towing of a legally parked car. The dominant police subculture dictated that the sergeant back the officer whether he was right or wrong. The sergeant followed departmental policy to the degree that it existed and then reverted to the role expectation of the dominant police subculture. The sergeant was much more willing to stay on good terms with the officer, with whom he would have to deal continually, than with the young man, whom he would never see again. The officer, having received the backing of the sergeant, then reacted in terms of his own accurate perception of dominant police subcultural role expectations and pushed the young man down the flight of stairs. Although there are legal sanctions against such actions, the officer fully understood that subcultural role expectations would completely support the action that he took.

Tulane City. Tulane City, an industrial urban community with a population of 97,000, has a large minority population and an unemployment rate of 19.3 percent. Its police department is administered traditionally and has very few binding policies and procedures. Police chiefs, who are selected politically from within the department, change with the election of each new mayor. Active political support of a successful mayoralty candidate is the only real qualification needed to become chief.

Five disgruntled and politically active former chiefs are currently serving in the department's hierarchy. Almost all of their energies are directed toward embarrassing the present chief, who has a high school education and no understanding of the principles of police administration. He sees himself only as a temporary caretaker of the office and realizes that soon, when a new mayor to whom he is not politically dedicated, takes office, he will be back with the troops and subject to the role expectations of a dominant police subculture that is totally incompatible with the democratic principles of constitutional government.

The dominant police subculture in Tulane City condones and encourages beating prisoners, accepting gratuities, and taking a public-be-damned attitude, which permeates the entire organization. Officers frequently refuse to answer calls, and a large detective force, grown lazy through the years, investigates only a small percentage of major crime, even though crime has risen 52 percent during the past year. Gambling is rampant throughout the city, and almost no effort is made to curtail it.

The department, although it consists of 168 sworn personnel and 12 civilians, has no organization chart, no internal affairs division, and no inspections unit. Except for personality conflicts between officers and supervisors, no one is suspended or otherwise punished unless involved in the commisssion of a serious crime that comes to public attention. The citizens of Tulane City are up in arms about their police department's ineffectiveness, but have discovered that no one within the department will listen to their complaints. The chief is coasting; he drives about the city in a new Cadillac and occasionally drops by the station to pick up his mail and luxuriate in his large, well-appointed office.

Police officers have successfully negotiated a contract which provides for time and a half overtime pay for court appearances. Because court appearances mean additional income, exhorbitant numbers of arrests are made, even for minor and insignificant violations. Many police officers, hiding away in the court house coffee shop, are unavailable when their cases are called and thereby increase their overtime incomes. One sergeant, the breathalyzer operator on the early-night tour, appears in court almost daily, although he is never called on to testify, because of a court policy which allows the prosecutor to introduce breathalyzer evidence; his court appearances are solely for the purpose of collecting overtime. Another officer drops by the court house frequently; he is allowed to sign an overtime chit for his services even when he has no case on the docket.

The Tulane City Police Department is in a shambles and works counterproductively to community interests. In every sense the department is unsophisticated operationally and administratively. Officers drink, carouse, and sleep on the job. Very little is right with the Tulane City Police Department.

The Tulane City Police Department is a good example of a police department completely out of control as a result of role expectations established by the dominant police subculture. The acceptance of these role expectations by the chief provides rationale for their acceptance by the whole department. If the chief had either the ability or the inclination to promulgate policies and procedures designed to change these role expectations, he would be ostracized from the department immediately on being relieved of command by a new mayor. Realizing that his life would be made unbearable, and possibly even placed in danger, when he returned to the ranks in a minor hierarchical position, he decided on the more comfortable approach of not rocking the boat. On that inevitable day when he will be fired as chief and replaced by another political caretaker, he will be welcomed back by his fellow officers as a hero. He may have difficulty, however, in looking at himself in a mirror.

Rixton. Rixton is a small community of 16,000 people and has a police force of 23. Police Chief Walton Eager came up through the ranks and is a pleasant man, but has little administrative ability. He promulgates all policy and procedures by tacking notices to a bulletin board already overcrowded wih memorabilia dating back several years. He makes no effort to determine whether his officers understand his policies and procedures, and officers feel no need to pay any attention to them.

The department has many excellent officers, who despite poor leadership conduct themselves in exemplary fashion. A small minority, however, cause some very severe problems. These six officers have their own police subculture and peculiar role expectations. The dominant police subculture in Rixton, although not predicated on officially established rules and regulations, is generally accepted by most of the police officers and dictates role expectations which are consistent with democratic processes. The minority police subculture is in conflict with the dominant police subculture; each group thinks that the other is ineffective.

The officers in Rixton refer to the two subcultures as *cliques.* Each clique operates according to its own role expectations, with neither clique particularly constrained by Chief Eager's policies and procedures. The minority clique perceives the police role as being largely militaristic. The following situations, involving minority-clique members, provide some interesting data on how role expectations and perceptions affect behavioral output.

1. Patrol officer Luigi Pasternak, a former marine who collects guns and believes that most people are criminals, received a radio call to mediate an argument at a gas station. On receiving the call, Pasternak said, "Good. Maybe I'll get a chance to crack someone's head."

2. Patrol officer Brodie Fishbaum, when asked what changes he would recommend to make the Rixton Police Department more professional, remarked, "I'd make it more military, have them all get haircuts, and have them wear combat boots." Commenting on his role, he said, "I like this (police work). This is just like being in the military. At least I think so. Pasternak and I think we are."

3. Patrol officer Moody Mickehaus, commenting on the fact that Brodie Fishbaum and Luigi Pasternak had been transferred to his shift, said, "Now that Fishbaum and Pasternak are back, you'll see a lot of arrests. We try to outdo each other."

These three conversations were typical of the way minority-clique members felt about themselves. Their attitudes and behavior were dictated by their own subcultural role expectations and were reinforced by the members of their small, but influential peer group. The fact that the dominant police subculture behaved differently in terms of different role expectations had very little effect on what they did.

Members of the minority clique were disturbed, however, that their group consisted of so few officers. Moody Mikehaus, for example, was forever comparing his own professionalism with that of other members of the department; he was terribly disturbed that they were not as professional as he perceived himself to be. He once remarked that he gets so upset about societal degeneration and his department's inability to deal with it that he sometimes has to drink himself to sleep. Although Moody Mikehaus considered himself to be professional, he was looked on by officers subscribing to the dominant police subculture as being dangerous.

The Rixton Police Department, with its two cliques of patrol officers, illustrates a department in which there is more than one set of role expectations. The fact that the dominant police subculture in Rixton was service-oriented and not militaristic was a fortunate quirk of fate. The minority clique, however, caused tremendous problems for the chief and a great amount of internal disharmony within the ranks of those officers who were trying their best to do their jobs properly. The real problem with the Rixton Police Department was Chief Walton Eager, who simply had no understanding of the situation and believed that a system is a method used to pick winners at a race track.

A more capable police chief would have had backing from the dominant police subculture and therefore would have had little difficulty in establishing departmental role expectations for all officers to follow. This would require either sensitivity education or the application of behavioral-modification techniques; it might also require firing Pasternak, Fishbaum, Mikehaus, and the other members of the minority clique. At the very least, it would require establishing viable control measures and a significant amount of feedback on their effectiveness. In other words, the problems could be resolved only through application of the systems approach to management.

These examples demonstrate the influence of dominant police subcultural role expectations as well as other subcultural role expectations

on the behavior and attitudes of police officers. The relationship between personally established and officially established role expectations
becomes apparent. How each police officer perceives his or her role is
all-important to behavioral output from an organizational standpoint.
Role expectations, if they are to impact positively on behavior, must be
consistently adopted by *all* departmental members. Dominant police
subcultures develop in order to fill the vacuums created by lack of
policy that defines role expectations and establishes behavioral constraints and parameters. If police administrators fail to define role
expectations and are remiss in their responsibilities to set behavioral
tolerances and limitations, they have only themselves to blame for the
inevitable behavioral chaos that will result.

STANDARD 1.5

POLICE UNDERSTANDING OF THEIR ROLE

Every police agency immediately should take steps to insure that every officer has
an understanding of his role, and an awareness of the culture of the community
where he works.

1. The procedure for developing policy regarding the police role should involve
officers of the basic rank, first line supervisors, and middle managers. Every police
employee should receive written policy defining the police role.

2. Explicit instruction in the police role and community culture should be provided in all recruit and in-service training.

3. The philosophy behind the defined police role should be a part of all instruction and direction given to officers.

4. Middle managers and first line supervisors should receive training in the police
role and thereafter continually reinforce those principles by example and by direction of those they supervise.

5. Methods of routinely evaluating individual officer performance should take
into account all activities performed within the context of the defined role. Promotion and other incentives should be based on total performance within the defined
role, rather than on any isolated aspect of that role.

National Advisory Commission on Criminal Justice Standards and Goals, *Police*
(Washington, D.C.: U.S. Government Printing Office, 1973), p. 34.

SELF–CONCEPT

Self-concept, another determinant of behavior in organizations, is defined as the image a person has of not only self, but also ideal self—how

he or she would like to be. Both aspects of this definition have important effects on the ways people act in organized situations.

A person's self-concept develops through interaction with other people. People learn who they are by watching how other people react to them.[5] Other people's behavior toward a person is the mirror in which one sees oneself; this behavior provides the data base from which a person forms his or her own self-concepts. Thus your own self-concept is formed in part by how other people behave toward you.

By carefully watching and analyzing the behavior of others, a person also learns what must be done in order to get more favorable reactions from others. In the process, one develops an ideal self-concept, comparing present self with ideal self. If an individual's ideal self-concept is too far removed from his or her real potential to achieve it, he or she may develop feelings of inadequacy and failure. On the other hand, if no one seems to expect very much, people are likely to develop too narrow or too conservative ideal self-concepts and, consequently, never reach their potential.

If individuals recognize the limitations of their real potential, they may be able to compensate for their inadequacies by working hard to overcome them. Cornelia Wallace, former wife of Alabama governor and unsuccessful presidential candidate George C. Wallace, summed it up nicely as follows:

> Any man who seeks the highest office in the land is overcompensating for some inadequacy. In my husband's case, it's probably because of his height. He's not a tall man—oh, I think he's 5 feet 8. I suppose he wants to prove he's a bigger man than the physical portrayal. Yes, some people call this a Napoleonic complex. But I say thank the Lord for people with complexes. They are doers who make the world go round.[6]

Not everyone compensates for inadequacies, whatever they might be, by running for President of the United States. People who recognize limitations imposed by inadequacies, however, often develop behavioral patterns designed, both consciously and unconsciously, to prove to themselves and to others that they are every bit as good or as capable as anyone else. In order to do this, they very often concentrate on developing what they know to be their strengths, with the hope that their limitations and inadequacies will be disregarded. If Mrs. Wallace was correct in her perception of her husband's compensatory motivation, what better way to prove oneself than by running for the presidency of the strongest and wealthiest nation in the world? Such activity could go a long way toward improving an individual's self-concept.

Because work is an important aspect of a person's self-concept, superiors are important participants in one's effort to achieve an ideal self-concept. By accurately appraising subordinates in terms of who they think they are and what they think they can become, a police chief is in a good position to understand their behavior and to make a positive contribution toward their personal and professional development. By carefully providing them with information about their progress toward achieving ideal self-concept goals and by encouraging them in every possible way to achieve these goals, a police chief can be assured of better work performance and greater productivity for the organization as a whole.

The relationship between behavior and self-concept is direct. As a general rule, most people evaluate situations and choose behaviors on the basis of how they think their self-concepts will be affected. Thus behavior perceived to satisfy or enhance ideal self-concepts is chosen; behavior perceived to be damaging to ideal self-concepts is rejected.

Individual behavioral problems are likely to arise when either or both of the following conditions prevail:

1. individuals are incorrect in choosing behavior that they believe will enhance their ideal self-concepts; and

2. individuals are incapable of exercising behavior that they believe will enhance their ideal self-concepts.

In the first instance, inaccurate perception of the facts involved in the situation may be blamed for an individual's choosing behavior that impacts negatively on self-concept. The young, idealistic police academy graduate, for example, who behaves on the job according to policies and procedures learned at the academy may abruptly discover that such behavior is not condoned by the dominant police subculture. The high school class clown whose behavior is reinforced by both teachers and students in the old home town may learn that similar behavioral patterns are unacceptable in the college or university milieu. Behavior predicated on inaccurate perception can have a devastating effect on the individual's ideal self-concept.

In the second instance, a person who is incapable of exercising behavior that will enhance ideal self-concept can become extremely frustrated over his or her inadequacies. The youngster who is uncoordinated and therefore a poor athlete can have his or her self-concept ruined by growing up in a neighborhood in which the peer group places a high value on being a good athlete.

Peer-group pressure dictates, in large measure, what an individual's ideal self-concept should be. In American society tremendous emphasis is placed on getting a good education; this ideal persists even though hundreds of thousands of college graduates are unemployed or underemployed. Someone growing up in a community in which education is the key to status will be virtually forced to get a college education in order to satisfy his or her own personal ideal self-concept. Frustration is the inevitable by-product of unreachable, and very often unreasonable, peer-group expectations.

Individuals who are able to cope with these frustrations often do so by overcompensating for what they perceive to be their own inadequacies. If the individual's efforts to overcompensate can be directed toward healthy and productive ends, a great deal can be achieved in making the individual a worthwhile contributor to society in general and to the organization for which he or she works in particular. It is management's responsibility to improve the individual employee's self-concept by providing realistic and reachable goals and objectives with which the individual employee can be comfortable and which will serve to enhance ideal self-concept.

MOTIVATION

One of the more important aspects of human behavior in organizations is motivation. Motivation refers to motives—what makes the individual behave in a certain way. Why does a person behave in a particular manner? The answer, as might be suspected, is not an easy one. The number and kind of motivational forces almost defy description.

Models of motivation Because we are interested in police officers who work in organizational settings, our primary concern here is *what motivates people to work?*. Theories that attempt to describe the process abound. Huse and Bowditch have outlined four general models of motivational systems: the *force and coercion* model, the *economic/machine* model, the *affective/affiliation* model, and the *growth–open system* model.[7]

Force and Coercion Model. According to the *force and coercion* model, human beings work because they have to in order to avoid pain and punishment. The parent who says to his or her child, "Learn your spelling words before supper, or you can't watch television tonight," is attempting to create motivation based on this model. Students who take required courses in which they are not interested study in order not to fail; examinations for the courses are constructed in order to force and coerce students to study. The once widespread institutions of serfdom and slavery were based on total compliance with the force and coercion model.

In American society forcing and coercing behavior are regarded as distasteful. For this reason and because force and coercion generally tend to debase human beings, this model has become the least popular motivational method. It is also the least effective; it encourages only the very minimum amount of work necessary to avoid punishment. It also breeds resentment and causes morale problems. In extreme cases this resentment and loss of morale can turn into open rebellion and even organizational sabotage.

There are instances in the police service, however, when force and coercion are the only methods that can be used to motivate desired behavior. If the dominant police subculture dictates role expectations which are diametrically opposed to organizational goals and objectives and if dominant police subcultural behavior conflicts with departmental policies, a police administrator might have to resort to force and coercion in order to maintain organizational stability. In those situations in which police officers are protected by outmoded civil service regulations, tenure, or strong union backing, force and coercion may very well be the only means by which a police administrator can demand behavior consistent with the police department's aims.

Economic/Machine Model. The *economic/machine* model suggests that human beings work in order to obtain the tangible rewards that employment offers. In the carrot-and-stick approach to motivation, the economic/machine model would represent the carrot, whereas the force and coercion model would represent the stick. According to the former theory, work is nothing more than a means to an end; it implies that if somehow everyone immediately became wealthy, no more work would be done.

The police chief who subscribes fully to the thesis of the economic/ machine model views police officers basically as machines designed to produce solely for pragmatic reasons. The chief is not particularly concerned about departmental employees except in terms of their performance and productivity. The main concern is efficiency, getting maximum return for minimum investment on a cost-effective basis. Although efficiency is important, especially in terms of prudent expenditure of the taxpayer's dollar, it cannot be looked on as the only basis on which to deal with workers.

Affective/Affiliation Model. Through the Hawthorne studies, a classic motivational research effort, it became apparent that immediate economic reward was not the only reason for individual productivity.[8] These studies demonstrated that social and psychological factors in the work setting have a considerable effect on performance. Specifically, the study found that the output of workers improved significantly when they were made to feel important and when they were consulted about job decisions.

These findings are at the heart of the *affective/affiliation* model of motivation. In other words, workers may be motivated to work because of their social needs—their need to work harmoniously with other people.

Growth–Open System Model. The *growth–open system* model of motivation grew out of the Hawthorne studies and their subsequent findings. This model incorporates much of the philosophy on which the economic/machine model is based; in addition, it gives consideration to those social and psychological forces (affective/affiliation model) that influence work behavior. This combination of the two other models is an *open system* because it recognizes and stresses that the work situation cannot be insulated from the outside world; it emphasizes the fact that the individual at work must be looked on as a human being influenced by the environment.

A central theme of the growth–open system model of motivation is that people work in order to satisfy certain human needs. Maslow has identified a five-level hierarchy of these needs. An adaptation of Maslow's hierarchy follows:

1. basic needs (food, clothing, shelter);

2. security needs (protection against physical and psychological threats to an individual's well-being);

3. societal/social needs (love, friendship, camaraderie, acceptance);

4. self-concept needs (recognition, respect, esteem); and

5. goal-realization needs (fulfilling individual potential and achieving ideal self-concept).[9]

After satisfying basic needs, an individual progressively seeks to satisfy higher-level needs (societal/social, self-concept, and goal realization needs). In other words, people fill their needs step by step in the hierarchy, moving from level to level. When one level of needs has been satisfied, it *generally* ceases to have strong motivational value. A person whose stomach is full, owns a home, and has job security is unlikely to be motivated by basic needs for food, clothing, and shelter. If the person feels secure physically and psychologically (level 2) and has societal/social and self-concept needs (levels 3 and 4), any additional motivation will probably derive from Maslow's fifth hierarchical level.

This, however, is an oversimplification; for most workers there is a vast amount of overlap between and among the various levels in the hierarchy of needs. Maslow's theory, then, can be applied only generally and cannot be used in an explicit way to categorize individuals. It is a very useful tool, however, for an administrator to use in attempting to gauge the hierarchical level at which *most* employees can be motivated. In fact, the implications of this theory for modern organizations are striking.

In the United States today, the basic needs of the great majority of employed workers are satisfied. This is not universally so; it is, however, generally so. Police pay scales in most jurisdictions within the United States are sufficient to meet police officers' most basic needs. Consequently, according to Maslow's theory, basic needs no longer have significant motivational value for police officers. Therefore, the police department that seeks to motivate its employees primarily through salary increases is applying a motivational technique that has little value.

In reality, however, this is only partially true. Many police officers, like other workers, have fulfilled their basic needs, but feel insecure about those needs being met in the future; the strength of police unions is a manifestation of this insecurity. The threat of having fulfilled needs cut off at any one of the five hierarchical levels is in itself a strong motivational force; only when that threat dissipates does an individual cease to be motivated at any given level.

But there is also another side to the coin. Many people today are leaving high-paying positions for jobs that, although they pay less, satisfy more important needs. Many incentive systems, offering more pay for more output, have failed to inspire greater productivity. With increases in worker mobility and public unemployment assistance, pay incentives have lost their grip on the American worker. Remember, however, that this is a generalization and therefore does not hold true for everyone. Many people are still strongly motivated by pay incentives even though they may also be responsive to factors higher in Maslow's hierarchy. Leavitt, for example, has noted that "wages and salary are not just money. They are indicators of progress, worth, and status. And they are equity measures, too, telling us whether our treatment relative to others and to our own performance is right and proper."[10]

The *growth-open system* model of motivation emphasizes the factors of attitudes, roles, self-concept, and human growth to be considered in attempting to achieve organizational goals and objectives. This model holds that human beings are neither machines to be directed and controlled nor totally free decision makers operating in a vacuum. The model maintains that behavior in work settings is a result of complex and interrelated motives which are not easily identifiable. Essentially, it recognizes that both behavior and motivation for behavior are *open systems*. As open systems, behavior and motivation have inputs, outputs, processes, and feedback, all of which are very personal to the individual and all of which are influenced by outside environmental factors.

A nonmodel of motivation   In discussing attitudes, roles, self-concept, and motivation, we have been seeking a better understanding of human behavior, especially in organized work settings. Such an understanding is elusive and difficult to conceptualize because each person's behavior is unique and very complicated. It is relatively easy to develop theories and models that explain behavior in a general sense, but these models often break down when applied to particular individuals. We must conclude, therefore, that there are no absolutes, no concrete principles that allow us to predict or to understand completely the behavior of others. Although Maslow's hierarchy of needs is a useful theory to explain much of the behavior that occurs in organizations, there are people with more money and more status than they could ever possibly exhaust, yet are still highly motivated to attain more of each.

Athos and Coffey have described what we will call a *nonmodel of human behavior,* which allows for a wide latitude of conscious and unconscious perceptions of self and situation and which seems almost universal in its applicability.[11] This nonmodel model, as it were, makes no attempt to be as prescriptive as a mathematical formula or, indeed, as definitive as the other models discussed; it is nonetheless very helpful in providing insights into behavior inexplicable through the application of other models. The three elements that make up this model can be summarized as follows:

1. A person's self-concept is determined by self-perception, perception being influenced by both conscious and subconscious factors.

2. A person's individual frame of reference is predicated on the way he or she perceives the world at any given time (including people, places, and things in the immediate environment) in combination with self-perception in a particular setting.

3. A person behaves in order to protect or enhance his or her feelings of security or adequacy in any given situation.[12]

If one uses this theory as a model, all behavior is logical, and all behavior can be explained. This nonmodel model is an extremely important concept to bear in mind when trying to understand behavior that is difficult to understand or that does not seem to conform to the norm. This model provides a rationale for the contention that all behavior is logical and that individuals who are behaving in particular ways are doing so according to what they think is best for them in particular situations as they see the situations. A person's behavior may seem irrational or even self-destructive, but for the person exhibiting it that behavior makes sense.

The nonmodel model makes allowances for differences between the way individuals see things and the way things really are. This difference is a product of perception.

PERCEPTION

People learn about other people, places, and things through information gathered by the sensory organs. The data base for perception is the individual's own way of seeing, hearing, touching, tasting, and smelling the environment.

People behave differently from one another in part because their sensory organs have varying capabilities. For example, the information gathered by people with excellent eyesight differs from that gathered by people with poor eyesight. The behavior of these two groups is based on different information. A person who is color blind, for example, has much less of an appreciation for the world's beauty than a person who sees a full spectrum of colors. People who are deaf perceive much less than people who are not; their behavior is predicated, in part, on what they hear, not on what others hear.

Although no one can accurately analyze the effect of sensory limitations on perception, and hence on behavior, it is safe to assume that perception and behavior are influenced to a remarkable degree by such limitations. The behavior of a person walking in the dark along a narrow, lonely road who hears a car approaching at a fast rate of speed would differ greatly from the behavior of a person who fails to hear the car; one would jump out of the way and the other would continue on walking.

Most sensory information needs to be interpreted before it can be used to design appropriate behavior. This interpretation of sensory data is perception.

Some of the perceptual process is carried out mechanically by the sensory organs. Your eyes, for example, sort out and arrange a steady flow of light so that you can see objects, people, color, and movement. This mechanical interpretation is very important, although people tend to take it for granted, becoming aware of it only when something such as an optical illusion deceives them.

Some perception is based on fairly straightforward learning. As your eyes present you with visual data on objects, for example, you learn to see and differentiate chairs, tables, books, automobiles, and a great number of other commonplace items. You learn to interpret the visual image of an object with four wooden vertical legs and a rectangular wooden top as a table, as something to eat from, play Monopoly on, or study at. In other words, you learn to perceive the object as a table, and you perceive it in terms of the varying ways you relate to it or use it.

Perception involves your own peculiar interpretation of sensory information; it includes both mechanical and learning processes. But the combination of these two processes is not enough to explain the wide variety of ways in which people interpret identical situations. Alexis and Wilson point out that "the information-gathering function is not a sequence of purely mechanical, routine physiological processes. Personalities and social needs are intricately woven into how people see things."[13]

To a large extent, then, people see things in terms of their attitudes, roles, self-concepts, and motivation. A police officer may perceive a drug addict as a criminal. To a doctor, the person is sick or perhaps a patient; to a psychologist, an addict with an emotional problem; to a drug dealer, a customer; to a parent, a wonderful child who is unable to cope with the stresses of society. In all instances, the addict is the same person, but is perceived differently by different people playing different societal roles. In each example, the personal attitudes held by the perceivers with respect to drug addicts and drug addiction would further differentiate their perceptions.

Similarly, a person's self-perception as the result of interaction with others may be a behavioral determinant. A person who has a concept of self as being intelligent may perceive going to school and taking examinations as enjoyable, rewarding experiences; a person who has consistently failed in academic studies, on the other hand, may perceive himself or herself to be considerably less intelligent, fear school, and freeze when taking examinations. Because of their different self-concepts, these two students will have markedly different perceptions of the same classes, instructors, and examinations.

Each person behaves so as to protect or enhance his or her perceived self-concept. It is important to understand that the way in which another person perceives a situation and subsequently behaves on the basis of that perception is very likely to be different from the way you perceive the same situation and subsequently behave on the basis of your perception. In a very real sense, your own perceptions obstruct your abilities to understand behavior in others. People tend to believe that other people should perceive and behave in exactly the same way that they perceive and behave. The administrator must overcome this tendency in order to deal effectively with the various kinds of behavior one can expect from individuals within an organization.

In addition, administrators must realize that perception is a *selective* process through which people accept or reject in automatic fashion what best or least suits their needs. Leavitt tells us that "people perceive what they think will help satisfy needs; ignore what is disturbing; and again perceive disturbances that persist and increase."[14] Perception controls interpretation of sensory information, blocks out bothersome information, and accents pleasing information.

People see things in terms of their personal attitudes, roles, self-concepts, and motivation. (Courtesy of the Wilmington Police Department, Wilmington, Delaware)

Another important aspect of perception is that it can be made more accurate through the utilization of feedback. A child who perceives a red-hot coal to be inviting and touches it gets immediate feedback in the form of pain; the pain "says" that the perception was inaccurate and that the child had better change that perception before being tempted again to touch a red-hot coal. Chances are excellent that the child will do so.

If you answered the door and saw a police officer, what would your immediate perception of the situation be? (Courtesy of the Wilmington Police Department, Wilmington, Delaware)

Unfortunately, feedback is not usually this direct and immediate. The good administrator, who sincerely wants to improve perception, must always actively seek information to either substantiate or correct initial perceptions of people and situations. There must be an awareness that perceptions may be inaccurate and that subordinates, individually and collectively, may perceive situations differently. Additionally, the good administrator must understand that varying perceptions are the major causes of behavioral differences among people.

COMMUNICATION

The attitudes, roles, self-concepts, motivation, and perceptions of others become known primarily through communication. Two people learn about each other, then, through the communicative process. It is through this process that people attempt to influence the behavior of others. Communication is the medium through which a police manager conducts day-to-day functions.

Communication provides information about the attitudes, roles, self-concepts, motivation, and perceptions of other people. (Courtesy of the Los Angeles County Sheriff's Department)

It has become fashionable in recent years to ascribe every possible kind of organizational malady to faulty communications or to gaps in communications. People who are likely to use communications as a scapegoat for all organizational difficulties do not fully appreciate or understand human behavior as it is affected by attitudes, roles, self-concept, motivation, and perception. Poor communications in organizational settings result from the total effect of thousands of interdependent variables which, working in concert, have behavior as their output. To say simply that an organization has communications problems, without considering other aspects of organizational behavior as these affect communications, is an oversimplification that cannot be justified under any circumstances. In fact, the administrator who uses the communications gambit as a rationale for organizational problems is, in effect, saying, "I don't know the real reasons that we are having problems, so I will conveniently blame our organizational difficulties on faulty communications." This is not to say, however, that poor communications do not cause problems; they do, just as all of the other five aspects of organizational behavior cause problems. The overemphasis that has been placed on communications as the major source of trouble is what cannot be justified.

STANDARD 16.4

INTERPERSONAL COMMUNICATIONS TRAINING

Every police agency should immediately develop and improve the interpersonal communications skills of all officers. These skills are essential to the productive exchange of information and opinion between the police, other elements of the criminal justice system, and the public; their use helps officers to perform their task more effectively.

National Advisory Commission on Criminal Justice Standards and Goals, *Police* (Washington, D.C.: U.S. Government Printing Office, 1973), p. 401.

For the purposes of our discussion here, communication simply means the way in which information is exchanged. Communication can be oral, verbal, or nonverbal. Oral communication occurs through the use of the spoken word. Verbal communication too is based on words and can be either written or oral. Nonverbal communication, by contrast, takes place without any use of words.

People tend to be much more aware of oral and verbal communication, although in actuality a great deal of information that is neither written or spoken is received and transmitted. Gestures, facial expressions, and body language are a few examples of nonverbal communication.

When police officer John Doe delivers a message that a family member has been killed in an accident, he does not approach the task with a broad grin on his face; rather, he communicates a sense of sadness and sympathy by controlling his facial muscles and by looking grim. If he fully understands the impact of nonverbal communications, he may remove his hat, hunch his shoulders a bit, bow his head, and give the recipient of the information a reassuring pat on the back. By doing so, he is communicating nonverbally. Without using words, he is in effect saying, "I respect you. I sympathize with you. I, too, feel sad. Please let me reassure you."

Different effects can be achieved through nonverbal communication even though the same medium of communication is used. If you are driving down the street and see a friend, you are likely to tap your horn two or three times, smile, and wave. By doing this, you are saying, "Hello there. Nice to see you." If, on the other hand, you are driving down the street and are abruptly cut off by a driver you do not know, you are likely to lean hard on the horn two or three times, grimace, and even possibly make an unfriendly gesture. In both situations you communicate nonverbally; in the first instance you use the horn to communicate friendship; in the second, to communicate anger. Both recipients fully understand your nonverbal messages, even though not a single word has been spoken.

The ability to receive nonverbal communication is especially dependent on the powers of observation. In the examples given above, one need not have acute powers of observation to understand the intended messages. But not all nonverbal communication is so obvious; much of it is very subtle and extremely difficult to interpret. People who have superior powers of observation and who understand the importance of nonverbal communication are much more adept than others in picking it up and in interpreting it correctly.

Whether the message is verbal or nonverbal, the information received is useless if the recipient is unable to interpret it accurately. Such interpretation involves perception. Physiological capacities, attitudes, roles, self-concepts, and motivations combine to determine how accurately a person receives information. Two individuals may receive the same message but perceive it differently. Faulty perception, therefore, is the main cause of organizational communication problems.

Most of a police chief's communication is verbal—either written or oral. The chief transmits information to subordinates and superiors and receives information from many other people. Communication is, in fact, the medium of management. It is the device by which management transmits and receives all information essential to organizational stability and well-being. Inasmuch as people speak to one another more often than they write to one another, most organizational communication is oral.

Oral, verbal, and nonverbal communication can be either one-way or two-way. One-way communication involves the transmitting of information; the reception of such information may or may not occur. Two-way communication involves: (1) the transmission and reception of information and (2) a retransmission of the information by the receiver to the transmitter, confirming the fact that the communication is fully understood. In two-way communication, the receiver is required to indicate what he or she perceived the message to be. The transmitter learns through this process whether or not the intended message was accurately received, which in effect implies accurate perception on the part of the receiver.

From a systems perspective, the essential difference between one-way and two-way communication is that the latter provides for feedback, a necessary element in maintaining a closed-loop system. In two-way communication the transmitter gets information (feedback) about the quality of the attempt to communicate, learning whether or not success was achieved in getting the message across. Two-way communication, therefore, has a distinct advantage over one-way communication: accuracy. Since accuracy is essential to the communicative process, a police chief should utilize two-way communication whenever possible. Because a receiver's accurate perception of a message as well as the confirmation of that fact are necessary elements if communication is to take place, it can be logically argued that two-way communication is the *only* real form of communication and that one-way communication totally misses the mark.[15]

The only apparent advantage of one-way communication is that it is faster; it involves fewer steps. If one considers the time lost as a result of organizational problems created by faulty communications, one-way communication is not a time saver in the long run. One-way communication serves a valid purpose in the police service only in emergency situations which require immediate action and in which a commanding officer has no time to evaluate through feedback whether or not orders are understood. It is only in such emergency situations that one-way communication becomes preferable to two-way communication and even then only when absolutely necessary.

Nothwithstanding its obvious faults, one-way communication is what is most frequently used by most people. There are numerous reasons for this. People find it difficult to understand that others do not perceive in exactly the same way that they do. Others are totally unaware that people perceive differently. One-way communication is easier and quicker. It also spares one the embarrassment of learning that he or she did not transmit and receive information perfectly.

Using one-way communication lets a person blithely assume that everyone understands everything he or she has written and said, and vice versa. Although these are very comforting assumptions and may make people feel very effective as communicators, nothing could be further from reality; people who make such assumptions are living in a dream world. Using two-way communications, on the other hand, provides a constant reminder of the fallibility and imperfections in communicating; all people are imperfect communicators. In two-way communication these problems can be overcome by recognizing them for what they are, which gives people the opportunity to become better communicators.

Both one-way and two-way communication can involve either writing or speaking; in some instances, they can involve both. Written messages generally have the advantages of being more carefully formulated and more permanent. Oral messages, however, are speedier and permit immediate feedback. On the negative side, written messages are more expensive and more time-consuming; if they are poorly written, conveying unintended ideas and questionable information, they accomplish nothing and may affect organizational goals and objectives in a negative way. Oral messages may have similar negative effects if the receiver is at all hesitant in asking questions to clarify meaning.[16]

The formal structure of communications as a system within the organizational framework will be discussed in a later chapter. Here, we are more concerned with communications as an interpersonal activity; as such, it requires technical proficiency in formulating and interpreting messages as well as an understanding of and a commitment to two-way communication processes. The latter requirement is every bit as important as the former. Even the most perfectly worded message can be misunderstood. Feedback is the only technique available which can ensure the transmitter and the receiver that they have the same perception with respect to the meaning of a given message.

A recent study has determined that 72 percent of a police officer's time is spent in some form of communication activity.[17] The percentage figure for police chiefs would probably be even higher; most of a police chief's time is spent in communicating. Success in management is clearly related to success in communicating. The police chief who is a poor communicator can never become a successful police manager. Drucker tells us that "the manager's . . . effectiveness depends on his ability to listen and to read, on his ability to speak and to write. He needs skill in getting his thinking across to other people as well as skill in finding out what other people are after."[18] In short, the effective manager needs to be an effective communicator.

SUMMARY

This chapter has emphasized the importance of attitudes, roles, self-concept, motivation, perception, and communication as elements of human behavior in organizational settings. These are just a few, but by far the most important, elements involved in human behavior. Controlling and manipulating human behavior in police organizations is an exceedingly complex task; a police manager's job would be an easy one if human behavior were less complex.

The police manager who is interested in reaching an objective understanding of the behavior of others must first come to a point of self-understanding and must develop an awareness of his or her own attitudes, roles, self-concepts, motivations, perceptions, and communication talents and understand that his or her own behavior is determined largely by these factors. Only then can the police manager really understand fully why others behave as they do.

DISCUSSION QUESTIONS

1. How important do you think it is for police managers to have a sound understanding of human behavior?

2. What systems are you a part of?

3. Try to identify your religious attitudes, or beliefs. Does your behavior directly match those beliefs?

4. Try to identify your prejudices. Are they rational or irrational, in your opinion? Try to figure out how and when you developed them.

5. What roles do you play? Try to put them in rank order from most important to least important. Are there situations in which your least important roles become very important?

6. As a police manager, how would you deal with the behavior of the Cod Bay sergeant and the patrol officer. What was the influence of role expectations on their behavior?

7. Suppose that you were a captain in the Tulane City Police Department, and the new mayor appointed you police chief. How would you deal with the dominant police subculture? How would you deal

with the former chiefs? Suppose you were just a middle-level manager, say, a patrol lieutenant, in the organization as it is described. How would you deal with the chief, the former chiefs, and the dominant police subculture?

8. Suppose you were a sergeant in the Rixton Police Department. How would you deal with the chief and with the dominant and minority police subcultures?

9. Examine your self-concept. Can you see your behavior as helping you get from who you are to who you want to be?

10. As a police manager, what impact do you think you would have on the self-concepts of the people who work for you?

11. Are there things that you cannot do, or at least not as well as you would like? How does this affect your self-concept?

12. Why do you think people work?

13. Would most people work if they did not have to in order to support themselves? Would you?

14. As a parent and/or son or daughter, what motivational model would you say was employed or is employed in your family?

15. As a police manager, what motivational model or models would you subscribe to?

16. What motivational model seems to be in operation in the organization in which you now work? In the classroom?

17. Using Maslow's hierarchy, what would you say are the needs most important to you in your present situation? Would your answer have been different five or ten years ago? How do you think you would answer this question ten years from now?

18. Can you think of any behavior that cannot be explained by the nonmodel of human behavior?

19. In what ways do police officers perceive things differently from other people, because of their role?

20. How do you perceive school and tests? Is your perception related to your experiences? To your self-concept?

21. As a police manager, in what ways do you or could you communicate nonverbally?

22. How well do you perceive nonverbal messages from others?

23. How conscientious are you in maintaining two-way communications? How important do you think two-way communications are for the police manager?

24. How good a communicator are you? Do you communicate better orally or in writing?

25. How well do you understand yourself?

REFERENCES

1. N. Maier, *Psychology in Industrial Organizations,* 4th ed. (Boston: Houghton Mifflin, 1973), p. 42.

2. Albert J. Reiss, Jr., *The Police and the Public* (New Haven, Conn.: Yale University Press, 1971).

3. Edgar F. Huse and James L. Bowditch, *Behavior in Organizations: A Systems Approach to Managing,* 2d ed. (Reading, Mass.: Addison-Wesley, 1977), p. 75.

4. A. G. Athos and R. E. Coffey, *Behavior in Organizations: A Multidimensional View* (Englewood, N.J.: Prentice-Hall, 1968), p. 155.

5. C. H. Cooley, *Human Nature and the Social Order,* rev. ed. (New York: Scribner's, 1922), p. 184.

6. M. Christy, "The Delicate Presence of Cornelia Wallace," *Boston Globe,* Feb. 24, 1976.

7. Huse and Bowditch, *op. cit.,* pp. 80–100.

8. F. J. Roethlisberger and W. J. Dickson, *Management and the Worker—An Account of a Research Program Conducted by the Western Electric Company, Hawthorne Works, Chicago* (Cambridge, Mass.: Harvard University Press, 1939).

9. A. H. Maslow, *Motivation and Personality* (New York: Harper & Brothers, 1954).

10. H. J. Leavitt, *Managerial Psychology* (Chicago: University of Chicago Press, 1972), p. 182.

11. Athos and Coffey, *op. cit.,* p. 154.

12. *Ibid.*

13. M. Alexis and C. Z. Wilson, *Organizational Decision Making* (Englewood Cliffs, N.J.: Prentice-Hall, 1967), p. 69.

14. Leavitt, *op. cit.,* p. 25.

15. W. Scholz, *Communication in the Business Organization* (Englewood Cliffs, N.J.: Prentice-Hall, 1962), p. 32.

16. H. Koontz and C. O'Donnell, *Principles of Management: An Analysis of Managerial Functions* (New York: McGraw-Hill, 1968), pp. 607–608.

17. T. R. Cheatham and K. V. Erickson, "Law Enforcement Communication Contacts," *The Police Chief* **12**, 3 (March 1975): 49.

18. P. F. Drucker, *The Practice of Management* (New York: Harper & Brothers, 1954), p. 346.

CHAPTER 8
GROUPS IN THE POLICE
ORGANIZATION

LEARNING OBJECTIVES

1. Cite the premise generally rejected by sociologists and the perspective that replaces it.

2. Identify the three elementary forms of everyday human behavior.

3. Differentiate between activities and interactions.

4. Identify the three basic elements of the group social system.

5. Characterize emergent-system behavior in terms of positive and/or negative influence on the organization.

6. Characterize the likelihood of an emergent system developing in an organization.

7. Identify three characteristics of emergent-system development.

8. Describe output limitation norms and the reasons for their development.

9. Identify three important consequences of the development of the emergent system.

10. Describe the relative importance of the three consequences of the development of the emergent system.

11. Identify a likely cause of an organizational situation in which the required and emergent systems are clearly at odds.

12. Identify a likely cause of an organizational situation in which the required and emergent systems are in complete harmony.

13. Characterize the relationship between group cohesiveness and productivity.

14. Define group cohesiveness.

15. Cite the condition on which the relationship between cohesiveness and productivity depends.

16. Identify the three varieties of intergroup behavior.

17. Characterize intergroup behavior involving police organizations in terms of win/lose situations.

18. Identify the likelihood of conflict between and among groups.

In Chapter 7 we discussed the individual in the police organization, with a view toward gaining some understanding of the complexities of human behavior. We talked about such things as attitudes, roles, self-concept, motivation, perception, and communication. An understanding of these aspects of human behavior is critical for the police manager, whose whole job involves getting things done through other people in the organization. In this chapter we will continue the discussion of human behavior in organizational settings, but from a slightly different perspective. Here we will focus on groups rather than individuals and their implications for organizational behavior and management.

The discipline of sociology—the study of groups and group behavior—characterizes humans as social beings and studies them as such. Sociologists generally reject the premise that humans are loners, rugged individualists who operate independently of their fellow human beings. Instead, sociologists argue that people form groups and that much of a person's identity is based on group membership. Although this is an oversimplification of the sociological viewpoint, it provides the necessary insight to begin to form some notions about the sociological perspective.

Although one school of thought maintains that people first grouped together in order to defend themselves against transgressors, it is also argued that people are by nature social beings and that they join groups because it is their natural inclination to do so. There is obvious merit to both points of view.

Sociologists argue that people cannot be studied individually apart from their group associations. They claim that what people do and how they behave is influenced by the group or groups to which they belong. *Webster's New Collegiate Dictionary* defines sociology as "the systematic study of the development, structure, interaction, and collective behavior of organized groups of human beings."[1] Sociological studies provide tremendous insight into how groups impact on individual behavior, a matter of great importance to anyone studying police organizations and the individuals who comprise them.

The organization itself is a group, a formal configuration to which managers, supervisors, and workers all belong. If the organization is large, there will be many subgroups within it, each subgroup comprising employees who also belong to the larger organization. Employees in all likelihood will also belong to a number of outside groups that have nothing to do with the organization which employs them. Except for cloistered nuns and contemplative monks, this rule applies almost universally. In some cases outside groups influence employee behavior and thereby affect job performance and attitude.

It is not our intention to make sociologists out of you or even to present an overview of sociological findings as they relate to the ways in which groups influence behavior. Rather than attempt to do justice to the myriad perspectives of sociologists on the subject, we have chosen the works of one highly respected sociological theorist, George C. Homans, whose systems theory of groups is solidly based on observable behavior and is readily applicable to groups within organizations.[2] In addition, Homans's theoretical approach is compatible with our viewpoint. Although there are many other ways of looking at groups within organizations, we hope that by focusing on one theorist who, in our view, has put it all together, we will be able to present a much more coherent discussion of the subject.

ELEMENTS OF BEHAVIOR IN GROUPS

Homans based his group theories on observable behavior. His approach, therefore, is straightforward and easily understood. He found that everyday behavior can be classified in terms of three elementary forms: activities, sentiments, and interactions.[3]

Activities are what people do alone. Activities also include what people do with other people, although there is no reaction or feedback from the other people involved. Observable activities might include walking, writing, sewing, typing, sleeping, stamp collecting, shaving, praying, bicycling, woodworking, bird watching, swimming, and jogging. These behaviors would be classified as activities whether the person engaged in them alone or with other people whose presence did not influence his or her behavior through reaction or feedback. Another example of an activity is the lecture method of teaching, in which the instructor presents information without allowing discussion or questions.

People in police organizations certainly perform a wide variety of activities. Operational duties such as "shaking doors" to see if they are secure, administrative duties such as counting parking revenue, and many other police organizational functions are essentially activities. They are activities because the reaction of others is not ordinarily an integral part of these duties.

Sentiments are attitudes, feelings, and beliefs and are observable in the sense that they are expressed directly or indirectly in the statements and behavior of the individual. Observable sentiments might include attitudes toward work and supervisors; feelings of alienation, anger, sadness, satisfaction, friendship, pity, embarrassment, lust, understanding, sympathy, and contrition; and religious beliefs. Obviously, everyone harbors his or her own sentiments, not all of which are clearly observable. This is no less true in the police organization than in any other.

Interaction is activity among and between people—the actions people take toward, for, and with other people where the resulting reactions of other people provide feedback information that becomes a part of the ongoing behavior. Some observable interactions are making love, playing basketball, riding a tandem bicycle, participating in a conversation, taking part in a committee meeting, attending a cocktail party, and leading a parent-teacher discussion group. In each case the individual's behavior is necessarily directed toward one or more other persons, forcing some response which becomes a factor in the individual's continuing behavior. Note that the substantive behaviors in activities and interactions can be essentially the same. For example, one can play basketball with a group in such a way that it is an activity, by ignoring the presence of others and refusing to interact. So it is not really the behavior as such, but the manner in which it is "enacted" that differentiates activities from interactions.

Police work and police organizational behavior are replete with interaction. Patrol officers regularly interact with their supervisors, other patrol officers, dispatchers, crime victims, witnesses, suspects, traffic violators, and numerous other people. Police managers interact with their subordinates, peers, and superiors and with various representatives of the general public. Records clerks interact with people wanting public information (such as lawyers, employers, and traffic accident victims), police officers wanting information, those who supply information, and their supervisors. Interaction is an extremely common mode of behavior in most organizations and particularly in those reliant on information, such as police departments.

The elements of behavior in groups, then, are activities, sentiments, and interactions. An activity is an acted-out behavior that ignores other people and is conducted without benefit of reaction or feedback. A sentiment is an attitude that is directly expressed or one that can be indirectly inferred from observable behavior. An interaction is an acted-out behavior that involves more than one person, with the reaction of one person to the behavior of another influencing subsequent behavior. In Homans's view, all aspects of behavior in groups can be classified in terms of these three behavioral elements.

Police work, and police organizational behavior, is replete with interaction. (Courtesy of the Los Angeles County Sheriff's Department)

BASIC ASPECTS OF THE GROUP SOCIAL SYSTEM

The elements of behavior in groups just discussed use the individual as the frame of reference. Individual behavior was classified in terms of the three elements. Building on these, we can identify three basic aspects of the group social system: the required system, the personal system, and the emergent system.[4] These aspects of the group social system look at behavior in groups from the point of view of the group.

The *required system* is composed of those activities, sentiments, and interactions which are necessary for group survival. This refers essentially to the mandates of the job itself and to the required tasks that must be performed in order for the job to be productive and remain worthwhile and viable. Part of the required system of a police organization, for example, includes activities such as writing reports and retrieving records, sentiments such as believing in the concept of due process of law and a positive attitude toward guaranteeing constitutional rights, and interactions such as questioning witnesses and settling family disputes. If the police system falls short in any one aspect of the required system, its chances of accomplishing its goals and objectives are severely diminished.

The *personal system* comprises all of the personal predispositions that members of an organization bring to the workplace. However much management would like its employees to be blank slates, or automatons, waiting to be programmed for the job at hand, in the real world people come already equipped with deeply entrenched ideas, expectations, values, beliefs, attitudes, prejudices, and feelings. All of these elements of the personal system have an important, though imprecise, influence on the behavior of people at work in organizations. In police organizations, for example, many members have in their personal systems deep ethnic, religious, and racial prejudices and attitudes which often run counter to the stated policies and legal requirements of the organization for which they work. Although their prejudices and attitudes may not be reflected in their official behavior, they nonetheless become a factor in the group social system.

The *emergent system* is composed of the sum total of the behavior in the group setting that is not required for the group's survival. It is the result of the collision that occurs when the personal system impinges on the required system. The personal needs of the members of an organization, as expressed by their ideas, feelings, and values, are rarely satisfied within the purely job-related activities and interactions of the required system. While at work, people are usually not content with just silently, steadily working. Their personal systems make them want to talk, take breaks, work slowly sometimes and quickly other times, and behave in many other ways that are not strictly in accordance with the required system.

Emergent-system behavior is sometimes counterproductive to the pursuit of organizational goals and objectives. In a police organization, for example, the emergent activity of "cooping" (sleeping on the job), the emergent sentiment that free restaurant food is a fringe benefit of the police officer's job, and the emergent interaction of addressing ethnic-group members with derogatory slurs all will have a negative impact on organizational effectiveness. These are all behaviors not demanded by the required system, which makes them emergent, and by their nature they retard the organization's attainment of its goals and objectives.

There are two important considerations about the emergent system. First, its development is inevitable. Given human nature and the complexities of individuals, no organization can exercise the degree of control necessary to eliminate it. Second, the emergent system is not necessarily and not always quite the negative influence that the examples above might suggest. Emergent interaction, for example, might result in improvements in the required system. Frequently, worthwhile and profitable suggestions are received by management from members of the organization who are not generally encouraged or required to contribute to the organization beyond their own narrow scopes of interest. An individual with special knowledge or insight, a commitment to efficiency and effectiveness, and a dedication to the organization might very well make a contribution in the form of emergent interaction which benefits the required system and the organization as a whole.

As an example of emergent behavior that is not necessarily counterproductive, one of the authors, while a police patrol officer, submitted to his chief a proposal for an antiburglary program. This was emergent behavior because the author's assignment was to the patrol division, with no planning or program-development responsibilities. The chief responded cordially that the proposed program was a good one, but that it would never work because of public apathy. A year later the chief asked the author and another patrol officer to explore outside funding possibilities for an antiburglary program he was devising, and another year later the program was initiated with federal funding. The chief's antiburglary program looked quite familiar to the author. The emergent behavior of submitting the program proposal had resulted in an innovative program that potentially could contribute to the organization's attainment of its goals and objectives. The route may have been circuitous, but the result seems to have been positive.

EMERGENT–SYSTEM DEVELOPMENT

The emergent system is composed of all the behavior in the group or the organization that is not necessitated by the required system. It is all the behavior, then, that is not required in getting the work done and in ensuring the survival of the group. Since these activities, sentiments, and interactions of the emergent system are "extras" and are not required, they are not taught in training or compiled in general-orders manuals. Individually, they are brought to the workplace by the people employed there. Collectively, in terms of the emergent system of the group, these behaviors must develop over time. This development of the group emergent system can be described in terms of three identifiable characteristics: elaboration, differentiation, and standardization.[5]

Elaboration is the initial stage of development of the emergent system; members of the group develop activities, sentiments, and interactions not mandated by the required system. This process is generated, as previously mentioned, by the inability of the required system to satisfy all of the personal needs of the members of the group as expressed by their ideas and values.

Imagine a police recruit training class, for example. On their first day of training, the recruits do not know one another, are in a strange environment where the rules are unknown, and are very eager to impress. In the first session of the training class, an instructor will probably advise the recruits of the procedures and rules and regulations by which they will be expected to abide. These will essentially constitute the required system of the training class. Gradually, the recruits will develop additional behaviors. Some may come forward to talk to instructors during class breaks. Some may cheat on exams. Especially in physical or firearms training, some recruits who are proficient may give unrequired assistance to other recruits who are having a difficult time. These and many other kinds of behaviors may develop even though the required system does not mandate them.

Differentiation refers to the process whereby the activities, sentiments, and interactions of the emergent system become valued differently. Some behavior is seen as furthering the formal and informal interests of the group; this behavior is highly valued. Other behavior is perceived as hindering the formal and informal interests of the group; as might be expected, this behavior is looked on as being objectionable and is likely to be suppressed.

In our example about recruit training, it is easy to imagine differentiation following the elaboration of emergent-system behaviors. Talking to instructors during breaks is often perceived as furthering individual but not group interests; as a result, the recruit class might come to value this behavior negatively, so that recruits who engaged in it would be labeled as "apple polishers" or worse, and the behavior would be held against them. On the other hand, if a majority of the recruits were genuinely apprehensive about exams, cheating might come to be valued highly because many would participate in it and thus gain advantage. Thus cheating could be seen as contributing to group interests.

Differentiation also includes the rank relationships between and among people in the group, the so-called pecking order. Rank within the emergent system may or may not be associated with formal rank in the required system of the organization. A police union leader, for example, may hold high rank in the emergent system and low rank in the required system. Similarly, status in the police recruit training class may or may not be related to formal success on exams.

While the activities, sentiments, and interactions of the emergent system are being differentiated according to their perceived value to the group, *standardization* is also occurring. As various behaviors are becoming identified as having value, most group members will tend to gravitate toward those behaviors. Norms develop in the emergent system that give group members clues and provide them with guidelines on which to base their behavior in certain situations. For example, norms develop concerning output limitations. In a police organization, the emergent system might adopt a norm that regulates the number of moving-violation citations (traffic tickets) issued by patrol officers during a given period of time. This norm would be adopted on the basis of experience; it would satisfy the minimum standards of the required system, and it would not put a particularly heavy burden on any member of the group.

Why would such a norm develop? Without it, different officers might be writing widely varying numbers of tickets. Management would see that some officers were writing many tickets and then would want to know why other officers were writing so few. Management might penalize those who wrote tickets infrequently and come to expect all officers to write as many as the few zealous ones were. So the output limitation norms develop. Pressure is brought to bear on the zealous ticket writers and the absolute gold-bricks, encouraging each type to more closely adhere to the group norm. If they fail to conform, in all likelihood they will be ostracized by the group, which would have the effect of making their work lives very difficult. This is particularly true in policing, where the support and assistance of fellow workers can be lifesaving. As a result, emergent systems in police organizations tend to have very strong norms, so that it is accurate to say that emergent-system standardization is well developed in most police organizations.

CONSEQUENCES OF THE EMERGENT SYSTEM

We have noted that the development of the emergent system in any organization or group is inevitable and that the emergent system can have both positive and negative effects. Also, we have discussed the process of emergent-system development, which includes elaboration, differentiation, and standardization. Next, we will mention three important consequences of the development of the emergent system that are of concern to administrators. As pointed out by Athos and Coffey, these consequences are productivity, satisfaction, and growth.[6]

Productivity is the output of the labor contributed by members of the organization. It involves both the quality and the quantity of the services that the organization is in business to provide. It should be obvious that productivity is the basic concern of the required system and that it is greatly influenced by the emergent system. As mentioned earlier, the emergent system frequently develops norms of output limitation; these often compete with the productivity standards of the required system.

Satisfaction involves how the members of the group feel about their work, the personal relationships and interactions they experience at work, and the rewards and costs associated with their group membership. Satisfaction is dependent on the makeup of the personal system of the group member, his or her position in the required system and rank in the emergent system, and the prevailing norms of the emergent system.

Growth involves both individual group members and the group social system. It implies change for the better. Individuals who cease to grow and groups that become stagnant experience a decline in creativity, enthusiasm, fresh ideas, and commitment. Growth for the individual means learning new concepts, experiencing new ideas, confronting new situations, meeting new people, increasing skills, and continuing in the process of maturation. Growth for the group means growth for its members, increases in physical size, continued development of the required system, and improvements in productivity and satisfaction.

Successful administrators must be concerned about all three of these consequences. If they neglect productivity, the primary concern of the required system, it is impossible for the organization to achieve its goals and objectives. If they neglect satisfaction, the emergent system will provide it, often to the detriment of productivity, through its own activities, sentiments, interactions, ranks, and norms. If they neglect growth, their organizations will not be prepared to deal with the changes that the future is sure to bring.

These concerns are critical for the police manager, who must constantly monitor productivity, especially in these times of local government belt-tightening. In doing so, however, the manager cannot ignore the matter of satisfaction. We all know of wonderful programs and ideas, in policing and other pursuits, that were sabotaged on implementation by the workers who were expected to put the ideas into action.

This kind of failure is often the result of single-minded attention to productivity and inattention to satisfaction. By the same token, satisfaction is not a guarantee of high productivity. Police managers must maintain a strong concern for both at the same time, a difficult but not impossible task. They must also show an interest in individual and group growth. They can do this by encouraging comment and criticism, strongly supporting education and training, and demonstrating a willingness to try different approaches to problem solving and decision making.

A study of the emergent system in an organization can provide insights into the caliber and climate of its management. If the emergent system is clearly at odds with the required system, as demonstrated by strong output limitation norms, highly divergent rank structures, and hostile management-employee relations, it is likely that management is concerned solely about productivity, to the exclusion of growth and satisfaction. If, on the other hand, the emergent and required systems are in complete harmony, an indication that management is neglecting the mandates of the required system, productivity is likely to be extremely low. At both extremes, severe management problems are likely. To avoid these kinds of situations and problems, the manager must learn to emphasize productivity, satisfaction, and growth all at the same time. Again, this is not a simple matter, but it is the ideal toward which managers must strive.

GROUP COHESIVENESS AND PRODUCTIVITY

It is often assumed, incorrectly, that there is a positive relationship between group cohesiveness and productivity. Empirical research has consistently shown that no such relationship exists.[7] Some cohesive groups are productive whereas others are not; some loosely knit groups are productive, whereas others are not.

Cohesiveness refers to the feelings of closeness and camaraderie that bind the members of a group together. Cohesiveness is the glue that holds the people of an organization together, working in the common interest. Cohesiveness is demonstrated by how well the group members get along with one another, how strongly they identify with the group, and the extent to which the norms of the group are accepted and followed. Two key indicators of cohesiveness within an organization are employee turnover and attendance. To some extent, cohesiveness is related to satisfaction: The more cohesive groups are, the more their members tend to be satisfied.

The relationship between cohesiveness and productivity is dependent on the similarity between the goals and objectives of the required system and those of the emergent system. Where the goals and objectives are divergent, the cohesiveness of the group will support the emergent system and its output limitation norms; this inevitably results in a curtailment of productivity.

Cohesiveness—feelings of closeness and camaraderie—binds the members of a group together. (Courtesy of the Jackson Police Department, Jackson, Mississippi)

The recent history of two American League baseball teams provides good examples of how productivity is influenced by cohesiveness and satisfaction and by the impact of the emergent- and required-system concepts. The Boston Red Sox won the American League pennant in 1967. Because the team members had considerable talent, they were expected to do well in subsequent years. They were a cohesive group made up of players and coaches who got along well with one another. They even got along well with the team owner, and satisfaction with the general situation reigned supreme. Following 1967, however, they developed a strong emergent system which resisted the efforts of a number of managers to effectively exercise control. The norms of the emergent system seemed to value high salaries and relaxed living to the exclusion of hard work and team play. This resulted in the team's failing to live up to expectations for seven consecutive years.

By contrast, the Oakland Athletics during this same period demonstrated very little group cohesiveness. Team members publicly fought with one another on a regular basis, and several failed to show up on time for spring training, due to salary disputes. They quarreled openly with owner Charles Finley, and some asked to be traded. Others played out their options and became free agents. But despite these continuing problems, the Athletics went on to win the World Series for three consecutive years, a feat that the Red Sox have never been able to accomplish in their entire history.

By what mysterious formula were the Athletics able to be so much more productive? That they were talented is, of course, indisputable. But, then, so were the Red Sox. Very simply, the Athletics were successful at preventing their lack of cohesiveness from interfering with the tasks and responsibilities and the goals and objectives of the required system. This was largely the result of good management, which insisted that the goals and objectives of the required system remain dominant over the goals and objectives of the emergent system. Although the team lacked cohesiveness in the club house, it achieved it to a remarkable degree on the field. This concept of success and productivity may be applied to all sorts of groups, including police organizations.

VARIETIES OF INTERGROUP BEHAVIOR

In addition to the relationships which exist between and among individual members of a group, a study of groups would be incomplete if it did not include the relationships between and among groups themselves. These relationships can run the gamut from perfect cooperation to bitter conflict. There are three basic factors involved in this spectrum of intergroup behavior; cooperation, competition, and conflict.

Cooperation refers to situations in which groups involved with one another get along, lend assistance whenever needed, share information, and generally work with one another toward a common goal. Cooperation allows the groups to be more productive and effective than they would ordinarily be if they worked alone.

Cooperation, however, is not always a positive factor and does not always provide the spark that ignites groups to superior performance. Athos and Coffey note that cooperation can lead to contentment and that "unlike contented cows, contented groups do not always achieve the best possible results."[8] Cooperation, then, can lead to groups' becoming lethargic and can negatively affect group productivity.

Competition is a factor which fits into the American creed somewhere between Kansas in August and blueberry pie. It is a cherished American value and the basis of the American economic system. It is understood that groups in competition vie with one another in order to achieve greater productivity, win, or accumulate greater portions of available resources. Competition can in some instances spur groups on to increased effort. On the other hand, the desire to win and the fear of losing can produce harmful effects among the competing groups. The ends may come to be seen as justifying the means, for example, and the fear of failure may prevent some groups from entering the competition at all.

Competition is deeply ingrained in all aspects of American society. (Courtesy of the Metropolitan Police Department, Washington, D.C.)

Conflict occurs as the result of competition for limited resources and rewards. It also arises between and among groups with incompatible goals and objectives. Groups in conflict tend to become more internally cohesive, distrust one another, characterize themselves positively in every respect, and stereotype competing groups as negative in every respect. Huse and Bowditch point out that such competition and conflict can be useful only in a clear win/lose situation where the groups involved are independent of one another, such as in the case of two advertising agencies competing for a particular account.[9] Where the groups involved are interdependent, as are two divisions of one organization, the winning group will be adversely affected by the failure of the losing group. In such an instance victory will always be accompanied by defeat.

Intergroup behavior involving police organizations is rarely of a win/lose variety, because police organizations are independent of very few groups in society. Even in dealings with organized criminal groups, a "victory" for the police would be accompanied by losses. Useful sources of information would be eliminated, known patterns of criminal activity would be replaced by more unpredictable patterns, and some restraining controls on particular types of criminal activity would be removed.

Police organizations are even more interdependent with more legitimate groups in society. Police competition for funds with other criminal justice agencies and social service agencies illustrates this. If the police were to "win" the competition with these other organizations for the limited resources available, it would certainly be a defeat for them in the long run. The criminal justice system, except for the police, would be unable to operate efficiently or effectively, so that suspected criminals would not be convicted, restrained, reformed, rehabilitated, or reintegrated into society in any meaningful manner. Also, the more general social service system would be unable to serve its clientele in a fashion designed to solve human problems. So the social climate and the criminal justice system would deteriorate, causing severe problems for the police—all because they "won" the competition for resources.

These two examples are not meant to imply that the police should leave organized crime alone and turn their budgets over to other organizations. They are simply offered as examples of the possible consequences of an all-out competitive approach in a highly interdependent society. With respect to the organized-crime illustration, the potential losses may be negligible when compared to the benefits of eliminating the problem. With respect to the other criminal justice and social service organizations, a healthy mixture of competition and cooperation may be a preferred approach to the issue of resource allocation.

Intergroup behavior involving groups within police organizations is also rarely of a win/lose variety. Competition to solve a criminal case may lead to an unwillingness to share information between, for example, the patrol and detective divisions. Each wants so badly to personally solve the case that everyone loses sight of organizational goals and objectives. In such a situation the pooling of information might well lead to an early solution, but the fear of not getting credit often prevents such cooperation. The competitive atmosphere may also be spurring investigative efforts, of course. The police manager must attempt to maintain a healthy balance between competition and cooperation.

Conflict between and among groups is inevitable. This includes conflict between and among groups in a single organization. The challenge for the administrator is to manage conflict so as to minimize its costs. The best way to accomplish this is to keep conflict out in the open, attempt to reduce stereotyping, move people internally on a frequent basis from group to group, actively seek input on conflict resolution from everyone involved, encourage group interaction, and seek participation from the members of individual groups on the establishment of organizational goals and objectives.[10] In other words, attempt to resolve conflict by actively promoting cohesiveness in the required system.

SUMMARY

It is impossible to understand human behavior without taking into consideration the influence of groups on people. Human behavior can be classified in terms of activities, sentiments, and interactions. The interdependence of these elements of behavior is reflected in the group social system, which is made up of the required, personal, and emergent systems. The emergent system develops because of the inability of the required system to satisfy all of the personal needs of group members. The development of the emergent system involves three identifiable characteristics: elaboration, differentiation, and standardization. The relationship between the required and emergent systems, and particularly the degree of congruence between their respective goals and objectives, influences productivity, satisfaction, and growth as well as the cohesiveness of the group. Group cohesiveness is also influenced by intergroup relations, which are characterized by cooperation, competition, and conflict.

The police administrator must understand the concepts presented in this chapter as well as their implications for the police organization in order to work successfully with the various groups that comprise the police department and the rest of society.

DISCUSSION QUESTIONS

1. Which characterization do you think is more accurate of the individual: a rugged individualist or a social animal? Why?

2. Think about the classroom situation in terms of group characteristics. What are the required and emergent systems?

3. In the text we argue that the influence of the emergent system on the organization can be either positive or negative. What is the influence of the emergent system in the classroom?

4. In your school and/or work career, have you encountered output limitation norms? In what situations? How did you react to them? How would you react as a manager?

5. As a manager, how would you go about emphasizing productivity, satisfaction, and growth all at once?

6. Describe some groups with which you are familiar in terms of their cohesiveness. Then assess their productivity. What seems to be the relationship between cohesiveness and productivity in these groups?

7. In the text we claim that conflict in organizations is inevitable. As a manager, how would you deal with it?

REFERENCES

1. By permission. From *Webster's New Collegiate Dictionary* © 1977 by G. and C. Merriam Co., Publishers of the Merriam-Webster Dictionaries.

2. George C. Homans, *The Human Group* (New York: Harcourt, 1950).

3. *Ibid.*

4. Anthony G. Athos and Robert E. Coffey, *Behavior in Organizations: A Multidimensional View* (Englewood Cliffs, N.J.: Prentice-Hall, 1968).

5. Homans, *op. cit.*

6. Athos and Coffey, *op. cit.*

7. Clovis R. Shepherd, *Small Groups* (San Francisco: Chandler, 1964), pp. 85–96.

8. Athos and Coffey, *op. cit.*, p. 207.

9. Edgar F. Huse and James L. Bowditch, *Behavior in Organizations: A Systems Approach to Managing*, 2d ed. (Reading, Mass.: Addison-Wesley, 1977), pp. 203–204.

10. *Ibid.*, pp. 210–213.

CHAPTER 9
LEADERSHIP IN THE
POLICE ORGANIZATION

LEARNING OBJECTIVES

1. Explain why leadership is an important concept for the police administrator to understand.

2. Differentiate among the terms "manager," "formal leader," and "complete leader."

3. Cite the three basic leadership functions.

4. Define the definition-of-structure function.

5. Compare upper-level and lower-level managers in terms of the definition-of-structure function.

6. State the coordination-control function.

7. Compare upper-level and lower-level managers in terms of the coordination-control function.

8. Define the goal- and norm-clarification function.

9. Cite the factor that separates managers from leaders.

10. Cite the five sources of influence.

11. Differentiate between the personal and position origins of coercion power.

12. Characterize the police manager's access to reward power.

13. Cite five general styles of leadership.

14. Cite the findings of studies that attempted to identify the personality traits and other personal characteristics that separate good leaders from bad ones.

15. Characterize the situational model of effective leadership.

16. Characterize leadership as an open or a closed system.

17. Identify some of the environmental factors that constrain the police leader.

Leadership is a difficult concept to define. To some, leadership is a science that can be mastered through study and practice. Others regard it as an art and maintain that leaders are born, not made. Some believe that leaders are respected and admired by their followers. Others believe that they are feared. It is not uncommon for people to believe that real leaders can be identified by their abilities to take charge in all situations. Others, who note that the captain of the football team is not always the president of the student council, believe that leadership talents pertain only to certain groups and that different group members will emerge in leadership roles in different situations in accordance with formal credentials, proven expertise, charisma, and range of contacts.

None of these perceptions of leadership is completely right or completely wrong. Because leadership is a factor that is involved in human behavior, it is not easily defined, described, or categorized. Any attempt to understand what a leader is must focus on functions, sources, styles, and theories of leadership, the topics discussed in this chapter.

Leadership is an extremely important concept for the police administrator to understand. In the police field leadership is critical as new organizational patterns emerge, the police attempt to adjust to rapid social change, large numbers of women and minority-group members join police departments, and the police are required to handle an ever-increasing and diverse range of social problems. The Police Foundation has noted that "progressive police leadership is essential both in terms of sensing the need for change and in managing the process of change."[1]

THE POLICE LEADER AS A SUBSYSTEM

One of the most important factors to consider in discussing leadership is that the leader is an individual whose behavior is influenced by a monumental number of variables. Thus as an individual, the police leader's behavior is influenced by attitudes, roles, self-concept, motivation, and perception and communication abilities.

A leader, like other individuals, also participates in a number of groups. Thus a leader may not only lead groups, but also be a nonleading member of other groups, including those made up of leaders. A chief of police, for example, might be a deacon in the Presbyterian Church, president of the state association of chiefs of police, a Rotarian, and a member of the International Association of Chiefs of Police. Aspects of group behavior and interaction, including conformity, cohesiveness, output limitation, cooperation, competition, and conflict all have their influence on the leader.

A police chief is a *formal leader;* that is, the chief has been designated as the person in charge and has been granted authority to command the people assigned to the police department. All other police managers are formal leaders too. The sergeant has formal authority with respect to commanding a squad or platoon, the shift commander has formal authority with respect to all the patrol officers and patrol sergeants working during a given tour of duty, and the director of the planning and research division has formal authority with respect to the members assigned to that division.

The terms *formal leader* and *manager* are very similar; in fact, all managers are formal leaders. But a formal leader is not necessarily a *complete* leader. There is considerably more to leadership than simply being given authority and being designated as the formal leader.

THE FUNCTIONS OF LEADERSHIP

Just as the terms *leader* and *police manager* are not synonymous, so too the functions of the leader and the police manager are not identical. In Chapter 5 we grouped the basic functions of police management into the categories of planning, organizing, staffing, directing, controlling, and system building. Here we will discuss leadership in terms of the following three functions:

1. definition of structure;

2. coordination control; and

3. goal and norm clarification.

Definition of structure   This leadership function is similar to the management functions of organizing, staffing, and system building. One of the principal tasks of a leader is to arrange people and jobs for the accomplishment of goals and objectives or, more simply, for the purpose of getting things done, defining the structure.

In a sandlot baseball game, for example, the team leader will assign the players their positions in the field and their places in the batting order. Similarly, the leader of a crime scene search will indicate the types of evidence to look for, the search method to be used, and the particular assignments of the personnel involved. In both instances the leaders are defining the structures of the tasks to be performed so that the members of their groups will have a better idea of what to do and how to do it.

A police patrol sergeant regularly exercises definition of structure when assigning officers patrol areas. The investigative supervisor performs the same function when assigning cases to detectives. But these examples are relatively minor in scope when compared with the definition of structure of command-level police managers, especially the chief of police.

Upper-level managers make the basic organizing, staffing, and system-building decisions that establish the limits on the definition-of-structure decisions of lower-level managers. In terms of patrol personnel allocation, for example, the upper-level managers determine how many officers there will be in the patrol division, how they will be distributed by shifts and squads, what methods and techniques of patrol will be utilized, and how the patrol areas will be drawn. Though lower-level patrol managers normally assign individual officers to their patrol areas, they perform the definition-of-structure function with less authority and on a much smaller scale than do upper-level managers.

Coordination control This leadership function includes the management functions of directing and controlling and involves most of the leader's routine decision making. Relations with other groups, coordination of the efforts of the people in the group, and supervision of the work of the group members are all part of coordination control.

Leaders of musical groups, for example, are responsible for seeing to it that the music of the individual musicians harmonizes into good group sounds. They will also decide what music to play and what engagements to accept. In making these and other day-to-day decisons, the leaders are providing coordination control.

As another example, the leader of a police union is expected to schedule and run the organization's meetings, make routine decisions that cannot be delayed until a meeting is held, maintain contact with other police unions, and represent the union in dealings with management. No matter how democratically this or any other group may be structured, someone will always be needed to provide coordination control.

Coordination control is exercised by police managers at all levels, but to a significant extent lower-level managers determine how effectively this leadership function is carried out. In theory, upper-level managers issue most of the directives and are responsible for controlling the organization. But because they are few in number and cannot be everywhere at once, upper-level police managers depend on lieutenants and, particularly, sergeants to implement organizational direction and control. Sergeants interpret directives for their squads and largely determine what control measures will be initiated. Sergeants perform most of the supervision in the organization, represent their squads in relations with other organizational subunits, and are also responsible for coordinating the efforts of the individuals in their groups. So in contrast to the leadership function of definition of structure, coordination control is more closely associated with lower-level police managers than with upper-level ones.

Goal and norm clarification This function of leadership is both the most important and the most difficult to provide. It is through this function that the leader assists the group in defining acceptable and unacceptable behavior and developing the objectives of group activity. In performing this function, the leader often cannot simply impose personal desires on the group, but must be sensitive to the goals and norms of individual group members and attempt to clarify and synthesize them into group goals and norms. This is an inordinately difficult function to perform; often, the only method available to leaders is to demonstrate through their own behavior the goals and norms that they perceive to be, or think should be, the goals and norms of the group. This is generally referred to as *leading by example.*

When the late President John F. Kennedy wanted Americans to become more conscious of physical fitness, he was photographed swimming and playing touch football. Through his own behavior, he attempted to influence the physical-exercise norms of the American people.

Another international leader who personally demonstrated goal and norm clarification was Ho Chi Minh. The following passage describes his North Vietnamese army.

> There is nothing to distinguish their generals from their private soldiers except the star they wear on their collars. Their uniform is cut out of the same material, they wear the same boots, their cork helmets are identical and their colonels go on foot like privates. They live on the rice they carry on them, on the tubers they pull out of the forest earth, on the fish they catch and on the water of the mountain streams. No beautiful secretaries, no pre-packaged rations, no cars or fluttering pennants . . . no military bands. But, victory, damn it, victory![2]

Goal and norm clarification is important at all levels of the police organization. The function that is least analagous to managing, it is also the most elusive. It is essentially the function that differentiates the formal leader, or manager, from the complete leader.

In Chapter 7 we pointed out that the way police officers look at their jobs and their responsibilities is not always based on organizational policy. Instead, police officers are often left on their own to define their roles, which they may do individually or with the assistance of established cultures and subcultures. Role expectations developed in this manner may or may not agree with those held by the chief and other police managers.

The establishment of role expectations is one example of goal and norm clarification. The manner in which role expectations are defined in a police organization is a good indicator of the condition of its leadership.

When role expectations are developed by individual police officers, management has defaulted on its leadership role. It may still be managing by providing definition of structure and coordination control, but it is not leading. It has turned over the important leadership function of goal and norm clarification to individual officers; in essence, the organization has told its members to lead themselves.

It is no wonder, then, that police officers turn to their colleagues for goal and norm clarification. The police culture, and/or its subcultures, takes up the function of defining role expectations. Its leaders effectively become the organization's leaders, at least with respect to this one leadership function.

This process has occurred not only in police organizations, but in many others as well. It illustrates that effective managing is relatively common, as compared with effective leading, which is relatively uncommon. The function of goal and norm clarification separates the leaders from the managers.

In hierarchical organizations the relative importance of the three leadership functions varies according to level. That is, the most important function for the leader of the entire organization will differ from the most important function for the leader of an organizational division consisting of only a few people. In general, the function of *definition of structure* becomes more important as one goes *up* the organization, whereas *coordination control* becomes more important as one goes *down* the organization. The importance of *goal and norm clarification* does not vary as widely, but remains as a vital function for leaders at *all* levels.

SOURCES OF INFLUENCE

Leadership involves influencing the behavior of others. It is through the use of influence that a leader attempts to coordinate and control, define structure, and clarify goals and norms. The sources of this influence will be discussed in terms of the following five categories of power:

1. position power;

2. coercion power;

3. reward power;

4. expert power; and

5. charisma power.[3]

Position power This source of influence is completely independent of the individual leader. This type of influence flows directly from the position held by the leader and accrues to any person who occupies the leadership position. When a person vacates the position, the influence is left behind for the successor.

The authority of police officers to regulate human behavior in certain situations is an example of position power. When they are sworn in, police officers are granted powers not held by other citizens. When they leave the job, they lose these powers; they have them only so long as they remain police officers. These powers will, however, be granted to their replacements.

Other holders of position power are basketball referees, baseball umpires, legislators, judges, ship captains, and police chiefs. Within all organizations position power is delegated to all kinds of positions in the form of authority.

Position power is a basic source of authority and influence for police managers. Through such administrative principles as division of labor and delegation of authority, police management positions inherit power. Thus the patrol sergeant's authority to assign squad members to patrol areas originates in the position, not the person. Similarly, the authority of the operations commander to coordinate the activities of the patrol, investigations, and traffic divisions comes from the position, not the person.

Coercion power This source of influence is based on the threat or actual delivery of punishment. Coercion power may be vested in the position held by the leader, or it may be a personal attribute of the leader.

Parents, for example, have certain *coercion power* stemming from their position; they can legally inflict corporal punishment on their children. In addition, parents have inherent coercion power if they are bigger and stronger than their children. When their children reach majority age, parents lose much of the coercion power of their position; the inherent coercion power of size and strength usually dissipates much sooner.

Police managers acquire coercion power through their control functions. Patrol sergeants coerce their subordinates by assigning unpopular patrol areas as punishment for behavior they do not appreciate, and they can also recommend more severe punishments. Upper-level managers, though more removed from the basic operations of the organization, have greater coercion power in the form of harsher punishments. In theory at least, the police chief has the most coercion power, inasmuch as only the chief has the authority to punish everyone else.

Coercion power in police organizations can also be personal in origin. Some police managers are feared because of their size, temper, or scathing tongue, though they might rarely use the coercion power of their position. Nonmanagerial personnel may also exercise coercion power within the police organization. Such use may be for personal gain or retribution, but it may also be exercised on behalf of the organization, the dominant culture, or a subculture. It may be used on behalf of the organization, for example, to bring into line a fellow officer who is giving the department a bad name by taking bribes, lying in court, or roughing up suspects. Coercion power may also be used on behalf of the dominant subculture to coerce an officer who refuses to participate in corrupt, dishonest, or brutal activities.[4]

Reward power   This source of influence is based on the ability of the leader to bestow rewards on other group members. As with coercion power, reward power may be an inherent characteristic of the position held by the leader. To a lesser degree, it may simply be a device developed by the leader to distribute as rewards some of his or her own personal property or finances.

The leader of a political machine, for example, traditionally wields influence in the form of government jobs and contracts to reward supporters; although the morality and ethics of such rewards are often questioned, the fact remains that jobs and contracts are used as a source of power by many political leaders. Those political leaders who are independently wealthy or who have financial support from large numbers of contributors might choose to pay supporters for their services and thus reward them for their loyalty and their assistance. Nelson Rockefeller was one such leader who exercised reward power in this way. Similarly, an employer who gives employees bonuses or salary increments is using reward power as a source of influence.

One of the difficulties of police management, and of public administration generally, is the relative unavailability of rewards. Police managers ordinarily cannot reward good performance with bonuses, salary increases, or even promotions. Civil service regulations and the realities of public finance prohibit such gestures, for the most part. For rewards, police managers can offer little more than a handshake and a pat on the back.

These kinds of rewards are not without value, however. Most people appreciate recognition and like being told that they have done a good job. In addition, modest benefits such as desirable assignments, days off, first choice of vacation times, recognition awards, and new equipment and supplies may sometimes be used by the police manager to reward good performance.

Expert power This source of influence derives from the skill, knowledge, and expertise of the leader. It is based on the leader's ability to accomplish difficult tasks that others would be either unable or unwilling to perform. Although the position held by the leader might serve to identify the expert, the influence the leader has comes directly from innate and learned talents.

At the scene where an explosive device has been found, for example, bomb-disposal technicians will very likely assume leadership because of their special training and skill. Even if they are the lowest-ranking officers at the scene, their expert power will give them considerable influence over everyone else present, regardless of their ranks or positions.

When officers or managers in staff positions want to exert influence on line operations, they often have to rely on expert power. Members of the planning and research unit who have discovered a pattern of criminal activity, for example, would rely on their expertise to try to convince the chief, the operations commander, patrol sergeants, and patrol officers to base future activities on their findings. The extent to which these individuals altered their work behavior as a result of these findings would depend on how much expert power they believed the members of the planning and research unit possessed. If their discovery turned out to be inaccurate or false, their expert power would diminish.

On the other hand, if criminal apprehensions were made as a result of their findings, their expert power would be strongly enhanced.

Charisma power This source of influence is drawn from the leader's personality, reputation, integrity, attractiveness, values, and general reputation. Leaders have influence over other people because of an almost ethereal quality about them which makes others want to believe in them and follow them.

Among the outstanding examples of charismatic leaders in recent history are Mahatma Gandhi and Martin Luther King. Both developed tremendous influence over large numbers of people even though their source of influence was restricted solely to charisma power. They had no significant position power, no expert power, and no capabilities to coerce or reward their followers; yet there was something about them as individuals that caused literally millions of people to believe in them and to follow them.

A person's personal qualities are the basis of charisma power. (Courtesy of the Los Angeles Police Department)

STYLES OF LEADERSHIP

The manner in which the leader exercises power and influence in order to carry out leadership functions is often referred to as leadership *style*. Certainly every leader's style is unique; it may even differ somewhat from situation to situation. For purposes of discussion here, we will define five general styles of leadership:

1. autocratic;

2. bureaucratic;

3. diplomatic;

4. participative; and

5. free-rein.[5]

Autocratic style The autocratic, or authoritarian, leader makes decisions and carries them out according to his or her own personal beliefs and without regard to precedent, rules and regulations, or the opinions of others. Autocratic leadership has the advantage of speedy decision making and works well if most group members are seeking to avoid responsibilities. It has the disadvantage of being associated with one-way communication and its attendant shortcomings. Inasmuch as the leader makes all decisions personally, this style will be unsuccessful if the leader is not an expert in a wide range of areas. The autocratic leader is almost always resented by those in the group who believe that they have something to contribute and who think that they should be consulted in decision making.

Bureaucratic style Bureaucratic leaders operate by the book, basing every move on a careful examination of the policies, procedures, rules and regulations, general orders, and other directives in effect in the organization. If they have any doubt as to the proper course of action, bureaucratic-style leaders will first consult their superiors or someone else likely to know the correct way to proceed. Bureaucratic leadership is consistent and fair; similar situations will be treated similarly.

The basic shortcoming of this leadership style is that it is not at all flexible. Operating by the book limits the leader's ability to adapt to changing circumstances and to react to the nuances and mitigating factors present in all situations. This kind of inflexibility often leads to resentment, as the people involved dislike not being treated as individuals.

Diplomatic style Diplomatic leaders make most of their decisions without consulting anyone. After decisions are made, they attempt to soft-sell them to the group, using gentle methods of persuasion and appeals to reason. By explaining to a group the reasoning behind a decision, a diplomatic leader often gets the group's cooperation in the execution of the decision. The group is likely to interpret the leader's efforts as a show of respect for its membership and abide by the decision as an expression of appreciation. On the other hand, if the leader does a poor job of selling the decision to the group, his or her efforts may seem to be an insincere gesture and will probably be resented. Diplomatic leaders also run the risk that some group members may view their efforts to explain their decisions as signs of weakness and insecurity.

Participative style This style of leadership emphasizes consulting group members before decisions are made; in some cases they may even make the decisions themselves. In either instance the members' inputs influence the decision-making process. As a result, there is ordinarily more support for the decision among the group members. There is also more information available for those making the decision, including information from the grass-roots level, where the decision will probably be carried out. Additionally, participation by group members contributes to their own personal and professional growth, making them better suited for future decision-making positions.

This style has the disadvantage of being time-consuming, however. It is also likely to establish cliques within groups, which can cause morale problems and even hinder the decision-making process. Furthermore, it provides leaders with a device by which they can avoid their own responsibilities. Finally, group members who are consulted and have their ideas rejected can become extremely resentful of the leader and eventually cause his or her downfall.

Free-rein style Free-rein leaders exercise a minimum of direction and control over their groups; they attempt to avoid making decisions whenever possible. Some group members are comfortable and productive in this kind of laissez-faire environment. Because individual group members are called on to make many of their own decisions, significant individual growth is possible. Professional people usually work very well within this kind of setting. On the other hand, some people cannot operate effectively in such an unstructured situation. Because the free-rein style of leadership provides for little control over the activities of group members, the risks involved are very high.

A recent research study surveyed all members of one police department in an attempt to identify the most preferred style of leadership and management.[6] The choices available to respondents on each item of the survey represented the full range of leadership styles. The study found that the choice of all ranks was a consultative style of leadership. In terms of the styles discussed above, this would be very similar to the participative, with some likeness also to the diplomatic, style. The consultative style was characterized by supportive (helping) relationships, substantial trust, delegated decision-making authority, and moderate interaction up and down the hierarchy.

THEORIES OF LEADERSHIP

Which kind of leader is likely to be the most successful? This question has drawn the attention of a large number of behavioral theorists. Early efforts to answer the question tended to focus on personality traits and other personal characteristics, attempting to identify those that were common in good leaders. Jennings sums up these efforts by stating that "fifty years of study have failed to produce one personality trait or set of qualities that can be used to discriminate between leaders and non-leaders."[7]

Attempts to identify one or another of the leadership styles as the most effective were also unsuccessful. McGregor hypothesized that the method of leadership used should depend on characteristics of the leader, the followers, and the organization as well as on the social, economic, and political milieu in which the leader operates.[8] An adaptation of guidelines developed by Loen is as follows:

1. use the *autocratic style* if you are an expert and in all emergency situations;

2. use the *participative style* only when group members are extremely capable; and

3. use the *free-rein style* when group members are capable of being productive when working independently.[9]

Research by Likert has indicated that a supportive type of leadership may be the most successful.[10] He found that leaders who genuinely tried to help their groups' members and who sought to develop cohesive groups with comprehensive goals were generally effective. Berkley agrees with this thesis, claiming that "the new organizational leader finds increasingly that he can obtain more from his subordinates by acting as their teacher rather than as their director."[11]

Most current thinking supports a situational model of good leadership; the kind of leadership that will be most successful will vary from one situation to another. One of the best known and most fully developed situational theories was advanced by Fiedler. He worked with two styles of leadership—*task-centered* and *group-centered*—and then sought to identify the factors in the situation that determined which style would be more effective.[12]

Fiedler identified three critical situational factors:

1. *leader-member relations;*

2. *task structure;* and

3. *position power.*

He characterized situations in terms of whether their *leader-member relations* were good or bad, their *task structures* were clear or vague, and whether the *position powers* of the leaders were strong or weak. Fiedler found that when all factors were positive (when leader-member relations were good, task structures were clear, and position power was strong), the *task-centered* leader was more successful. When all factors were negative (when leader-member relations were poor, task structures were vague, and power position was weak), the *task-centered* leader again was more successful. When the factors were mixed, the likelihood of the *group-centered* leader's being more successful increased.

Some applications of Fiedler's theory are very specific in prescribing leadership styles for particular combinations of good or poor leader-member relations, clear or vague task structures, and strong or weak position powers. These practical applications of the theory, however, have yet to be validated. But the answer to the question: *Which kind of leader is likely to be the most successful?* is clear from Fiedler's research. It all depends.

THE ENVIRONMENT OF POLICE LEADERSHIP

Leadership, as an element of human behavior, is an open system, influenced by and having influence on its environment. It would be much simpler to understand, and much easier to provide, if it were exercised in a vacuum, but such is not the case.

In performing leadership functions, police managers are constrained by external factors. In defining the structures of their organizations, they are limited by budgetary considerations, and political pressures often dictate their allocation of personnel and their design of patrol areas. Coordination control is greatly restricted by the natural human desire to avoid and evade direction and control. Goal and norm clarification has as its boundaries the goals and norms of the entire society, and within these limits police cultures and subcultures further constrain the influence of the manager.

The position power available to police managers is determined by their superiors and is thus susceptible to change. Even the chief has superiors (the mayor, city manager, city council, public safety director) who can alter the power of the chief's position. Coercion power, the ability and/or authority to punish, is strictly limited by civil service regulations, due process guarantees, and the criminal law. Reward power, as we noted earlier, is also limited by civil service and the budget. Expert and charisma power are more clearly vested in the person, but nevertheless their exercise is also constrained by human, organizational, and political factors.

These are some of the reasons why leadership is difficult to provide in police organizations. Police leaders operate in an environment that includes the constraining influences of politics, law, other interdependent agencies, police fraternal organizations and unions, budgets, and human behavior. It is not an easy task to provide definition of structure, coordination control, and, particularly, goal and norm clarification in such an environment.

SUMMARY

At the outset of this chapter, we indicated that leadership is not easily defined, described, or categorized. There are a number of functions that leaders perform, a number of ways that they go about performing them, and a number of theories about which ways are the best. Although it has been the subject of considerable research over the years, leadership remains one aspect of human behavior about which not very much is known.

A long time ago, a Chinese sage named Lao-tzu said something about leadership; although his research design is not clear, we still take him at his word:

> As for the best leaders, the people do not notice their existence. The next best, the people honor and praise. The next, the people fear; and the next, the people hate. . . . When the best leader's work is done the people say, "We did it ourselves." [13]

STANDARD 7.7

IMPORTANCE OF POLICE ADMINISTRATOR

In addition to directing the day-to-day operations of his agency, the police adminis-trator has the responsibility to exert leadership in seeking to improve the quality of police service and in seeking to solve community-wide problems of concern to the police. The position of police chief should be recognized as being among the most important and most demanding positions in the hierarchy of governmental officials.

American Bar Association Project on Standards for Criminal Justice, *The Urban Police Function,* Approved Draft (New York: A.B.A., 1973), pp. 14–15.

DISCUSSION QUESTIONS

1. Do you think that leaders are born or made? Why?

2. Do you think that the best leaders are respected and admired or feared?

3. How would you describe the difference between a manager and a leader?

4. The three basic leadership functions are definition of structure, co-ordination control, and goal and norm clarification. How do these relate to the chief of police? To an administrative captain? To a patrol sergeant?

5. In what ways can a police manager exercise the leadership function of goal and norm clarification?

6. What is the condition of leadership in organizations with which you are familiar?

7. Compare the following officials in terms of sources of influence: police officer, patrol sergeant, patrol captain, chief of police, mayor, judge, prison warden, probation officer, assembly-line super-visor, and company president.

8. Identify some charismatic leaders. What gives them their power?

9. Which leadership style best suits you as a follower? As a leader?

10. What is your theory about which kind of leader is likely to be most successful?

11. Analyze your present work situation according to the three critical

factors in Fiedler's theory. Which kind of leader does the situation seem to call for? Does the present leader operate that way? Is the present leader successful?

12. How can police leadership be effective, given all of the environmental constraints that limit it? As a police leader, how would you deal with all the constraints?

REFERENCES

1. *Experiments in Police Improvement: A Progress Report* (Washington, D.C.: Police Foundation, 1972), p. 18.

2. J. Roy, *The Battle of Dienbienphu* (New York: Harper & Row, 1965), p. 304.

3. J. French and B. Haven, "The Basis of Social Power," in *Group Dynamics: Research and Theory*, 3rd. ed., ed. D. Cartwright and A. Zander (New York: Harper & Row, 1967).

4. An excellent example of this is P. Maas, *Serpico* (New York: Bantam Books, 1972).

5. J. Owens, "The Art of Leadership," *Personnel Journal* **52**, 5 (May 1973): 393.

6. R. Reams, J. Kuykendall, and D. Burns, "Police Management Systems: What Is an Appropriate Model?" *Journal of Police Science and Administration* **3**, 4 (December 1975): 475-481.

7. E. E. Jennings, "The Anatomy of Leadership," *Management of Personnel Quarterly* **1**, 1, (Autumn 1961): 2.

8. D. McGregor, *Leadership and Motivation* (Cambridge, Mass.: MIT Press, 1966), p. 73.

9. R. O. Loen, *Manage More By Doing Less* (New York: McGraw-Hill, 1971), p. 111.

10. R. Likert, *New Patterns of Management* (New York: McGraw-Hill, 1961), p. 7.

11. G. Berkley, *The Administrative Revolution: Notes on the Passing of Organization Man* (Englewood Cliffs, N.J.: Prentice-Hall, 1971), p. 85.

12. F. Fiedler, "Engineer the Job to Fit the Manager," *Harvard Business Review* **43**, 5 (September-October 1965): 115-122.

13. Quoted in R. Townsend, *Up the Organization* (New York: Knopf, 1970), p. 99.

PART IV
THE FLOW PERSPECTIVE

The two chapters of Part IV discuss the flow perspective of police administration. This perspective emphasizes organizational interactions rather than structures, principles, or people. Another way of characterizing this approach is by considering it to be process-oriented. A visual display of this perspective would be a flow chart of information channels and decision making.

Chapter 10 addresses communication and information flow in the police organization. Information is probably the most important "resource" utilized by a police department. All sorts of management and operational activities depend on the timely availability of pertinent information. In order to ensure the provision of such information, the police manager must carefully design an information system. Although information systems may incorporate computers and other sophisticated automatic data-processing equipment, the true test of the system is its reliability in providing needed information.

In Chapter 11 policies, procedures, and rules and regulations in police organizations are discussed. These forms of managerial guidance provide the flow of direction from management to employees. We argue that such guidance is critical in policing, because the complexity and variety of the tasks performed preclude complete predetermination of police behavior, while the importance and sensitive nature of those tasks require that management exercise some direction and control. This problem of the management of police discretion is a continuing one in law enforcement, for which there certainly is no one best solution. It is the sort of problem that police managers will always wrestle with, but never solve.

CHAPTER 10
COMMUNICATION AND
INFORMATION FLOW IN
THE POLICE ORGANIZATION

LEARNING OBJECTIVES

1. Compare the complexity of interpersonal and organizational communications.

2. Cite an example of unofficial communication in an organization.

3. Differentiate between formal and informal organizations.

4. Cite a reason for the development of the informal organization.

5. Compare the efficiency and effectiveness of official and unofficial communications.

6. Cite examples of good and bad influences of unofficial communications.

7. Identify the three directions of organizational communications.

8. Identify the main barrier to effective downward communications.

9. Compare the perceptions of subordinates and superiors with respect to upward communications.

10. Cite the reason for the growing importance of lateral organizational communications.

11. Cite the basic obstacle to effective lateral communications.

12. Define the substance of communications.

13. Characterize the importance of information in an organization.

14. Differentiate between open-loop and closed-loop communications and information systems.

15. Define the principle that identifies the decision maker.

16. Identify five common decision-making errors.

17. Characterize the decision-making system.

In Chapter 7 we discussed communication as an important element of human behavior; we said, in effect, that communication works in concert with roles, attitudes, self-concept, motivation, and perception to provide behavior as an output. We further indicated that communication is an involved and complex function for individuals to perform and that it is not often performed well.

If communication from one individual to another is a problem, consider the possibilities for difficulty in attempting to communicate with large numbers of people. In the organizational setting there are countless situations in which one individual must communicate with several others, groups of individuals must communicate with other groups, and groups must communicate with individuals. Severely complicating these processes of communication are the many and diverse roles played by individuals, superiors, subordinates, peers, group members, and competitors. These roles, in turn, influence the motivations of the participants and serve to impede good communication. Organizational communication, therefore, is much more complex than interpersonal communication.

ORGANIZATIONAL COMMUNICATION

Organizational communication is much more than a simple compilation of all of the interpersonal communication that takes place between and among members of an organization. It cannot be explained solely on the basis of the principles of interpersonal communications discussed in Chapter 7. Although these have a direct bearing on organizational communication, they must be considered in terms of some other organizational concepts.

Scholz has correctly maintained that "communication in an organization must be viewed as a system."[1] After discussing the channels, directions, and barriers of organizational communication, we will focus on communication and information systems and their provisions for feedback. Both interpersonal and organizational communications are dependent on feedback to ensure accuracy in the transmittal and reception of messages.

COMMUNICATION CHANNELS

In many organizations the best sources of information are secretaries. They type all the memoranda and letters, take notes at meetings, place and receive many telephone calls, answer questions when the boss is absent, and open most of the mail. They are key participants in a number of communication processes, and they have access to a great amount of information. People within the organization who want to get information without going through official channels can probably get the information they want if they know the right secretary.

Anyone who has ever served in the armed forces knows that sergeants, not generals, win wars. This, of course, is a facetious way of saying that much of what is accomplished in organizations is accomplished in unofficial ways. In the military, sergeants are the people who have the information and who are usually in a position to act on it. Many a soldier who knew the right sergeant could find out what was going on, have orders changed, and be sent to an exotic assignment; information unofficially obtained and put to the right use can be extremely useful.

In similar fashion, people who work skillfully within an organization can often get their messages through to someone else in the organization in an unofficial way. A police officer who is displeased with the sergeant, for example, can relay that displeasure to the chief simply by talking about the sergeant in front of the right people; the right people, in this instance, are those who have access to the chief and who take pleasure in spreading disparaging remarks.

These are examples of how unofficial communication can impact on people within an organization; such communication takes place in a milieu usually referred to as the *informal organization* (see Fig. 10.1). As opposed to communication that takes place in the *formal organization* (see Fig. 10.2), which may or may not be truly realistic, informal organizational communication is much more likely to be a manifestation of real activity and real information. The activity and information may or may not be in furtherance of organizational goals and objectives, but they are, nonetheless, real.

A formal organization chart establishes formal communicative relationships between superiors and subordinates and between peers at the same organizational levels. The organization that confines itself solely to these official communication channels will, in effect, starve its people for information. What happens in most organizations is that an informal organization develops for the purpose of facilitating unofficial communications. Organization members at all levels eventually learn to get the information they need; they learn to do this without going through official channels and without upsetting the formal organization.

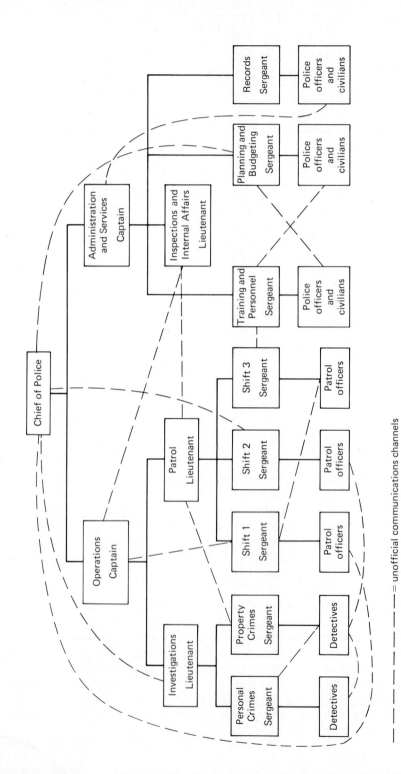

Fig. 10.1. The informal organization.

- - - - - = unofficial communications channels

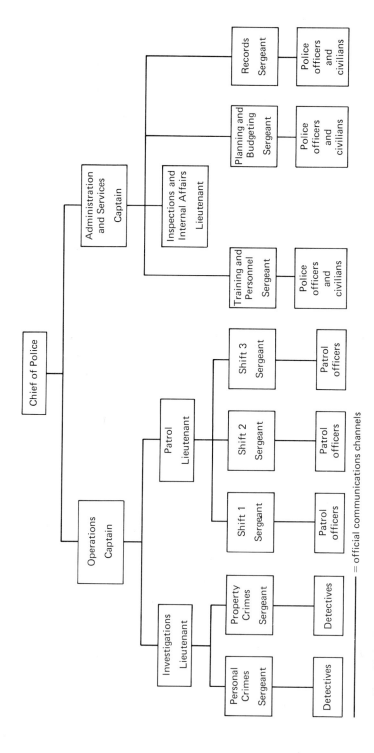

Fig. 10.2. The formal organization.

= official communications channels

As might be expected, the unofficial communication channels that develop are often more efficient and more effective than officially established channels. Unofficial communication channels are usually capable of passing information along more quickly; they can skip entire levels of the organization and avoid the red tape that the formal organization imposes on the communication process. The content of messages unofficially delivered is often clearer than the content of official messages; unofficial messages do not have to be enshrouded in official language or be designed to please readers along official communication channels.

Although unofficial communication channels are essentially neutral structures, their existence can exert both positive and negative influences on the organization as a whole. They can serve to enforce output limitation norms, spread rumors, pilfer confidential information, and generally create organizational turmoil. On the other side of the coin, unofficial communication channels have prevented many an organization from collapsing and disintegrating. They alert superiors to problems that middle managers do not recognize, choose to ignore, or attempt to hide. They provide information to decision makers when official communication channels are clogged. They allow competent people with incompetent supervisors to do their jobs, and they facilitate speedy communication in crises when official communication channels, even if they are working, are too slow.

Many police chiefs instinctively fight the informal organization, failing to recognize that it has probably developed because of the shortcomings of the formal organization, a matter which embarrasses them and affects their self-concepts. Secure and resourceful chiefs will recognize organizational inadequacies as the reason for the development of unofficial communication channels and will revise the structures and procedures of the formal organization so that efficient unofficial communication channels become, by proclamation, official. If they are unable to do this, they should at least attempt to recognize the value of these channels for the communication of information vital to the stability of their organizations. As Whitehead has noted, "if some department is in fact habitually obtaining information from another by unofficial means, this rather suggests that the information is found useful, and a few procedures for obtaining it with less trouble might be devised."[2]

COMMUNICATION DIRECTIONS AND BARRIERS

Communications in a formal organization can go up, down, or across (see Fig. 10.3). Downward communications go from supervisor to

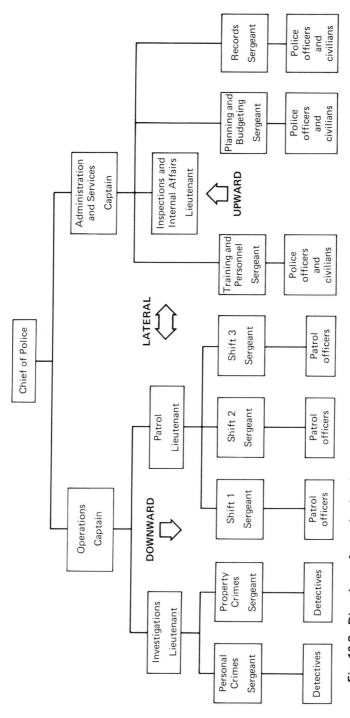

Fig. 10.3. Directions of organizational communication.

subordinate down the chain of command. Upward communications go from subordinate to supervisor up the chain of command. All other communications go laterally across the organization.

Downward is the most traditional and accepted direction of organizational communication. Downward is the direction in which orders are given and authority exercised. It is the direction in which police chiefs, command-level personnel, and supervisory personnel communicate with and through their subordinates.

The main barrier to effective downward communication is the chain of command. According to this principle of management, a police chief who wishes to get a message to a patrol officer at the operational level must transmit that message down the chain of command, through each level of management. A police chief who wants to tell a patrol officer to dress more neatly, for example, must give the message to the proper captain, who in turn gives it to the proper lieutenant, who gives it to the proper sergeant, who gives it to the patrol officer. Passing as it does through so many people, the message is likely to become distorted. Each person within the chain of command perceives the message differently, interprets its meaning differently, and transmits it with varying accuracy. Also, because each person in the chain is in an authority position with respect to the next recipient of the message, each tends to add his or her own contribution. With so many perceptions, interpretations, transmissions, and personal contributions involved, it is the rare message that finally arrives at its destination intact.

An example of how a message might go from a police chief to a patrol officer is outlined below.

1. *Chief to Captain:* "Captain, while I was driving through the city this morning, I saw Patrol Officer Burl App doing traffic duty at the corner of Center and Main. There was a rip in his coat; his hat was back on his head; he was smoking a cigarette; his pants were unpressed; and his appearance was sloppy. You give him this message from me: 'Shape up or ship out!'"

2. *Captain to Lieutenant:* "Lieutenant, the Chief talked with me this morning about Patrol Officer Burl App. He was mighty upset. Seems he saw App out on the street someplace and he looked pretty sloppy. He was also smoking a cigarette, which is against every regulation in the book. I've seen him a number of times myself when he needed a shave and a good shoe shine. Tell him he better get on the stick."

3. *Lieutenant to Sergeant:* "Hey, Sarge, the Captain was telling me about your man App this morning. I guess the Chief is pretty upset with him—wants him to shine his shoes and get a shave. By the way,

you tell him for me that nobody around here likes his attitude. Seems like he's in a dream world all the time. Tell him to get back down here to earth or we'll look for ways to bring charges against him."

4. *Sergeant to Patrol Officer:* "Say, App, I've got a message here for you from the Chief. He wants you to know that he doesn't like your attitude and he wants you to get your shoes shined."

5. *Patrol Officer:* "Who, me, Sarge?"

Upward communications undergo this same distortion as they pass through levels of the organization. But they are beset by many other distorting forces as well, largely because upward communications go directly against the grain of organizational authority. In upward communications, employees are giving supervisors information which may eventually be used in evaluating them. If the information is accurately communicated, it could reflect adversely on either the employee or the quality of his or her performance. Upward communications, therefore, are likely to be distorted at their inception.

It has been noted that supervisors generally tend to think that their subordinates feel free to discuss problems with them, whereas a much smaller percentage of subordinates believe that such an open relationship actually exists.[3] Employees often feel that it is dangerous for them to express their true feelings, that to disagree with their superiors will negatively affect their chances for promotions, that management is not really interested in their welfare, and that they will not be rewarded for good ideas.[4] Maier has suggested that although supervisors regard their jobs as positions of responsibility, subordinates view their supervisors' jobs as positions of power.[5] Because of apprehension about how supervisors will use their powers, subordinates attempt to keep them in the dark, cover up problems, avoid taking chances, protect one another, and generally play it safe.[6]

Gonzales and Rothchild have identified four common organizational characteristics which further thwart upward communication:

1. banish or otherwise decimate whistle-blowers and boat rockers— those employees who expose intolerable conditions, corruption, incompetence, and other problems in the organization;

2. place safe and loyal employees above and below troublemakers in the organization's hierarchy, thus effectively silencing them;

3. ask questions the answers to which are predetermined, giving management an appearance of being concerned about problems without actually confronting them; and

4. decline to inform management about what is actually going on because of a belief that management would probably not understand anyway, or worse, that management might try to become directly involved and thus further complicate matters.[7]

Gonzales and Rothchild conclude that "from an agency perspective, the bureaucrat's main job is not only to hide facts from the public, but also to keep them from fellow bureaucrats up the line."[8] The very nature of organizations almost precludes effective upward communication.

Lateral communications are all those organizational communications that do not go up or down the chain of command. They may be between line and staff units, coequal units, employees within a particular unit, or even between different organizations. Although they are extremely important elements in the communicative process, lateral communications are often overlooked. With organizations performing ever more complex operations, managers at all levels are less able to coordinate their subordinates via the chain of command. The more complex an organization becomes, the greater the need for lateral communications among subordinates so that all involved can know exactly how their particular work fits into the organization and where they fit on the team.

The very nature of hierarchical organization is an obstacle to lateral communications. All hierarchies operate on the principle of vertical authority—authority that comes down from the top through communications. In lateral communications, authority is absent; its place is taken by persuasion. Hierarchies encourage specialization, a factor which is detrimental to lateral communications, inasmuch as specialists usually have their own frames of reference, loyalties, and languages. Additionally, the general division of the hierarchy into subunits is a barrier to lateral communications, with each subunit fighting for a larger share of organizational resources and a more prominent organizational position in the relative scheme of things. The huge size of the modern organization makes it difficult for any unit to ascertain who has the information it needs or who needs the information it has.[9]

One must also consider the basic problems involved in communication between any two individuals in addition to the obstacles with respect to downward, upward, and lateral communications. Most organizational communications boil down to series of interpersonal communications being conducted within the organizational milieu and impacted on by organizational communication channels, directions, and barriers. (Recall that feedback is the device used to clear the lines of interpersonal communications so that the communicating parties can be aware of whether or not they understand one another and whether or not messages have been received as sent.) Because interpersonal communications are major factors in organizational communications, feedback is also an essential element in keeping organizational communication lines unclogged.

COMMUNICATIONS AND INFORMATION SYSTEMS

The substance of communications is information. Regardless of whether the direction is downward, upward, or lateral, what is communicated is information.

Information is an extremely important resource in any organization. Accurate information is needed at every organizational level. Without accurate information, good decisions cannot be made, good plans cannot be formulated, and good strategies and tactics cannot be devised; in general, no one can perform the job satisfactorily if accurate information is unavailable. As Johnson, Kast, and Rosenzweig have noted, especially with respect to governmental service organizations, "the flow of information is the critical element. Information must flow to the key decision points where action is taken with regard to a service to be performed . . . ."[10]

Information gets from one place to another in an organization through communications. The messages containing the information can be written or oral. Of great importance, however, is whether or not the communications system carrying the messages is *open loop* or *closed loop.* If the communications system is open loop, providing for no feedback and no evaluation of messages, the organization will be run on the basis of inaccurate information. If the communications system is *closed loop,* providing for feedback and evaluation of messages, the organization will be run on the basis of accurate information. The necessity for a *closed-loop* communications system is obvious.

One of the most important tasks for any organizational administrator, therefore, is the development of a good, *closed-loop* communications and information system. Such a system is a fundamental and necessary factor for organizational stability. If administrators are deprived of information about how their organizations are running, they will be unable to run them properly. Their communications and information systems must be designed so that communication barriers are minimized, problems are identified quickly, and reliable information is available to decision makers. The creation and maintenance of such a system can be difficult, costly, and time-consuming, but the results invariably make the effort worthwhile.

The most important aspect of the communications and information system is feedback. The number of methods and techniques that can be used to improve organizational communications is endless, but they will all fail if feedback is not used as the foundation of the system. Feedback ensures that the system will in fact be a system. Communications and information systems may utilize radios, telephones, intercoms, charts, graphs, automatic data-processing equipment, memoranda, elaborate rules and regulations, carefully formulated policies, and computers, but these means of communication are merely tools, and their use does not a system make. As James Q. Wilson has observed, "even those departments with the most modern technologies—including IBM machines, punched cards, computer tabulations, and the like—were administered by men who by and large used the numbers thus produced merely to compile annual reports, satisfy the FBI's need for data, and keep track of . . . operating expenses."[11]

STANDARD 24.3

DATA RETRIEVAL

Every police agency should establish a cost-effective, compatible information system to collect, store, and retrieve information moving through the agency. The use of such a system should be directed toward crime reduction without sacrificing local autonomy.

National Advisory Commission on Criminal Justice Standards and Goals, *Police* (Washington, D.C.: U.S. Government Printing Office, 1973), p. 578.

As Wilson points out, the increased technological sophistication of police departments has been used largely for routine data storage and retrieval. This is needed, certainly, but the mere presence of the machinery does not create a communications and information system, even though it might give that impression.

For example, let us consider how a communications and information system might be utilized by the captain in charge of the operations division in the deployment of patrol personnel. The captain needs information on which to base decisions, a means by which to communicate decisions, and information on how well those decisions are being carried out and how well they are working.

It is the function of the communications and information system to solve these problems for the captain and to provide the information needed to do the job. If regular procedures for tabulating patrol activity exist, the information needed to make deployment decisions can easily be made available. Through a *closed-loop* communications sytem, the captain's decisions can be transmitted with little difficulty to all concerned operational personnel. Through reports, meetings, inspections, and other control processes, compliance with decisions can be monitored. Through the analysis of work-load information and changing activity trends, the continued validity of original deployment decisions can be studied. And, returning full circle, the communications and information system can provide the data necessary for the subsequent reformulation of original deployment decisions. The system is used continuously to improve current deployment practices.

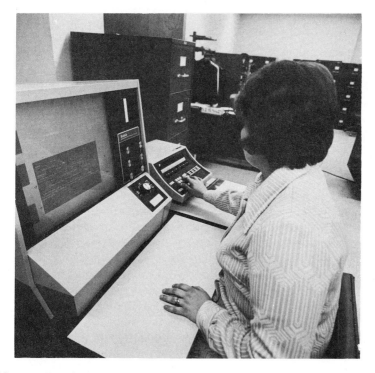

Many police departments use communications and information systems to keep administrators informed. (Courtesy of the Jackson Police Department, Jackson, Mississippi)

In developing a communications and information system, several considerations are important.[12] In order to demonstrate concern about the system and to provide the authority necessary to overcome obstacles, the top management of the police organization should be involved in the development of the system from its beginning. The project team members who design and implement the system should be carefully chosen on the basis of both their skills and their standing in the eyes of their colleagues.

An important first step in the design stage should be an analysis of the way in which information is currently processed in the organization. This is an essential step because it provides a true picture of formal and informal communication channels presently in existence; those that are useful and viable may be incorporated into the new system's design. An additional consideration is the necessity of relating newly developed automated communicative processes to long-established organizational clerical procedures. Finally, all personnel should be fully trained in the use and operation of and rationale for the new communications and information system.

COMPUTERS

Computers are an enigma to most people; they are either overwhelmingly impressed by them or terribly afraid of them because they have no idea how they work. Computers, however, are nothing more than very complicated business machines which are capable of performing certain prescribed functions very quickly. Computers are no more capable than the people who program and operate them; they can do nothing for which they have not been programmed. In a very real sense, computers are tools which have great capabilities when used by capable people. In many organizations, some police departments included, computers have become little more than automated filing cabinets.

There has been much speculation on the long-range impact of computers on organizations. It has been argued that computers will bring about the eventual elimination of middle management because they make information available to top management. Others argue, on the other hand, that computers may increase the importance of middle management because they make better information available at the same time that direct supervision is being deemphasized. Still others argue that neither of these trends will materialize; rather, they foresee present organizational patterns continuing, with computers serving to better inform all levels of management.[13] Regardless of which trend finally wins out, it is important to keep computers in their proper perspective. They are useful machines that are capable of providing large amounts of information very quickly. But they are only machines, certainly not demons or gods.

Computers have great capabilities when used by capable people. (Courtesy of the Metropolitan Police Department, Washington, D.C.)

DECISION MAKING

The decision-making process is completely dependent on the communications and information system of an organization. Decision making must be based on accurate and reliable information provided by the system.

The determination as to who makes what decisions is based on the organization's structure and the pattern of authority delegation within it. In Chapter 4, we discussed the *authority-level principle,* which is based on the premise that authority exists within organizations at all levels and that only those decisions that cannot be made at a given level because of lack of authority should be referred upward in the organization for resolution. The authority-level principle, in effect, demands that decisions be made at the lowest possible organizational level by the person at that level who holds the authority for making decisions. As Reddin puts it, "the decision-making process should be pushed down to the lowest possible level in an organization."[14]

A systematic process can easily be developed to make the authority-level principle operational. This process involves, as pointed out in Chapter 4, a reporting procedure which demands that all officers at all departmental levels write weekly reports on problems that have surfaced at their respective levels and which they or their superiors have been unable to solve through decision making.[15] These weekly reports are passed along to those persons within the organization to whom the individual officers report. Saxenian suggests that superiors hold problem-solving sessions with subordinates after receipt of reports.[16] Problems that cannot be solved through decision making at each respective level within the organization are pushed upward for solution. Reports and meetings at all organizational levels become the media for problem solving and decision making. Through such a system, problems that are not solved and which surface later can be traced to the individual or individuals within the organization who had the authority to solve them but failed to do so. Thus the principle of accountability can be put into effect; individuals who have the authority to make decisions but fail to make them can be held accountable for their failures.

This systematic process is an excellent procedure for decision making and problem solving at all organizational levels where the authority exists to make definitive decisions and to solve problems. If the process is carefully monitored through feedback, relatively few problems should work their way upward through the organization to the chief; most of them will have been solved through decision making at lower organizational levels.

Regardless of who makes decisions, some will be made poorly. Nigro points out that there are five common errors in decision making. The following is an adaptation of the five common errors that Nigro has identified:

1. the tendency to focus on immediate problems, needs, and issues to the exclusion of long-range considerations;

2. the tendency to deal with problem symptoms rather than with problem causes, thereby favoring simplistic solutions;

3. the tendency to make decisions on the basis of one's own past experience and personal judgment rather than on empirical evidence and consultation with colleagues;

4. the tendency to base decisions on preconceived ideas rather than on facts; and

5. the tendency to avoid responsibility and avoid making decisions by referring problems to someone else.[17]

These common errors demonstrate the need for a decision-making system. Prior to making a decision, the person who has both the authority and the responsibility to make it must make the effort to assemble as much information as possible. This person must get not only facts, but also the opinions of all concerned individuals. On arriving at a decision, the decision maker must carefully communicate it through the organization, using the established communications and information system. Next, the person must examine feedback to determine how well the decision has been understood and how well it is being carried out. Feedback must also be used as the basis for making the continuing adjustments in the decision and as input for future decision making.

Decision makers can overcome the common errors in decision making only by gathering as much information as possible about the problem before they make their decisions and by carefully monitoring feedback once those decisions have been made. Decision making is an extremely important function within any organization and must be approached from a systems perspective.

SUMMARY

The flow of communications and information within any organization is an important and often overlooked element of management. Except for the knee-jerk tendency to attribute almost every conceivable organizational difficulty to "communication problems," very little attention is generally given to communications and information systems.

Good communications, whether interpersonal or organizational, are totally dependent on good feedback. Without it, communications are tentative and inaccurate; with it, communications are confident and sure.

In problem solving and decision making, the key ingredient is information. As Hodge and Hodgson have noted:

Information is the essential factor with each organizational level. At the policy level, higher management needs information to formulate strategic plans and to evaluate them. At the planning level, information is required to convert strategy into tactics. ... At the operational levels, information is required to carry out production. ...[18]

DISCUSSION QUESTIONS

1. What roles are played by official and unofficial communications and the formal and informal organizations in systems with which you are familiar?

2. Do you think that the informal organization usually helps or harms?

3. The main barrier to downward and upward communication is the chain of command. Should the chain of command be eliminated? Why or why not?

4. Why do supervisors think that subordinates feel free to communicate upward to them, when in fact most subordinates fear such communication?

5. Think of communications and information flow in organizations with which you are familiar. Is the flow open or closed loop in nature? Do decision makers know whether their information is accurate? Do the decision makers find out about the impact of their decisions? Do order issuers know whether their orders are understood? Do they find out whether their orders are carried out?

6. Do you know of organizations that use sophisticated information-processing equipment? How do they make use of the information supplied? Do they use the information only for reports and to impress outsiders, or do they use the information regularly in making decisions?

7. What do you think of computers?

8. Again think of organizations with which you are familiar. Do they make decisions rationally (based on goals and objectives, identification and analysis of alternatives, testing, implementation of most favorable alternative, and evaluation of results), or traditionally (examination of existing situation, review of possibilities consistent with realities, and choice of one possibility)?

REFERENCES

1. William Scholz, *Communication in the Business Organization* (Englewood Cliffs, N.J.: Prentice-Hall, 1962), p. 33.

2. T. N. Whitehead, *Leadership in a Free Society* (Cambridge, Mass.: Harvard University Press, 1936), p. 78.

3. Rensis Likert, *New Patterns of Management* (New York: McGraw-Hill, 1961), pp. 46–47.

4. Alfred Vogel, "Why Don't Employees Speak Up?" *Personnel Administration* (May–June 1967): 20–22.

5. Norman R. F. Maier, *Psychology in Industrial Organizations,* 4th ed. (Boston: Houghton Mifflin, 1973), p. 582.

6. *Ibid.*

7. Jack Gonzales and John Rothchild, "The Shriver Prescription: How the Government Can Find Out What It's Doing," *Washington Monthly* (November 1972): 37–39.

8. *Ibid,* p. 36.

9. Felix A. Nigro, *Modern Public Administration* (New York: Harper & Row, 1965), pp. 197–199.

10. Richard A. Johnson, Fremont E. Kast, and James E. Rosenzweig, "Designing Management Systems," *Business Quarterly* (Summer 1964), as quoted in Peter P. Schoderbek, ed., *Management Systems* (New York: Wiley, 1967), p. 117.

11. James Q. Wilson, *Varieties of Police Behavior–The Management of Law and Order in Eight Communities* (Cambridge, Mass.: Harvard University Press, 1968), p. 62.

12. Charles R. Work, "The Prosecutor's Guide to Automation," *The Prosecutor* 7, 6 (1971): 479–480.

13. Ernest Dale, *Organization* (New York: American Management Association, 1967), pp. 271–273.

14. Thomas Reddin, "Are You Oriented to Hold Them?" *The Police Chief* (March 1966): 16.

15. Hrand Saxenian, "Prescription for Old Fashioned Leadership," *Business Horizons* (Fall 1965): 45–53.

16. *Ibid.*

17. Nigro, *op. cit.,* pp. 178–183.

18. Bartow Hodge and Robert E. Hodgson, *Management and the Computer in Information Control Systems* (New York: McGraw-Hill, 1969), p. 2.

CHAPTER 11
POLICIES, PROCEDURES, AND
RULES AND REGULATIONS IN
THE POLICE ORGANIZATION

LEARNING OBJECTIVES

1. Explain why organizational guidelines are especially important in policing.

2. Explain why organizational guidelines are difficult to apply to police work.

3. Compare policies to procedures, rules, and regulations in terms of specificity.

4. Identify the four sources of organizational policy.

5. Identify the two major sources of externally imposed policy.

6. Identify the five key stages in the development of originated policy.

7. Cite several important considerations in the actual development of policies.

8. Compare procedures to policies, rules, and regulations in terms of specificity.

9. Describe the unusual characteristic of police organizations with respect to discretion.

10. Cite some good and bad points of standardized procedures.

11. State the real difficulty in police-procedure development.

12. Differentiate policies, procedures, and rules and regulations in terms of the behavior they guide and the degree to which they require adherence.

13. Describe the types of situations to which rules and regulations should apply.

14. Cite three reasons why police administrators should not attempt to formulate guidelines as if they were operating in a vacuum.

In Chapter 5 we discussed policies, procedures, and rules and regulations as outputs of the directing process. We said that policies and procedures are guides to thinking and action, respectively, and serve as general guidelines for officers to follow in the conduct of their duties. We pointed out that there is no distinction, in fact, between the words *rule* and *regulation*. Unlike policies and procedures, rules and regulations are binding mandates that all officers must follow in the conduct of their duties. Recall that we did not discuss policies, procedures, and rules and regulations in any great depth. Here we will attempt to evaluate these methods of direction in a much more comprehensive fashion.

STANDARD 1.3

POLICE DISCRETION

1. Every police agency should acknowledge the existence of the broad range of administrative and operational discretion that is exercised by all police agencies and individual officers. That acknowledgement should take the form of comprehensive policy statements that publicly establish the limits of discretion, that provide guidelines for its exercise within those limits, and that eliminate discriminatory enforcement of the law.
2. Every police chief executive should establish policy that guides the exercise of discretion by police personnel in using arrest alternatives.
3. Every police chief executive should establish policy that limits the exercise of discretion by police personnel in conducting investigations, and that provides guidelines for the exercise of discretion within those limits.
4. Every police chief executive should establish policy that governs the exercise of discretion by police personnel in providing routine peacekeeping and other police services that, because of their frequent recurrence, lend themselves to the development of a uniform agency response.

National Advisory Commission on Criminal Justice Standards and Goals, *Police* (Washington, D.C.: U.S. Government Printing Office, 1973), pp. 21–22.

In the police field, policies, procedures, and rules and regulations are extremely important. They are, in effect, statements which define role expectations for police officers. As previously pointed out, the police officer is given powers not granted to the ordinary citizen. Because they possess extraordinary powers, the police represent a potential threat to freedom. It can therefore be argued that the police need to be restrained by explicit and carefully defined directions which will guarantee that they will play their roles in accordance with departmental rather than personal role expectations. At the very least, the police in a democratic society should be expected to play their roles within the confines of legal constraints; they must certainly be expected to abide by the laws they are committed to enforce. In addition, because police departments are service-oriented public agencies which impact significantly on public safety and public protection, they must work according to well-defined, specific guidelines designed to ensure that police officers will conform consistently to behavior that will enhance public safety and protection.

Their vast powers make the police a potential threat to individual freedom. (Courtesy of the Jackson Police Department, Jackson, Mississippi)

One must also consider the fact that the police task is characterized by the enormous degree of discretion afforded individual officers in the exercise of their duties. The incredible variety of situations that police officers encounter, the omnipresence of danger in their work, their need to settle problems informally, and the variable personal skills that individual officers bring to their work all mitigate against narrow, unbending behavioral requirements.

The goal of any police chief must be to find the middle ground between unlimited discretion and total standardization. This is not an easy task, but it can be accomplished through an understanding of the proper applications of policies, procedures, and rules and regulations.

STANDARD 2.2

ESTABLISHMENT OF POLICY

Every police chief executive immediately should establish written policies in those areas of operations in which guidance is needed to direct agency employees toward the attainment of agency goals and objectives.

3. Every police chief executive should provide written policies in those areas in which direction is needed, including:
   a. General goals and objectives of the agency;
   b. Administrative matters;
   c. Community relations;
   d. Public and press relations;
   e. Personnel procedures and relations;
   f. Personal conduct of employees;
   g. Specific law enforcement operations with emphasis on such sensitive areas as the use of force, the use of lethal and nonlethal weapons, and arrest and custody; and
   h. Use of support services.

National Advisory Commission on Criminal Justice Standards and Goals, *Police* (Washington, D.C.: U.S. Government Printing Office, 1973), p. 53.

The case for the need to have clear behavioral guidelines in police organizations has been made time and again in recent years. In 1967 the President's Commission on Law Enforcement and Administration of Justice recommended that "police departments should develop and enunciate policies that give police personnel specific guidance for the common situations requiring exercise of police discretion."[1] In 1972 the American Bar Association asserted that "police discretion can best be structured and controlled through the process of administrative rule-making by police agencies. Police administrators should, therefore, give the highest priority to the formulation of administrative rules governing the exercise of discretion . . . ."[2] In emphasizing the need for clear police policy, the Police Foundation pointed out in 1972 that "despite some progress in the last five years, police agencies still tend to keep major policies ambiguous and invisible rather than risk discussion and controversy by following overt administrative guidelines."[3]

The police role is much too ambiguous to become totally standardized. But it is also much too important to be left totally to the discretion of individual officers. The following discussions of *policies, procedures,* and *rules and regulations* should shed some light on the manner in which police chiefs can harness, but not choke, their employees.

ORGANIZATIONAL POLICY

Policies are more general than procedures, or rules and regulations. Policies are primarily guides to thinking rather than to action. They are especially important as guides to decision making. Therefore, policies should reflect the purpose and philosophy of the organization and help interpret that purpose and philosophy for its members.

Koontz and O'Donnell have identified four sources of organizational policy which help immeasureably in understanding the dimensions of what policy actually is:

1. originated policy;

2. appealed policy;

3. implied policy; and

4. externally imposed policy.[4]

Originated policy emanates from within the organization itself, usually from top management, but often from other levels of management as well. Loen has identified five key stages in the development of originated policy:

1. define long-range purpose;

2. define managing philosophy;

3. define policies in areas where repeated decisions are made;

4. determine how policy will be enforced; and

5. specify how exceptions to policy will be handled.[5]

Appealed policy also comes from within the organization. Somewhat like the common law, appealed policy develops haphazardly as decisions are appealed or simply passed up the chain of command. As with the law, unwritten and written precedents are established which gather force with time and use. These appealed policies are often confusing, conflicting, and uncoordinated.

Implied policy derives from the impression given by the organization's actions rather than its words. If, for example, the expressed originated policy of a police department is that promotions are based on merit when, in fact, only the chief's friends get promoted, the implied policy is that *it is not what you know that counts, it is whom you know.*

Externally imposed policy originates outside of the organization. The two major sources of externally imposed policy are other governmental agencies and employee organizations. The federal government, for example, has imposed the policy that personnel selection, assignment, and promotion will be made without discrimination according to race or sex. Employee unions are instrumental in establishing policy with respect to hours of work, pay, and grievance procedures. Such policies are all externally imposed.

In order for an organization to develop coherent policy, these four types of policy must be consolidated. To this end, appealed policy must be recognized and then incorporated into originated policy. Implied policy should be minimized through the simple act of honoring originated policy. If originated policy is carefully adhered to by management, the development of implied policy will be severely hindered. Finally, externally imposed policy must be accepted as binding and included in organizational policy.

With regard to the actual development of policies, several considerations are important.[6] Policies should reflect organizational goals, objectives, and plans. Under no circumstances should any policy exist that does not serve a useful purpose. Inasmuch as policies are guidelines for clear thinking and decision making, they should be consistent. They should also be flexible so that they may be applied to varying situations and changing times.

Policies must be carefully distinguished from *procedures* and *rules and regulations.* Policies should also be committed to writing as a prerequisite, although not a guarantee, of clear thinking and clear understanding. All policies should be thoroughly explained to all personnel, and feedback should be sought to ensure understanding. Finally, policies should be controlled, added to, adjusted, and deleted according to the requirements of changing circumstances.

ORGANIZATIONAL PROCEDURES

Procedures are more specific than policies. As the means for carrying out policy, procedures are, in effect, guides to action. According to Wilson and McLaren, a procedure is "more specific than a policy but less restrictive than a rule or regulation. . . . [It] describes a method of operation while still allowing some flexibility within limits."[7]

Most organizations abound in procedures. Police organizations, for example, have investigative procedures, patrol procedures, booking procedures, arrest procedures, radio procedures, filing procedures, roll-call procedures, sick-leave procedures, promotional procedures, evidence-handling procedures, reporting procedures, and many more procedures which describe specific methods of operation. These procedures are action plans or designs for implementing policy. They are not totally inflexible, but they do describe rather detailed methods for carrying out policy.

Koontz and O'Donnell have noted that in most organizations procedures multiply and become more exacting at lower organizational levels.[8] They ascribe this to the need for closer control, the advantages of detailed instructions, the reduced need for discretion, and the applicability of the philosphy that there is *one best way* to accomplish routine tasks. Although this theory may hold true in business organizations, it does not in police organizations. Police patrol officers operate at the lowest organizational level; yet their work is far from routine and requires enormous discretion. Because of this unusual characteristic of police organizations, James Q. Wilson, for one, has concluded that precise, positive guidance in the form of detailed procedures cannot realistically be made available in many circumstances.[9]

Loen has further pointed out that in general, an abundance of standardized procedures tends to discourage initiative and imagination.[10] Stultifying procedures can unnecessarily complicate jobs and make it difficult to attract and keep capable and enterprising employees. On the other hand, procedures can decrease the time wasted in figuring out how to accomplish tasks and thereby increase productivity. They can also ensure a continuing level of quality output. Finally, good procedures can help cut training costs because they describe in an explicit way what actions an employee is expected to take.

As with policies, a middle ground must be sought in procedure development. Many aspects of the police task lend themselves to relatively detailed procedures. The bulk of police work is routine, especially administrative and auxiliary service activities. It is an easy matter to develop procedures for these. The real difficulty in police procedure development is with those aspects of police work that are not routine and in which individual discretion is required.

It is all but impossible, for example, to develop a prescriptive procedure that confidently prepares a police officer to deal with all armed offenders. What if the weapon is a knife, a gun, a prizefighter's fist, or an automobile? Is the suspect a man, a woman, or a juvenile? What difference does this make? What is the crime that the suspect is *alleged* to have committed? Is the suspect fleeing, fighting, or surrendering? Has the suspect been identified so that he or she could be found later if capture is avoided? Is it night or day? Does the police officer have help? Is the suspect likely to harm innocent citizens?

The extreme danger, the multitude of variables, the unanticipated circumstances, and the unpredictability of human nature make it almost impossible to specify in advance exactly how a police officer should act. Nonetheless, some guidance must be provided; the guidance should probably be in the form of a policy rather than a procedure. A policy would serve to guide the officer's thinking in the situation, but would permit some flexibility in the action taken. In a sense, a policy has some procedural overtones, while still allowing flexibility. Through training, police organizations must get their police officers to internalize such policy so that they can develop procedures on the spot that are in keeping with the organization's goals and objectives.

A good example of a combination of policy and procedure on the use of force and weapons is one currently in use in Falmouth, Massachusetts. It is presented below in its entirety, with some minor amendments for the purpose of clarity and reproduction.

1. POLICY

The Police Department is given special powers to use force by physical means and by firearms and other weapons. With the rapid growth of the country's cities, private citizens have increasingly entrusted to law enforcement agencies their rights to use violent force. Not to have done so would have continued and perhaps made worse the lawlessness and general violence which was common before the appearance and growth of metropolitan police departments.

The stakes for the proper execution of the responsibility to hold weapons and use them only with restraint and when necessary are very high. Abuse by police officers of the use of force violates the trust the public has given to the police and leads citizens injured or offended by such abuse to revoke that trust. Once this happens, people increasingly take matters into their own hands and dispense force and violence themselves. Such a situation has disastrous consequences for the peace of any modern, civilized community.

No other area of police work is so sensitive as this or as important to the implementation of the department's peace-keeping mission. In no other area is the exercise of sound judgment by the individual police officer and conformity to departmental policies and procedures more necessary.

2. GUIDELINES AND PROCEDURES

Use of Firearms in Particular Situations

A police officer is to:

1) use only the minimum amount of force which is consistent with the accomplishment of duties and is to exhaust every other reasonable means of apprehension or defense before resorting to the use of firearms;

2) never discharge a firearm in the performance of duties except under the following circumstances:

   a) to defend self or another from attack which the officer has reasonable cause to believe could result in death or serious physical injury;

   b) to apprehend one who has committed or attempted to commit a felony in the officer's presence, providing that the felony involved an actual or threatened attack which the officer has reasonable cause to believe could result in death or serious bodily injury;

   (*Note:* If the felony described above is not commited in the officer's presence, the officer is to have sufficient information to know as a virtual certainty that the suspect has committed the felony.)

   c) to kill a dangerous animal or an animal that is so badly injured that humanity requires its removal from further suffering;

   d) for target practice or competition on an approved range under supervision;

3) never use firearms to fire a warning shot or in cases involving only misdemeanors.

Reports

1) Whenever discharging a firearm, except when practicing with it, a police officer must submit as soon as possible afterwards a written report to the chief.

2) The report must include the following:

   a) the names of the officer and other persons concerned;

   b) the circumstances under which the firearm was used;

   c) the nature of the injury inflicted, if any; and

   d) the care given afterwards to the injured.

Furnishing, Holding, Maintaining, and Inspecting Firearms

1) Revolvers are furnished by the department to all members of the force. A police officer is to carry a loaded revolver at all times when on duty.

2) A police officer is to keep the firearm clean and in a condition ready for use.

3) If a firearm issued to an officer is defective or in need of repair, the firearm should be taken to the sergeant in charge of the shift or supervisor immediately and, if necessary, a substitute firearm obtained.
4) If in need of extra cartridges for any reason, make out a requisition and give it to the shift commander.
5) While on duty use only those firearms and ammunition supplied by the police department or approved by the chief.
6) Once a month, all sergeants are to inspect the service revolver of personnel under their supervision.

Proficiency in the Use of Firearms
1) Each officer is to qualify with the revolver twice a year in accordance with a standard established by the chief of police.
2) A notation of each such qualification on the record of the particular officer is to be made. This notation is to include the date of qualification and the record of the instructor.

Clubs
The designation "clubs" includes both the baton and the longer riot club. A police officer is to
1) if uniformed, carry the baton on duty at all times and carry the riot club only when the commanding officer so directs or when the officer believes the situation may require its use rather than the use of the baton;
2) when the use of force is necessary to effect an arrest, exhaust other options (hands, claw, handcuffs, aerosol sprays, etc.) before using the club (in these situations, the officer's own good judgment is most important as to what means is called for);
3) never use a club to "stop" a suspicious person;
4) whenever striking a person with the club, follow the same report procedure as described above for situations in which a firearm has been discharged;
5) obtain clubs from the operations officer via the chain of command.

Aerosol Sprays or Similar Devices
1) Aerosol sprays or similar devices are to be considered defensive weapons and are to be used as such with discretion and care.
2) When the use of aerosols or the club would be equally adequate and appropriate in a particular situation, aerosol sprays or similar devices are to be used.
3) Aerosol sprays and similar devices are intended primarily for use in those cases in which:
   a) the officer is attempting to subdue an attacker or a violently resisting suspect; and

b) the law permits the use of necessary force and in the given case aerosol sprays or similar devices are the most suitable means to apply such force.

4) They are to be used in demonstrations, riots, and other civil disorders only under the direction of a superior officer.

5) When using aerosol sprays or similar devices in any of the situations described above in which it is so permitted, the officer's use is to be subject to the following regulations:

a) apply aerosol sprays or similar devices to subjects more than three feet away, using them at lesser distances only under emergency conditions;

b) limit the duration of application to the absolute minimum required to effectively control the subject (normally, this requires no more than a one-second application);

c) exercise great care in use on persons who confine themselves in closed vehicles and who resist being taken from closed vehicles;

d) in cases where persons have confined themselves to closed vehicles, use only as the last resort in preventing injury to subjects and officers;

e) in instances where used on persons in closed vehicles, accomplish removal from vehicles as quickly as possible after the application of a spray;

f) do not use under any circumstances on persons who are sick or intoxicated or who are not in possession of their normal protective reflexes, such as being able to blink, hold their breath, or turn away from the applied stream;

g) applying aerosol sprays or similar devices to persons incapable of protecting themselves can result in grave injury to such persons out of proportion of harm threatened by such persons; they should not be used in such situations;

h) never use aerosol sprays or similar devices indiscriminately or in anticipation against more threats of violence or resistance, on persons secured and properly in custody, or to "stop" persons from fleeing.

6) Follow-Up Procedures After Use

a) Assist subject in custody to wash basin and advise to wash exposed areas with cold water and not rub eyes.

b) If any extreme situation exists where the officer believes that medical treatment is needed, the sergeant in charge will be notified.

c) The treatment needed will be decided on by the sergeant in charge;

d) When an officer is exposed to aerosol sprays or similar devices, the same procedure will be followed.

7) Reports
   a) Whenever a member of the force uses an aerosol spray or similar device on any person, regardless of whether that person is apprehended, the same report procedure is to be followed as described above for situations in which a firearm has been discharged.
   b) When involved officers are treated for exposure to aerosol sprays or similar devices, they are responsible for having this fact noted on the journal, together with information relative to the time of the exposure and the treatment.
8) Acquisition of Aerosol Sprays and Similar Devices
   a) Obtain aerosol sprays and similar devices from the operations officer, via the chain of command.
   b) Carry such devices at all times on duty as required.
   c) Whenever in need of additional supplies of aerosol sprays or similar devices, make out a requisition and give it to the shift commander, who will be responsible for promptly informing the operations officer of the requisition.[11]

This policy is flexible while at the same time prescribing definitive procedures that *must* be followed in *all* cases. It allows the police officer to use discretion and judgment within limitations which, in the use of force and weapons, the officer must be able to do. Furthermore, it is a sensible way for a police chief to establish role expectations and to guarantee that the department's goals and objectives will be carried out.

The various ways in which force and weapons are used demonstrate the need for policy and procedure to place limitations on what police officers do and to spell out the extent to which they are allowed to operate within the confines of departmental expectations. There is a need for policy and procedure to govern all kinds of police activity, while at the same time giving the officer a certain amount of behavioral latitude, depending on circumstances. This is precisely why the police job is so difficult to perform well, precisely why police officers must have good judgment, precisely why police officers need to be thoroughly trained, and precisely why sound and well-understood policy is essential. It takes a well-trained person with exceedingly good judgment to follow policy and to exercise discretion wisely time and time again.

ORGANIZATIONAL RULES AND REGULATIONS

Rules and regulations are specific managerial guidelines that leave little or no room for discretion. They either require or prohibit specific behavior on the part of organizational employees. Whereas policies are *guides* to thinking and procedures are *guides* to action, rules and regulations are *mandates* to action.

The requirements that uniformed officers wear their hats whenever they get out of their patrol vehicles, that they not smoke on the street, that they be in court 30 minutes prior to the opening of sessions to confer with prosecutors, that they not accept gratuities, that they take a specified time for lunch breaks, and that they appear for roll call are a few examples of rules and regulations. These requirements leave no room for discretion and mandate that specific actions be taken. There will, of course, always be instances in which some rules or regulations may be waived; these, however, are few and far between. A regulation specifying that all officers appear for roll call, for example, might be waived by a commanding officer or a supervisor who, for whatever good reason, believes it necessary for certain officers to report directly to fixed posts rather than to stand roll call. Officers handling an emergency call during the 30 minutes prior to the opening of court could not be expected to leave the emergency situation before it is resolved because rules and regulations require them to be in court to confer with prosecutors 30 minutes prior to the opening of court. By and large, however, rules and regulations are mandates that police officers must follow.

Inasmuch as rules and regulations require certain, specific behavior that is essential to departmental stability, it is necessary that they be enforced strictly in accordance with established disciplinary measures. The viability of rules and regulations will depend on the fair and impartial application of these disciplinary measures. There is no quicker way for a police department to degenerate and for morale problems to build than through the unfair and partial application of disciplinary measures as these relate to rules and regulations. They must, therefore, be reasonable and fully in keeping with organizational goals and objectives. There are many police departments in the United States that have rules and regulations that are outdated and that are rarely, if ever, enforced.

A few rules and regulations governing the activities of officers working in a community of over 20,000 people in the year 1974 are presented below to give you some appreciation of the ridiculousness of some rules and regulations in existence in American police service within recent years.

1. A patrolman shall, during his tour of duty, report by telepone any information of importance.

2. Members of the department shall not carry umbrellas . . . while in uniform on active duty, except when otherwise directed by proper authority. . . .

3. Members of the department shall not smoke while in uniform, and in public, either on or off active duty; nor in any police buildings, except in private offices or in the . . . squad rooms thereof; nor in the police garages, nor shall they chew tobacco while in ranks, either during roll call or while marching to duty. . . .

4. Members of the department when in uniform and when going with other members in a body to perform any duty, or when returning therefrom, shall march in military order.

5. Members of the department shall report immediately by telephone to the commanding officer, the particulars in all cases of accident involving injury or damage to property on the public streets, sidewalks, alleys, or other public places which may come to their attention.

6. Members shall avoid expressing any opinions on religious, political, or other questions, the nature of which is controversial. . . .

7. Members shall not actively participate in politics.

8. In radio-equipped police cars, only properly licensed radio operators shall operate the transmitter.

9. A radio-patrol car shall be called twice only by the dispatcher.

10. Length of coat shall be two inches below the knee . . . .

11. The regulation police puttee shall be black in color and of a style approved by the chief of police.

12. The members of the regular force shall wear the regulation . . . State Police Sam Brown belt. Other members of the department shall wear the 2¼ inch wide black Sam Brown belt with 4 Deerings . . . .

13. A member of the force shall tender and return the personal salute prescribed by the United States Army Drill Regulations. Members of the board of selectmen, chief of police, superior officers and sergeants are entitled to the salute. An operator of a police vehicle will salute only when the vehicle is stopped for some other purpose. In a moving vehicle all members will salute with the exception of the operator. The salute will be tendered by the subordinate, and smartly and promptly acknowledged by the superior.

These rules and regulations are unreasonable and outmoded. It is difficult to conceive of a group of police officers today chewing tobacco and carrying umbrellas while marching to duty, saluting everyone in sight, reporting important information by telephone and not radio, expressing no controversial opinions of a religious or political nature, using their police radios only if they have a license, and walking about with puttees, Sam Brown belts, and coats two inches below their knees. These rules and regulations are right out of a script from a Keystone Cops comedy. To put it mildly, they are unreasonable; yet there are many police departments in the United States whose rules and regulations are equally ludicrous.

Rules and regulations must be fair, reasonable, pertinent and in keeping with the times. Therefore, they must be subject to change and must be updated periodically. The police department must be careful not to allow rules and regulations to interfere materially with an officer's use of discretion in unpredictable situations. They must apply only to those specific situations that are essentially unchanging and predictable. Unless they are so limited, officers will be hampered in the performance of their duties and will come to regard rules and regulations as both bothersome and invalid.

Furthermore, the number of rules and regulations should be kept to a minimum because of their unbending and coercive nature. If rules and regulations are allowed to proliferate unchecked, management is, in effect, saying to its employees, "We are telling you exactly what and what not to do because we do not have confidence in your abilities to act responsibly." If such a message is transmitted to employees, they must either acquiesce or rebel; in neither instance will they remain active partners in the effort to accomplish organizational goals and objectives.

Once again, that elusive middle course must be sought. Some rules and regulations are obviously necessary. These should be confined strictly to nondiscretionary matters in which no behavioral latitude whatever can be granted. It should be the function of policies or procedures to govern activities in which behavioral latitude may be allowed and in which interpretive discretion is essential. Management, then, must be careful not to overdo it when it comes to constrictive rules and regulations. On the other hand, it must be equally as careful to establish precise, dogmatic canons affecting behavior that should, under all circumstances, be restricted. The achievement of a delicate balance between the two is essential to departmental stability. Whenever possible, management must allow for individual discretion and hence professional growth. As Reddin so aptly puts it:

> Certainly we must have rules and regulations and procedures and they should be followed. But they are no substitute for initiative and intelligence. The more a man is given an opportunity to make decisions, and in the process to learn, the more rules and regulations will be followed.[12]

FORMULATION OF ORGANIZATIONAL GUIDELINES

The formulation of policies, procedures, and rules and regulations for a police department has an important effect on not only the department, but also individual police officers and the community in general. The manner in which these guidelines are developed can be as crucial as the guidelines themselves.

Several sources of organizational policy have already been noted. These reflect the fact that police departments are open systems, are affected by their environments, and receive inputs from external systems. Any given police department receives inputs from its parent governmental system, the community, the courts, employee groups, professional police organizations, and many other special- and general-interest groups.

STANDARD 4.5

METHOD OF POLICY-MAKING

In its development of procedures to openly formulate, implement, and reevaluate police policy as necessary, each jurisdiction should be conscious of the need to effectively consult a representative cross-section of citizens in this process.

American Bar Association Project on Standards for Criminal Justice, *The Urban Police Function,* Approved Draft (New York: A.B.A., 1973), p. 9.

Because the police administrator receives inputs from so many different quarters, it is unwise to develop policies, procedures, and rules and regulations without giving serious consideration to both external and internal constraints. There are three good reasons why guidelines should not be formulated as if the police administrator were operating in a vacuum.

First, the police administrator must recognize that the police department is a part of the executive branch of a democratic government. People who are intensely involved in the selection of those who make the law can be expected to show tremendous interest in those who enforce it and to demand that police officers be responsive to their interests. Aware that their tax dollars pay police salaries, citizens expect some consideration in return. The police administrator must therefore take into consideration community input in the formulation of policies, procedures, and rules and regulations.

The nature of our governmental system, however, tends to lead many citizens to expect preferential treatment at the hands of the police. To argue in favor of the police administrator's considering community input in the development of organizational guidelines is *not* to argue against impartial application of the law. Legitimate community interests must be given consideration.

Second, in formulating organizational guidelines, the police administrator must be aware of the importance of the resulting development of strategies designed to promote guideline adherence. The only effective way of doing this is to involve those who will be affected by the guidelines in their development. This kind of democratic, participative involvement can help considerably in promoting guideline acceptance. This gives the members of the department a better understanding of the rationale behind the guidelines and a stake in their successful application.

STANDARD 6.2

POLICE OFFICER CONTRIBUTION TO POLICE POLICY

Policemen, as individuals and as a group, have a proper professional interest in and can make significant contributions to the formulation and continuing review of local law enforcement policies within individual communities. Methods should be developed by police administrators, therefore, to ensure effective participation in the policy-making process by all ranks including the patrolman who, because of his daily contact with operational problems and needs, has unique expertise to provide on law enforcement policy issues.

American Bar Association Project on Standards for Criminal Justice, *The Urban Police Function,* Approved Draft (New York: A.B.A., 1973), p. 12.

Third, the involvement of numerous concerned parties in the formulation of guidelines is likely to result in better guidelines. Community involvement in policy formulation, for example, will almost invariably result in better policy because it is much more likely to be universally accepted than is policy developed by the police alone. The involvement of organizational employees in the development of procedures will result in better procedures because it is the people who actually do the work who know the most about how it can best be done.

Police administrators should not be concerned that the involvement of the community and of organizational employees will be considered an abdication or usurpation of their authority. Their authority originates in the community, and they are expected to use it in the community's best interests. The community should have a say in determining what these best interests are. Police administrators accomplish the goals and objectives they establish for their organizations through their employees, who should have their say in how these are best achieved. Meeting responsibilities by sharing authority is an indication of strength and wisdom, not abdication.

SUMMARY

Policies, procedures, and *rules and regulations* are distinctly different and have distinctly different applications. Policies are guides to thinking. Procedures are guides to action. Rules and regulations are mandates to action. The following brief examples pertain to telephone use.

Policy   Contacts with citizens over the telephone are important aspects of police-community relations. The only contact that many citizens have with the police is telephone contact. Therefore, the behavior of each officer on the telephone reflects on the entire department. All officers are expected to be courteous and helpful when dealing with the public over the telephone.

Procedure   When answering the telephone, all officers will:

1. identify the department;

2. identify themselves by rank and name;

3. ask: "May I help you?";

4. ascertain the nature of the call as quickly as possible;

5. request the name and telephone number of the caller, address where service, if any, is requested, and other pertinent information;

6. repeat these to the caller to confirm accuracy;

7. time stamp and fill out a dispatch slip.

Rules and regulations   No officer will use profanity, racial epithets, or other derogatory remarks when dealing with the public over the telephone. In all cases where the public may be argumentative or otherwise abusive over the telephone and in all cases where complaints about police service or police officers are made by the public over the telephone, officers will, on satisfying callers' immediate needs for services, refer all such calls to the commanding officer of the shift. All officers will be polite to all callers regardless of circumstances.

There is a great need for clear policies, procedures, and rules and regulations in police departments. Conformity to such guidelines is important, and therefore they must be well defined and understandable. Much of police work is routine and easily standardized. Those parts of the job that are not routine are much too important to be left completely to the discretion of the individual police officer. Deciding what parts of the job are routine and what parts of the job are not become critical decisions for the police administrator. The administrator's overall success may very well be predicated on his or her ability to make such decisions.

DISCUSSION QUESTIONS

1. To what extent do you think police work is susceptible to organizational guidelines?

2. In organizations with which you are familiar, does there exist implied policy which is at odds with formal, originated policy?

3. As a police manager, how would you react to externally imposed policy?

4. Are you aware of organizations with policies that do not contribute toward goals and objectives?

5. What are some procedures of the educational organization that apply to you as a student? Some rules and regulations?

6. It has been suggested that an abundance of standardized procedures tends to discourage initiative and imagination. Do you agree? Why?

7. What kind of organizational guidance would you, the police manager, provide to your officers for dealing with armed offenders?

8. How would you, as police manager, enforce organizational rules and regulations?

9. Are you familiar with any organizations that continue to maintain outdated rules and regulations? What are some of these outdated guidelines?

10. We recommend that police administrators seek input from the community and police employees when developing organizational

guidelines. Do you agree with this recommendation? How would you carry it out?

11. How can a police administrator, when developing organizational guidelines, take community interests into consideration and yet remain impartial and objective?

REFERENCES

1. President's Commission on Law Enforcement and Administration of Justice, *The Challenge of Crime in a Free Society* (New York: Avon, 1968), p. 267.

2. Advisory Committee on the Police Function of the American Bar Association Project on Standards for Criminal Justice, *The Urban Police Function* Approved Draft (New York: American Bar Association, 1973), p. 8.

3. *Experiments in Police Improvement: A Progress Report* (Washington, D.C.: Police Foundation, 1972), pp. 14–15.

4. Harold Koontz and Cyril O'Donnell, *Principles of Management: An Analysis of Managerial Functions* (New York: McGraw-Hill, 1968), pp. 178–180.

5. Raymond O. Loen, *Manage More By Doing Less* (New York: McGraw-Hill, 1971), pp. 86–89.

6. Koontz and O'Donnell, *op. cit.*, pp. 193–195.

7. O. W. Wilson and Roy C. McLaren, *Police Administration,* 3rd ed. (New York: McGraw-Hill, 1972), p. 130.

8. Koontz and O'Donnell, *op. cit.*, p. 88.

9. James Q. Wilson, *Varieties of Police Behavior–The Management of Law and Order in Eight Communities* (Cambridge, Mass.: Harvard University Press, 1968), pp. 278–279.

10. Loen, *op. cit.*, pp. 91–92.

11. Falmouth Police Department, *Rules and Regulations,* (Falmouth, Massachusetts, as adopted from the Rules and Regulations of the Cambridge Police Department, Cambridge, Massachusetts).

12. Thomas Reddin, "Are You Oriented to Hold Them?: A Searching Look at Police Management," *The Police Chief* (March 1966): 17. Reprinted with permission of the International Association of Chiefs of Police.

PART V
ORGANIZATIONAL
IMPROVEMENT

The first two chapters in Part V present information on methods currently being used to effect organizational improvement; Chapter 14 poses some of the basic and insoluble issues and dilemmas in police administration. One of the main purposes of Part V is to integrate the several perspectives of organizational analysis and management discussed in this text. Although we discussed police administration in terms of three main perspectives—traditional, human, and flow—the successful manager must recognize the interdependence and interrelatedness of these approaches. In order to manage systematically, chiefs and other police administrators must develop their abilities to analyze their organizations from all of these perspectives more or less simultaneously. Police managers who choose to ignore one or more of these approaches are likely to witness the breakdown of their systems.

Chapter 12 discusses methods of organizational improvement currently used in business, industrial, and public management. The discussion virtually ignores the police, focusing instead on organizations in general. We argue strongly that police managers who ignore all but specifically police-related practices and literature unnecessarily limit their learning and experiences. We certainly agree that police administration encounters some unique problems and has unique needs; however, many aspects of police administration are also quite common to management generally, and it seems stubborn and foolhardy not to borrow whatever might be successfully applied.

In Chapter 13 the general approaches to organizational improvement previously presented are applied to the police. This chapter does not have to deal all in theory and ideal circumstances, though, since many police departments actually have been experimenting with organizational improvement in recent years. Despite the fact that the discussions are brief, the evidence seems overwhelming that many general approaches to organizational improvement are applicable in whole or in part to the police service.

Chapter 14, our concluding statement, considers some of the basic issues confronting police administrators. The chapter is not a practical one in the sense that solutions to problems are offered. Rather, we suggest that the issues defy resolution, that they are timeless and basic. An understanding and appreciation of these issues, however, is crucial for the police administrator. Just as we would not care to be served by a president who did not understand the intractable dilemmas of democratic government, so do we believe that police managers should appreciate in their heads and hearts the central issues of policing and police administration in a free society dedicated to ordered liberty.

CHAPTER 12
CONTEMPORARY APPROACHES
TO ORGANIZATIONAL
IMPROVEMENT

LEARNING OBJECTIVES

1. Identify the origin of the concept of the worker as something more than a human machine.

2. Contrast Theory X and Theory Y.

3. Explain the failure of regular improvements in salary, fringe benefits, and job security to result in increased productivity and higher morale.

4. Cite the basis for Drucker's Management By Objectives.

5. Cite the role of information in Management By Objectives.

6. Identify and contrast hygiene factors and motivators.

7. Describe job enrichment.

8. Cite three key factors in participative management.

9. Cite two compelling reasons for involving all employees in the process of running an organization.

10. Characterize organization development (OD) in terms of the previously discussed approaches to organizational improvement.

11. Identify the role of the change agent in organization development.

12. Describe laboratory training.

13. Identify and characterize the organizations from which classical theorists drew their conclusions.

14. Identify the currently popular one-best-way approach to organizational structure.

15. Describe the contingency theory of organizational structure.

16. Cite the factor in organizations that limits both the descriptive and predictive value of models.

17. Define operations research.

In the preceding chapters we discussed organizations from the perspectives of structural design, human behavior, and flow. We attempted to describe the wide range of factors involved in organizations. You should now have a rather clear understanding of what an organization is. Such an understanding, however, brings you, historically speaking, to about the year 1950. Since then a great number of new ideas and theoretical concepts have been advanced to more comprehensively describe the managerial process in organizations. Some of these have further refined basic principles discussed earlier; others have contradicted them completely. Some of the basic assumptions about authority and hierarchy, for example, have been challenged, and some organizational principles have been roundly criticized as infringements on personal freedom.

The organization as we know it today is much different from the organization of 1950. This is understandable. The fact that organizations are open systems means that they are affected by changing environmental influences. The environment today is much different from that of 1950. Organizations must necessarily be different if they are to be responsive to changing societal demands.

Many observers believe that the organizational turmoil and loss of respect for authority evident in recent years are indicators of social degeneration and organizational disintegration that threaten the very foundations of society. Other observers see these conditions as temporary aberrations of a society in the state of cultural lag, changing so rapidly that its institutions have been unable to keep up with the change and respond to it meaningfully. Still others see these trends producing an administrative revolution which will increase personal freedom as the organization becomes a "shelter without walls."[1]

In this chapter some of the major contemporary approaches to organizational improvement will be discussed. We hope that you may begin to appreciate just how complex the management function has become.

THE HUMAN DEVELOPMENT APPROACH

The Hawthorne studies of the 1920s introduced the concept that the worker is something more than a human machine. These studies provided a foundation for what eventually became the human relations movement, which characterized the worker as a social being with human needs and which demanded that management treat its employees more humanely. An overview of human development approaches is given in Table 12.1.

Table 12.1   Human development approaches

Approach	Key Theorist	Summary
Human relations	Roethlisberger *et al.*	Hawthorne studies; recognition of the social needs of workers
Theory X and Theory Y	McGregor	Need hierarchy; worker self-direction and self-control
Management By Objectives	Drucker	Goals and objectives for direction and control
Job enrichment	Herzberg	Importance of the work itself; motivation from work
Participative management	Likert	Democratic management; supportive and advisory supervision
Organization development	Bennis	Organizational improvement as change; integrated strategies

Traditional theorists considered the human relations movement to be managerial permissiveness, branding it as an abdication of managerial authority, which had heretofore been considered the glue which held organizations together. Other theorists came to view the human relations movement as a cosmetic public relations gimmick and claimed that it involved no real changes in the patterns of organizational authority.

Neither group of theorists was correct. In retrospect, the human relations movement can be credited with improving the workplace considerably and with contributing to the improvement of employee compensation and other work benefits. Most important, the movement was the first step toward recognizing that the human element in an organization is not comparable to inert resources such as money, machinery, and raw materials. Organizational productivity became dependent on treating workers with dignity and with respect. The human relations movement was here to stay.

Theory X and Theory Y   Douglas McGregor was one of the first observers to suggest that the human relations movement and the debate over the relative merits of "hard" and "soft" management were missing the point.[2] He argued that the basic assumptions of management had not changed, and he forcefully contended that these basic assumptions were invalid.

McGregor called the conventional view of management's task Theory X. The assumptions behind Theory X are as follows:

1. people do not like to work and will avoid work whenever possible;

2. people must be forced to work; and

3. people are inherently unambitious and irresponsible, seek security, and expect to be directed in their work.[3]

McGregor conceded that most workers behaved just as the Theory X assumptions indicated. But he argued that the organizational climate created by Theory X managers predetermined workers' behavior. He believed that management's view of workers as lazy, stupid, and irresponsible and management's treatment of workers on the basis of that view made it all but impossible for workers to display interest, intelligence, and energy.

In arguing that the assumptions of Theory X did not accurately characterize the motivation and basic nature of organizational employees, McGregor drew on the findings of Abraham Maslow, whose findings were discussed in Chapter 7.[4] Basically, Maslow found that human behavior is motivated by a hierarchy of needs: basic needs, security needs, societal/social needs, self-concept needs, and goal-realization needs. Maslow contended that a satisfied need ceased to have any motivational value. The human need for air, for example, is basic, but it does not motivate behavior except in circumstances where a person's supply of air is withdrawn.

McGregor saw that Theory X assumptions and management were based on the belief that workers are still motivated primarily by basic and security needs. Because Theory X assumptions were incorrect, management became frustrated when regular improvements in salary, fringe benefits, and job security did not result in increased productivity and in higher morale. But McGregor pointed out that for almost all workers, basic and security needs were satisfied. The major motivational needs of most workers, therefore, are societal/social needs, self-concept needs, and goal-recognition needs.

McGregor also pointed out that for needs to have a motivating effect at work, the opportunity must be present to satisfy these needs *at work*. Although an individual's after-hours activities might satisfy certain needs, they have no motivating effect in the workplace. Although a man may be president of the Little League, a director of the Junior Chamber of Commerce, and a 32nd degree Mason and thereby satisfy some of his needs on the top side of the need hierarchy, such satisfaction plays no role whatever in motivating him to do his job; these needs must be satisfied where he works if he is to be motivated to do his job well.

Armed with Maslow's findings on motivation, McGregor proposed Theory Y as an alternative to Theory X. The general assumptions on which Theory Y is based are as follows:

1. It is natural for workers to expend energy in work that they enjoy.

2. If work is satisfying, it will be performed well; if it is not satisfying, it will be looked on as punishment and will be avoided.

3. Control and punishment are not the only methods to motivate work.

4. Workers are totally capable of directing themselves toward the accomplishment of goals and objectives to which they are personally committed.

5. There is a direct relationship between worker commitment and the rewards associated with the achievement of goals and objectives.

6. Rewards emanate from the satisfaction of motivational needs as these relate to the effort expended on the achievement of goals and objectives.

7. If conditions are right, workers will not only accept responsibility, but also seek it.

8. Laziness and disinterest in work are the result of bad experiences, not innate human behavior.

9. Most people are ambitious and are capable of working innovatively and productively in organizational settings.

10. Modern management uses human potential to an extraordinarily limited degree.[5]

The essential difference between the two theories is that Theory X emphasizes external control of worker behavior, whereas Theory Y emphasizes self-control and self-direction. Theory X proponents treat employees like children; Theory Y proponents treat them like mature adults. Considering the fact that management has been treating employees like children for many generations, McGregor conceded that it would take considerable time for both managers and workers to grow accustomed to Theory Y. McGregor concludes that Theory X "fails because direction and control are useless methods of motivating people whose physiological and safety needs [what we have called *basic* and *security needs*] are reasonably satisfied and whose social, egoistic, and self-fulfillment needs [what we have called *societal/social, self-concept,* and *goal-recognition* needs] are predominant."[6]

Management By Objectives   Another approach to management that differed sharply from Theory X was developed by Peter Drucker. He called his approach *Management By Objectives,* which like Theory Y is based on self-control. Drucker saw his approach as a means of obtaining higher work standards and greater productivity along with stricter accountability.[7]

Management By Objectives is based on Drucker's observation that people work hardest when they have a clear goal in mind and when they can see a direct relationship between their efforts and the accomplishment of that goal. Moreover, Drucker argued, when employees have a clear understanding of the goals of the organization and when they see how their own work contributes to achieving those goals, they can then be counted on to establish objectives for their own work accomplishment. The task itself provides substantial direction and control, and employees will strive to achieve their objectives and hold themselves accountable to such objectives.

Drucker noted that the modern organization is characterized by factors that encourage misdirection. Specialization, as one example, tends to divert employee loyalty and effort away from the organization as a whole and toward the particular specialized areas. Instituting Management By Objectives, Drucker argued, can overcome factors of misdirection by emphasizing the goals of the organization as a whole as well as ways that subunits contribute to their achievement.

Drucker points out that in order for employees to exercise self-control and self-direction, they need information on a regular basis by which to measure their progress. A semiannual or annual performance evaluation will not suffice. Employees need such information much more frequently, and it should be available to them without their having to go to an immediate superior for it. In short, the employee's job should be systematically structured so that direct feedback is periodically available to the employee for progress measurement.

Drucker also contends that there is nothing "soft" about Management By Objectives. With its emphasis on self-direction and self-control and its aim toward higher standards and greater productivity with stricter accountability, it requires much more from employees than they had previously been expected to give. Drucker is convinced, like McGregor, that in general people like to work, want to work, want a feeling of accomplishment, and are capable of intelligent direction. Drucker sees management's task as more one of removing organizational impediments to motivation than one of providing motivation.

Job enrichment   A third approach to management and organizational improvement that springs from motivational theory is *job enrichment.* The principal theorist for this approach has been Frederick Herzberg.[8]

Herzberg studied a number of techniques for motivating workers: increased wages, human relations training, and employee counseling. He found that such techniques served only as short-term motivators and that some even seemed counterproductive. He also studied work behavior and isolated two sets of workplace factors which bear on employee satisfaction and dissatisfaction. The dissatisfiers included company policy and administration, supervision, work conditions, salary, personal life, status, security, and work relationships with supervisors, subordinates, and peers. These he called *hygiene factors.* The satisfiers included achievement, recognition, the work itself, responsibility, advancement, and growth. These he called *motivators.* He found that the alleviation of the dissatisfiers tended to make employees happier but no more motivated. He concluded that motivation comes only from the satisfiers.

The implications of Herzberg's studies should be clear. Through salary increases and employee counseling, management may be able to decrease employee dissatisfaction; such decreases, however, will promote no motivation. Motivation can be achieved, according to Herzberg, only through those factors he calls *motivators.*

Job enrichment is the restructuring of work itself in terms of motivators. It is much different from job enlargement, which gives each worker more work to do, and it is much different from job rotation, which simply shuttles the worker from one unenriched job to another. Job enrichment can be accomplished, according to Herzberg, by taking the following steps:

1. reduce controls but increase accountability;

2. assign workers to established, definitive work units or projects;

3. provide sufficient authority for workers to accomplish tasks within a milieu of freedom;

4. furnish workers with productivity reports directly on a periodic basis without involving supervisors as intermediaries;

5. give workers tasks that are more difficult and challenging than tasks previously assigned; and

6. allow workers to become experts by giving them specialized tasks. [9]

Central to the job-enrichment approach is the concept that needs that motivate work behavior can be satisfied at the workplace. Townsend, in agreeing with this approach, asks us to "look at the rewards we're offering our people today: higher wages, medical benefits, vacations, pensions, profit sharing, bowling and baseball teams. Not one can be enjoyed on the job. You've got to leave work, get sick, or retire first." [10]

Robinson notes, however, that job enrichment is not an organizational panacea, although he and other managers have found that it is a useful approach to organizational improvement, particularly as it offers workers a greater sense of pride in their work. [11] Job enrichment must be considered an important input to the managing process.

Participative management   Another human development approach to organizational improvement that has received generous praise in recent years is *participative management*. This approach is based on including nonmanagerial employees in the managing process.

The extent to which employees of an organization can be involved in the managing process varies widely. Some factories in Europe, for example, are run by councils made up entirely of elected representatives of the employees. In other organizations some members of the boards of directors are elected by the employees. Elsewhere, supervisors are appointed by employees. In some organizations, the appointment of supervisors is subject to employee veto.

Although the degree of involvement may vary, then, there are numerous examples of employee participation in management. To many traditional managers the idea of employees participating in the managing process has seemed radical, even revolutionary. Looking at the idea objectively, however, it is no more revolutionary than having citizens participate in their own governments, an idea which was also considered revolutionary when it was first advanced.

Likert, in studying a number of organizations, found that a consensus existed among managers that the most effective organizations they had known were open, democratic ones.[12] Likert identified three key factors in participative management. The first was that the relationship between supervisor and subordinate should be a supportive type of relationship, with the supervisor emphasizing the helpful rather than the authoritarian aspects of his or her role. The second factor was that decision making in organizations should be democratic and group-centered and that decisions made by groups under these circumstances should be forwarded to management by the democratically chosen group leader. The third and most important factor in participative management was the advisory role played by the supervisor in devising work goals and norms and in acting as a liaison between employees and management in attempting to accommodate the objectives of each.

There are two outstanding and practical reasons why management should involve its employees in the process of running the organization. One is that participation gives employees a greater feeling of belonging and a stronger commitment to their work. The second is that the involvement of employees in management tends to increase the efficiency and effectiveness of the organization.

It makes absolutely no sense for managers, who in many instances are years removed from the operational aspects of their organizations, or for staff specialists, who make recommendations from safe distances, to go about making arbitrary, unilateral decisions, oblivious to the thoughts and feelings of the people who actually do the work. In many organizations decisions are still made this way; such decisions, for the most part, are bad decisions and impact negatively on organizational goals and objectives. Management that is committed to unilateral decision making today is management that will probably not survive. Even good unilateral decision making is ineffective because it lacks the full commitment of the people charged with implementation responsibility.

Boyd has noted that "businessmen have . . . known that workers can achieve extraordinary productivity increases by finding ways to do their jobs better or faster or cheaper."[13] The manager who wants to take advantage of employee ingenuity, initiative, and talent does so by involving employees as much as possible in the management of the organization. Although the manager may be criticized for being soft and for abdicating responsibility, especially in traditional organizations, such criticism must be absorbed in return for greater efficiency and improved effectiveness through employee participation in the managing process. These techniques really work.

Organization development Warren Bennis has described *organization development,* or OD, as "an educational strategy employing the widest possible means of experienced-based behavior in order to achieve more and better organizational choices in a highly turbulent world."[14] If that sounds just a little bit hazy, it is not really Mr. Bennis's fault. OD means many things to many people and defies simple definition.

OD is not actually a separate and distinct approach to human development in organizations. That is, OD programs include, in whole or in part, Theory Y, Management By Objectives, job enrichment, and participative management. Consider the following set of OD assumptions, for example, in light of the other approaches we have discussed:

1. people need to grow in their jobs and to realize their potentials;

2. once people's basic needs have been satisfied, they will work energetically, seeking challenge and assuming responsibility;

3. effectiveness and efficiency in organizations may be enhanced through the organization of work designed to meet human needs;

4. the more open organizational communications are, the greater the degree of personal and professional growth experienced by employees;

5. open confrontation as a means of resolving conflict achieves employee growth and the accomplishment of organizational goals far better than does unilateral conflict resolution;

6. as people begin to care for one another openly and honestly within group frameworks, it becomes easier to handle organizational problems in constructive rather than destructive fashion;

7. the structure of an organization and the kinds of job requirements within it can be changed to better meet individual, group, and organizational needs, goals, and objectives; and

8. problems relating to the design of organizations are directly responsible for personality problems within them.[15]

An important ingredient of OD is its treatment of growth and development as change. It takes note of the fact that many organizational employees are quite comfortable with the way things are presently done and are therefore resistant to changes no matter how logically they are presented or how obviously advantageous they are to employee welfare.

As people begin to care for one another openly and honestly within group frameworks, it becomes easier to handle organizational problems in constructive rather than destructive fashion. (Courtesy of the Cincinnati Police Department)

A key figure in the OD process is the so-called *change agent.* Usually an objective and impartial outside consultant, the change agent is hired by the organization to oversee OD. Unlike the ordinary consultant, who is hired for a limited period of time to study organizational problems, the change agent, or OD consultant, contributes expertise on an ongoing basis, acting as a resource person and advisor to management and suggesting programs and strategies for organizational improvement while at the same time developing the organization's own capacity to grow and to manage change. The OD consultant seeks to become fully aware of the organization's particular culture and to adapt OD assumptions and principles to the realities of the organization.

In developing the organization's capacity to improve and to deal with change, the OD consultant often makes use of some variation of an approach called *laboratory training.* This technique is designed to provide groups of people with insights into their own behavior, the behavior of others, and group dynamics. It is much like sensitivity training and education (see Chapter 7). The central feature of laboratory training is the training group, or T-group, which usually consists of 10 to 15 people who work together in an organization. The only distinction between sensitivity training and laboratory training through the T-group is that laboratory training is always intraorganizational, whereas sensitivity training may be either intraorganizational or interorganizational.

The T-group meets in seclusion for a period of two days to three months. It is guided and advised by an experienced sensitivity trainer, who intervenes in the group as little as possible, but provides ongoing direction. The group is given very little structure. It establishes its own agenda and elects its own leadership. The actions of the group become the subject of analysis, with the trainer emphasizing the need for participants to be open and honest in their exchanges. Group members are pressed to focus on the motivations for their own behavior and on their relations with others.

The outcome of T-group training is usually an emotional experience; it is therefore as difficult to describe as it is to measure its impact. Coghill has reported that participants show an increase in listening ability, an improved understanding of others, a capability of making better contributions in group situations, and an increase in tolerance and flexibility.[16]

However, the success of T-group or laboratory training is dependent on the extent to which participants are willing to commit themselves openly; consequently, the results vary widely. Also, the technique has become identified with "soft" approaches to management and is held in disfavor by strict management traditionalists. This is unfortunate, because T-group training, if properly conducted, can go a long way toward indoctrinating employees in new roles and in the acceptance of new responsibilities. We are among those who believe that laboratory training is the foundation on which organization development is built. Because it shows employees how to be receptive to change and how to adapt to it in terms of their own personal and professional growth, it is an absolute OD imperative.

The emphasis of the OD approach is on growth and change. Any organization attempting OD must be careful to tailor its programs to organizational realities, avoiding prepackaged cure-alls. There are no prescribed procedures in organization development; herein lies its strength. OD must be applied to different organizations in different ways in accordance with the identification of dynamic factors that are not universally found in all organizations. OD relies on openness and candor at all times and in all situations. It must therefore be an ongoing approach, as changing personnel, jobs, circumstances, and demands continually upset established relationships. OD operates on the valid assumption that organizations are and always will be in varying stages of turmoil. The assumptions on which OD is based represent nothing more than techniques that may be applied, given the right circumstances and an enlightened and sensitive management, in organizational improvement.

THE STRUCTURAL–DESIGN APPROACH

In our concern for the people who make up an organization, we must be careful not to forget the organization itself. The way in which an organization is structured has an important bearing on its ultimate efficiency and effectiveness. In recent years the preeminence of behavioral scientists in the organizational-improvement field has tended to obscure the importance of structure; this is unfortunate, but true.

Early structural theorists advanced a *one-best-way* approach to organizational arrangement. They relied on principles of hierarchy, such as chain of command, unity of command, span of control, and division of labor, to popularize the pyramidal organizational form. These theorists contended that this was the best way to organize any undertaking, whether it be a social club or General Motors; as a result, social clubs and General Motors were organized for years in much the same way. Structural theorists have had a tremendous influence on large numbers of organizations and the way they have developed.

Recently, however, a contingency theory of organizational structure has been gaining prominence. Much like Fiedler's leadership theory (see Chapter 9), this contingency theory holds that situational factors require different organizational structures for different circumstances. This contingency theory will be discussed in detail after a brief description of classical theory.

Classical theory   March and Simon have noted that classical organizational theory tends to view the employee as an inhuman instrument performing preassigned duties; employees came to be looked on, there-fore, as constants rather than as variables.[17] This unusual perspective is sometimes referred to, as mentioned earlier in this text, as the machine-economic model, because it perceives human beings as machines and recognizes only their economic motivation. It is easy to see how this conception of the worker leads to a *one-best-way* approach to organiza-tion and management.

The early classical theorists drew their conclusions from the promi-nent organizations of their day—the Church and the military. These organizations were structured along pyramidal lines, with authority resting at the apex; indeed, the Church and the military are still struc-tured in much the same way. This kind of organization is called *central-ized organization* because authority is centralized at the top of the hierarchy.

In more recent years the sheer size and complexity of organizations literally forced those in authority to share their authority. As authority is dispersed throughout an organization, that organization becomes a *decentralized organization.* A pattern of decentralization currently in vogue is capsulized in the phrase "centralize policy making; decentralize decision making."

Just as early classical theorists postulated that centralization was the only way to organize properly, many contemporary theorists now claim that decentralization is the only way to go. General Motors has been extremely successful in operating from a decentralized base. The fact that its Pontiac Division, for example, is totally separate from its Oldsmobile Division and that the divisions compete with each other has provided both autonomy for its divisions and stability for the corpora-tion. The Ford Motor Company, which for years operated as a central-ized organization, took a page out of General Motors' book and decentralized several years ago; it could no longer afford the luxury of centralized authority. Since decentralizing, the company has become much stronger and more competitively viable. Even the Roman Catho-lic Church, in which centralized authority was for centuries always looked on as a key to its success, has decentralized in many respects. Bishops now make decisions which would have been looked on as being strictly within the province of Rome two decades ago. Parish councils have been established in many local Roman Catholic churches to make decisions affecting the local level at the local level. Decisions about faith and morals are centralized in Rome; just about everything else is decentralized in dioceses and parishes. From an organizational stand-point, this increases effectiveness. Theorists who argue in favor of decentralization claim that organizations should be as *flat* as possible, meaning that authority should be decentralized so that fewer levels of management are needed and so that decisions may be made where the action is.

These modern classical theorists are right—some of the time. But the variety of tasks that different organizations perform, the difference in sizes of organizations, and the varying environments in which they operate provide substantial rationale for the position that no one particular structure is best for all. Therefore, organizations should be structured in terms of their individual needs, goals, and objectives in accordance with factors that peculiarly characterize them and impact on their productivity.

Contingency theory In 1964, Chris Argyris predicted that "organizations (of the future) will tend to vary the structures that they use according to the kinds of decisions that must be made."[18] More recently, Leavitt asserted that there is no ideal structural design; structure, he said, must be contingent on variables such as tasks, environment, people, and technology.[19] He further suggested that organizations must be structured so that they are adaptable and capable of self-modification.

The principal proponents of the *contingency theory* have been Lawrence and Lorsch.[20] They studied a number of different organizations in a variety of fields, attempting to relate success to type of organizational structure. They concluded that there is no one best way to structure all organizations. The most efficient and effective organizations they found were structured to fit the environments in which they operated.

Lawrence and Lorsch advanced the theory that any organization can be located at some point along an environmental continuum that stretches from situations of stability and certainty to situations of instability and uncertainty. They suggested that traditional hierarchical structures tend to be more successful in stable and certain situations, whereas more decentralized and flexible structures are preferable in situations of instability and uncertainty.

Just as OD recognizes that approaches to human development must be tailored to organizational realities, the contingency theory forces abandonment of the one-best-way approach to structure in favor of the situational approach. In each organizational situation, the variables involved must be considered in structuring the organization to fit its environment. The contingency theory, therefore, is built around the proposition that an organization's structure is *contingent* on the specific variables affecting the specific organization. Because contingency theory is based on an *it-all-depends* approach, it is a flexible theory that is extremely useful in structuring all organizations. Because it is flexible, it is an excellent approach.

THE FLOW APPROACH

The third general approach to organizational improvement is concerned with the processes of information and work flow. The *flow approach* looks laterally at the manner in which tasks are accomplished. It is by far the most systems-oriented of the three general approaches in terms of both its analytical aspects and its prescriptions for organizational improvement.

As we pointed out repeatedly in Chapter 10, the key to effective information and work-flow processes is feedback. Feedback, which characterizes the closed-loop system, allows the people who are passing information and doing the work to know how well they are performing. It provides them with the opportunity to correct dysfunctional processes that are hampering progress long before problems reach crisis proportions.

The flow approach to organizational improvement also tends to be the most technical of the three general approaches. Its use of computers, operations research, and mathematical models can be mind-boggling to the manager who is a generalist and who is unfamiliar with technical approaches to management. It is for this reason, as much as any other, that the flow approach has failed to live up to its early billing as the solution to nearly every organizational malady. Many organizational improvement programs have failed because they attempted to superimpose an integrated systems design on a traditional hierarchical organization without laying the proper groundwork. These programs did not take into account organizational realities such as satisfaction with the status quo, fear of technical innovations, costs of established techniques, and uncertainty about how to use newly designed systems and newly available information. If nothing else, these unfortunate experiences have highlighted the need to explain systems approaches in language everyone can understand. They have also demonstrated the importance of fitting flow approaches to organizational realities.

The value of the flow approach to organizational improvement cannot be overemphasized. Because it is systems-oriented, it is an extremely important tool that must be mastered and used. Its potential, which has barely been tapped, is great.

Models   Everyone knows that a model airplane is a scaled-down, simplified facsimile of a real airplane. In somewhat the same way, an organizational model is a scaled-down, simplified facsimile of a real organization. An airplane model is built with wood, plastic, and glue; an organizational model is built of information, variables, equations, and assumptions.

It is possible to construct a rather precise model of an airplane because the makeup and operation of real airplanes is very clearly understood. If we understood organizations nearly as well, we could also build precise organizational models. But such is not the case.

In constructing an organizational model, one must first carefully analyze information and work flow, resource allocation, decision making, material consumption, and numerous other factors that in one way or another impact on the organization. From this analysis relationships between and among factors can be uncovered and equations developed which reflect these relationships.

Once an accurate model of the present operation of an organization has been developed, it can be used to make predictions about future operations and alternative programs. The effects of changes in any of the factors involved can be investigated through the use of the model. For example, the model could be used to predict the consequences for the entire organization of reassigning a group of employees.

It is the human element in organizations that limits both the descriptive and predictive value of models. In order to develop a model that establishes relationships and equations involving human behavior, assumptions must be made. In a resource-allocation model, for example, assumptions must be made about the amount of work that can be accomplished by varying numbers of workers. But the dynamics of individual and group behavior are such that worker productivity can vary widely in seemingly identical situations. All of the factors that interact in finally determining why people do what they do and how they are likely to react cannot be reduced to mathematical formulas and computer models.

Nevertheless, models do have great value, particularly if those who construct them and work with them understand their limitations. Just as with management information systems, the development of models requires a careful analysis of the ways in which an organization presently operates and the manner in which tasks are currently accomplished. This analysis is useful in and of itself; it usually reveals some astonishing insights into organizational defects. Although the human element severely restricts the predictive value of models, there are in most organizations numerous subsystems which are predominantly inert and which can be greatly improved on, based on the predictive capacity of well-built models.

Operations research A flow approach to organizational improvement that makes use of models and other scientific techniques to optimize the performance of an organization as a system is *operations research* (OR). Jenny has described OR as the "application of the scientific method, of quantitative analysis, and of mathematical models in order to provide executives with the best possible answers concerning managerial problems under their control."[21]

Just as with models, the viability of OR is limited by the unpredictability of human behavior in organizations. Nonetheless, it may be successfully applied to the following organizational problems:

1. allocation of resources;

2. deployment of personnel;

3. replacement of resources;

4. conflict management;

5. data collection and planning;

6. improvement of clientele relationships; and

7. handling of requests for service.[22]

Operations research, which is sometimes referred to as management or administrative science, holds great promise for improving organizations and their components from a systems perspective. Skills and techniques in the application of science and mathematics must necessarily be developed by managers who expect to put OR to productive use.

SUMMARY

A sampling of approaches to organizational improvement has been presented in this chapter from three different perspectives: human development, structural design, and flow. It should be understood that each perspective, or approach, has its committed disciples and its vocal critics.

Today's managers interested in improving their organizations can pick and choose from a plethora of programs; we have outlined and described some of those we believe to be important. Police chiefs, in attempting to improve their departments, should avoid at all costs the *one-best-way* mentality and instead draw intelligently from all approaches and methods available, tailoring these to the realities of their organizations and the environments in which they operate. This means that police chiefs, in order to be effective, must seek an integrated approach to organizational improvement, drawing on applicable aspects of the human development, structural-design, and flow perspectives simultaneously. If an integrated approach is not used, gains made in one subsystem will be frustrated by blockages in others. The effort to improve the organization must be systematic, moving ahead on all fronts at once.

DISCUSSION QUESTIONS

1. Organizations and authority do not seem to be as well respected to-day as they once were. Why? What do you think is the future implication of this trend?

2. Which set of assumptions—Theory X or Theory Y—is closest to your personal opinion of human nature? Which set of assumptions does your teacher seem to hold?

3. Do you agree that the physical and security needs of most Americans are satisfied? If you do agree, how would you explain labor strikes and demands for higher wages?

4. Do you find that the presence of goals and objectives motivates you to work harder? Is there a difference between goals that someone else has set for you and goals that you have set?

5. How would you enrich some jobs with which you are familiar? How would you enrich an assembly-line job? The police job? A secretary's job?

6. Why do you think that we support democracy in government but question its usefulness in other types of organizations?

7. Would you work harder for a supervisor who gave you advice and was generally helpful or one who was constantly looking over your shoulder to make sure that your nose was to the grindstone?

8. How do you react to change? Do you welcome it like a fresh breeze or dread it like a tornado?

9. Consider organizations with which you are familiar in terms of centralization and decentralization. Which classical structure do they most closely fit? Can you think of any organizations that demonstrate the contingency approach?

10. How successful do you think theorists will ever be at developing models of human organizations?

REFERENCES

1. George E. Berkley, *The Administrative Revolution: Notes on the Passing of Organization Man* (Englewood Cliffs, N.J.: Prentice-Hall, 1971).

2. Douglas McGregor, "The Human Side of Enterprise," *Management Review* **46**, 11 (1957): 22-28.

3. Douglas McGregor, *The Human Side of Enterprise* (New York: McGraw-Hill, 1960).

4. Abraham Maslow, *Motivation and Personality* (New York: Harper & Brothers, 1954).

5. McGregor, *The Human Side of Enterprise, op. cit.*

6. McGregor, *Management Review, op. cit.,* pp. 14-15.

7. Peter Drucker, *The Practice of Management* (New York: Harper & Brothers, 1954).

8. Frederick Herzberg, "One More Time: How Do You Motivate Employees?" *Harvard Business Review* (January-February 1968): 53-62.

9. *Ibid.,* p. 59.

10. Robert Townsend, *Up The Organization* (New York: Knopf, 1970), p. 140.

11. John F. Robinson, "Job Enrichment: What It Is," *Supervisory Management* **18,** 9 (September 1973): 5.

12. Rensis Likert, *The Human Organization: Its Management and Value* (New York: McGraw-Hill, 1967).

13. Marjorie Boyd, "How We Can Bring Back Quality: Sharing A Piece of the Action," *Washington Monthly* **5,** 12 (February 1974): 24.

14. Warren G. Bennis, *Organization Development: Its Nature, Origins, and Prospects* (Reading, Mass.: Addison-Wesley, 1969), p. 17.

15. Edgar F. Huse and James L. Bowditch, *Behavior in Organizations: A Systems Approach to Managing,* 2d ed. (Reading, Mass.: Addison-Wesley, 1977), pp. 386-387.

16. Mary Ann Coghill, "Sensitivity Training: A Review of the Controversy," *Key Issue Series,* (Ithaca: New York State School of Industrial and Labor Relations, Cornell University, December 1967).

17. James G. March and Herbert A. Simon, *Organizations* (New York: Wiley, 1958), p. 29.

18. Chris Argyris, *Integrating the Individual and the Organization* (New York: Wiley, 1964), p. 211.

19. Harold J. Leavitt, *Managerial Psychology* (Chicago: University of Chicago, 1972) p. 309.

20. P. Lawrence and J. Lorsch, *Organization and Environment: Managing Differentiation and Integration* (Boston: Harvard University Graduate School of Business Administration, 1967).

21. Hans H. Jenny, "Applications of Operations Research," *Linear Programming and the Theory of the Firm* (New York: Macmillan, 1960).

22. *Ibid.*

CHAPTER 13
POLICE ORGANIZATIONAL
IMPROVEMENT

LEARNING OBJECTIVES

1. Identify a defense mechanism attitude often used by the police to deflect public criticism.

2. Cite one of the first popular avenues to police organizational improvement.

3. Describe LEEP and its impact.

4. Characterize the evidence relating education to police organizational improvement.

5. Cite the representativeness rationale for higher education for the police.

6. Describe the police agent program of the Baltimore Police Department.

7. Describe the unrealistic and dangerous aspects of police professionalization.

8. Characterize patrol officer investigation in terms of job enrichment.

9. Define team policing.

10. Characterize team policing in terms of the various approaches to organizational improvement.

11. Characterize police work in terms of its inherent qualities.

12. Cite some applications of participative management in police organizations.

13. Cite examples of organizational improvement through both decentralization and centralization.

14. Cite frequent but questionable bases for additional personnel requests.

15. Cite some rational indicators on which personnel requirements and allocation can be based.

16. Identify some applications of operations research to police organizational improvement.

The police in America today have some severe organizational problems. Numerous investigating commissions have found the quality of American police service to be generally inadequate. One of the primary, underlying reasons for this inadequacy is the backwardness and ineffectiveness of traditional police organizations, which is compounded by extremely strong resistance to change in not only the ranks, but also the supervisory and administrative echelons of many police departments. The old way of doing things is the most comfortable way of doing things; change, which challenges initiative and ingenuity, inevitably upsets the status quo and the comfortable approach.

Police departments in the United States have been closed to public scrutiny for so long, operating in almost total isolation with little or no accountability for their actions, that they find it very difficult to accept public criticism and adjust accordingly, especially if such adjustment involves radical change. As a defense mechanism, the police in this country have developed an attitude that only they understand their problems and that consequently only they can provide solutions to them. They lose sight of the fact, however, that they may be too close to the forest to see the trees. Although many police officers go to college and take police courses and read magazines and books that have the word "police" in their titles, they remain an insular subculture quite distrustful of outside interference. If business organizations were to react as the police do to the inputs of outside experts, they would quickly go bankrupt. Although the police may have unique expertise in handling certain operational problems, their training and orientation in no way prepare them to work effectively with management problems; with these, they need help from outsiders who have expertise in organizational management.

The police administrator who has just finished reading Chapter 12 in this book, for example, may see little application of organizational improvement approaches in police departments. In Chapter 12 the word "police" was infrequently used. Yet these approaches have been found to be successful in a wide variety of organizations. They translate the latest findings on human behavior and systems theory into practical, workable approaches to managing everything from a hot dog stand to the Polaroid Corporation. They have enthusiastic supporters among both academicians and managers of public and private organizations. They certainly apply to police organizations.

During the last few years, primarily as a result of pressure and persuasion generated by such organizations as the Law Enforcement Assistance Administration, the International Association of Chiefs of Police, and the Police Foundation, the police have begun to appreciate the need for their organizations to be open systems, constantly interchanging information and ideas with the rest of society. To be sure, the police still have a long way to come along the road of reentry into the mainstream of society, but the journey seems to have begun.

In this chapter we will discuss briefly some police organizational improvements that have been made in recent years. Note that most, if not all, are applications of general improvements presented in the preceding chapter.

Imaginative and intelligent police administrators must over the coming years begin to realize that a wealth of information and programs is available to them once they overcome the traditionally based impulse to reject organizational improvement methods not specifically labeled "police methods." Organizational improvement methods are universal in their application and must be looked on as such as the police attempt to adjust to the rapidly changing needs of a rapidly changing society.

EDUCATION

One of the first popular avenues to police organizational improvement was higher education for police officers. Some of the advantages of sending police officers to college and of accepting college graduates at the entrance level are listed below:

1. an enhanced understanding of police functions and the police role;

2. an increased knowledge of the importance of police in society;

3. an improved sensitivity for the problems of people;

4. a better ability to communicate;

5. the development of skills;

6. an improved capability for exercising discretion;

7. the refinement of analytical qualities;

8. the consideration of moral and ethical implications of police work; and

9. the development of personal values which are consistent with police organizational goals and objectives in a democracy.[1]

With the establishment of the Office of Law Enforcement Assistance in 1966 and later the Law Enforcement Assistance Administration, some strong impetus was given to making the need for police education a reality. The leading figure in this movement was Patrick V. Murphy, then the Assistant Director of the Office of Law Enforcement Assistance. Murphy prodded and guided a grant panel established by Attorney General Nicholas Katzenbach to provide seed money for various police educational efforts throughout the country. As a result, various regional and local training and educational programs were started with federal government money. Even on the grant panel, there was some strong opposition to sending police officers to college, a reflection of the time-honored assumption that only police officers should train police officers. Murphy won out, however, and started what has become a massive influx of police officers to colleges and universities.

At about that same time, James Stinchcomb, a staff member of the International Association of Chiefs of Police, and Congressman William R. Anderson of Tennessee were collaborating on a House bill which for the first time introduced the possibility of providing scholarships and government-supported loans to police officers interested in pursuing academic degrees. Anderson was successful in convincing the Johnson administration of the value of his proposal, and the Law Enforcement Education Program (LEEP) became incorporated in the Safe Streets Act. The rest is history. Thousands upon thousands of police officers who otherwise never would have had a chance to go to college entered the halls of ivy to be exposed to ideas and techniques which were, for the most part, foreign to the heretofore isolated police subculture. The police, whether they knew it or not, were being dragged screaming into the twentieth century.

Once the idea of college-educated police officers became accepted by the police themselves and by others who were at first somewhat skeptical, it became almost universally considered desirable. An equally desirable trend was the recruitment into police organizations of individuals already possessing college degrees. Taken together, these twin avenues for upgrading police personnel were believed to hold great promise.

Those observers who expected the college experience to have an immediate and dramatic effect on police officers and police organizations have largely been disappointed. The full value of police educational programs will not be fully realized by the police service for

ON-WESLEY DISTRIBUTION CENTER

SERVING

ADDISON-WESLEY PUBLISHING COMPANY, INC.

UR ORDER NUMBER	INVOICE NO.
04	8237811

LTD
AU ST

/56125

BENJAMIN / CUMMINGS PUBLISHING COMPANY, INC.

RETURN POSTAGE GUARANTEED

TERMS: NO CASH DISCOUNT		(M)	IA.
NET	CON DAYS	00	4
F.O.B. POINT OF SHIPMENT			

OR WILL BE MAILED SEPARATELY WHICH IS EITHER ENCLOSED PLEASE PAY FROM INVOICE **THIS IS YOUR PACKING LIST**

BIN	TITLE CODE	LOOSE	CTN	CTN P.U
	AL06777	1		22

	A
NUMBER OF CARTONS FOR LOOSE BOOKS	B

AL CARTONS A + B

ADDISON-WESLEY PUBLISHING COMPANY, INC.

BENJAMIN / CUMMINGS PUBLISHING COMPANY, INC.

E DO NOT MARK OR STAMP
OOKS BEFORE INSPECTING
THIS SHIPMENT.
BOOKS CANNOT BE RETURNED

PACKING LIST

CONSIGNMENT 011

PAGE	INVOICE DATE	CUSTOMER'S ORDER NUMBER	
01	03/17/80	2788	04

TO
ADDISON-WESLEY PUBL LTD
53 BEDFORD SQUARE
LONDON WC1B 3DZ
ENGLAND
LONDON WIR 2LR ENGLAND

ACCOUNT NUMBER	T.S.	TERR.	COLLEGE	CNTY.	SH ST.	SHIP VIA
KH 0123 430 9 00	41					PRT.M/

QUANTITY	AUTHOR AND TITLE	SUGG. PRICE
1	SHEEHAN INTRO POLICE AD	15.95
	2-18-053-1	

FORMAL BILLING FOLLOWS FROM
OUR LONDON OFFICE
CONSIGNMENT, TRANSFER OF STOCK TO LO

INVOICE
TO
FOLLOW

CHG POSTAGE TO 4-7000-600-8602-0
CONSIGNMENT INVOICE

MESSAGE TO WAREHOUSE

LBW
FCW

			TOTAL BOO
303722	8237811		
1	INVOICE NO.		

03/17/
BLUE/T

perhaps another two decades, when, in our opinion, educated police officers will be not only desirable, but also mandatory.

The evidence relating education to police organizational improvement today is inconclusive. This is probably the result of a settling-down process and of the need for adjustment to what for the police is a new, startling, and revolutionary trend. Sterling, for example, found that higher education seems to be associated with some undesirable effects on police attitudes and behavior.[2] Anyone familiar with the police service can readily understand the problem. Police officers who are naturally self-centered, arrogant, pompous, and egotistical are likely to have these qualities reinforced through education, becoming the world's greatest authorities on myriad subjects while flaunting their degrees in the faces of their fellow officers.

The experience of getting a baccalaureate degree can be a heady experience for an individual who never expected to get one and who works with a large number of people who have never had the experience. Although the baccalaureate degree should teach an individual how little, as opposed to how much, one knows, it does not always work that way in practice. Hence the degree can change behavior and attitudes so that they work counterproductively to organizational interests. Until the degree becomes a mandatory requirement at the entrance level and only after all police officers have their degrees will behavioral and attitudinal changes level off and not cause organizational problems.

There is some indication even now, however, that education positively affects police performance. Sparling concluded, after reviewing research in the field, that "it appears that increased education is likely to have a general positive effect on the performance of police officers."[3]

The police task is a very specialized one requiring tremendous discretion and judgment. What a police officer needs to know in order to perform that task is comparable to what doctors, lawyers, clergy, marriage counselors, teachers, and businesspeople need to know in order to perform their respective tasks. There is no question but that education must eventually impact positively on the police service; it is only a matter of time until it does.

Another factor that provides significant rationale for police officers to have a higher-education experience is one of representativeness. Saunders notes that "the most compelling argument for higher educational standards for police is the steadily rising educational level of the general population."[4] Ramsey Clark, former Attorney General of the United States, agrees: "We need to draw more than half of our police from colleges merely to begin to reflect a common experience with the public served."[5]

It may also be true that, the police socialization process notwith-standing, an improved police management capability will become evi-dent as college-educated officers achieve greater representation in supervisory and command positions. For the time being, however, the advocates of college education for the police must rely more on their instincts that it is beneficial than on any hard research data that would fully support that supposition.

One police organization that has developed a comprehensive pro-gram to attract college graduates is the Baltimore Police Department. This effort was spearheaded by Police Commissioner Donald D. Pomerleau and the late Major Lon R. Rowlett, Director of the depart-ment's Personnel Division. After being accepted at the entrance level, completing the basic training course, and serving as patrol officers for one year, college graduates become eligible for reclassification as police agents. In the department's rank structure, this position is equivalent to that of patrol officer, but the police agent gets an immediate and sub-stantial raise in pay and is reassigned from general patrol duties to either a more challenging operational post or a staff position. Police agents' assignments are rotated frequently so that the agents will get a broad background in the workings of the organization from an experiential standpoint. As might be expected, this new program has enjoyed great success, and police agents assigned to it have done extremely well on competitive promotional examinations.

Surprisingly, the Baltimore Police Department is one of the few in the country to adopt such a program, even though the idea was ad-vanced as a positive recommendation by the President's Commission on Law Enforcement and Administration of Justice in 1967. While other police departments attempt to satisfy basic and security needs in an effort to motivate their officers, officials in Baltimore are motivating their officers by attempting to satisfy needs higher up on the hierarchi-cal scale. That few other departments have followed suit provides sufficient evidence to confirm our contention that most police adminis-trators strongly resist change, even if such change has been proved beneficial and especially if such change is the recommendation of outsiders.

Many police departments throughout the country have initiated pay-incentive programs, rewarding their officers for having achieved certain levels of higher education. Although incentive programs based on educational achievement reward lower hierarchical needs and are not in and of themselves strong motivators for doing a more effective job, they have for the most part accomplished the purpose of exposing more police officers to the higher-educational experience. Massachusetts passed the following law establishing guidelines for its cities and towns to develop pay-incentive programs based on educational achievement:

> There is hereby established a career incentive program offering base salary increases to regular full-time members of the various city and town police departments, the division of state police in the department of public safety, the capitol police and the metropolitan district police, as a reward for furthering their education in the field of police work.
>
> Police career incentive base salary increases shall be predicated on the accumulation of points earned in the following manner: one point for each semester hour credit earned toward a baccalaureate or an associate degree; sixty points for an associate degree; one hundred and twenty points for a baccalaureate degree; and one hundred and fifty points for a degree of master or for a degree in law. All semester credits and degrees shall be earned in an educational institution accredited by the New England Association of Colleges and Secondary Schools or by the Board of Higher Education.
>
> Base salary increases authorized by this section shall be granted in the following manner: a three percent increase for ten points so accumulated; a six percent increase for twenty-five points; a ten percent increase for forty points; a fifteen percent increase for sixty points; a twenty percent increase for one hundred and twenty points; and a thirty percent increase for one hundred and fifty points so accumulated.
>
> Any city or town which accepts the provision of this section and provides career incentive salary increases for police officers shall be reimbursed by the commonwealth for one half the cost of such payments upon certification by the board of education. The board of higher education shall certify the amount of such reimbursement to be paid to such city or town from information filed on or before September the first of each year with said board, on a form furnished by it, by the chief of police, or one of similar rank, of the city or town police department. The board of higher education shall also certify the amount of the career incentive salary increase to be allocated to the state police, the capitol police and the metropolitan district commission police from information filed with said board on or before September the first of each year. . . .

Many Massachusetts communities, the Massachusetts State Police, the Capitol Police, and the Metropolitan District Commission Police accepted the provisions of this statute and instituted incentive programs. The results have been astonishing. Thousands of Massachusetts police officers are now either college graduates or college students. In some departments nearly all officers have become college students. Although the impact of their educational experiences will probably not be felt for several years to come, at least a beginning has been made which in the long run cannot help but improve police services and enhance the talents of individual police officers. Education for the police is here to stay.

PROFESSIONALIZATION

A much ballyhooed approach to police improvement that goes hand in hand with education is *professionalization.* This approach means many things to many people. Unfortunately, it has too frequently become merely a catchphrase for police requests for more respect, higher salaries, and better equipment and for public demands for higher standards, more devotion to duty, and the elimination of corruption.

To the extent that the police dream of professional status equal to that of doctors and lawyers, their dreams are unrealistic and even somewhat dangerous. They are unrealistic because the police service will never develop the bodies of knowledge, entrance requirements, or lucrative pay scales of these other professionals. They are dangerous because they imply that the police believe that they can be granted the same degree of self-regulation and autonomy that these other professions enjoy.

As they think about becoming professionalized, the police must bear in mind their unique position in the democratic scheme of government. As a general description of efforts to upgrade personnel, professionalization is a worthy element of police organizational improvement programs. But professionalization methods must in no way be designed to wrest control of the police from the people and their elected representatives. The tendency of the police to hide behind the cloak of professionalization as a means of escaping public scrutiny and avoiding accountability to the public has some frightening aspects. This is the greatest danger in professionalizing the police, and it must be taken into account in the process.

This is a good time, *before* the police are professionalized, to establish safeguards and to ensure continuing accountability. In large measure the responsibility for this lies with police administrators. Should they arrive at the point where they disregard public input and established political controls under the pretense that they are the professionals and that therefore they know best, it is time for their removal. The truly professional police administrator must recognize the need for operating an open police system which is receptive to public concerns and amenable to established political controls. Otherwise, professionalization is a meaningless concept which has as its only purpose keeping the public at arm's length, not at all a healthy situation in an open democracy.

In actuality, however, the police will probably never be professionalized. Pointing to the fact that the police are not professional, James Q.
Wilson indicates that professional people have a tendency "to govern
themselves through collegial bodies, to restrict the authority of their
nominal superiors, to take seriously their reputation among fellow professionals, and to encourage some of their kind to devote themselves to
adding systematically to the knowledge of the profession through writing and research."[6] Although they may hone their discretion capabilities, develop job skills, and achieve certain educational levels (all of
which are professional criteria), the very nature of their work in the
public sector makes it unlikely, if not impossible, for them to meet
other requirements on which professionalization is based.

Many police officers today look on themselves as professional, but
have no real understanding of what the word really implies. The concept of professionalization, however, has value to the police service
because it dictates the necessity for personal and organizational
improvement; although it is a goal unlikely to be achieved, at least
from a classical frame of reference, it serves as a strong motivator for
improvement.

JOB ENRICHMENT

One major effort toward job enrichment in the police service is the return of the investigative function to patrol personnel. This allows patrol
officers to follow preliminary investigations through to their ultimate
conclusion rather than having to refer such investigations to others for
follow-up. In job-enrichment terms, such a procedure provides officers
assigned to the patrol division a complete rather than a partial unit of
work with which to become involved. Most police officers welcome
this; there has always been a strong general resentment to surrendering
interesting cases to investigative specialists.

Team policing, another job-enrichment effort which many regard as
the way of the future, increases authority and accountability at the
lowest operating levels of the organization; it is fully in consonance
with job enrichment and satisfies high-level hierarchical needs. It is a
decentralized, and hence a relatively new approach to the policing process. What it does, in effect, is institutionalize police discretionary authority through the formation of units which are autonomous and
which establish their own working procedures. These units, which are
assigned to a specific police problem and/or a specific geographical area,
develop their own strategies and fully control their own destinies.

If such units can reduce crime, establish better community relations, or accomplish other tasks to which they are assigned, team members become highly motivated to perform even better through the recognition they receive and the job satisfaction they achieve. Their motivation springs from something other than basic and security needs. This is job enrichment of the highest caliber and is an approach which offers much promise for the future.

There have been many team policing efforts made in the United States. Some of them have been successful, others have not. The Police Foundation has taken an interest in the concept and has made in-depth evaluations of team policing projects in seven American cities (Holyoke, Massachusetts; Richmond, California; Dayton, Ohio; Syracuse, New York; Detroit, Michigan; Los Angeles, California; and New York City) in order to provide pertinent information and relevant data on why some projects succeeded and others failed.[7]

Team policing incorporates concepts from Theory Y,[8] Management By Objectives, participative management, organization development, classical and contingency structural theory, and the flow approaches to organization development. It is, therefore, more than a job-enrichment approach; it is an integrated approach inasmuch as it seeks to improve the organization from the human development, structural-design, and flow perspectives.

In Syracuse, New York, team policing is credited with reducing crime, reducing the fear of crime, and increasing the morale of the police.[9] In Dayton, Ohio, team officers had higher crime-clearance rates and higher property-recovery rates than did nonteam officers.[10] In New York City, the team concept was responsible for relieving boredom, stimulating officers to greater efforts, improving the relationship between the police and the community, and developing a healthy competitive spirit between and among teams.[11] In New Brunswick, New Jersey, a team policing project was able to effect a remarkable drop in the crime index, which in turn was reflected in increased attendance at nighttime church and social activities.[12] In San Bruno, California, team policing was accompanied by decreases in crime, departmental sick leave, personnel turnover, and overtime; increases in traffic enforcement and patrol vehicle mileage; and a resounding satisfaction with the program among the officers of the department.[13] Although some team policing efforts have failed because of poor planning, poor strategies, and ineffective implementation, the general success of such efforts is legend.

Berkley has argued that team policing "may well turn out to be the most significant innovation in police work since Sir Robert Peel

Police work is, for the most part, fascinating. (Courtesy of the Metropolitan Police Department, Washington, D.C.)

established the unarmed London constabulary."[14] Berkley may, indeed, be right. Team policing is a device that should and will be used increasingly by the police as they discover the impact it can have on police productivity.

Although team policing is not a concept that can be applied to all communities, especially small ones, it is unlikely to be dismissed as a fad and is, if adopted, likely to provide job enrichment for thousands of police officers presently locked into traditional and unrewarding organizational frameworks.

Although much has been written on and said about police productivity, a concept which we view as being almost synonymous with police organizational improvement, it is safe to say that it will never be fully achieved unless police administrators implement job-enrichment programs in their organizations. Productivity, according to Kuper, "refers to the relationship between the resources used and the results produced."[15] Because human resources are the most important resources, it is obvious that the environments in which they operate must be enriched. This is the task of job enrichment.

Job enrichment is achieved only through the realization and satisfaction of upper-level hierarchical needs. The fact that these needs have not been recognized or satisfied is a sad reflection on the abilities of traditional police administrators. Police work is, for the most part, fascinating work. That police administrators have succeeded in making it humdrum and mundane and lacking in rewards and recognition is a signal that something is terribly wrong. As Reddin puts it, "We give too little thought to the work itself. Work must be more than congenial; it must be absorbing, meaningful, and challenging. There just isn't any 'work' as inherently rich in these qualities as policework."[16] Capable police administrators, anxious to achieve organizational goals and objectives, must look hard for ways to enrich the jobs of everyone in their commands.

PARTICIPATIVE MANAGEMENT

Participative management is the basis for many team policing projects. Some teams choose their own supervisors, and in nearly all instances the entire team participates in the establishment of goals, selection of patrol and other operational modes, and development of work schedules. Decision making is almost always a team project.

Participative management is also being introduced in police organizations in which team policing is not a dominant operational style. The Police Foundation reports, for example, that the Kansas City, Missouri,

Police Department, in connection with patrol strategy experiments, has discovered great interest in the development of participative-management models.[17] In 1973 the California Highway Patrol implemented a participative management effort in conjunction with a *management by results* program. When the program was introduced, the commissioner of that organization, pointing to the need for job satisfaction, stated: "Participative management recognizes that the greatest amount of untapped talent and ability is probably in the lower ranks in any organization. Traditional police authoritative methods of management tend to waste this potential."[18]

In police circles such a viewpoint tends to be startling and almost revolutionary. The traditional viewpoint holds that only high-ranking officers have anything of value to offer. Yet in nonpolice organizations, the tenets of the commissioner's view have been accepted for years. That the police have been backward in implementing participative-management programs is evidenced by the fact that they exist in very few police departments. There is a scant amount of literature in police journals on the subject, and few police administrators have examined and tested its potential. We may conclude, however, based on the success of participative management in nonpolice organizations, that it can serve as a very useful tool to police organizational improvement if only the police will give it a try.

REORGANIZATION

Many police organizations have benefited in recent years from simple reorganization. We have noted previously that the concern of behavioral scientists with human behavior in organizations cannot be permitted to obscure the importance of structure. Although a few progressive police departments are experimenting with the most modern improvement approaches, many other departments are just beginning to discover some of the most basic and unsophisticated principles and functions of management. This is evidenced by the fact that many police departments, even in this day and age, do not have simple organization charts. Although it is difficult to believe, many police chiefs functioning today have never read a book on the subject of police administration. This is obvious from the manner in which they administer their departments.

Reorganization, or restructuring, is basic to organizational improvement, but is an impossible task if the police administrator is unfamiliar with the most rudimentary elements of police structure. In such cases consultants are usually called in from the outside to make recommendations. Very often these consultants have an extremely difficult job because they make recommendations based on principles of management which no one in the police department, including the chief, understands. This constraint, coupled with the traditional police reluctance to change, makes departmental restructuring a difficult and sometimes even impossible job. Yet as a rule restructuring is essential for improvement.

STANDARD 7.10

POLICE DEPARTMENT ORGANIZATION

More flexible organizational arrangements should be substituted for the semimilitary, monolithic form of organization of the police agency. Police administrators should experiment with a variety of organizational schemes, including those calling for substantial decentralization of police operations, the development of varying degrees of expertise in police officers so that specialized skills can be brought to bear on selected problems, and the substantial use of various forms of civilian professional assistance at the staff level.

American Bar Association Project on Standards for Criminal Justice, *The Urban Police Function,* Approved Draft (New York: A.B.A., 1973), pp. 15-16.

DECENTRALIZATION

One element of many reorganization plans has been decentralization. It is, for example, a fundamental aspect of team policing, placing increased authority, responsibility, and accountability directly on the shoulders of team members who work the streets. But decentralization is an important concept to apply to more traditional police organizations as well.

In Dallas, Texas, for example, the centralized investigations unit was disbanded, and detectives were assigned instead to the commanders of each of the city's police districts.[19] This move was greeted enthusiastically by participants and resulted in higher crime-clearance rates and better response times to crime scenes. The success of decentralized investigative services spurred the department to decentralize traffic, juvenile, and drug-enforcement units.

Decentralization, however, does not always work so well. In New York City, by contrast, the exposure of widespread patterns of corruption in the police department convinced the police commissioner to remove detective and other plainclothes units from the control of precinct commanders and to place these operations within specialized district and citywide units.[20] But this centralization of structure was effected simultaneously with a renewed commitment to decentralized accountability, placing the onus on unit commanders to develop anti-corruption programs of their own and holding them responsible for their implementation.

As with all police organizational improvement methods, the decision of whether to use decentralization depends on circumstances. Whenever feasible, it should be used; as an improvement device, it enhances the realization and satisfaction of upper-level hierarchical needs and gives police employees a greater sense of participation and involvement in the management of their own careers.

PERSONNEL ALLOCATION

Recognizing that police departments will never have sufficient monetary resources to hire all the personnel they could use, the need for rational personnel allocation becomes clear. In the past, police administrators based their requests for additional personnel on highly questionable but rarely questioned indicators such as crime rates, national average figures, and subjective evaluations of needs. In many instances they allocated their personnel according to traditional and political considerations. It is not at all unusual, for example, to find unnecessary police personnel assigned to city wards represented by politically powerful city councillors or to sections of a community which are particularly vocal in their demands for community services generally. This has resulted in the expenditure of unnecessary funds and the irrational allocation of personnel.

STANDARD 8.3

DEPLOYMENT OF PATROL OFFICERS

Every police agency immediately should develop a patrol deployment system that is responsive to the demands for police services and consistent with the effective use of the agency's patrol personnel. The deployment system should include collecting and analyzing required data, conducting a workload study, and allocating personnel to patrol assignments within the agency.

1. Every police agency should establish a system for the collection and analysis of patrol deployment data according to area and time.
    a. A census tract, reporting area, or permanent grid system should be developed to determine geographical distribution of data; and
    b. Seasonal, daily, and hourly variations should be considered in determining chronological distribution of data.

2. Every police agency should conduct a comprehensive workload study to determine the nature and volume of the demands for police service and the time expended on all activities performed by patrol personnel. The workload study should be the first step in developing a deployment data base and should be conducted at least annually thereafter. Information obtained from the workload study should be used:
   a. To develop operational objectives for patrol personnel;
   b. To establish priorities on the types of activities to be performed by patrol personnel; and
   c. To measure the efficiency and effectiveness of the patrol operation in achieving agency goals.
3. Every police agency should implement an allocation system for the geographical and chronological proportionate need distribution of patrol personnel. The allocation system should emphasize agency efforts to reduce crime, increase criminal apprehensions, minimize response time to calls for services, and equalize patrol personnel workload. This system should provide for the allocation of personnel to:
   a. Divisions or precincts in those agencies which are geographically decentralized;
   b. Shifts;
   c. Days of the week;
   d. Beats; and
   e. Fixed-post and relief assignments.
4. Every police agency should establish procedures for the implementation, operation, and periodic evaluation and revision of the agency's deployment system. These procedures should include provisions to ensure the active participation and willing cooperation of all agency personnel.

National Advisory Commission on Criminal Justice Standards and Goals, *Police* (Washington, D.C.: U.S. Government Printing Office, 1973), p. 199.

In recent years, however, many police administrators have recognized the need for basing personnel requirements and allocation on established patterns of crime, activity statistics, and citizen requests for service according to time and place of occurrence. Through careful accumulation and analysis of activity data, the police administrator can allocate personnel when and where such personnel are actually needed and can authoritatively argue for personnel increases based on statistical proof.

In large departments this process can be computerized. In small departments the accumulation and analysis of activity data can be mathematically computed in relatively simple fashion. What this amounts to, in the most elementary terms, is adding up the time spent on servicing various categories of activity that takes place on certain days at certain times in certain geographical areas of a community and determining the number of officers needed to service this activity, based on an analysis of the time actually used. Although the process may sound extremely involved, it is not. It is a process that can easily be handled by anyone who has achieved an eighth-grade proficiency in mathematics. It is also a process that is essential for police organizational improvement.

OPERATIONS RESEARCH

The application of operations research (OR) and mathematical models is a recent development in police organizations, particularly with respect to personnel allocation and patrol strategies. A major project designed to apply OR to the resource-allocation problems of the Chicago Police Department found that "allocation problems of law enforcement agencies are amenable to operations research and systems analysis methods."[21] The report on the project went on to say that units "similar to the Operations Research Task Force of the Chicago Police Department should be established and actively supported within every major law enforcement agency."[22]

Another project used a computer simulation model to evaluate seven different patrol strategies.[23] The researchers used the model to apply each of the patrol strategies to the data base developed by the Chicago project. The strategies were then tested for average travel time, queue wait for nonpriority calls, average response time, and response time for high-priority calls. The researchers discovered that removing personnel from routine patrol for assignment to tactical patrol did not seem to have the desired effect of improving response time to high-priority calls.

This is the type of finding that OR and mathematical models can provide. They have the capability of providing a fast and relatively accurate appraisal of aspects of operations and administration never heretofore examined in a precise way.

Some amazing results emanate from the use of carefully constructed mathematical models. A computer in the Quincy, Massachusetts, Police Department, for example, when fed information from a developed model based on a rash of handbag snatches in that city, advised detectives to go to a certain store at a certain time on a Friday afternoon and wait. The skeptical detectives followed the computer's instructions and went to the store at the designated time, convinced that they were engaging in an exercise in futility. Within 30 minutes their suspect was under arrest, resulting in the clearance of a number of crimes. The model had worked. The computer had been right.

SUMMARY

This chapter has briefly touched on a few police organizational improvement concepts which we regard as being some of the most meaningful approaches to upgrading police departments. You should be aware that there are literally hundreds of other efforts being made in departments all over the country which impact on the desire of police agencies to improve their services. The availability of funding from the Law Enforcement Assistance Administration over the past several years has prompted large numbers of police administrators to concentrate their efforts on improving their operations. The establishment of the Police Foundation has further served as an impetus for improvement, and that organization has made some remarkable research inroads in challenging traditional practices. Its studies of the value of preventive patrol in the Kansas City, Missouri, Police Department, for example, have exploded some time-honored myths about patrol effectiveness as a crime-prevention device and have opened debate on a police practice which had previously been taken for granted as a necessary, but costly, operational procedure.[24] The fact that research is being conducted and that innovative programs are being tried is a strong indication that the police service has made a commitment to improve itself.

Police administrators must develop a sound understanding of the general approaches to organizational improvement, as discussed in this chapter and in Chapter 12, take a long look at their own organizations, and attempt to tailor programs of organizational improvement to fit the unique characteristics of their departments. In conclusion, we pass along the following advice from the Police Foundation:

> If new ideas for improving the delivery of police services are to be developed, and if good ideas are to be spread, "the need to build an organization capable of continuing change" is critical. Rank-in-file officers must, whenever possible, be involved in both the planning and implementation of each project. "Street insight" is a vital ingredient in initiating and evaluating any program. Such involvement also strengthens the ability of police agencies to manage the process of change. Unless the individual police officer regards himself, not as an outsider to the project taking place about him, but as an individual with a personal stake in the project's successful outcome, the prognosis for any experimental undertaking is poor.[25]

DISCUSSION QUESTIONS

1. In the text we state that the police often refuse to consider suggestions or criticism offered by people who are not police officers. The attitude of the police often is that only they understand their work,

their problems, and the necessary solutions. Why do you think the police often feel this way? Do you think that this attitude is good or bad, overall, for policing? Why?

2. What do you think would be the ideal educational level for police officers? What do you think is a realistic level? In what ways do you think a college education helps and/or hurts a police officer?

3. What do you think about the police desire for professional status? Can they achieve it? Should they?

4. If you were a police manager, in what ways could you "enrich" the patrol officer's job? The detective's? The sergeant's? The dispatcher's? The records clerk's?

5. Ideally, on what should personnel requirements and allocation be based, do you think? How does this ideal approach compare with the ways in which police strength is distributed in your community?

6. A number of approaches to police organizational improvement are discussed in this chapter. Are any of them in use in your area? Do you know of some police organizations in need of some improvement? What seems to be their weaknesses? Which approaches to police organizational improvement might be helpful in correcting their problems?

REFERENCES

1. James W. Sterling, "The College Level Entry Requirement: A Real or Imagined Cure-All," *The Police Chief* **41**, 8 (August 1974): 28.

2. *Ibid.*, pp. 28-31.

3. Cynthia L. Sparling, "The Use of Education Standards as Selection Criteria in Police Agencies: A Review," *Journal of Police Science and Administration* **3**, 3 (September 1975): 335.

4. Charles B. Saunders, *Upgrading the American Police: Education and Training for Better Law Enforcement* (Washington, D.C.: Brookings Institution, 1970), p. 89.

5. Ramsey Clark, *Crime in America* (New York: Simon and Schuster, 1970), p. 147.

6. James Q. Wilson, *Varieties of Police Behavior: The Management of Law and Order in Eight Communities* (Cambridge, Mass.: Harvard University Press, 1968), p. 30.

7. Lawrence W. Sherman, Catherine H. Milton, and Thomas V. Kelly, *Team Policing: Seven Case Studies* (Washington, D.C.: Police Foundation, 1973).

8. George E. Berkley, "Theory Y Comes to the Police," paper presented to the annual convention of the American Society for Public Administration, April 1973.

9. *Ibid.*

10. Thomas R. Tortoriello and Stanley J. Blatt, "Client Service: Implications for Organizational Change," *The Police Chief* **41**, 11 (November 1974): 36-38.

11. Edwin J. Donovan, "Response to the Community: A Neighborhood Police Team Profile," *The Police Chief* **42**, 3 (March 1975): 32, 74-77.

12. John T. O'Brien, "The Neighborhood Task Force in New Brunswick, New Jersey," *The Police Chief* **42**, 6 (June 1975): 48-49.

13. William Cann, "Our 4/40 Basic Team Concept," *The Police Chief* **39**, 12 (December 1972): 56-64.

14. Berkley, *op cit.*, p. 7.

15. George H. Kuper, "Productivity: A National Concern," in *Readings on Productivity in Policing,* ed. Joan L. Wolfle and John F. Heaphy (Washington, D.C.: Police Foundation, 1975), p. 2.

16. Thomas Reddin, "Are You Oriented to Hold Them?: A Searching Look at Police Management," *The Police Chief* **33**, 3 (March 1966): 20. Reprinted with permission of the International Association of Chiefs of Police.

17. *Experiments in Police Improvement: A Progress Report* (Washington, D.C.: Police Foundation, 1972), p. 31.

18. Walter Pudinski, "Managing for Results," *The Police Chief* **40**, 1 (January 1973): 39. Reprinted with permission of the International Association of Chiefs of Police.

19. *Experiments in Police Improvement, op cit.,* p. 24.

20. *The Knapp Commission Report on Police Corruption* (New York: Braziller, 1972).

21. *Allocations of Resources in the Chicago Police Department* (Washington, D.C.: Government Printing Office, 1972), pp. xiii, xiv.

22. *Ibid.*

23. Jerry L. Carlin and Colin L. Moodie, "A Comparison of Some Patrol Methods," *Police* **16**, 12 (August 1972): 27-31.

24. George L. Kelling, Tony Pate, Duane Dieckman, and Charles E. Brown, *The Kansas City Preventive Patrol Experiment: A Summary Report* (Washington, D.C.: Police Foundation, 1974).

25. *Experiments in Police Improvement, op. cit.,* p. 23.

CHAPTER 14
BASIC ISSUES IN POLICE
ADMINISTRATION

LEARNING OBJECTIVES

1. Identify some sources of diversity in American society.

2. Describe the issue of the objectives of policing.

3. Cite the two basic sources of conflict in police administration as noted by James Q. Wilson.

4. Identify some of the ways in which society "checks" the police.

5. Cite the main argument in opposition to community control of the police.

6. Define "due process of law."

7. Cite the trend with respect to due process.

8. Discuss the managerial implications of due process.

9. State some reasons why productivity and effectiveness are difficult measures to apply to policing.

10. Identify the outstanding feature of police work.

11. Cite several realities of police work and police organizations that must be considered in designing an approach to the management of discretion.

In this concluding chapter we will discuss some of the basic issues in police administration. For the most part, these issues have long been recognized, but not resolved. Their stubborn refusal to retire from the scene qualifies the issues as being *basic*.

Some of the issues transcend police administration and go to the heart of the American social and governmental system. For example, one of the basic issues in police administration that we will discuss is due process of law. As we will see, due process has important ramifications for the internal workings of the police organization and for police relations with the public (especially criminal suspects). It is a basic issue because it is being constantly redefined by the courts; the general trend has been to widen its scope and enlarge the arena of its application. But of course due process is an issue today in many fields other than police administration. The application of due process requirements to posttrial criminal justice activities, for example, is a controversial problem that has recently become a focal point for discussion. Probation, parole, and imprisonment are all undergoing significant changes as a result.

Outside of the criminal justice system, due process is now applicable to disciplining students in school, management actions toward employees, and the activities of government regulatory agencies. In all of these cases the application of due process requirements has been designed to protect the rights of individuals from unfair and arbitrary action by the government and other organizations. The question of how much due process protection the individual should get, as opposed to the necessity for government and other organizations to act according to their perceptions of the general welfare, is a basic issue in the American social and political system.

In the following sections, we will discuss a number of issues which, like due process of law, have been around for a long time, still persist, and probably will never be resolved. Not all of the issues are likely to be as timeless as due process of law, but all seem basic to police administration.

THE OBJECTIVES OF POLICING

Unlike such countries as England and Japan, the United States is an extremely heterogeneous nation. Citizens are of many races and national origins, and some are relatively recent arrivals. As a consequence, diverse customs, cultures, and languages can be found in America, often within single communities. The size of the United States and the mobility of its people also contribute to population diversity. Many urban dwellers are recent arrivals from the rural South, and lately numerous affluent city residents have moved to the suburbs and beyond, to rural areas. Also, despite more than 200 years of democratic government and capitalist economics, some citizens are very rich while others are very poor. In these and many other ways, we are a diverse people.

One of the consequences of all this diversity is a lack of agreement about the goals and objectives of policing. Although it is true that in very general terms agreement can sometimes be reached, such is not usually the case when one becomes the least bit specific. We can all agree, for example, that a primary goal of the police is the maintenance of order. But this means something a little bit different to each of us. To some people maintenance of order includes the shutting down of noisy parties after 10 P.M. To others, especially those who party frequently, it does not mean quite the same thing. When is noise a disturbance, and when is it the harmless natural product of people having a good time? When has order been broken, such that it must be restored? We all have our own ideas about where we would draw the line.

In addition to holding different opinions of the meanings of the broad goals and objectives of policing, people also give them different priorities. Some people feel that the primary objective of the police should be the prevention of crime. Others would place the provision of emergency services first. Still others would nominate order maintenance. In fact, almost every objective of policing has proponents who would claim it as the most important.

Every police officer has probably had occasion to experience this lack of agreement in society about the most important goals and objectives of the police. A typical experience develops as follows. A citizen calls the police station or complains to a local political figure that automobiles regularly run through a nearby stop sign, thus endangering children in the neighborhood. Whatever channel the complaint follows, it will eventually be communicated to a patrol officer. Desiring to please the community and to correct the hazardous situation, the officer will normally attend to the problem by monitoring the intersection and ticketing motorists who fail to stop for the sign. From the motorists ticketed will be heard the familiar refrain: "Why aren't you out catching real criminals, officer, instead of bothering law-abiding citizens like me? Rapes and robberies are rampant, and you are harassing me for a minor traffic offense. What do you think we are paying you for, anyway?" In trying to respond to a problem identified by one citizen, the officer runs afoul of other citizens. And, of course, if the officer had not responded to the complaint about the trafffic at the intersection, the complaining citizen would have become more irate. The officer quickly learns that, because of the lack of agreement about the priorities of the various goals and objectives of policing, not everyone can be satisfied.

This lack of agreement influences police administration in much the same way that it consternates the patrol officer. Police chiefs and their managers are regularly contacted by citizens and citizen groups who want police action (or inaction) of one sort or another. Because the police have limited resources, responding to one request usually means ignoring another. Emphasis on one objective requires deemphasis of another. If the general public or its political representatives agreed about the priorities of the objectives, it would be easy for police administrators to respond correctly and to be popular. But because of the lack of agreement, police administrators often have to make difficult choices that guarantee, either way, that they will displease some portion of the community.

This discussion is not meant as an apology for any shortcomings or flagrant abuses in police administration. However, it must be acknowledged that in many communities there is no agreement about what the police are to accomplish, or at least about which objectives the police are to emphasize. Given this reality, the controversial nature of policing and police administration in many communities should not be surprising.

MEANS AND ENDS CONTROVERSIES

One important implication of the inability to agree on the objectives and priorities of policing concerns responsibility and accountability. If there is no agreement about what the police are to accomplish, how can they be held responsible and accountable for the accomplishment of anything? And if the society cannot agree, for what kinds of accomplishments can the police manager hold police employees responsible and accountable? How can one measure the success of the police organization or of individual police officers?

With respect to these questions, James Q. Wilson has noted two basic sources of conflict in police administration.[1] One, which we have already discussed, is the lack of agreement about the "ends" to be obtained through order maintenance. Public expectations vary widely concerning the appropriate degree of order that the police should strive to maintain. The second source of conflict centers on the "means" by which the police enforce the law.

In their efforts to detect crime, apprehend offenders, and recover stolen property, the police must follow certain rules. These rules drastically restrict the means by which the police can go about enforcing the law. Examples of these kinds of restricting rules include the need for probable cause in order to arrest, the need for a warrant in order to conduct many kinds of searches, and the requirement that the police advise a suspect, prior to questioning, of the right to remain silent and be assisted by counsel. Although the actual restrictions imposed on the police by recent Supreme Court cases have been exaggerated, it is a basic characteristic of the legal system that the police are restricted in the "means" by which they can enforce the law.

These restrictions are imposed on the police for very important reasons. Historically, the police have often been used by governments for repressive purposes. The American Founding Fathers experienced this at the hands of the British. On winning independence, then, it was natural that they should incorporate limitations on police power into the Constitution, which they did, largely in the Bill of Rights. Basically, these limitations and restrictions are designed to protect individual citizens from capricious or unjust government action, including police action.

These restrictions limit the ability of the police to enforce the law. They were intended to. That they are necessary and invaluable, we certainly agree. But, realistically, they do limit law enforcement. This inescapable fact has important consequences for police administration.

The matter of responsibility and accountability is again brought to mind. First, the public cannot agree on the ordering of the objectives of policing. Second, the police are restricted in the means available for enforcing the law. Thus we do not know what to hold the police accountable for, nor can we fairly hold the police accountable for law enforcement accomplishments, because we restrict them so.

From the perspective of the management of police organizations, parallel problems arise. First, the ends, or objectives, that police officers should accomplish cannot be clearly enumerated. Second, police officers are restricted in the means available to them for accomplishing law enforcement ends. Thus the organization is hard put to hold its employees responsible or accountable for the accomplishment of much of anything at all.

As a result, modern approaches such as Management By Objectives are difficult to apply to policing. Such approaches are based on definable objectives and the measurement of progress toward them. But if society cannot agree on the objectives and restricts progress toward them (hazy as they are), such approaches as Management By Objectives may be inherently inapplicable to policing or, at best, extraordinarily difficult to apply.

In systems terms, the output of policing, and its relationship to desirable objectives, is very difficult to identify and measure. It may be more natural, then, to concentrate on inputs and processes which can more readily be identified and measured and for which police organizations and police officers may be more legitimately held responsible and accountable. Skolnick has reached this same conclusion, albeit via a different route.[2] He argues that the police should be evaluated not in terms of crime control, but rather in terms of their adherence to the rule of law.

We cannot offer a solution to this means/ends controversy. But it does help illustrate another basic issue in police administration. Just as there is a lack of agreement about the objectives and priorities of policing, so also are the police restricted in the methods and techniques that they can use to enforce the law. These are both conditions that will persist and that will complicate the administration of policing.

PUBLIC CONTROL OF POLICING

Earlier we discussed the autonomy issue raised by police professionalization. The police, in their efforts to attain higher status, have sought professional recognition of the sort afforded doctors and lawyers. One of the characteristics of that sort of professionalism is autonomy, which is made possible through self-regulation. But as we have noted, serious questions must be raised regarding autonomy for the police.

Police officers are among the most powerful people in society. Within certain restrictions, as have been discussed, they can arrest, search, detain, eavesdrop, wiretap, and use force up to and including that which can cause death. They have the authority to restrict freedom, a possession that Americans have traditionally guarded very jealously.

Because of the enormous power of the police, society has "checked" them in several ways. Constitutional principles restrict their activities. The laws they enforce are created by elected legislators. Police budgets are presented by the executive branch, but approval and alterations are the prerogative of legislative bodies. Police chiefs are usually appointed by the executive branch of government, but are often subject to legislative approval. Police enforcement of the law is reviewed on a case-by-case basis by the judiciary. Citizens whose civil rights have been violated by the police may bring civil suit. And police officers alleged to have committed crimes may be tried in the criminal courts.

It is not clear in what ways professional police autonomy would alter these checks on police power. It is clear that the police are powerful, however, and that these checks were designed to control police use of their extraordinary authority.

In contrast to professional autonomy for the police, some arguments have been heard for greater restrictions on police power and/or greater community control of the police. Some years ago the use of civilian review boards was frequently proposed as a means of controlling police power. These boards would review complaints about the exercise of police authority, make decisions about upholding or dismissing such complaints, and levy punishments on offending officers. Police officers were vehement in their opposition to this scheme, arguing that civilians are incapable of appreciating the complexities of the police job and thus unqualified to stand in judgment of police actions. Police opposition to civilian review boards was influential enough to prevent their adoption in some communities, such as New York City, where strong political and grass roots support had been gathered in support of the boards.

Another proposal has been to increase community control over the police. This has been particularly noticeable in large cities, where the proposal would shift control of the police from city hall to the various neighborhoods. The rationale for this proposal is that different neighborhoods may want to be policed differently, but that large citywide forces are unable to be responsive to such local desires. James Q. Wilson has pointed out, however, that neighborhood control of the police could prove to be very troublesome.[3] Local neighborhoods might well use the police as a tool against races, classes, or other groups in instances when these groups are negatively perceived. The power of the police could very easily be used to subvert the law for what some people might perceive to be the benefit of the local neighborhood.

Again, we cannot resolve the issue of the proper scheme for public control of the police. The problem of "who guards the guards" has long existed and promises to remain. It is an issue with which police administrators will probably always wrestle.

DUE PROCESS OF LAW

We have already touched briefly on the issue of due process of law. The concept itself holds that the government may not arbitrarily or unfairly deprive a citizen of life, liberty, or property. Arbitrary or unfair means are simply those that do not equate with due process of law. So as the term itself implies, due process does not require any particular outcome or action, but rather a proper process.

Due process can be called a basic issue because of its vagueness. Although mentioned more than once in the Constitution and its amendments, due process is not defined in the document. As a result, the concept has been defined by the courts as the necessity arose, and the definition has varied over the years. The precise applicability of due process is also not prescribed in the Constitution and so has also been subject to changes in judicial interpretation and philosophy.

In general, the trend with respect to due process of law has been to expand the range of its applicability. As noted earlier, it has recently been applied to the posttrial stages of the criminal justice process, an area previously regarded as off-limits to judicial interference. Similarly, due process of law with respect to pretrial stages of the criminal justice system now includes Miranda warnings prior to questioning, prompt review by neutral, detached persons of probable cause for arrest, and public counsel for indigent defendants at the preliminary hearing.

Due process of law also has managerial implications for the police administrator. The concept either has been, or inevitably will be, applied to various internal disciplinary processes in many jurisdictions. It may be applied through statute, as in Maryland, which has a Police Officer's Bill of Rights that requires hearings and other procedural safeguards pursuant to allegations of misconduct against officers. Or it may be introduced through labor negotiations, with police unions winning for their members specific disciplinary and grievance procedures. Due process may also be internalized in civil service regulations in some jurisdictions; it is commonly believed, and probably to some extent it is true, that current procedures are so involved that it is virtually impossible to fire or even discipline a civil servant. Finally, on top of statutory, labor relations, and civil service guarantees, it is likely that the courts will also contribute to the requirement for due process in police disciplinary proceedings. The idea that all people, be they criminal suspects, millionaires, minority-group members, students, or police officers, have the right to be treated fairly and nonarbitrarily by the government and other organizations is deeply rooted and surely with us to stay.

PRODUCTIVITY AND EFFECTIVENESS

We have already discussed two aspects of the police productivity and effectiveness issue, which are that we cannot agree about what the police are supposed to accomplish and that we severely restrict the means by which the police can attempt to accomplish their law enforcement objectives, whatever they are. Not knowing just what the police are to achieve, we are hard put to measure their effectiveness. This problem and the restrictions placed on their activities make it difficult also to gauge police productivity.

Nevertheless, the public certainly expects the police to be productive and effective, especially in these times of budgetary belt-tightening.

Unfortunately for the police, productivity and effectiveness are both output-oriented concepts. As such, they are perplexing to the police administrator.

Consider the matter of police patrol. Historically, it was assumed that police officers, whether in cars or on foot, prevented crime by moving about their assigned areas, thereby giving the impression of police omnipresence. The recent Kansas City Preventive Patrol Experiment, however, could find no evidence to support this traditional belief.[4] Additionally, Richard Larson has demonstrated that the probability of a police officer's intercepting a crime in progress through random patrol is very, very slight.[5] Taken together, these two findings certainly call into question the productivity and effectiveness of routine police patrol.

Research findings have challenged the presumed productivity and effectiveness of routine police patrol. (Courtesy of the Los Angeles County Sheriff's Department)

Very few communities, of course, are presently willing to eliminate their police patrols. On the one hand, there is the lingering belief that police patrol must prevent some crime and that without it a community would be easy prey to opportunistic criminals. Other considerations are voiced in favor of police patrol, however. Some argue that the community is reassured by the sight of officers on patrol and by the belief that when they are out of sight, they may be only around the corner. Also, it is argued that the officer who regularly patrols a beat learns the tempo of it and the best means of attending to its problems and inhabitants.

Some of these arguments for patrol, of course, are at least as applicable to modern programs such as team policing as they are to traditional preventive patrol. The important aspect of the arguments, however, is that they are basically process- and input-oriented. They refer to the way that an officer "handles" the problems on the beat rather than to outcomes of police actions. And to the extent that they do apply to outputs, these are mostly intangible. It is very difficult to specify the outcomes that result from an officer's awareness of the tempo and the inhabitants of the assigned patrol area.

We argued before, and return to the same point, that the police must to some extent be evaluated in terms of process, as opposed to output. The output of policing that consciously and conscientiously adheres to the rule of law may be very difficult to measure and if measurable will not document the critical elements of interest. To a large extent the evaluation must be based on the process of policing lawfully, outputs notwithstanding.

The acceptance of this contention will not make such interests as productivity and effectiveness go away, needless to say. Within the rule of law and taking into consideration such intangibles as knowledge of the community, the police certainly should be as productive and effective as possible. The determination of the most effective and productive methods of police operations and the evaluation of the effectiveness and productivity of police officers, units, and agencies will certainly be of increasing concern to police administrators in the coming years. In such efforts the police will undoubtedly have the assistance, whether requested or not, of various kinds of efficiency and management experts and social scientists as well as the input from individual citizens and citizen groups. Whether employed by police agencies, budget bureaus, or research organizations, these technical assistants will greatly improve the ability of the police to measure their outputs; citizens also will undoubtedly impact on outputs. The issue will remain, though, of the tradeoff between these outputs and the intangibles and process concerns. For assistance in addressing this issue, the technical experts will probably be of little value to the police administrator; the citizen, on the other hand, may be of great value. The citizen may very well be the ultimate judge of output viability if, together with police administrators, some agreements can be reached between police and community on productivity expectations. And it should be emphasized that this issue can only be addressed, not completely resolved. It is another of those issues that will unquestionably outlive all current and aspiring police administrators.

THE MANAGEMENT OF DISCRETION

Probably the most outstanding feature of police work is the vast amount of discretionary authority vested in the operational practitioners of the craft. In most other organizations discretionary authority decreases from the top to the bottom of the hierarchy. The opposite is true in police organizations. The lowest-ranking employees, patrol officers and detectives, have the most authority and discretion.

How does an organization go about directing and controlling employees who possess vast discretionary authority? We have discussed a number of approaches to this problem in the text. Applicants are carefully screened. Recruits are trained. Employees are supervised. The policies and procedures promulgated guide behavior and thus limit and structure discretion. Inspections determine adherence to guidelines. Control processes discipline those who deviate. And so on.

Despite traditional management practices such as these, the problem of directing and controlling employees who possess such vast authority has persisted. In the text we have also discussed some modern and promising new approaches. Employees who are treated as if they are capable of self-direction and self-control may be more likely to exhibit such positive characteristics. Employees who have clear objectives to strive for may also exhibit greater self-direction and self-control. Education may hold some promise for preparing people to wisely exercise discretionary authority. Finally, participative management, besides injecting valuable employee input to the decision-making process, also may encourage stronger employee commitment to organizational goals and objectives.

We cannot resolve the issue of how best for the police organization to manage discretion. We can only strongly suggest that the approach taken must account for the present realities of police work and police organizations. One such reality is that police work is highly variable and unpredictable; this should strongly suggest that detailed procedures and rigorous training will never be so comprehensive as to prescribe the proper action for every conceivable situation. Another reality is that police work is presently attracting more and more college-educated

Probably the most unique feature of police work is the vast amount of discretionary authority vested in operational personnel. (Courtesy of the Department of Public Safety, Lakewood, Colorado)

people; this should suggest that greatly limiting police discretion could alienate many police officers who sought the job specifically because it offered opportunities for initiative and decision making. Still another reality is that close supervision of field forces has never been attained and probably never will be; patrol officers and detectives take action in the field alone, or at best in the company of another of like rank, and even the diligent supervisor is likely to arrive some minutes after the crucial decision has been made or the critical action taken. The listing of the realities of police work and police organizations could go on, but hopefully the point has been made. These kinds of factors must be kept firmly in mind by police administrators as they design their approaches to the management of discretion.

Police work is highly variable and unpredictable. (Courtesy of the Savannah Police Department, Savannah, Georgia)

The proper management of police discretion is another of those issues that will not meekly surrender to technical solution. As the realities of police work change, as the expectations of the public and of police employees change, and as time passes, adjustments will have to be made to even the most successful approaches. Police managers of the future will have to struggle with the problem of supplying their field personnel with sufficient discretion to meet the uncertainties and the unpredictables, while at the same time maintaining direction and control. Such will always be one of the basic tasks of the police administrator.

SUMMARY

In this chapter we have discussed a number of issues in police work which have not been fully resolved and which, indeed, may never be fully resolved. For this reason, we call these *basic* issues. Among these basic issues are the objectives of policing, which at best are hazy and poorly identified; the restricted means that the police use to achieve questionable goals and poorly defined outputs; the necessity for public control of the police as the police tend to move toward greater professionalism and autonomy; the nebulous concept of due process of law as it is continually being redefined by the courts and as it is applied both by and to the police; the changing attitude toward police effectiveness and productivity as these are affected by new knowledge and citizen involvement; and the problems involved in attempting to deal with the delicate balance that exists between maintaining direction and control on the one hand and managing discretion on the other.

DISCUSSION QUESTIONS

1. Do you think that society will ever reach anything approaching full agreement about the objectives and priorities of policing? What do you think are the most important reasons for the current lack of agreement?

2. As a police chief, how would you handle the competing requests from the public and its representatives for police services? How would you establish your organization's priorities?

3. As a police manager, how would you evaluate the performance of your employees? As a citizen, how do you evaluate the performance of your police department?

4. Some people think that the police do a good job of controlling themselves. Others disagree and want greater public control of the police. Where do you stand on this age-old issue? What mechanisms do you think ought to be used to handle public complaints about police abuses?

5. Police patrol officers and detectives, the lowest-ranking employees in their organizations, have vast discretionary authority. As a police chief, how would you go about devising a system for managing that discretion and those employees?

REFERENCES

1. James Q. Wilson, "Dilemmas of Police Administration," *Public Administration Review* (September/October 1968): 407–417.

2. Jerome H. Skolnick, *Justice without Trial: Law Enforcement in Democratic Society* (New York: Wiley, 1966).

3. James Q. Wilson, *Thinking About Crime* (New York: Basic Books, 1975), pp. 118–120.

4. George L. Kelling *et al., The Kansas City Preventive Patrol Experiment: A Summary Report* (Washington, D.C.: Police Foundation, 1974).

5. Richard C. Larson, *Urban Police Patrol Analysis* (Cambridge, Mass.: MIT Press, 1972).

CASE STUDIES

CASE 1
THE ENERGETIC CHIEF

Bruce Williams was appointed Chief of the Westerburg Police Department 15 years ago. A very principled person, Chief Williams is looked on with tremendous respect in his community of 15,000 people. He is a Deacon in the First Methodist Church, a member of the Rotary Club, and a member of the Board of Directors of the Y.M.C.A. Although approaching 60 years of age, he is physically fit and jogs four miles every day. A member of the department, which now numbers 28 officers and one civilian secretary, for the past 35 years, Williams came up through the ranks to his present position.

Although he is well accepted in the community, he has great difficulty in getting along with his police officers and is considerably frustrated because the department is not functioning smoothly. Officers are often criticized in the press; although he has never been the focal point of such attacks, he would like to minimize the effects of this bad publicity. He would sincerely like to do a better job running his department, but has almost given up in the attempt. But not quite!

In an effort to improve the department, Williams devotes almost all of his time to its problems. He is at his desk promptly at 8 A.M., usually works right through his lunch hour, and never goes home to dinner before 7 P.M. Occasionally he jogs his four miles during the day, but most often he postpones this ritual to the late night hours. It is not unusual to see him running through the streets of Westerburg at midnight. He almost always drops by the station after he finishes running, no matter what time that might be. Occasionally at night and always on the weekends, he prowls the streets in his own departmental car, supervising the activities of his officers. On a Saturday night, he can usually be found in his car or in his office until 2 or 3 A.M.

Because his wife died five years ago and because his four children are grown and settled, running the department effectively and efficiently has become almost an obsession with him. The people of the community see this as overwhelming dedication on his part and feel grateful that they have a police chief of his caliber and commitment. Many of the citizens of the town, knowing him as they do, find it difficult to understand why their police department is not a better department and why the department is oblivious to citizen concerns. Williams is so highly respected that no one has ever considered that the department's problems stem from his own mismanagement.

The department's table of organization has one lieutenant, four sergeants, and twenty-three patrol officers. Lieutenant Augustino "Gus" Severino is commanding officer of the 4 P.M. to midnight shift. He is two years younger than the chief and joined the department two years after the chief. He and the chief have been traditional rivals for promotion over the years, and Severino has never succeeded in topping the chief in a promotional examination. This rivalry has caused a schism between the two men. Severino has become bitter and never misses an opportunity to be critical of Williams, both as a police officer and as a person. The two men talk to each other only when it becomes officially necessary.

Although the chief feels hurt over this situation, he makes a concerted effort never to criticize the Lieutenant, but has given up on the possibility of developing a personal relationship with him. The chief is not personally bitter, and would like to mend fences if he thought that this would be possible.

Severino, on the other hand, has one ambition in life: to become chief. He is, however, not a particularly dedicated police officer and is much more interested in his self-advancement than in the police department. Because he requires very little by way of work from his officers, he gets along well with most of them and would generally have to be considered the leader of the emergent system. All four sergeants and most of the patrol officers are in his corner. As a result, what he does has the approval of most officers, and what he says is generally followed.

Departmental personnel see Severino as a "real cop" and the chief as a "do-gooder who was promoted beyond his capabilities." The chief fully understands how he is looked on by the department and believes firmly that the only way to combat the problem is to stay on top of it. In fact, the chief has taken only two vacation days in the last five years.

The chief is known as a strict disciplinarian, whereas Gus Severino leans over backwards to cover up officers' mistakes. The sergeants fall in line behind Severino, thinking that one day he might become chief. Besides, a few citizen complaints are easier to handle than the wrath of subordinates. On one occasion, when a prisoner was brutalized with two fellow prisoners and a newspaper reporter as witnesses, the shift sergeant, acting as commanding officer, and several patrolmen lied under oath at the public hearing on the matter. The chief suspended the sergeant and all officers involved for 60 days, but the suspension was reversed on a technicality by the Civil Service Commission.

On another occasion a citizen coming to the station to report that his car had been stolen discovered to his amazement that the desk officer, the only officer present in the station at the time, was sound asleep at the desk. When the chief investigated the matter, three patrol officers, the shift sergeant, and Gus Severino all signed written statements affirming that they were present at the station when the citizen came in and that the desk officer was wide awake and alert.

The most serious cover-up occurred when a 17-year-old high school student reported to Chief Williams that she had been raped the previous evening by an on-duty patrol officer. There were no witnesses. The incident occurred in the back of a police car in an isolated sand pit in the town. The officer involved had a considerable reputation as a Romeo and had recently been divorced by his wife on the grounds of adultery. A physical examination of the girl indicated positively that she had been raped. Chief Williams's investigation of the incident included written statements from four patrol officers, the shift sergeant, and Gus Severino that the accused officer had been assigned to desk duties that night and never left the police station until he was relieved of duty because of illness at 10 P.M., one hour after the incident occurred. Although semen stains were found in the back seat of the police car involved in the rape, nothing could be proved against the officer. Chief Williams was held in considerable contempt by his officers because he brought charges against the officer involved. Based on the testimony of the officers, the case was dismissed and the chief further humiliated.

"I've got to stay on their backs all the time," Chief Williams is frequently heard to say. "Even if I leave town for a day or stay away from the department for a few hours to attend a Rotary meeting, all hell breaks loose."

Chief Williams is a chief from the old school and is proud of it. "What's ruining the police service today is these young college kids," he says. "I don't know what they're teaching them in college these days; permissiveness, I think. Why, I'd take one good old-time cop to any ten of these young punks any day."

The chief himself never took advantage of any educational opportunities. A 1936 graduate of Westerburg High School, his education stopped there. "You don't need an education to be a good police chief," he is fond of saying. "Education does nothing but confuse the issues. Look at me. I've done pretty well, and I've never received a day of police training in my life."

Yes, look at him. The fact that his police department is disorganized is evidenced by the fact that it has no organization chart. In fact, he has never seen an organization chart; he has no idea what one looks like, let alone what one is used for.

He does everything himself. He refuses to delegate any authority to anyone because he is afraid of what might happen. He and his secretary do all of what he calls the "paper work" of the department. "There's no one in this department I can rely on," he says. "If I did, they'd just mess it up. It's easier to do myself."

His philosophy dictates that he control everything. All official decisions are made by him. All equipment and supplies are handed out by him. If the members of the department need tear gas and riot equipment in an emergency situation, oxygen to refill empty oxygen tanks, bullets for their weapons, or even flashlight batteries, they have to see him. If he is unavailable, the equipment and supplies are unavailable. If a tire on a police car blows, the purchase of a new tire has to be cleared by him. In fact, he makes the purchase personally. Lieutenant Severino and the sergeants have no authority to make any meaningful decisions. The chief does not believe that they have the capability.

Additionally, there is no chain of command within the Westerburg Police Department. Officers communicate officially only when they are moved by the urge. The chief frequently gives direct orders to patrol officers and encourages them to by-pass their supervisors in communicating with him. He calls this "keeping the lines of communication open" and envisions it as contributing to police effectiveness in the department.

The department has no established policies and procedures and uses as a guideline an outmoded (1947) set of rules and regulations. When the chief wishes to establish a policy or disseminate a procedure, he writes out a memorandum, which he usually types himself, and tacks it to a bulletin board which most officers rarely look at. Most of these policies and procedures are ripped off the bulletin board and thrown away shortly after they are posted.

The chief makes no effort to determine whether or not his policies and procedures are followed unless a violation comes to his attention as the result of a citizen's complaint. When violations of policies and procedures are discovered inadvertently, perhaps by the chief in one of his nocturnal patrols, the officer or officers involved are reprimanded orally, and no further action is taken. In most cases the policy or procedure involved is missing from the bulletin board and cannot be found.

Although its chief is energetic, well-meaning, and dedicated, the Westerburg Police Department has some serious problems. What steps would you take to solve them?

DISCUSSION QUESTIONS AND PROJECTS

1. What is the department's major problem?

2. If you were Chief Williams, what steps in what order would you take to solve your problems?

3. Draw an organizational chart for the Westerburg Police Department, using what you know about the organization as a point of departure.

CASE 2
THE PERIPATETIC
SERGEANT

John Crummerine is a sergeant on the Brushboro Police Department. Brushboro is a community of 40,000 people. The department consists of 45 patrol officers, 8 sergeants, 4 lieutenants, 2 captains, and 1 chief. A simple organization chart of the department is given in Fig. 1.

The department is an excellent organization. Chief Donald W. Slocum has his bachelor's degree in criminal justice from Michigan State University and is a graduate of the F.B.I.'s National Police Academy. Since becoming chief four years ago after a national search to replace the retiring chief, he has been successful in shaping up the department, and it is now looked on as a model municipal police agency. Chief Slocum is fourth vice-president of his state's association of police chiefs. He has written numerous articles for national police publications and is presently writing a book on police administration. He is considered by everyone who knows him to be a thoroughly knowledgeable and innovative police leader. Also, he is well liked by his officers and commands the admiration of his community.

He has one problem: Sergeant John Crummerine. Crummerine, who has been in the department for almost 35 years, is the department's senior officer in terms of service. He was a close personal friend of the previous chief. John Crummerine has two problems: an aversion for work and a propensity for consuming large quantities of alcohol both on and off the job. Additionally, Crummerine is not at ease with the world unless he is walking. Police cars give him a feeling of claustrophobia, and he has never been able to adjust to the fact that police service today is necessarily highly mobilized.

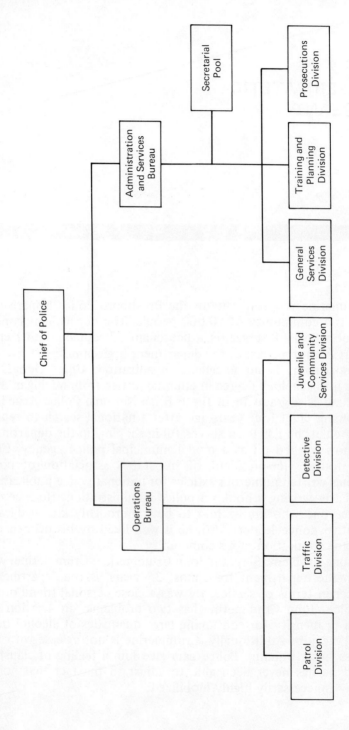

Fig. 1. Organization chart of the Brushboro Police Department.

As a patrol officer, a position in which he served for 30 of his 35 years on the job, he was always assigned to a walking beat, never to a car. When he became a sergeant five years ago because of his friendship with the former chief, he was the only sergeant in the department who was excused from mobile supervisory duties. He continued to walk his downtown beat and was assigned "supervisory responsibilities" over the one patrol officer who had the contiguous foot beat. It was common knowledge that the two men never saw each other. Crummerine was constantly on the move, strolling about in his beat area. This also gave him frequent opportunities to visit and pass the time of day with his many friends in taverns, pool rooms, and liquor stores along the way. Toward the end of any given tour, John could usually be seen swaying to and fro in an alcoholic stupor on his way back to the station. Because he was a likable fellow who never made an arrest and who never became involved in anything but a little light conversation with his beat clientele, he received very few complaints over the years and was generally accepted as the character he obviously was.

Enter Chief Donald W. Slocum. An advocate of motorized patrol and a critic of foot patrol in relatively peaceful communities of Brushboro's size, Slocum waited for six months before making any changes in the department. During those six months, he studied the department's problems. John Crummerine surfaced as one such problem almost immediately. The first change made by Slocum was to eliminate walking beats and to assign all patrol supervisors and patrol officers to motorized responsibilities. The second change he made was to reassign the sergeant in charge of the General Services Division to the Patrol Division and replace him with Sergeant John Crummerine. He reasoned that the elimination of walking beats would increase the department's patrol capabilities, that all supervisory patrol personnel should be mobile, and that Sergeant Crummerine, given his peculiar problems and interests, might become a more productive member of the department if he were given an inside job, which by its very nature would tend to curb the sergeant's wayward appetites. Although he anticipated that Crummerine might not be ecstatic about his new assignment and might not accept its challenge with relish and enthusiasm, in his wildest dreams he never anticipated what actually happened.

John Crummerine was a member in good standing of the Brushboro Police Brotherhood, a collective bargaining unit which was very strong in Brushboro and which, through its attorney, made absolutely certain that every provision of the contract between the Brushboro Police Brotherhood and the City of Brushboro was followed to the letter. The union contract contained a seniority clause stipulating that seniority would be the basis on which officers would choose both shift and work assignments. Sergeant John Crummerine was not only the senior member of the department, but also its senior sergeant. His seniority was indisputable. In no uncertain words, the Brotherhood attorney spelled this out for Chief Slocum. Crummerine refused the transfer.

Slocum was forced to rescind his transfer order. He was not, however, forced to rescind his order eliminating all walking beats and assigning all patrol personnel, including supervisory personnel, to mobile units.

Slocum transferred Crummerine from his walking beat to a supervisor's car. In the meantime, the chief had issued policies and procedures governing the activities of patrol sergeants.

Slocum anticipated serious difficulties with Crummerine once the transfer had been effected, but to both his surprise and relief, Crummerine seemed to adjust to his new role very well. He could be seen at all hours darting about the city in his patrol car, meeting his every obligation and fully subscribing to the chief's new policies and procedures. Although there were a few unauthenticated reports that Crummerine was occasionally visiting his old haunts for a "quick one," his drinking never really surfaced as a problem. Not, at least, for four years!

The chief's first indication that Crummerine was back to his old tricks came about as the result of a late-night inspection of patrol operations conducted by the chief himself. While touring the city, he noticed Crummerine's supervisor's car parked on Main Street. Inasmuch as no calls had been received for service in the Main Street area over the preceding hour, the chief felt that perhaps this situation warranted his attention. It was 10 P.M. as the chief pulled into a supermarket parking lot across the street from where Crummerine's vehicle was parked. There was no sign of Crummerine. In fact, there was no sign of Crummerine for the rest of the night. Shortly after midnight, when the shift changed, the chief saw the midnight shift sergeant, Henry Dalrymple, walking down the street toward the patrol supervisor's car. Arriving at the car, he got in, started up the motor, and drove off.

The following day, the chief, armed with this information, called to his office the commanding officer of the 4 P.M. to midnight shift, Lieutenant Nicholas Charos.

"Where was Crummerine last night, Nick?" he asked.

Charos gave the chief a sheepish grin. The grin asked the question: How much does he know?

"Why the sheepish grin, Nick? What do you know that I don't know?"

"Well, Chief, I guess you know," said the lieutenant.

"Know what?"

"I guess you know what's been happening with Crummerine."

"I don't know what's been happening with Crummerine unless you tell me what's been happening with Crummerine," said the chief.

"I don't want to get the old guy in trouble," said Charos.

"Well, why don't you assume that the old guy is in trouble and we'll take it from there."

"Gee, Chief, I didn't think it was that serious. I would have brought it up before if I had. You know, the old guy is having trouble at home, and I just didn't want to add to his problems."

"But you know, Nick, that the old guy is a police officer—no, a police sergeant—and that makes him special in my book. That means he has responsibilities. If he's not meeting them, he *should* get in trouble."

"Yeah, but, gee, Chief, I _____ ."

"Nick, will you stop pussyfooting around with me. You're his commanding officer and you have responsibilities, too."

"Okay, Chief. Okay. Don't start threatening me. I'm just an innocent party to this whole thing and it's not that serious."

"What's not that serious?" demanded the chief.

"Okay, Chief, I'll lay it out for you. The old guy's wife is a lot younger than he is, and she wants to go out all the time—to the movies, dancing, out to dinner, to cocktail parties. She even wants to go to Disneyland and go on all the rides. Can you imagine the old guy going to Disneyland and going on all the rides?" Charos smiled. "I tell ya, Chief, she's drivin' him bananas. And then there's his kid, his only kid. Always was a nice kid, but the old lady is driving the kid right through the wall. The kid got on the sauce pretty bad, and that killed the old guy because the problem kinda runs in the family, and the kid got involved in a hit-and-run property damage over in Lakeport, and he's up on charges, so the roof's fallin' in."

"Too bad, but what's that got to do with what Crummerine is doing on the job?"

"Well, you know, Chief, he's sorta lettin' up. Nothin' serious, but sorta lettin' up."

"Where was he last night between 10 and 12?"

"You know about that?"

"Why don't you tell me about that?"

"If I *have* to."

"Look, Nick, I'm the chief. You're a lieutenant. You work for me, right?"

"Why don't you tell me what you know about last night, Chief, and then _____ ."

"No, Nick. You tell *me* what *you* know about last night."

"Well, Crum came in late for work to begin with ____ ."

"How late?"

"An hour or maybe an hour and a half."

"Does that show on the Attendance Roster?"

"Well, Chief, no it doesn't. We didn't want to cause him any trouble, so ____ ."

"So you covered for him?"

"Yeah, I guess you could say that we sorta ____ ."

"*Sorta*!!! You *covered* for him. Go on."

"Well, Chief, you know that he's back on the sauce and that he ____ ."

"Nick, how could I know he was back on the sauce if you didn't tell me he was back on the sauce?"

"I guess I just assumed you knew, Chief. Anyway, he's back on the sauce pretty good and, you know, when he's on the sauce, all he wants to do is walk around, walk, walk, walk. He won't take a car. It's like the old days. He goes down on the old beat and walks all night. It's like he could solve all his problems by walking them off. What do you say to a guy when he tells you he's got problems and he needs to get away from the job for awhile and walk them off. Do you say, '*No, you can't; I'm not going to let you.*'? Maybe you can be tough like that, Chief, but not me. I gotta go with a guy for awhile."

"How long has this been going on?"

"Couple months. Maybe three. It's his wife, Chief. A real witch. We gotta help him. That's the way I see it."

"Did he take a car out last night?"

"Yeah. He took the patrol supervisor's car, like he always does."

"Then what?"

"Well, what he does, Chief, is park it someplace and go for a walk. You know, he visits his friends."

"What time did he go for a walk last night?"

"Gee, Chief, I dunno, I really dunno."

"You *dunno*? You're his shift commander and you *dunno*?"

"Yeah, Chief, I really mean that. I dunno. I really don't."

"Did you have radio contact with him last night?"

"Gee, Chief, I really dunno. I could check the radio log ____ ."

"I have the radio log right here on my desk, Charos, and it doesn't show any contact at all. What do you have to say about that?"

"I dunno, Chief. I really dunno."

"So Crummerine left the station last night an hour or an hour and a half after you came on duty, and you haven't seen him or heard from him since?"

"I guess you could put it that way, Chief. But I know he's okay. I know _____ ."

"You know he's okay? How do you know he's okay? You clairvoyant, got ESP?"

"Come on, Chief. Crummerine does this all the time. He always shows up for work the next day."

"He does this all the time?"

"Yes, sir."

"You mean once he leaves the station, that's the last you see or hear from him, every night?"

"That's about it, Chief. I know it sounds a little screwy, but that's the way it is."

"Captain Wallbanger is commanding officer of the Operations Bureau, right?"

"Right."

"In the chain of command, you report to him. Right?"

"Yes, sir. Right."

"I assume that Captain Wallbanger is fully apprised of this problem. Right?"

"Yes, sir, he is."

"He's *what*?"

"He knows about it, sir."

"All about it?"

"Yes, sir. All about it."

"I can't believe it. Who told him?"

"I told him, sir. He's the officer I report to in the chain of command, like you said. Your policy is that we pass along to him any problems we can't solve. This problem has been passed along just like your policy says."

"I can't believe it. Wallbanger knew about this?"

"Yes, sir, he did. I assumed, I guess, that maybe he told you and that was how you knew about it."

"He didn't know about last night."

"Yes, sir, he did."

"How did he know about last night?"

"I called him on the telephone and told him. That's your policy, sir. Everytime Crummerine takes off, I always call the captain and tell him."

"And what does he do?"

"I guess he doesn't do anything. I had assumed that he at least told you about it. That's the policy, sir."

"Yes, Charos, I know, *that's* the policy."

DISCUSSION QUESTIONS AND PROJECTS

1. Identify the specific problem or problems Chief Slocum has.

2. Should Chief Slocum take any action against Lieutenant Charos? Explain.

3. Should Chief Slocum take any action against Captain Wallbanger? Explain.

4. What should Chief Slocum do to strengthen the police department?

5. Do you believe that Lieutenant Charos's feedback will prove helpful to Chief Slocum? Why?

6. Is Sergeant John Crummerine Chief Slocum's major problem?

7. In definitive fashion, outline your solutions to the problems Chief Slocum has.

CASE 3
THE YULETIDE
REMEMBRANCE

Ever since becoming a member of the Emmetville Police Department, Patrolman Walter Whitty had strong pangs of conscience whenever he saw his fellow officers of all ranks accepting gratuities. He had not only learned that accepting gratuities violates the police officer's Canon of Ethics, but had been taught since childhood that nobody ever gets something for nothing.

His education in practical police work got a severe jolt the first night he was assigned to duty. Teamed with partner John "Gunner" Paquette in a black and white, they left the station house at 4:10 P.M. and headed toward their sector in the northeast section of the city. Looking back on that first tour of duty, Walter often wondered how he was able to hide the pride he felt at actually becoming a police officer. It was something he had always wanted to be, ever since he was a kid. He sat there in the passenger seat with his brass polished and his shoes shined and felt a sudden surge of satisfaction; at long last he had achieved his goal. He *was* a police officer with a whole career of interesting, dignified, and rewarding work ahead of him. There would be no stopping him now. He would work hard, advance in rank, and become a truly professional law enforcement officer.

As the black and white pulled out onto Highway 19, heading north, Gunner was the first to speak. Gunner was an experienced officer and generally considered one of the department's best. At age 35, with ten years of street experience behind him, he was a very self-assured, confident man.

"Just got out of the academy, right, kid?"

"I graduated last week," Walter replied.

"Then you understand what our relationship is going to be over the next eight weeks."

"Yes I do. You're my FTO. I learn it all from you."

"Right, kid. You learn it all from me. A field training officer can show you more in one week than you learned in 16 weeks at the academy."

"I believe it," said Walter somewhat skeptically.

"The first thing I should tell you, kid, is that you forget everything they told you at the academy—everything."

"Everything?" asked Walter.

"Everything," said Gunner.

"I guess I don't understand exactly what you mean," said Walter.

"Well, kid, they do police work one way at the academy and we do it another way on the street. There's a lot to learn on the street that don't exactly jibe with what they told you at the academy."

"Like what?" asked Walter.

"Like I'm gonna show you right now," said Gunner as he wheeled into the parking lot of a franchised hamburger restaurant.

"Let's go in and have a cup of coffee just to settle the nerves." Gunner pulled the car behind the restaurant. The two officers got out of the car and went into the kitchen of the restaurant.

"The first lesson you learn," said Gunner, "is that you always pull the car into the back of the restaurant, and you always go into the kitchen. As long as you have the portable radio with you, you never sign off the air."

"Why?" asked Walter. "I don't think I understand."

"The first rule of the road," said Gunner "is that the less they know about where you are or what you're doing, the better off you are."

"We sure didn't learn that in the academy," said Walter. "We were taught that we always went into restaurants through the front door and that we always signed off the air if we were going for coffee or for a lunch break."

"Right, kid," smiled Gunner. "Those are the policies, the rules we're *supposed* to follow. "You will soon learn that the department's policies and the rules of the road are always different."

Gunner was right at home in the kitchen. He knew the restaurant manager and all the kitchen help. He took two large paper cups and filled them with coffee.

"How do you take yours, kid, cream and sugar?"

"Black," said Walter.

Gunner handed Walter a cup of steaming black coffee and put a generous supply of cream and three teaspoons of sugar into his own cup.

"Walter Whitty meet Yancy Beauregard," said Gunner, pointing with his coffee cup toward the man with "Manager" in big red letters on his hat. "Yancy, this is Walter Whitty, one of our new men that I'm gonna train."

"Pleased to meetcha," said Yancy as he flipped a batch of burgers over on the grill. "You got a good teacher. Gunner here is the best. We got no trouble as long as Gunner's in a car nearby."

"That's right," Gunner laughed. "Our response time ain't bad when *trouble down here, right Yancy?"

"Right, Gunner. You always get here in a hurry."

"Good community relations, right kid?" Gunner was looking expectantly at Walter, his eyebrows raised and a big smile on his lips.

Walter nodded, thinking back on the lectures he had had at the police academy on good community relations. They had never covered what went on in the back rooms of hamburger joints.

"You stick with me, kid," said Gunner "and you'll learn a lot about good community relations."

"Right," said Yancy. "There's nobody knows more about good community relations than Gunner. When we need him, he's there."

"Right," said Gunner. "When you need me, I'm there, right, Yancy?"

"Right," said Yancy.

"By the way," said Gunner, "do you think I could swing by in a couple hours and pick up some goodies for the wife and kids?"

"Sure," said Yancy. "If I'm not here, I'll leave word with Durk that it's okay. Anything you want Gunner, you know that."

"I know that," said Gunner. "I hate to put the bite on you so often, but the wife and kids are sick of fried chicken and fish and chips and pizza from all of those other restaurants all the time. Once in a while, they like a good hamburger feed."

"I hope they enjoy it," said Yancy.

"They'll *love* it," said Gunner. "The kids are wild about your hot apple pies. I usually swing by the Open All Nite and pick up a quart or two of ice cream for the pie. Nothin' like good, wholesome food for growin' kids."

"Right," said Yancy.

"Well, we gotta go fight crime," said Gunner. "Call us if you have any trouble with those motorcycle kids hanging around out front."

"I'll call you Gunner, and thanks," said Yancy.

Walter reached for his wallet as Gunner moved toward the door.

Gunner looked around in disbelief. "What are you doing, kid?" he asked.

Walter fumbled for a bill.

"What are you doing, kid?" Gunner repeated.

"Just paying for the coffee," Walter said.

Yancy dropped three double cheeseburgers on the floor and stared at Walter.

"You gotta excuse him, Yancy," said Gunner. "He's just a rookie, and they gotta lot to learn about street sense."

"It's always on the house in here, young fella," said Yancy. "Least we can do for the officers in blue." Yancy picked the cheeseburgers off the floor and threw them back on the range. "We'll fry off the dirt," he said.

Walter left without paying, feeling a deep sense of remorse that he hadn't insisted.

Back in the black and white, Gunner said, "Don't ever do that again, kid. Don't ever embarrass me like that again."

Walter said nothing.

During the first night on the job, Walter learned what Gunner had meant by the *rules of the road.*

At 6:30, they returned to the restaurant and picked up 10 double cheeseburgers, 7 orders of french fries, 7 malts, and 14 hot apple pies. On their way to Gunner's house, they stopped at the Open All Nite. Walter watched Gunner through the large plate glass window as he went to the ice cream freezer, picked up a gallon of ice cream, and waved at the cashier as he walked by without paying.

"Doesn't that bother you just a little?" asked Walter when Gunner was back in the car.

"Just a fringe benefit of the job, kid," said Walter. "Everybody does it."

"But rules and regulations say that _____ ."

"Kid, what'd I tell ya. Forget what they taught you in the academy. What you learn from your FTO is what's important. Save you a lot of headaches if you just go along with the system."

After they had made their delivery of "goodies," Gunner said, "Okay, kid. Now it's chow time for us. What'a ya feel like?"

"I'm not very hungry," said Walter.

"How about Chinese? Egg Foo Yung. Chicken Chop. Fried Rice. Pork Strips. Don't that make your mouth water?"

"Okay," said Walter.

"You don't like Chinese, kid?" asked Gunner.

"I love Chinese," said Walter.

Walter learned the rules of the road very thoroughly over the following two months. He paid for absolutely nothing he ate or drank while on the job, and he watched Gunner negotiate for a free lawn hose, grass seed, garbage can, wallpaper, cinder blocks, window panes, spark plugs, lawn chairs, and sport shirts.

"Look at it as good community relations," Gunner would say. "You couldn't *buy* better community relations."

After Walter left Gunner and the field training program, he became a full-fledged police officer. He was terribly confused about the wide gap that existed between departmental rules relating to gratuities and the rules of the road. Gunner did such a good job teaching him the rules of the road that he was convinced that all of the other officers subscribed to the *take-what-you-can-get* philosophy. Once on his own, however, he paid for everything. He found that this was extremely difficult to do and developed something akin to a guilt complex as a result. Rationally, this made no sense at all. Who ever heard of someone's developing a guilt complex because of scrupulously following departmental policy? But the department didn't care. Nobody cared. The policy was there for window dressing, nothing more.

After Walter had been on the job for two years, *he* became a field training officer. He gave his rookies a different kind of field training than he had received from Gunner. Rules and regulations and policies and procedures were drummed into the heads of his recruits. For seven years, Walter remained a field training officer. Ever so gradually, Walter's image within the department began to change. Whereas he had always been ostracized for the fastidious manner to which he subscribed to departmental rules, now he was being looked on as a kind of hero by the younger members of the department.

The Emmetville Police Department was relatively small (38 total complement), and within nine years of Walter's becoming a patrol officer, he had been promoted to sergeant and had achieved considerable stature as a no-nonsense, strictly-by-the-book professional. After years of worrying about how his fellow officers looked down on him, he was now in a position where he could enjoy his professional self-image. He had completed a community college program in law enforcement and was on his way to the baccalaureate degree when something happened that changed his life.

While at college, he heard a lecture on police unionization. He became interested in the idea and did a term paper on the police union movement. He presented the idea of a police union to his band of followers, who now numbered over 50 percent of the department. They liked the idea and commissioned Walter to develop a union in

Emmetville. When the chief heard about Walter's efforts, he chastised him severely and transferred him to the graveyard shift. Angered by the chief's actions, Walter's followers urged him to form a union immediately and assured him of their votes in an election. Walter became somewhat of a martyr and was elected first president of the union. The town of Emmetville challenged the right of the officers to organize. The case went to the State Board of Labor Arbitration for a decision. The board ordered a new election to be held under its supervision and assured the fledgling union that if over 50 percent of the department's members voted for a union, a union could be officially established. When the final votes were counted, 73 percent of the department had voted for the union. Once again, Walter became its president.

Under Walter's direction, the union flourished, winning for its members increased insurance benefits, higher pay, longer vacations, seniority for work shifts, and time and one-half for all overtime work. In a very short time, everyone in the department joined the union. Walter was a hero.

The time had come to challenge the rules of the road. Only a few officers now still followed those rules, Gunner Paquette among them. The worst offenders were the older officers. Even the chief violated his own gratuity policy. Every year at Christmas time, merchants would bring to the chief's office bottles and even cases of liquor. The chief, after earmarking the select stock for his own liquor cabinet, played Santa Claus with the rest, doling it out equally among the officers who gathered at his door at 4 P.M. every Christmas eve. Each year, fewer and fewer officers appeared at his door. Gunner and his pals, however, were always there waiting at the door. Everybody got at least seven bottles. Perhaps this was the opportunity that Walter had been waiting for.

He called a meeting of his union and proposed that the union write to all the merchants in town who were traditionally accustomed to sending a so-called Yuletide remembrance and request that this year, instead, they make a contribution to the Children's Cancer Fund. This would be a way to impact on the gratuity problem from the chief right on down the chain of command. A few of the old-timers grumbled at the rear of the room, but everyone else agreed with Walter that this was an excellent idea.

"Maybe this is a good way to remind the chief that he should follow his own policies," said one of the officers during the discussion.

"We'll make him eat that gratuity policy of his," said another officer. "And at the same time, we'll divert some much needed money to a good cause."

"And *that's* good community relations," said Walter, watching Gunner grimace at the rear of the room.

The letter went out:

The Yuletide season is upon us, and we, the members of the Emmetville Police Union, wish you and yours happy holidays as well as a healthy and prosperous New Year.

Over the past several years, the merchants of this town have been very generous, and we have received large numbers of gifts from you. We have appreciated this very much. It is wonderful to know that we have so many good friends.

Because our police department has a policy against our accepting gratuities, we would like to ask you if you would take the money you would ordinarily spend on presents for police officers and, instead of buying us presents as is your custom, send this money to the Jimmy Fund to help the thousands of little children who have cancer.

We pledge not to accept any gifts this year from the business community, and we ask you to pledge your support to the Jimmy Fund. Such a pledge would indeed make us very happy.

This letter was sent on November 21, just 34 days before Christmas. It was signed by Walter Whitty. Ten days later, on December 1, merchants in Emmetville received the following mysterious, unsigned letter:

We are writing this letter to inform you of the establishment of the Emmetville Police Department Yuletide Gift Committee. This committee is being established to give you an opportunity to continue your generosity to police officers, as has been the tradition for so many years.

We know that a few of our fellow officers have contacted you expressing their disinterest in receiving gifts. This, of course, is a free country, and our fellow officers have the right to take any position they wish to on the matter. We want you to know, however, that those of us who are members of the Yuletide Gift Committee are sincerely grateful to you for your many kindnesses of the past. Furthermore, we would like to see this wonderful tradition continued.

Therefore, we will continue to welcome your gifts and appreciate your generosity.

Happy Holidays!

On December 8, over the signature of the Emmetville Police Chief, the following notice appeared on the bulletin board at the police station:

SEVERAL BUSINESSPEOPLE IN THE COMMUNITY HAVE CONTACTED ME ABOUT WHETHER OR NOT OFFICERS IN THIS DEPARTMENT ARE

RECEPTIVE TO ACCEPTING GIFTS DURING THIS HOLIDAY SEASON.
I WOULD APPRECIATE IT IF ALL OFFICERS WHO ARE INTERESTED
IN ACCEPTING GIFTS THIS YEAR WOULD SIGN THIS NOTICE ON OR
BEFORE DECEMBER 12TH.

The chief himself and six other officers signed, indicating that they
would accept the gifts. One of the signatures was that of Gunner
Paquette.

DISCUSSION QUESTIONS AND PROJECTS

1. Discuss the ramifications of problems that obviously exist within
   the Emmetville Police Department.

2. Discuss the department's required and emergent systems. How does
   each operate for or against the best interests of the organization?

3. What inputs does the Emmetville chief have to the basic functions
   of police management?

4. What relation does the chief's value system have to the way the department functions?

5. What inadequacies of leadership does the chief exhibit?

6. Of the five general styles of leadership, which one does the chief
   most closely follow?

7. Is Walter Whitty a leader? If yes, why? What style of leadership
   does he follow?

8. Discuss the organizational policies of the Emmetville Police Department.

9. Discuss the Emmetville Police Department in terms of Theory X
   and Theory Y.

10. Is there any hope for the Emmetville Police Department? Explain.

CASE 4
THE CHIEF WHO
PLAYED KING

Walden Center, a town of 14,000 people, is 20 miles from Central City and serves as a residential bedroom community. It is a highly homogeneous community of relatively affluent citizens who take great pride in their town and local government. Before World War II, Walden Center had been a small, rural town of 6000. Its rural character is still evident, and small farms, woodlands, and open space abound.

Until now, there have never really been any problems between Walden Center citizens and their town government. The town is administered by a town manager appointed by three elected selectmen. The town manager is the appointing authority for all town governmental departments, including the police department. Therefore, the town manager has the power to hire and fire.

Walden Center is the type of town that has grown slowly, so just about everyone in town knows everyone else. Disputes over how the town is run and its fiscal affairs are hammered out by its citizens at the annual town meeting, which is, in effect, Walden Center's legislative branch of government. This system of government has worked well for Walden Center because it has given every interested citizen a definite say in how the community is run. Because of lack of bureaucracy, it has been relatively easy over the years to resolve any problems that might have arisen simply by calling the town manager or appearing before the board of selectmen at one of their weekly meetings.

Two years ago, Hap Hollingsworth, who had been Chief of Police in Walden Center for about as long as anybody could remember, retired. An amiable, congenial man, Hap's door was always open to anyone who wanted to see him. He was a master at resolving disputes and had a knack for satisfying everyone's interests. The members of his police department both loved and respected him, and although he had no formal rules and regulations or policies and procedures, he was able to control the activities of his officers simply because they all knew "what Hap wanted." Although his given name was Granger, everyone, including his officers, called him "Hap," a nickname that precisely fitted his personality.

When Hap retired the town manager recommended to the board of selectmen that they conduct a national search for the chief's position, reasoning that they should seek out the best possible person for the job. Hap's act would be a hard one to follow, the town manager had said. Inasmuch as the new chief would be reporting directly to the manager, he wanted someone who knew something about the intricacies of police administration to handle the job.

The board was reluctant to agree to this request, and citizens were in something of an uproar about appointing a "foreigner" as their new chief. The issue centered on the concept of local control, and many people thought that this would be lost if a stranger was appointed to the position. The officers in the department joined forces with the more vocally opposed citizens in demanding that the appointment be made from among those officers already in the department. The town manager persisted, quoting a textbook on police administration by Sheehan and Cordner to support his thesis.

Hap Hollingsworth resolved the question by suggesting that the national search be conducted, but that all members of the department be given equal opportunity to be considered for the position.

At a meeting of the board of selectmen when the controversy was at its height, Hap said, "I have never read this book the town manager talks about by Sheehan and Cordner. As a matter of fact, I've heard that the book is controversial and that a lot of chiefs don't like their approach, but I am in favor of getting the best person we can get. To tell you the truth, I think the next chief will come right from within the department. I know of a handful of Walden Center police officers who could take over the job tomorrow and probably do a better job than I'm doing right now." That was just like Hap—always praising his officers.

Hap carried the day, and the board voted unanimously to begin the national search. The board appointed a search committee consisting of five citizens and appointed Hap to chair the committee. Advertisements were placed in the *New York Times,* the *Central City Gazette,* and *The Police Chief* magazine. Everyone was astounded that 178 applications were received for the position. Of the 178, 14 were from Walden Center's 26-member department. The choice was narrowed to seven candidates; one was from Walden Center, one was from Central City, two were from police departments in the state, and three were from out-of-state police departments. Although Hap felt strongly that four other candidates from the Walden Center Police Department should be considered, he was voted down by the majority of the members of the search committee.

Professor W. O. Whittemore from Central City University's Department of Police Administration was retained to write an examination to be administered to the seven finalists.

The out-of-state candidates were flown in at the expense of Walden Center and put up at the Tan Dog Inn, a local colonial hotel that boasted that Martha, not George, Washington had slept there. The examination was given at 8 A.M. on a Saturday morning and lasted two hours. By 1 P.M. on the same day, Professor Whittemore handed the results to the search committee, which began interviewing candidates 30 minutes later. The committee had asked the town manager to become a member of the oral board interview panel.

The Walden Center officer had scored lowest on the written examination, scoring 52 out of a possible 100. The Central City officer had a 61; the two candidates from in-state departments had 66 and 68, respectively. The three candidates from out-of-state departments received grades of 57, 76, and 98, respectively.

The interviews of candidates began with the committee armed with the test results. In a short meeting convened just prior to the start of the oral board, Professor Whittemore briefed the committee members on the examination results. He strongly urged that only the candidates with the 76 and 98 grades be considered seriously for the position. He indicated that the examination was a relatively easy test which anyone with any good understanding of police administration should have passed at a very high level. On the basis of this advice, the committee, in private session, decided to look seriously at only two candidates—those scoring 76 and 98 in the examination. The decision to do this was not unanimous. Hap Hollingsworth was the lone dissenter. He believed that all of the candidates should be considered equally.

At the completion of the orals late Sunday afternoon (the committee had adjourned at 7 P.M. on Saturday evening), the candidates were ranked by each committee member solely on the basis of the oral interviews; however, it can be assumed that the impact of the examination grades influenced the rankings. The officer from Central City was ranked seventh; the officers from in-state departments who received

66 and 68 were ranked fifth and sixth, respectively; the out-of-state candidate who received a 57 on the examination was ranked fourth; the Walden Center officer was ranked third; the out-of-state officer who received a 98 on the examination was ranked second; and the out-of-state officer who received a 76 on the examination was ranked first.

The appointing authority, the town manager, asked that each committee member seriously consider who, among the top three candidates, should be chosen for the position and called a meeting for the following Wednesday evening to advise him on a final decision. On Wednesday evening, the committee met with the manager and voted 4 to 1 to appoint the out-of-state officer who had achieved a grade of 76 on the examination and who ranked as first choice on Sunday evening. Again, Hap Hollingsworth was the only dissenting voice. He voted for the Walden Center officer.

The town manager said that with all due respect to Hap's position, he would go along with the choice of the committee majority and expressed confidence that this type of new leadership, someone from the outside, would provide the department with the kind of leadership it needed. Although he said that he was impressed by the 98 score achieved by the out-of-state officer, he emphasized that the committee's feeling that this officer did not possess leadership qualities automatically eliminated him.

On the following day, after contacting each member of the board of selectmen, receiving their approval, and getting a commitment from them to offer the new chief a five-year contract, he made a public announcement in the local press. The news release read:

> Walden Center Town Manager J. Reid McWhinney announced this morning the appointment of Luke P. Grinnel of Candlelight, California, as the town's new police chief. Grinnel was chosen after a national search in which 178 police officers applied for the position. He succeeds Chief Granger Hollingsworth, who will retire next month.
>
> Chief Grinnel is presently a lieutenant in the Candlelight Police Department and has come up through the ranks. He is a police science graduate of Long Beach State College and is currently pursuing studies for his master's degree at the Univeristy of Southern California.
>
> The new chief is the author of a number of articles in police journals and has served as a consultant on law enforcement to the governor of California.
>
> He and his wife, the former Barbara Jane Mizzlehoff, have five children. He will assume his new duties on August 1.

After the choice was announced, all of Walden Center was abuzz about the new chief. The reaction of townspeople was decidedly favorable, and the board of selectmen commended the search committee and Hap Hollingsworth for their efforts in "selecting the best person in the country for the job." Feelings were a little hurt in the police department, but Hap assured the officers that Chief Grinnel "was a good man with an excellent background."

"Things will work out just fine, you wait and see," said Hap.

In retrospect, history was to prove Hap, the search committee, the town manager, and the board of selectmen wrong. Things didn't work out just fine.

Luke Grinnel descended on Walden Center something like the 1938 hurricane. All spit and polish and armed with the latest theories of good police administration practice, he moved immediately to establish rules and regulations for the department. In a speech before the Rotary Club three weeks after his arrival, he criticized the department publicly and Chief Granger Hollingsworth's leadership particularly.

"The Walden Center Police Department looks to me like the Mexican Army," he said. "It is disjointed. It is disorganized. It has no procedures. It is a disaster. And I assure you, the townspeople of this great town, that things are going to change and change for the better at the Walden Center P.D."

Chief Grinnel's remarks, along with a picture of him in uniform, graced the front page of the *Central City Gazette* that night.

As you might expect, morale among police officers in Walden Center sank to a low ebb. No one had a good word to say about the new chief. For the first time in his life, old Hap looked down in the dumps.

"Hap, what have you done to us?" asked one officer who met him on the street. "We're supposed to get a professional police chief, and you went and gave us Adolph Hitler."

"I'm sorry, Randy," said Hap. "I'm truly sorry, but what can I do?"

"Maybe you could make a statement to the papers or see the board of selectmen or the manager and tell them you made a mistake."

But Hap was too principled a person to tell anyone that he had been the only member of the committee to oppose the new chief's nomination. He suffered in silence.

In the meantime, Grinnel issued new policies and procedures almost daily. "You're going to learn how to do it the right way even if I have to hammer it into your heads," he was fond of saying.

He had not been on the job a month before he had established an organization chart and a rigid chain of command. "If you want to communicate with me in the future," he said, "you do it through the chain of command. No more open-door policy here. Patrol officers report to their sergeants, the sergeants to their lieutenants, and the lieutenants to me. That's the way it's done in police departments all over the country, and that's the way it will be done here."

Once after a briefing session at a roll call in which the new chief complained bitterly about the time-honored practice in Walden Center of allowing officers to get out of their patrol cars to carry on conversations with citizens on the street, a practice with which he thoroughly disagreed, he finished up the session by asking, "Any questions?" One officer, an old-timer who had been on the force for 21 years, asked, "But shouldn't we go through the chain of command if we want to ask you questions, sir?"

Without a bat of an eye, Grinnel retorted, "You've got three days punishment duty for that. What's your name?"

"Blaney, sir."

"Three days punishment duty for your insolence, Blaney, and that will teach the rest of you who's running the show here."

Grinnel had not been on the job two months before the town manager and the board of selectmen were flooded with complaints. Not only police officers, but also citizens were complaining.

One little 80-year-old lady who had retired 15 years earlier as the town's librarian and who knew everyone in the community went to the police station by taxi to see the chief about finding her lost cat. She had tried to reach the chief by phone, but was told by the officer answering the telephone that the chief didn't take complaints like that and that he'd "get into a peck of trouble" if he put the call through. When she arrived at the station, the desk officer told her that she would have to go through the chain of command to see the chief. She had never heard of the chain of command. She argued, but to no avail. In desperation, she wrote to the board of selectmen and to the town manager. On the following Monday evening, she appeared at the selectmen's meeting and wondered aloud "what on earth, gentlemen, is this chain of command that a taxpaying citizen has to go through to talk to the chief of police?" She never did find her cat.

In another instance, the president of a local bank who was also scoutmaster of Troop 8 went to the station to meet with the chief to make plans for police coverage of the Boy Scout Council's annual regional jamboree, which was to be held the following week at the high school stadium. With over 1000 youngsters expected to be participating, the availability of emergency services and extra police coverage was of extreme importance. The desk officer informed the scoutmaster that the chief didn't handle such matters himself and that he would have to see Lieutenant Billingsley, who was head of the new Operations Division. Lieutenant Billingsley would be available in two weeks when he returned from vacation.

"But I can't wait two weeks," said the scoutmaster. "The jamboree is next Saturday."

"Sorry, sir," said the desk officer, "I can't help you. I'd like to, but I'd get into a lot of trouble if I did. It's not in my job description."

"Job description, hell," said the scoutmaster. "You tell the chief I want to see him and I want to see him now."

"Okay," said the desk officer, but it won't do any good. Billingsley handles everything like that. That's the chief's policy."

"The chief's policy be damned," said the irate scoutmaster. "Who does he think he is?"

"You wait here," said the timid desk officer. "I'll tell the chief you want to see him."

He returned in less than a minute.

"Sorry, sir. Like I said, he said to see Lieutenant Billingsley."

"But Lieutenant Billingsley is on vacation. How can I see Lieutenant Billingsley?"

"The chief said he thinks he's home and to call him there. He'll take care of everything."

The scoutmaster called the town manager and issued a complaint against the chief. The town manager called the chief and asked him, as a special favor to him, if he would see the scoutmaster.

"He's an important guy in town," said the town manager. "He's president of the First National Bank and he's on the finance committee. I think it would be wise to see him."

Reluctantly, the chief agreed, explaining to the manager that he thought it unwise to interfere with the responsibilities of his people once he had delegated them the authority to carry out his orders.

At the meeting between the chief and the scoutmaster, the chief lectured the scoutmaster on the principle of delegation of authority. Then the chief called Lieutenant Billingsley, whom he found at home painting his house, and said, "Billingsley, get down here right away. Some scoutmaster is here about a jamboree this Saturday. Do you know anything about it? You don't? Well, you should, Billingsley. This is an annual affair, and you should have been on top of it. Get yourself down here right away and take care of it. What's whose name? The scoutmaster? I don't know, wait a minute. What's your name, mister? His name is Francini. He'll be here when you get here."

After he had hung up the telephone, the chief stood up, indicating that the meeting was over.

"He'll be down in about a half an hour, Mr. ____, Mr. ____"

"Francini."

"Yes, he'll be down in about a half hour. Let me know if he doesn't handle everything to your satisfaction, and I'll get on his back."

"How will I let you know?" asked Francini. "Write you a letter?"

DISCUSSION QUESTIONS AND PROJECTS

1. Did Walden Center make a mistake in hiring Luke P. Grinnel as its new police chief? Why?

2. What specifically are Chief Grinnel's problems?

3. If you were Chief Grinnel's best friend, what would you advise him to do?

4. Was the screening process through which Chief Grinnel was hired appropriate to the needs of the town?

5. Had you been chairman of the search committee, what would you have done differently?

6. If you were a member of Chief Grinnel's police department, how would you personally react to his administration of the department?

7. Break up into small groups of four. Assume that one of you is town manager and that three of you are members of the board of selectmen. Discuss through role playing how you would resolve the problem.

8. Inasmuch as the chief reports directly to the town manager, choose one of your classmates to role play the town manager's position and another to role play the chief's position. Conduct a meeting in which the two discuss the town manager's concerns.

CASE 5
THE NERVOUS PLANNER

You are one of 200 police officers assigned to the Randall City Police Department. You joined the department ten years ago and have advanced in rank to lieutenant. During your career, you have been assigned to numerous responsibilities, including patrol, investigations, property, and communications. On receiving your baccalaureate degree this past June from Randall City College, you were called to the chief's office and informed that you were to be given one of the most responsible positions in the department, Director of Planning. Although you have many misgivings about your capabilities to handle such an assignment and are quite nervous about it, you agree to accept.

Randall City has a population of 100,000 people. It is largely a residential community, but does have some light industry in the Friendly City Industrial Park area. Randall City has always been known as the "Friendly City" and pretty much lives up to that name. For a community its size, it has a relatively low crime rate and few real police problems. The police department is a good one and boasts few internal problems. Its officers are dedicated and extremely enthusiastic. Because of its lack of general police problems, it has never had a Director of Planning. You are its first.

The immediate situation that prompted the chief to appoint you came about as a result of the new mayor's concern about spiraling budget costs. In attempting to pinpoint areas in which money could be saved, the chief decided that his first effort will be made in the area of patrol personnel allocation. The department uses all two-officer patrol cars. Almost all of the patrol officers like the two-officer system, and although the chief has often been tempted to do away with it in favor of all one-officer cars, he has hesitated to do so for fear of what this might do to morale. Morale, incidentally, is at a very high level.

The department operates on a three-shift basis: midnight to 8 A.M. (shift 1); 8 A.M. to 4 P.M. (shift 2); and 4 P.M. to midnight (shift 3). The city has nine patrol sectors, designated by letters; at least nine patrol cars are always on the road and, depending on the availability of personnel, usually several more as well. Citizens are very satisfied with the department and often comment on seeing patrol cars "all over the place." The department has 18 marked vehicles.

The chief believes that activity in the city does not warrant the number of officers currently assigned to the patrol function. He is certain that the midnight to 8 A.M. shift can be substantially cut and feels reasonably sure that the 8 A.M. to 4 P.M. shift can also be cut, but he needs figures to back up his feelings. Your first assignment is to provide him with these figures and to give him data which will indicate exact numbers of patrol officers needed to service activity on each of the three shifts.

An additional problem is the department's lack of capability to handle calls and to engage in general patrol activities when shifts change. There is sometimes a 20-minute delay in servicing calls that come in at 11:50 P.M., 7:50 A.M., and 3:50 P.M. You are requested to work out a system to alleviate this problem.

After thinking several days about how to proceed, you finally decide that it will be necessary to collect data on the amounts of time that it takes patrol officers to service various types of calls, recognizing that certain types of calls take longer to service than others. Getting these times will be no problem, because the communications division has been time-stamping complaint cards for years. Information is available on what time each call was received, what time it was dispatched, what time the assigned officers went out of radio service at the scene, and what time the officers came back into service at the conclusion of the call. Your only problem is to attempt to categorize the different types of calls. After much study, you decide on the following categories: *Part I Crimes, Part II Crimes, Incidents, Accidents, Arrests,* and *Hospital Runs.* Patrol officers in your department are always assigned to calls that fall into one of these six categories.

Your next step is to determine what the average length of time is for servicing calls in each category. This is easy. You take the complaint cards for three months and add up all of the times time-stamped in each category and divide by the number of calls in each category. This gives you an average time for each category. Recognizing that some calls will take longer than others and wanting to be fair, you decide to allot slightly more time on an average than your hard figures, the actual average time spent, indicate. After completing this task, you draw up a table showing your figures (see Table 1).

Table 1. Average amounts of time spent in and allotted to servicing activity categories

Category	Time Spent	Time Allotted By You
Part I Crimes	22.3 minutes	25 minutes
Part II Crimes	16.2 minutes	20 minutes
Incidents	15.7 minutes	20 minutes
Accidents	23.5 minutes	25 minutes
Arrests	19.6 minutes	20 minutes
Hospital Runs	17.9 minutes	20 minutes

Now that you know how much time you will allot for each categorized activity, you must determine how many activities within each category occur each year on each of the three shfits. While gathering this information, it occurs to you that it might prove beneficial to determine the amount of activity per year by actual hourly time of occurrence. The possibility of recommending overlapping shifts to compensate for time lost during shift changes might be better accepted if this kind of detailed information were available. Additionally, if your study is to be a fully detailed personnel allocation effort, while you are in the process of determining how many officers you need per shift, why not use the same activity statistics to determine where and on what day of the week the activity takes place?

Rather than accumulate data for the year, you decide that three months of activity will be a sufficiently substantial sample. Inasmuch as three months represent one-quarter of a year, you can interpolate your annual activity statistics by multiplying your activity figures for three months by 4. This should provide a reasonably accurate estimate of all activity for a year.

Wanting to estimate activity somewhat on the high side, you choose two relatively busy representative months to compensate for seasonal changes in activity. You choose July as a busy summer month, December as a winter month with high accident and crime frequency, and May as a month which is fairly representative of other months from an activity standpoint. These months are chosen on the basis of your experience as a police officer and not on the basis of any hard data which will support your position.

You collect your data by thoroughly reviewing daily radio logs for each of the three months chosen and compiling activity by category and by time of day for each of the three shifts (see Table 2).

Table 2. Three months of police activity by time of occurrence, by shift

Shift 1

Time of Occurrence	Part I Crimes	Part II Crimes	Incidents	Accidents	Arrests	Hospital Runs	Totals
12:00–1:00 a.m.	91	183	311	31	32	32	680
1:00–2:00 a.m.	72	146	264	32	24	26	564
2:00–3:00 a.m.	40	144	224	35	20	23	486
3:00–4:00 a.m.	37	72	129	11	19	9	277
4:00–5:00 a.m.	15	23	67	8	5	8	126
5:00–6:00 a.m.	12	12	56	7	1	8	96
6:00–7:00 a.m.	27	16	64	6	3	12	128
7:00–8:00 a.m.	31	13	61	14	5	10	134
Totals	325	609	1,176	144	109	128	2,491

Shift 2

Time of Occurrence	Part I Crimes	Part II Crimes	Incidents	Accidents	Arrests	Hospital Runs	Totals
8:00– 9:00 a.m.	59	58	244	23	5	17	406
9:00–10:00 a.m.	44	55	212	20	9	13	353
10:00–11:00 a.m.	49	58	209	16	11	16	359
11:00–12:00 p.m.	50	57	203	18	15	18	361
12:00– 1:00 p.m.	47	59	193	27	15	23	364
1:00– 2:00 p.m.	59	74	221	21	32	22	429
2:00– 3:00 p.m.	70	61	222	26	25	19	423
3:00– 4:00 p.m.	63	59	172	21	18	25	358
Totals	441	481	1,676	172	130	153	3,053

Table 2. (cont.)

Shift 3

Time of Occurrence	Part I Crimes	Part II Crimes	Incidents	Accidents	Arrests	Hospital Runs	Totals
4:00– 5:00 p.m.	117	120	267	36	45	18	603
5:00– 6:00 p.m.	103	126	200	47	38	30	544
6:00– 7:00 p.m.	97	109	238	30	46	21	541
7:00– 8:00 p.m.	100	115	274	22	59	25	595
8:00– 9:00 p.m.	106	157	263	25	52	26	629
9:00–10:00 p.m.	113	166	287	27	78	29	700
10:00–11:00 p.m.	107	128	243	36	86	26	626
11:00–12:00 p.m.	73	142	186	31	95	21	548
Totals	816	1,063	1,958	254	499	196	4,786

You follow the same procedure for plotting activity figures for place of occurrence and day of occurrence (see Tables 3 and 4). Although the chief did not give you these specific assignments, this information will prove useful later in determining daily patrol personnel deployment.

Table 3. Three months of police activity by place of occurrence, by shift

Shift 1

Sector	Part I Crimes	Part II Crimes	Incidents	Accidents	Arrests	Hospital Runs	Totals	% of Total Activity
N.W.	52	74	167	13	14	9	329	13%
C.W.	44	66	129	13	6	9	267	11%
S.W.	18	47	110	10	2	8	195	8%
N.C.	43	119	139	20	17	23	361	14%
C.	42	46	135	24	16	21	284	11%
S.C.	34	102	145	19	9	11	320	13%
N.E.	37	68	119	20	14	12	270	11%
C.E.	31	45	115	11	27	22	251	10%
S.E.	24	42	117	14	4	13	214	9%
Totals	325	609	1,176	144	109	128	2,491	100%

Table 3. (cont.)

Shift 2

Sector	Part I Crimes	Part II Crimes	Incidents	Accidents	Arrests	Hospital Runs	Totals	% of Total Activity
N.W.	62	45	168	20	8	15	318	10%
C.W.	63	49	291	28	5	18	454	15%
S.W.	52	40	141	22	8	11	274	9%
N.C.	43	71	191	22	3	28	358	12%
C.	27	51	217	16	3	17	331	11%
S.C.	44	73	157	10	3	15	302	10%
N.E.	55	61	191	20	5	17	349	11%
C.E.	51	49	183	18	92	16	409	13%
S.E.	44	42	137	16	3	16	258	9%
Totals	441	481	1,676	172	130	153	3,053	100%

Shift 3

Sector	Part I Crimes	Part II Crimes	Incidents	Accidents	Arrests	Hospital Runs	Totals	% of Total Activity
N.W.	138	94	194	28	26	15	495	10%
C.W.	108	109	212	51	15	18	513	11%
S.W.	59	86	194	15	15	14	383	8%
N.C.	94	179	256	28	57	33	647	13%
C.	75	108	189	16	23	29	440	9%
S.C.	77	127	234	29	24	27	518	11%
N.E.	79	123	211	21	24	10	468	10%
C.E.	103	150	276	38	296	34	897	19%
S.E.	83	87	192	28	19	16	425	9%
Totals	816	1,063	1,958	254	499	196	4,786	100%

Table 4. Three months of police activity for all three shifts by day of occurrence

Day	Part I Crimes	Part II Crimes	Incidents	Accidents	Arrests	Hospital Runs	Totals
Sunday	231	328	699	74	115	62	1,509
Monday	242	249	594	77	82	67	1,311
Tuesday	252	289	656	77	112	79	1,465
Wednesday	192	253	626	52	84	55	1,262
Thursday	235	303	742	84	89	76	1,529
Friday	226	319	746	92	140	72	1,595
Saturday	204	412	747	114	116	66	1,659
Totals	1,582	2,153	4,810	570	738	477	10,330

You now take all of your activity by category for the three months, add it together on a per shift basis, and multiply by 4. This gives you a reasonably accurate estimate of shift activity by category for a year. Because different categories of activity require different amounts of time to service (see Table 1), you must then take the number of activities in *each* category and multiply that number by the number of minutes you have allotted in Table 1 for servicing each category of activity. For example, 325 Part I crimes have occurred on Shift 1 for the three-month period. Multiplying 325 by 4 gives you a projection that approximately 1300 Part I crimes will occur in one year. By multiplying 1300 by 25 minutes, you can determine that it takes 32,500 minutes for patrol officers to service all Part I crimes for the year. By dividing 32,500 minutes by 60 (the number of minutes in an hour), you can determine that it takes 542 hours for patrol officers to service all Part I crimes for the year. Table 5 shows the number of hours spent by each shift in servicing activity in Randall City for one year.

Table 5. Hours of police shift activity for one year

Shift	Part I Crimes	Part II Crimes	Incidents	Accidents	Arrests	Hospital Runs	Totals
Shift 1	542	812	1,568	240	146	171	3,479
Shift 2	735	642	2,235	287	174	204	4,277
Shift 3	1,360	1,418	2,611	424	666	262	6,741
Totals	2,637	2,872	6,414	951	986	637	14,497

These figures, however, represent only the time needed to handle calls for service. Consideration must also be given to the fact that police officers are involved in many activities other than the servicing of calls. They direct traffic, check vacant buildings, write reports, patrol the community, enforce speed laws with radar, take coffee and lunch breaks, assist motorists, research laws, obtain search warrants, gas patrol vehicles, check equipment, confer with fellow officers, check school bus operations, and become involved in myriad other activities that do not reflect in the time statistics which appear in Table 5. When determining personnel requirements for the patrol function, it is therefore necessary to build into officers' work schedules sufficient time to engage in these peripheral activities. Time must also be made available to handle work overloads that are unpredictable and to provide back-up assistance for fellow officers. Patrol officers must be available for unusual and unforeseen circumstances that require their availability on a moment's notice. Considering these factors, it is unrealistic to base shift personnel strength solely on the actual activity and called-for services reflected in the daily radio logs. Time must be allotted for those additional hours officers need to perform their additional responsibilities. This additional time is referred to as *buffer time.* Buffer time accommodates overload, relief, patrol, and incidental activities.

For every hour patrol officers spend in making investigations at the preliminary level and in servicing calls, two additional hours should be allowed each officer as *buffer time.* Multiplying the number of hours actually spent in servicing activity by 3 gives the number of hours needed to accommodate all buffer time and all actual activity on each shift by category for one year (see Table 6).

Table 6. Hours of police shift activity for one year including buffer time

Shift	Part I Crimes	Part II Crimes	Incidents	Accidents	Arrests	Hospital Runs	Totals
Shift 1	1,626	2,436	4,704	720	438	513	10,437
Shift 2	2,205	1,926	6,705	861	522	612	12,831
Shift 3	4,080	4,254	7,833	1,272	1,998	786	20,223
Totals	7,911	8,616	19,242	2,853	2,958	1,911	43,491

Rather than work with annual figures, however, you determine that it would be easier to make your personnel calculations on a monthly basis. In order to ascertain the number of patrol hours needed on a per month basis, you simply divide your annual figures by 12 (see Table 7).

Table 7. Hours of police shift activity for one month, including buffer time

Shift	Part I Crimes	Part II Crimes	Incidents	Accidents	Arrests	Hospital Runs	Totals	% of Total Activity
Shift 1	136	203	392	60	37	43	871	24%
Shift 2	184	161	559	72	44	51	1,071	30%
Shift 3	340	355	653	106	167	66	1,687	46%
Totals	660	719	1,604	238	248	160	3,629	100%

You can now see that shift 1 (midnight to 8 A.M.) is approximately one-half as busy as shift 3 (4 P.M. to midnight) and that shift 2 (8 A.M. to 4 P.M.), although busier than shift 1, is much less busy than shift 3. It is apparent that a personnel adjustment is in order. Certainly the shifts should not be staffed with almost an equal number of officers, as is now the case.

In order to determine the exact number of officers needed to handle shift activity, it is first necessary to calculate the exact number of hours taken off each year by the 166 officers assigned to the patrol division. Because the amount of time taken off by patrol officers significantly impacts on the availability of officers assigned to the patrol function, a review of all time off taken by the 166 patrol officers must be made. You must establish a *time-off factor* for the patrol component of the department in an effort to determine the number of patrol officers necessary to be assigned to each shift to compensate for the time off taken by officers assigned to regularly established beats. Each shift must be staffed with a sufficient number of officers to compensate for all time off taken by all officers assigned to the shift. If this is not done, the chances of having shifts frequently understaffed can become a very real problem in attempting to provide a level of service consistent with identified needs.

Once this task has been performed and once shifts are properly staffed to compensate for the anticipated absence of personnel, a relatively consistent level of service can be maintained. The *time-off factor* is an instrument of measurement which you can use to determine the number of patrol officers needed to staff each shift fully, cover each patrol beat consistently, and compensate completely for all officers away from the job for whatever reason.

In calculating the *time-off factor* for Randall City, you work on the premise that every patrol beat assignment must be filled on a 24-hour basis, 365 days a year. Patrol officers, however, do not work 365 days a year. They work considerably less. In Randall City, they take from 21 to 26 days off each year for vacations. In addition to the 104 days they would normally take off each year regularly (two days out of each seven), Randall City police officers have been successful in negotiating a contract which places them on a four- and-two work week; this means that instead of taking two days off out of each seven, they actually take two days off out of each six. This gives them an additional 17 days off each year. They also take sick leave, injury leave, no-pay days, and leaves of absence. Occasionally, some officers are suspended. All of this time represents substantial time away from work. Each officer, there-fore, is available for work many fewer hours than the maximum num-ber of hours if he or she were to work eight hours a day, 365 days a year. The number of hours not worked, however, must be provided for by assigning a sufficient number of officers to each shift to compensate for time off.

You decide to determine the Randall City *time-off factor* before you determine the number of beats needed to accommodate activity on each of the three shifts. In order to do this, you must determine the number of work days lost per year by all 166 officers assigned to the patrol function (see Table 8).

The number of days lost per year by the 166 patrol officers is 26,371. The number of hours lost per year (210,968) is determined by

Table 8. Patrol officer time lost by day for one year

Time-Off Category	Work Days Lost per Year
Vacation Leave	3,583
Days Off	17,264
Sick Leave	1,765
Injury Leave	663
4 & 2 Loss	2,822
Suspensions	103
No-Pay Days	131
Leaves of Absence	40
Total	26,371

multiplying the number of days lost per year (26,371) by 8 (the number of hours in one work day). The number of hours lost every month by the 166 patrol officers (17,581) is determined by dividing the number of hours lost per year (210,968) by 12 (the number of months in a year). The average number of hours lost every month by each of the 166 patrol officers (106) is determined by dividing the number of hours lost each month (17,581) by 166 (the number of patrol officers).

If one patrol officer worked one eight-hour shift every day for one month, he or she would work 243 hours. These 243 hours are referred to as the *basic police officer month*. The *basic police officer month* is calculated by dividing 365 (the number of days in a year) by 12 (the number of months in a year). There are 30.4 days, or 243 hours, needed to cover each beat for each eight-hour shift each month. Put another way, there are 243 hours needed to staff one patrol beat fully for each one-month period.

Working with the *basic police officer month* as a standard, it is relatively easy, you discover, to determine the number of hours that each patrol officer is available to work each month. By subtracting the average number of hours that each patrol officer is off each month (106) from the number of hours needed for one patrol officer to cover one beat for a month (243), it can be determined that each Randall City patrol officer will be available for duty 137 hours per month. By dividing the number of hours in the *basic police officer month* (243) by the 137 hours each officer works on an average each month, the Randall City *time-off factor* (1.77) can be determined. This figure means, in effect, that .77 percent of one patrol officer is needed to compensate for time off taken by each officer.

By multiplying the *time-off* factor (1.77) by the number of beat officers needed to handle all activity on a given shift, you arrive at the number of officers who should ordinarily be assigned to that shift to compensate for time off. Although this might seem to be a rather involved process to determine shift strength, it is essential if any degree of consistency is to be achieved in staffing beats fully and providing services according to identified demands.

You now have the necessary information to make some preliminary estimates of the number of officers needed to staff your three shifts. You proceed by making use of information in Table 7.

1. *Shift 1:* A total of 871 hours is spent each month by patrol officers on shift 1. By dividing 871 by the *basic police officer month* (243), it may be determined that 3.6, or 4, car beats are needed on shift 1. If the department continues with its present policy to staff each patrol vehicle

with two officers, eight officers will be needed to handle all patrol car activity on shift 1. Adding the two walking beats to the four car beats gives a total of ten patrol officers who will be needed to staff all beats. Multiplying the ten patrol officers by the *time-off factor* (1.77) indicates that 18 patrol officers should be assigned to shift 1. A total of 55 patrol officers is currently assigned to the shift.

2. *Shift 2:* A total of 1071 hours is spent each month by patrol officers on shift 2. By dividing 1071 by the *basic police officer month* (243), it may be determined that 4.4, or 5, car beats are needed for shift 2. If the department continues with its present policy to staff each patrol vehicle with two officers, ten officers will be needed to handle all patrol car activity on shift 2. Adding the two walking beats to the five car beats gives a total of 12 patrol officers who will be needed to staff all beats. Multiplying the 12 patrol officers by the *time-off factor* (1.77) indicates that 22 patrol officers should be assigned to shift 2. A total of 55 patrol officers is currently assigned to the shift.

3. *Shift 3:* A total of 1687 hours is spent each month by patrol officers on shift 3. By dividing 1687 by the *basic police officer month* (243), it may be determined that 6.9, or 7, car beats are needed on shift 3. If the department continues with its present policy to staff each patrol vehicle with two officers, 14 officers will be needed to handle all patrol car activity on shift 3. Adding the three walking beats to the seven car beats gives a total of 17 patrol officers who will be needed to staff all beats. Multiplying the 17 patrol officers by the *time-off factor* (1.77) indicates that 31 patrol officers should be assigned to shift 3. A total of 56 patrol officers is currently assigned to the shift.

Quite naturally, you are astounded by these calculations. They indicate that you need 71 police patrol officers to handle all of the activity on all three shifts. The department, therefore, is 95 officers overstaffed. You must have made some terrible error in mathematics somewhere along the way. You check and recheck your computations. They appear to be right. They couldn't be. If only you had a computer, maybe it would come out differently. You take a trip to Randall City College and run your figures through the computer there. The computer parrots back your own computations. No question about it, they are correct.

Having a large amount of excess personnel to work with, you refer to Table 9 and see that the shift workload is heaviest for all three shifts at shift changes. Table 9 also indicates that from 4 A.M. to 8 A.M. activity drops off markedly.

Table 9. Percentage breakdown of work activity by hour of day

Shift 1

	May	July	Dec.	Total	% of Shift Activity	% of Daily Activity
12:00– 1:00 a.m.	182	235	263	680	27%	7%
1:00– 2:00 a.m.	140	183	241	564	23%	5%
2:00– 3:00 a.m.	118	176	192	486	19%	5%
3:00– 4:00 a.m.	71	97	109	277	11%	3%
4:00– 5:00 a.m.	33	51	42	126	5%	1%
5:00– 6:00 a.m.	35	31	30	96	4%	1%
6:00– 7:00 a.m.	35	37	56	128	5%	1%
7:00– 8:00 a.m.	38	34	62	134	6%	1%
Total	652	844	995	2,491	100%	24%

Shift 2

	May	July	Dec.	Total	% of Shift Activity	% of Daily Activity
8:00– 9:00 a.m.	120	122	164	406	13%	4%
9:00–10:00 a.m.	120	111	122	353	11%	3%
10:00–11:00 a.m.	114	119	126	359	12%	4%
11:00–12:00 p.m.	99	116	146	361	12%	4%
12:00– 1:00 p.m.	105	130	129	364	12%	4%
1:00– 2:00 p.m.	141	133	155	429	14%	4%
2:00– 3:00 p.m.	117	151	155	423	14%	4%
3:00– 4:00 p.m.	113	114	131	358	12%	3%
Total	929	996	1,128	3,053	100%	30%

Shift 3

	May	July	Dec.	Total	% of Shift Activity	% of Daily Activity
4:00– 5:00 p.m.	228	192	183	603	13%	6%
5:00– 6:00 p.m.	198	180	166	544	11%	5%
6:00– 7:00 p.m.	188	180	173	541	11%	5%
7:00– 8:00 p.m.	196	199	200	595	13%	6%
8:00– 9:00 p.m.	198	206	225	629	13%	6%
9:00–10:00 p.m.	201	263	236	700	15%	6%
10:00–11:00 p.m.	171	247	208	626	13%	6%
11:00–12:00 p.m.	156	210	182	548	11%	5%
Total	1,536	1,677	1,573	4,786	100%	46%

It seems obvious that there is a need to have half the patrol officers assigned to shift 1 report for duty at 11 P.M. and half at midnight; half the officers assigned to shift 2 report at 7 A.M. and half at 8 A.M.; and half the officers assigned to shift 3 report at 3 P.M. and half at 4 P.M. This will be one of your recommendations to the chief.

Although the total amount of activity does not warrant any additional patrol cars or the assignment of any more than a total of 71 patrol officers on all three shifts to accommodate all activity, the fact that patrol shifts are currently overstaffed suggests the possibility of assigning a number of additional officers to one-officer cars to not only increase patrol capability and visibility but also handle many of the routine calls that do not present any appreciable degree of danger and that do not necessitate the services of more than one officer.

After thinking about the matter, you make the subjective judgment that 15 additional one-officer car beats can be created. You decide to distribute nine of these beats evenly among the three shifts. You add one additional one-officer car beat to shift 2, two additional one-officer car beats to a new split shift to run from noon to 8 P.M. (shift 2A), and three additional one-officer car beats to a new split shift to run from 8 P.M. to 4 A.M. (shift 3A). Also, you reduce the number of two-officer cars on shift 3 from seven to six and thereby put two additional one-officer cars on the road during shift 3. Your new beat assignments for the patrol division appear in Table 10.

Table 10. New patrol assignments by shift.

	Assignment	No. of Partol Officers Assigned to Beats
Shifts 1 and 3A	4 two-officer cars	8
	3 one-officer cars	3
	2 walking beats	2
	3 one-officer cars (midnight to 4 A.M.)	3
Total	12 beats	16
Shifts 2 and 2A	4 two-officer cars	8
	4 one-officer cars	4
	2 walking beats	2
	2 one-officer cars (noon to 8 P.M.)	2
Total	12 beats	16

Table 10. (cont.)

	Assignment	No. of Patrol Officers Assigned to Beats
Shifts 3 and 3A	6 two-officer cars	12
	5 one-officer cars	5
	3 walking beats	3
	3 one-officer cars (8 P.M. to midnight)	3
Total	17 beats	23

The *time-off factor* of 1.77 suggests that a total of 94 patrol officers be assigned to the patrol division. The breakdown of patrol assignments for each shift is given in Table 10. The full complement of officers assigned to each shift, computed by multiplying the number of patrol officers assigned to beats on each shift by 1.77, is presented in Table 11. It should be noted that you have been liberal in assigning an additional officer if the figure to the right of the decimal point is 3 or more.

Table 11. Full complement of officers assigned to shifts.

	No. of Patrol Officers Assigned to Beats		Full Complement Assigned
Shift 1	13	(x 1.77 = 23.01), or	23
Shift 2	14	(x 1.77 = 24.78), or	25
Shift 3	20	(x 1.77 = 35.4), or	36
Shift 2A	2	(x 1.77 = 3.54), or	4
Shift 3A	3	(x 1.77 = 5.31), or	6
Total			94

According to your calculations and new personnel allocation plan, the Randall City Police Department can be reduced by 72 patrol officers. You write a report, present all of this information to the chief, and suggest that your plan be implemented.

DISCUSSION QUESTIONS AND PROJECTS

1. How do you think that the chief should use the report?

2. Should the chief implement the recommendations contained in the report?

3. Knowing that you are the director of planning, how do you think that your fellow officers will respond to you once they learn that there is a possibility that 72 patrol officers will be laid off?

4. How will you respond to them?

5. If you were to change the recommendations in any way, what changes would you make?

6. Would it be possible to reduce the patrol force even further? How could this be done? Would it be wise? Would it result in significant financial savings?

7. Why, in your opinion, is Randall City so grossly overstaffed?

8. Do you think that the new mayor of Randall City will be pleased with your recommendations? Why?

9. How do you think that the information found in Tables 3 and 4 could be used?

10. By how many police officers could you reduce the force if you went to all one-officer cars? Would this be a good move? Why or why not?

11. Do you think that you could conduct a personnel allocation study in your own police department if requested to do so by the chief? If you do, turn to Case 6.

CASE 6
THE PRESCOTT VALLEY
PROJECT

Prescott Valley is a town of 18,000 people and has a police department of 42 officers, 30 of whom are assigned to patrol duties in one-officer cars. This well-run town boasts the lowest property tax rate in the state. When its town manager, Janice Cady, hears about your personnel allocation study in Randall City, she seeks you out and asks if you will assist her in conducting a similar study in Prescott Valley. After clearing this request with your chief and getting his approval, you show Cady how to get the necessary activity information as well as the time-off information needed to determine the Prescott Valley time-off factor. Because Prescott Valley is considerably smaller than Randall City, you ask that she provide you with a four-month rather than a three-month sample of activity. You also request that this be done by shift.

In two months Cady returns with the activity figures and time-off information for the Prescott Valley Police Department. You tell her that within a few minutes you will be able to determine what her personnel requirements are.

Although you question the amounts of time allotted to servicing activity categories, Cady assures you that although these times seem to be excessively long, she herself conducted the time study and the figures are accurate. Because there is no investigations division in the department, patrol officers follow through themselves on all investigations involving Part I and Part II crimes. Also, Prescott Valley is a large community geographically (67 square miles), and officers spend more time responding to calls. The community has no hospital, so the injured and sick must be transported to Randall City Hospital; this also increases activity time. The town has an ambulance which is staffed by the police department. Additionally, the town has no lock-up facilities, so prisoners must be transported to the jail at Randall City for booking; this increases the time allotted to the arrest category.

Table 1 shows the average amounts of time spent in servicing activity categories. Table 2 shows four months of shift activity by category. Table 3 shows the time lost by day for one year by the 30 officers assigned to the patrol function in Prescott Valley.

Table 1. Average amounts of time spent in servicing activity categories

Category	Time Spent
Part I crimes	4 hours
Part II crimes	2 hours
Incidents	3/4 hour
Accidents	3 hours
Arrests	1 hour
Ambulance runs	1 1/2 hours

Table 2. Four months of police activity, by shift

Shift 1

Time of Occurrence	Part I Crimes	Part II Crimes	Incidents	Accidents	Arrests	Ambulance Runs
October	2	8	66	5	6	4
December	6	4	60	12	2	6
February	1	3	41	6	4	8
July	13	1	121	12	7	5
Totals	22	16	288	35	19	23

Shift 2

Time of Occurrence	Part I Crimes	Part II Crimes	Incidents	Accidents	Arrests	Ambulance Runs
October	8	33	99	26	20	16
December	13	37	97	44	10	19

Table 2. (cont.)

Shift 2 (cont.)

Time of Occurrence	Part I Crimes	Part II Crimes	Incidents	Accidents	Arrests	Ambulance Runs
February	7	23	87	30	7	27
July	13	15	150	28	8	11
Totals	41	108	433	128	45	73

Shift 3

Time of Occurrence	Part I Crimes	Part II Crimes	Incidents	Accidents	Arrests	Ambulance Runs
October	13	33	124	35	10	8
December	17	27	137	41	23	12
February	5	14	81	32	7	8
July	26	12	232	37	10	11
Totals	61	86	574	145	50	39

Table 3. Time lost by day for one year

Individual Time-Off Factors	Officer Days Lost Per Year
Vacation leave	325
Days off	3120
Bereavement days	1
Sick leave	317
Injury leave	20
Military leave	10
Holidays	116
Court days	179
Total	4088

DISCUSSION QUESTIONS AND PROJECTS

1. What is the Prescott Valley Police Department's time-off factor?

2. How many car beats are needed to accommodate activity on shift 1? How many patrol officers should be assigned to shift 1?

3. How many car beats are needed to accommodate activity on shift 2? How many patrol officers should be assigned to shift 2?

4. How many car beats are needed to accommodate activity on shift 3? How many patrol officers should be assigned to shift 3?

5. Should the fact that the Prescott Valley Police Department provides ambulance service for the community impact on personnel requirements? If so, how?

6. On the basis of question 5, would you like to recalculate your figures?

7. Should the fact that Prescott Valley encompasses 67 square miles of area impact on personnel requirements? If so, how?

8. On the basis of question 7, would you like to recalculate your figures?

9. On the basis of any recalculations you may have made, how would you change your previous recommendations?

10. In your opinion, is the Prescott Valley Police Department over-staffed or understaffed? Explain.

INDEX